Feminism
in the
Heartland

Feminism
in the
Heartland

Judith Ezekiel

The Ohio State University Press

Columbus

This Book Belongs To:

Andrea Renaker

Library of Congress Cataloging-in-Publication Data

Ezekiel, Judith, 1956–
    Feminism in the heartland / by Judith Ezekiel.
        p.cm.
Includes bibliographical references and index.
    ISBN 0-8142-0903-3 (hardcover: alk. paper)—ISBN 0-8142-5098-X (pbk.:
alk. paper)
1. Feminism—Ohio—Dayton. 2. Dayton (Ohio)—Social conditions. I. Title.
    HQ1439.D39 E94 2002
    305.42'09771'73–dc21
                        2002005532

Cover and text design by Janna M. Thompson-Chordas.
Type set in Adobe Sabon.
Printed by Thomson-Shore.

9 8 7 6 5 4 3 2 1

Contents

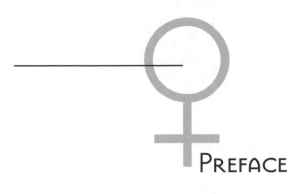

PREFACE

D AYTON, OHIO. A typical American city. The "heart of Middle America." Dayton has been described as everything from "a nice place to raise kids" to "the archetype of nowhere" that looks like postwar Dresden. As novelist and former Daytonian John Baskin wrote: "Dayton sat in the inexact geography of the national mind like a mirage, an unformed vision on the imagined expanse of flat Midwestern plains. In this picture, it seemed pleasant, sleepy, dull. . . . Dayton had begun to occupy prime real estate in the national subdivisions of symbolism. Dayton had, God forbid, become an idea. This idea was that Dayton had become Middle America. People weren't exactly sure where Dayton was, or even what it was, but it was The Heartland."[1]

In 1970, demographers Ben Wattenberg and Richard Scammon suggested in *The Real Majority* that the typical voter was "a forty-seven-year-old wife of a machinist living in suburban Dayton, Ohio." The Dayton *Journal Herald,* with the help of a local machinists union, identified her in the person of Bette Lowrey; *Life* and scores of other publications made a celebrity of Lowrey. Since then, literati such as Ray Bradbury, Kurt Vonnegut, Garry Trudeau, and Marcia Muller have used Dayton as the hometown for their Middle American characters. In analyzing the press, Noam Chomsky invoked an imaginary "editor of a newspaper in Dayton, Ohio" to exemplify what happens in Middle America. In the television series *Dynasty,* Krystal's dirty secret was that before her rise to fame and fortune, she had been a mere secretary in Dayton.[2]

Dayton has long been a prime spot for opinion polls. Reporters for media ranging from the *New York Times* to the British Broadcasting Corporation flock to Dayton when elections approach. As Dayton votes, they say, so does America. Similarly, as Dayton buys, so does

America; market studies are big business in the city. As a child in Dayton, I assumed that all grocery stores let their customers taste food before buying it and that everybody got at least three free samples a week of products such as foot deodorants. Dayton's fame as a testing ground stretched across the Atlantic to France, where I now live. Upon first venturing into a suburban shopping mall near Paris, I was overwhelmed by a feeling of déjà vu. Like Charlton Heston in *The Planet of the Apes*, I sank (figuratively) to my knees and groaned, "My God, I'm back!" Indeed, French industrialists traveled to Dayton to study its malls.[3]

I lived in Dayton until 1973, when I left to attend the University of Michigan. A few years later, I moved to France, where I have lived ever since. Often in my travels, people assume that since I am a feminist, I'm from a big American city. When they learn I was born and raised in the Heartland, they view me as an oddity. Feminism, with its subversive connotation, was long considered an unlikely phenomenon for Dayton, Ohio. In the 1980s, when I started my research, my subject met with laughter even in Dayton. I began to wonder if I had imagined the political effervescence around me. I wrote this book in part to answer that question.

Another question rapidly arose about the nature of this movement. As feminism became mainstream, outsiders conceded that if Dayton was average, and if feminism was a national phenomenon, then it had to be happening in Dayton. However, they assumed, in what I call the fashion-designer view of history, that it would be a milquetoast version of the exciting big-city movements. It is common knowledge that New York fashion trends take several years to make it to department stores in the Heartland, and when they do they have been diluted for popular consumption: the satin transformed into double-knit polyester, the bright colors muted, the skirts never as short or as long. This has become a "common sense" view of social movements: radical ideas may work well in the big cities, but they need to be toned down for the Heartland. The only brand of feminism that could take hold in Middle America had to be "liberal feminism." Only bread and butter issues of equal rights could have appeal.

In an alternative view, often taken by historians, Heartland feminism was a small-scale version of the "national" movement. However, what is called national is in fact big-city feminism, based on the events and personalities in America's urban and intellectual centers, most often New York and to a lesser extent Boston, Washington, D.C., and Chicago. Judith Hole and Ellen Levine, in their invaluable early study, set the stage when they declared: "[T]he movement in New York is so varied and protean in character it can in some sense serve as a microcosm of the movement as a whole." Alice Echols's influential book *Daring to Be Bad* focused on East Coast groups "because with few exceptions these were the groups that made significant theoretical contributions." Echols continued, "While some of the conflicts I recount here were peculiar to New York, the major debates over the left, class, race, elitism, and lesbianism occurred everywhere. . . . Although the details of my analysis might vary from region to region, I believe the essence of the argument would remain unchanged."[4] Quite an assertion given the dearth of information on these other regions!

Some of these works provide excellent studies of a specific part of the movement, but they remain inadequate as overarching explanations of an immense, multifaceted grass-roots movement in a decentralized country. The amalgam of the experiences, writings, and organizations of a few visible leaders and those of feminists across the nation makes the assumption that feminist ideas take on the same meaning in different times and places. This negates the experiences of millions of women. Sociologists and political scientists have done better at avoiding this trap. In the past decade, invaluable studies have appeared, such as those brought together in Myra Marx Ferree and Patricia Yancey Martin's *Feminist Organizations: Harvest of the New Women's Movement.*[5] But these writings, generally on specific case studies or social movement theory, do not fill the need for more history.

Few book-length histories based on primary-source material have been published on the second-wave movement. In 2000, historians Rosalyn Baxandall and Linda Gordon wrote that "[y]ou can count on your fingers the scholarly studies and well-researched journalism about the American women's movement."[6] This comes as a surprise to people with superficial knowledge of the question because of the extensive bibliography. In fact, most accounts use the same few books based on primary sources and original research, and they are quoted so often that they have become gospel. I have come across descriptions of an event backed by three different citations—each of which can be traced to the same book. This process creates an illusion of historiographic consensus.

One of the enshrined narratives of the movement tells of its emergence in two parts, often described as ideological divisions, with what called itself women's liberation on one side and liberal feminism on the other. Another way of analyzing the movement's configuration has been structural, dividing it into a younger branch with its small groups and an older branch with its traditional organizations. Most of these narratives portray the liberal or bureaucratic branch as the earliest and most successful.

Dayton's story differs. Only one part emerged, challenging the universality of this narrative, and the only way I can characterize it is as liberationist, just as the movement characterized itself. Neither the fashion-designer view nor the Dayton-as-a-microcosm assumption proved accurate. Demands for equal rights did not give birth to or sustain feminism in Dayton. The keys to understanding the movement were to be found among far-reaching ideas and practices: the consciousness-raising group, the link between the personal and the political, and the innovative, prefigurative structures. It was precisely the limiting of these ideas and practices that weakened the movement. "There must always be a blueprint for the future," David Bouchier has argued. "[M]ost people will not commit their time or energies to a cause unless they can see it leading toward a better life for themselves or their children. This means, in the fullest and most positive sense, a utopia."[7] My study suggests that without utopian vision, a movement is doomed. It gives a glimpse of some feminist utopias as they evolved in Dayton.

The movement in Dayton, although difficult to dismiss as a lunatic fringe, is not presented here as typical (a paradoxical notion that would make Dayton both conservative and progressive, stable and innovative). Rather, it offers a building block, a new facet to the history of feminism that will create space for new voices and challenge the hegemony of previous models.

This study concentrates on the history of four successive, overlapping organizations that were central to the women's movement in its first decade: the umbrella organization, Dayton Women's Liberation, which in turn created the second group, the Dayton Women's Center; the third group, Dayton Women Working, an offshoot of the Center; and finally a reproductive rights coalition, Freedom of Choice. In addition, three of the many parafeminist groups—an abortion referral service, an abortion clinic, and a rape crisis center—provide examples of how feminist initiatives are institutionalized outside the movement.

The book is structured chronologically, both to show how these organizations unfolded in time and to render the depth and complexity of the movement. Chapter 1 tells the story of the consciousness-raising process among the founders of the second wave, the creation of Dayton Women's Liberation, and the peculiar configuration of the city's movement. The second chapter traces the life of DWL during a period when, despite innumerable offshoot groups and projects, the movement was one. It discusses the many issues addressed, the actions undertaken, and the innovative structure developed, all integral parts of the organization's utopian philosophy. Chapter 3 shows the group creating, then being eclipsed by, the new Women's Center. The movement entered a new era with the creation of a physical space, increased feminist visibility, and the growing importance of a service orientation. The Women's Center became a new nucleus, but it was also the site of the first major internal rift, ostensibly between founding feminists and a second generation of socialist feminists, which resulted in the demise of the mother organization. Chapter 4 looks at a developing context of the movement: the increase of parafeminist groups, offshoots of the movement in the middle of the decade. Three groups are examined to illustrate different outcomes of what later came to be called mainstreaming. In the fifth chapter, we see how the Women's Center continued to serve as a nucleus and maintain a sense of movement unity for several more years. The necessity of maintaining a utopian vision while providing services and engaging with local institutions proved to be a difficult line to tread, which helps explain why the Center later lost its central position in the movement. Chapter 6 tells the story of an offshoot of the Center, Dayton Women Working, that intentionally separated from the rest of the movement, illustrating how the subject "woman" was no longer one. This organization, a laboratory for socialist feminists and a relay of a national movement, diverged from previous groups in its narrower focus and its rejection of prefigurative structure. It raises issues of linkage between gender, race, and class. The final chapter introduces the rise of the antifeminist New Right and the threat it posed to feminists in Dayton. In response, the first major coalition, Freedom of Choice, brought together a broad spectrum of activists, including liberal women, to defend reproductive freedom.

Woven through the study of the organizations are the stories of a handful of their key activists, thanks to oral history interviews, many life stories, with fifty-nine people. We meet a population that is significantly more diverse than what is described elsewhere. Three generations stand out, characterized by their political trajectories rather than sociological profiles: a first generation of founding liberationists; a group of socialist feminists in the mid-decade; and toward the end of the period, a cohort of liberal women. Contrary to many studies, these women are named here. I felt strongly about avoiding the use of pseudonyms so that the subjects would assume their places in history and maintain more control over their stories. Their integrity as characters allows them more easily to contest my telling. Of particular interest to me was what led women in the Heartland to break with familiar life styles and take the risk of becoming feminists—or to borrow Jane O'Reilly's term, "What went 'click'?"[8]

When reading much of the existing body of literature on feminism of the 1960s and '70s, I feel exhausted and frustrated at the violent conflicts that rocked the movement. Perhaps this is how it was in other cities (although the stress on leaders with public images and positions to defend no doubt exaggerates these fights even within the most contentious groups). Dayton's movement had its share of conflicts, some internecine and sterile, others productive confrontations of ideas. Yet even for those activists most affected by what was worst in the movement, there were no regrets. The conflicts never overshadowed the elation of the liberating experiences, the tangible bonds of sisterhood, the transformations in their lives, and the conviction that they could and would change the world.

⟩

Acknowledgments

Many people have contributed to this work. Above all, I am indebted to my "subjects." They opened up their archives and often their homes to me. They have shared memories, feelings, and perceptive thoughts about the movement they forged. Several of them read and critiqued various drafts of the manuscript. They have impressed me again and again with their intelligence and honesty about the strengths and weaknesses of this movement and their own involvement. In addition to the dozens of names mentioned, there were hundreds of other important activists; they are the heroes of this story. It is my most heartfelt desire that they recognize themselves and their movement in the following pages.

Special thanks to Claire Moses who wouldn't let me give up; to Howard Zinn for his loving support and his inspiring radicalism; to Thierry Lang who always believed in this project; to Anne Lovell, Liliane Kandel, and Lisa Marie Hogeland who read and commented on various drafts; and to the Stanford University Institute for Research on Gender where I was a visiting scholar in 1994. Thanks to the Ohio State University Press editors for their suggestions and their enthusiasm.

My gratitude to my family: to Bernice Ezekiel Brant who has been my staunchest supporter and who contributed her extraordinary knowledge of Dayton, and to Bernice and Bertram Brant for their hospitality; to Jonathan Ezekiel for his constant encouragement and expert advice about the publishing world; to Michael Ezekiel who brought radicalism into the family; and to my beloved Clara and Eizo, who from birth learned to let Mama work and who await this book with impatience.

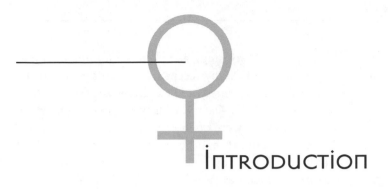

Introduction

In Dayton, Ohio, as in many cities, the social movements of the 1960s —civil rights, Black Power, and the New Left—served as midwife to the women's movement. The local and the national scene intertwined to provide the context, the ideas, and the events that were to affect the movement in its formative years.

At the beginning of the sixties, Dayton was still overcoming the climate of conservatism and political repression that had swept the country during the previous decade. The American Civil Liberties Union had been decimated, with only a handful of active members. The city's birth control clinic, created in 1935, had been closed in 1955.[1] Radicals had been purged from the unions. A history of Dayton, written in 1963 by a member of the chamber of commerce and prefaced by the editor of the so-called liberal *Dayton Daily News,* recounted how the Congress of Industrial Organizations had been faced locally with the same "threat" as it had nationally: within and without, "Reds" were being discovered, members of "the international Communist conspiracy to destroy the United States government and the American economic system." Local unions, the author proclaimed, valiantly fought this menace.[2] In the early sixties, little trace could be found of progressive activism.

The civil rights movement broke through this repressive culture.[3] A small chapter of the National Association for the Advancement of Colored People had existed in Dayton for decades and continually fought for civil rights. It campaigned for voter registration, community improvement, and desegregation of the police department and of public facilities. By the late fifties and early sixties, the movement was gaining strength both locally and nationally.

In Dayton, although "whites only" signs had disappeared, blacks could by no means be assured decent service in any restaurant. And in employment, education, and housing, attitudinal and institutional racism had barely been touched. Many recent arrivals to the city at the time, both black and white, commented on the extreme segregation they encountered. The vast majority of Dayton's black population lived on the West Side, where conditions were often poor. A 1966 mayor's committee and public hearing reported that the West Side had substandard housing, rat-infested neighborhoods, and inadequate transportation, schooling, and recreational facilities.[4]

In the early 1960s other civil rights groups appeared, including a local chapter of the Congress of Racial Equality (CORE) in 1962 and subsequently a Non-Violent Direct Action Committee. As CORE cofounder Jesse Gooding said, there was "a lot of feeling among young males and females that the NAACP wasn't aggressive enough, and . . . that we needed more direct action and confrontations with the system." CORE was short-lived but highly visible. One campaign targeted a downtown Dayton department store that despite its large black clientele had only an estimated fourteen blacks employed in its some three thousand public-contact positions.[5] Black civil rights activists picketed the store, and many were arrested.

Throughout the sixties, many whites, including future feminists, were involved in the civil rights movement. The NAACP had always had white board members, but Gooding, later president of the local NAACP, recalled an increase in white membership and financial support by the early sixties. Among the issues that attracted whites, the most important were open housing and desegregation in education.

City government response to the black community's demands was slow. Dayton's city commission/manager system had been instituted at the beginning of the century, supposedly as the answer to the political corruption and centralization of the mayoral systems and party machines. Nonpartisan municipal government did temper the party patronage system, but it also disenfranchised Dayton's ethnic and racial minorities by eliminating what had been an active ward system, and by requiring more expensive, citywide campaigns for commission candidates.[6] The city's business elite filled the political void created by nonpartisan government, according to local reporter Richard Emmet Daley. Daley stressed the role of the secretive thirty-member Area Progress Committee, founded in 1961 and "composed entirely of financial-industrial-commercial leaders. . . . The vast majority live near each other in the affluent suburbs, outside the central city, and consider themselves politically conservative."[7]

In 1962, the city commission established the Human Relations Council "to keep peace and good order and harmony among the citizens of Dayton . . . [to] avoid intergroup tensions and to promote tolerance and goodwill, and to ensure equality of treatment and opportunity to all."[8] But the council's staff was limited to two persons, and its goal was to obtain voluntary cooperation from businesses. The council published a report in 1963 charging discrimination in the city's employment policy and drafted what was to become Dayton's Code of Fair Practices, which prohibited discrimination in city employment and services. Only in 1967 was the Human Relations Council authorized to initiate and investigate complaints.[9]

By the midsixties, blacks' patience was wearing thin. Gooding attributed Dayton's disturbances to reactions against racist violence, particularly against civil rights activists, and to knowing that the system would not handle the situation fairly.[10] The issue of police brutality, by no means a new one, came to a head when a black man, Robert Barbee, was shot by a Dayton policeman who thought the pipe in Barbee's pocket was a gun. When white Unitarian minister and civil rights activist James J. Reeb was murdered in Selma, Alabama, in 1965, a large demonstration, with black and white church support, was held in Dayton. In 1966 rioting followed the shooting of a black by a white. The National Guard was called in, and 130 people were arrested. Several disturbances followed in 1967, and again after Martin Luther King's assassination the following year.

In 1967, the President's Advisory Commission on Civil Disorders traveled to Dayton to investigate and reported being told: "Key decision-makers in the Dayton power structure—particularly Mayor Dave Hall and the All Dayton Committee—have little genuine, effective concern for the city's Negro population. . . . By the same token, Dayton Negroes have developed deep hostility toward those who call the shots for the city."[11]

Unrest in the black community, Dayton's status as a testing ground, and the fund-raising abilities of city government administrators resulted in the city's becoming a prime recipient of federal pilot programs. Several of these programs were grouped together under the heading of Model Cities, intended to create prototypes for economic and racial progress in urban centers. Money was granted to projects based on recommendations of elected neighborhood priority boards. These boards were adopted by the city government as a means of taking into consideration the needs of specific communities, and later played an important role in supporting one feminist initiative.

Riding this wave of relative liberalism, a new, innovative superintendent of the public schools was appointed in February 1968. One of Wayne Carle's major tasks was the desegregation of the schools; that year, projects were defined to redistribute teachers and to bus some students.[12] The backlash began immediately. In the November 1969 election, right-wing, segregationist Save Our Schools candidates won three of the four empty slots on the seven-member school board. With the black vote divided over several candidates, for the first time in several years not one black was elected to the board of a school system that was almost 40 percent black. The board nevertheless voted a desegregation resolution in 1971, but the following year Save Our Schools won a majority, ousted Carle, and overturned the resolution.[13]

By the middle of the decade, the civil rights movement was changing as young blacks nationwide began to see power, not rights, as the issue. These changes were to have a profound effect on the emerging New Left in Dayton and subsequently on the women's liberation movement.

Black Power meant a lot of different things. For latter-day members of the Student Nonviolent Coordinating Committee[14] and the Black Panthers, it meant the end of pacifism and the beginning of blacks' using whatever means necessary to defend themselves when threatened or attacked. More applicable to the budding women's liberation movement, Black Power meant eliminating internalized oppression. SNCC president Stokely Carmichael recalled watching Tarzan movies in his youth and cheering on the title character as he beat up black natives. "Today, I want the chief to beat the hell out of Tarzan and send him back to Europe," he said.[15] Another important lesson for future feminists was the need for autonomous organizing. Black Power partisans argued that blacks should organize among themselves to strengthen and improve black communities, as opposed to supporting an integrationist approach—which often meant allowing blacks into a white world on white terms.

White civil rights activists were not welcome in Black Power groups. "We cannot have the oppressors telling the oppressed how to rid themselves of the oppressor," Carmichael wrote. Black Power advocates were telling whites that what had been called the Negro problem was, in fact, a white problem: "[M]ost liberal whites react to 'black power' with the question, What about me? rather than saying: Tell me what you want me to do. . . . White supporters of the movement [have been] afraid to go into their own communities—which is where the racism exists—and work to get rid of it. . . . They admonish blacks to be nonviolent; let them preach nonviolence in the white community. They come to teach me Negro history; let them go to the suburbs and open up freedom schools for whites."[16]

In Dayton, sympathetic whites took Black Power advocates' lessons to heart and sought to do antiracist organizing in white communities. One group, including future feminists, created an organization called Summer in the City (SITC) that was aimed explicitly at confronting white racism.[17]

Work against racism was but one element in the rise of a broad spectrum of political activism, called by sociologists the youth revolt and often divided into the counterculture and the New Left. For much of the decade participants thought of such activism as "the Movement." The disillusionment of post–World War II baby boomers—including white Northerners who went south to participate in the civil rights movement—was similar to the alienation of the 1950s beat generation. As children of a selectively affluent society, they opposed the conformity of the American Dream and the "little boxes" of the suburbs. In addition, they discovered injustice—racism, repression of free speech, and rapidly, imperialism—that was opposed to what they had been taught about America. Instead of retreating into individualism, as the beats did, they decided to change not only their lives but also the world.[18]

In 1969, Daytonian Charles Radican wrote: "The movement was a child of moral passion. A rapidly growing number of American war babies became incensed at the knowledge that they had been misled and betrayed by their country, their parents and their schools. They saw that America, far from being a bulwark of peace and justice in the world, was the largest single obstacle to that goal. . . . Nothing short of total revolution on all sides—political, economic, spiritual, cultural—is needed in this country. . . . The people must rise up out of their stupor and take responsibility for the establishment of a truly democratic and spiritually dynamic society. TO LOVE WE MUST FIGHT!"[19]

The New Left was a politically conscious, radical segment of the movement. It was called "new" by its early, more politically experienced protagonists to distinguish it from the old Left and its Communist Party, nearly eliminated under the weight of extreme repression and by its dogmatism and allegiance to the Soviet Union. Many who followed equated "new" with good and "old" with the lies they had been taught. While leftist political parties did emerge or resurface, the numerous ad hoc committees and loose organizations and the general anarchic movement typified the era. Many New Leftists thought that the working class had sold out and turned conservative,[20] so they looked toward the lumpen proletariat and oppressed minorities, in particular blacks, as the vanguard.

Nationally, the movement first exploded into the public eye in the form of the Free Speech Movement at the University of California Berkeley in 1964. Over the following year the small group Students for a Democratic Society saw its ranks swell, the influx sparked by the escalation of the Vietnam War, the beginning of large-scale bombings, and the draft.[21] Although the movement has often been mistakenly reduced to its antiwar components, the war—as a symbol of all that was evil in America—was beginning to overshadow racism as the single issue which mobilized the largest numbers of people.

Dayton's first demonstration against the Vietnam War, according to organizer Bill Mooney, took place at the University of Dayton. Mooney recalled a hostile reception, but also one brave ROTC student with a sign reading, "Should we be in Vietnam?" The student, Mooney said, was subsequently court-martialed.

However, Dayton's universities were not the locus of the movement. Although they had small student organizations and underground newspapers, neither the conservative Catholic University of Dayton nor the commuter college Wright State University provided much radical culture or free space for the movement. Only Antioch College, some twenty-five miles away in the village of Yellow Springs, might have played this role. Radical Antioch traversed the 1950s true to its nineteenth-century commitment to racial equality (although less so to its feminist heritage[22]). It attracted progressive people to the area, some of whom later settled in Dayton. Yellow Springs was a mecca for area radicals, artists, and freethinkers. Yet Antioch influenced Dayton's social movements far less than most outsiders assume, no doubt because its work-study program resulted in a transient student population.

In 1966, the Quaker American Friends Service Committee began what was to be a long tradition of holding weekly silent vigils in downtown Dayton to protest the war. Summer in the City, initially organized to fight white racism, quickly converted to antiwar activism. By the late sixties, Dayton had a number of left-wing, antiwar, and student groups alongside the antiracist groups: the Dayton Peace Committee, Vietnam Veterans Against the War, and a support group for the United Farm Workers and its grape boycott. Significantly, rather than a chapter of Students for a Democratic Society, Dayton had Citizens for a Democratic Society. These groups meshed with the counterculture—the record and head shops, the open-air concerts, and the Community Switchboard, which handled inquiries about drug problems, venereal disease, "crash pads," and upcoming protests. The local movement spawned several underground newspapers, one of which, the *Minority Report,* was to be the seedbed for Dayton's first feminist group.

In late 1968, at a farm outside Dayton, a small group of friends and acquaintances met to discuss the need for an alternative news source. The group swelled rapidly, drawing in radical and liberal activists, including some journalists from the local dailies and the campus-based underground papers. The ambitious goal was "to create a viable alternative paper," as opposed to a supplement or opposition to the daily newspapers.[23] The first issue of the *Minority Report* "hit the streets and the campuses of Dayton [with] campus, community, and national news from a slightly different viewpoint than that espoused by the *Dayton Daily News* and the *Journal Herald*" and with "book and music reviews, interviews, cartoons, pictorials, and all sorts of other groovy things."[24] The paper was a professional-looking monthly (and later a biweekly) tabloid financed by street sales and advertisements from head shops and book, record, and crafts stores. Its downtown office was usually packed with people. Some twenty-five to thirty-five people, drawn from a pool of more than a hundred, constituted its core group. The group was almost all white, despite working relations with some black activists.

The *Minority Report* was a success. Circulation estimates ranged from four thousand to more than ten thousand.[25] It was the center for radical activism in Dayton and the de facto local correspondent for the New Left nationally. Staff members held discussions, wrote leaflets, and organized protests.

Shortly after its creation, a group of radicals who saw the paper as a tool for political organizing became prominent on the staff. As these hard-liners pushed the paper further to the left, some of the liberal participants and professional journalists withdrew. Different positions began to crystallize among the remaining staff members, in particular on the issue of culture and its relationship to the Left. This tension led to a culture-politics rift that reflected developments nationally, as it became clear that drugs, sex, and rock 'n' roll did not always rhyme with revolution.[26] Among those to leave the *Minority Report* was its cofounder, Bill Mooney. He remembered his interest in poetry and literature being condemned for having "no revolutionary meaning." Mooney, who loosely defined himself as libertarian, opposed the hard-liners' political rhetoric and their "correct line." Two of the few professional journalists to remain on staff pointed out a clash in style: the hard-liners, they said, wanted to replace the journalistic language with a more rhetorical style. Despite the tension, the *Minority Report* continued to be successful and was the rallying point for the city's radical activists, but the split later influenced Dayton's feminist movement.

In the *Minority Report,* another development that mirrored national events was in the making: the emergence of the women's liberation movement. . . .

REBIRTH
Dayton Women's Liberation

"Women's Liberation—
Call Cheryl 278-6271"

T HIS MODEST one-line advertisement announced the beginning of the women's liberation movement in Dayton, Ohio. Printed in the *Minority Report* in the fall of 1969, it initially was a tentative invitation to take part in informal discussions. It metamorphosed into a call to join a nationwide movement via a new organization—Dayton Women's Liberation. The movement transformed the lives of women in Dayton through its utopian vision by expanding the boundaries of their consciousness, helping them move inward into their psyches and outward into new arenas of thought and action. This chapter tells the stories of several of the key founders of this first organization, their political and personal itineraries, and their consciousness-raising. The consciousness-raising groups they founded became the form and content of the new movement, a movement that differed from those described elsewhere. In the first year, these feminists, like many across the nation, took their independence from the social movements they came from, yet with far less acrimony than elsewhere. This is but one example of the distinctive configuration of Dayton's movement. In particular, the new group showed that radical, utopian vision and innovative organizational structures could and did mobilize women in the Heartland.

The "Cheryl" whose number appeared in the advertisement, Chewerl Radican, had never heard of women's liberation before the summer of 1969. It was a man, a coworker at the *Minority Report,* who first brought it to Radican's attention. Male leaders had been wondering whether the issue warranted attention in the paper, and they asked Radican for her opinion. Baffled, she exclaimed, "Whaaat? What's that?" Her coworker handed her a special issue of *motive* magazine on women's liberation.[1] "He gave me that magazine, and Dayton was never the

I

same!" Radican recalled. Before she finished the first article, Radican was a women's liberationist. "I devoured every word. It all hit home. . . . It was a very weird experience because <u>it was simultaneously like reading something new and like reading something I had always known.</u> At times [it was] almost like . . . someone was writing down what's in my head. . . . That term 'click' didn't come in for several more years, but that was multiple orgasms of 'click.'"

Radican's revelatory experience mirrored that of many women across the nation as they read their first feminist text, be it Beauvoir, Friedan, Millet, or others. However, it is not surprising that it was *motive*, the magazine of the progressive University Christian Movement, that had such an impact on Radican. The opening editorial by Joanne Cooke could have been written with Dayton in mind. Cooke's autobiographical introduction emphasized the "normalness" of her background. She had been in the Girl Scouts, church youth groups, and student councils. Her father was a minister and an officer in the Air National Guard.[2] Cooke's conversion to feminism had occurred when she was sent by *motive* to cover a national women's liberation conference.

Like Cooke, Radican also had a transformative experience when sent to cover a national conference—an underground press conference in Ann Arbor, Michigan, in 1969. When a women's caucus was convened, she jumped at the occasion.[3] "That was my first meeting of women, and that was an incredible experience. It got to be a huge group, all talking at once, all so excited about the whole thing." The experience provided Radican with both a taste of sisterhood and a model for feminist organizing.

Like Cooke, Radican as a youth had been influenced by the military. She had been born in nearby Cincinnati, but as an army brat had lived in different American cities. Her parents were lower-middle-class Kentucky hillbillies (as she put it) who had taught her to believe in justice and equality. These ideals took on new meanings when, as a young girl, she and her family moved to Turkey. In 1957, at age ten, she witnessed U.S. military escalation and the arrival of the "ugly American" who shocked her by "whistling at the Turkish women and being obnoxious." The experience "tuned [her] into the world and into respect of different cultures."

After returning to the U.S., Radican was captivated by John F. Kennedy and sympathetically watched the growing civil rights movement from afar. Like Cooke, Radican also was involved in church activities. In high school, she decided to join a church group and sought out one that discussed social issues.

A highly intelligent child, Radican became the first member of her family to go to college. It was in a Bible literature class at the University of Cincinnati that she met her future husband, Charles. In 1968, the Radicans got involved in the tail end of the civil rights movement, in the antiwar movement, and in the campaign to elect antiwar candidate Eugene McCarthy. (An hour after their wedding, they swung by McCarthy headquarters to pick up the leaflets they would distribute upon return from their honeymoon.) During this period, politics and church blended together. The couple tutored black ghetto children through a campus ministry program, and their most intense exposure to both movements was at a University Christian Movement conference in Cleveland.

Radican moved to Dayton that same year, following her husband, who had enrolled at the United Theological Seminary. Rejecting the traditional role of minister's wife, she commuted to Cincinnati to complete her B.A. in psychology and began working at the *Minority Report*.

Radican was impulsive, quickly absorbing new ideas, embracing new causes, and becoming impatient with those who were slow to understand. She soon made the connection between her readings on women's liberation and her personal life, calling up experiences that she realized were examples of sexism. She angrily remembered the college counselor who tried to dissuade her from entering the "male field" of psychology, and a girlfriend whose wealthy parents refused to pay her college tuition, saying that women had no need for higher education. Radican began to see the inequalities in her marriage and those of her radical friends. Upon reading an article on sexism in the Left, particularly the methods male radicals used to silence women at meetings, she realized that "that was going on right here, and it had to stop!"

Radican, all "fired-up and energized," armed with the rudiments of an analysis of women's oppression, a taste of the solidarity of an all-woman's caucus, and a goal of rectifying the situation in the Left, began working on other women at the *Minority Report,* particularly Robin Suits, Jan Griesinger, and Kathy Kleine. Radican gave them *motive* magazine and other literature to read, but none of the women were immediately converted.

For Robin Suits, the question of women's liberation was not totally new. Living at the mailing address of the *Minority Report,* she received the underground press from around the country, and by 1969 many papers devoted space to the issue. Indeed, on several occasions the *Minority Report* had mentioned, in fairly favorable terms, women's

3

Robin Suits

organizing in the New Left as well as the women's liberation movement. Suits agreed that women's oppression existed, but placed it second to other struggles. In any case, she knew it did not apply to her: she was "one of the boys." Women's liberation, she feared, was "a lot of personalistic stuff that was going to gum up the Left" and divert it from the important issues of capitalism and racism.

Although at eighteen Suits was the youngest of the group, she had been politically active for years. Suits was a "pink-diaper grandbaby" from an affluent family. Her grandfather had been a socialist in the 1930s, and her parents had close friends in the Communist Party. In addition, having grown up in a university town in Michigan, she was exposed to social movements early and attended her first protest by age eleven. In 1966, then sixteen, Suits participated in a project with other white youths, living in and renovating a community center in the slums of Chicago. That summer was filled with intensive political education as she attended rallies, heard Martin Luther King Jr. speak, and simultaneously learned about Black Power.

Suits moved to the Dayton area to attend Antioch College in Yellow Springs, a haven for political progressives for more than a century. Suits had chosen Antioch because of its reputation as radical, but although many students identified with the New Left, she was disappointed to discover little activity on campus. Antioch's work-study program created a transient student body, and many students invested their political energy in their workplaces, Suits believed. Campus life centered on drugs and free love, and she heard men make comments such as, "Why would a chick go to Antioch if she didn't want to ball?" She found this unfair, but her own personal problem. Suits first went to Dayton through the college's work-study program to become a part of the Summer in the City, a group fighting white racism. By 1969, when Dayton Women's Liberation began, she had dropped out of college to devote herself full time to "the Revolution."

Bright and articulate, Suits was an active member of the *Minority Report* and the Dayton Left. She shared a house with her lover and two other male leftist "honchos." Part of her devotion to the revolution consisted of supporting the three men with her meager salary from working at a photo shop and doing all the cooking and cleaning. Her home front did not make her immediately receptive to the idea of women's liberation.

Jan Griesinger recalled she was uninterested in reading about women's liberation and unimpressed by Radican's consciousness-raising experience. "I didn't really think it affected me, and I thought there were more important problems," she said. In her midtwenties at the time, she had been politically active for years.

Griesinger grew up as one of five children in an affluent, suburban Chicago family. Her father, the "first generation off the farm," had gone to college and become an attorney. Her college-educated mother was a full-time homemaker. Her parents were progressive Young Republicans and very involved in their Methodist church.

Griesinger's first glimmers of political consciousness came from witnessing, through a church camp and a high school exchange program, the difficult lives many blacks led. In the early sixties, when she was a student of philosophy and religion at conservative DePauw University, she became active against the racism to which the few black students on campus were subjected. For example, when it became known that local barbershops would not cut blacks' hair, she participated in the ensuing pickets. Far more, national developments affected her; in 1963, when a bomb killed four children in a black church in Birmingham, Alabama, Griesinger was "catapulted into action" and helped organize protests. Like most of the students interested in civil rights, she was attracted to the campus Christian youth group.

In a freshman English course, Griesinger wrote a paper on the problems of being a minister's wife—problems she assumed she would encounter. Upon graduation, she did get married, although not to a minister, and followed her husband to the Cincinnati area, where his family lived. There, she worked in an all-white church for a short time, but even her mild attempts to bring the congregation into contact with black people were judged too radical, and she finally resigned. In the early years of her marriage, she felt "isolated in the suburbs and hooked into [her husband's] family." Nevertheless, by 1966 Griesinger had helped pen an antiwar resolution in a statewide church meeting, and by "Vietnam Summer" in 1967 she had plunged into antiwar organizing. She became active in Clergy and Laity Concerned about Vietnam and helped found and chair Cincinnatians for Peace.

This reawakening corresponded to the beginning of Griesinger's renewed student life and increased independence. In 1967 she began commuting to Dayton to attend the United Theological Seminary. Rather than marry a minister, she had decided to become one herself. By this time, she and her husband, who was not politically active, were moving apart. As it became apparent that divorce was imminent, she began transferring her activist energy to Dayton, and she moved there shortly after. By 1969, she was a central figure to the *Minority Report* and the Dayton Left.

Griesinger became close friends with the Radicans, and Chewerl Radican particularly prodded Griesinger on the subject of women's liberation, with little success at first. Having competed well in the male-dominated field of theology, Griesinger was convinced that she was already liberated. In addition, unlike her impulsive friend, she tended to be cautious about new ideas, slowly incorporating them and then instead of talking, she acted.

Of all the women at the *Minority Report,* the most receptive to the ideas Radican espoused was Kathy Kleine, who immediately believed they made "all the sense in the world." However, while Kleine had no theoretical objections, like Suits and Griesinger she did not consider herself oppressed. Kleine, in her early thirties, was happily married, had small children, and "had always worked." She thought she had "the perfect life," but said that many of her friends were "haranguing [her] on the phone day and night because of their oppression—which they did not, of course, define as such." It was these women, trapped in the housewife syndrome, that Kleine hoped to free.

Kleine had come to the Midwest from New York in 1954 to attend Antioch, one of the rare places where a spirit of resistance to the repressive cold war culture reigned. At the time, though not a member of a political party, Kleine called herself a socialist. After graduation, she and her new husband found jobs in the Dayton area. For social more than religious reasons, Kleine became active in the Unitarian Church as well as in organizations such as the League of Women Voters. During the early sixties, Kleine was, as she later put it, "a good liberal" and as such was sympathetic to the civil rights movement. She was particularly affected by the 1964 murders of three civil rights activists in Mississippi; one of the victims, Michael Shwerner, was the brother of a former Antioch classmate.

Kleine pushed her church to support progressive causes. When the antiracist group Summer in the City was organized, she fought for the Unitarian Church to offer its facilities. She later joined the *Minority Report* project. When Radican spoke of sexism on the paper's staff, Kleine, whose personal life was somewhat independent of the Left community, was the first to recognize that there were problems.

Radican, impatient in these heady times of rapid transformations, believed that her friends were insufferably slow to see the light. But it was only a matter of weeks before Kleine, Suits, and Griesinger agreed to hold a meeting to discuss women's liberation. They invited a few friends and women from the Left. There was no doubt that the meeting should draw from the radical community: that was where the women's energy was invested and where they were experiencing unfair treatment. But they also believed that the New Left had to be a model of new, liberated life styles, and that feminism had to be an extension of their revolutionary politics and made up of revolutionary women. Only Kleine extended invitations beyond this milieu, drawing in some of her "discontented housewife" friends.

In September 1969, some twenty women came together in the living room of Kleine's house in Dayton View, one of the city's only integrated neighborhoods and home to many progressives. The women were white, between twenty-five and thirty-five years old. About half were married, and quite a few had children. Virtually none were college students at the time.

As the evening began, many of the women were skeptical, and few were ready to admit that they were personally "unliberated."[4] But all hesitations vanished as they "got personal" and timidly began to recount experiences of unfair treatment, wondering if they were relevant. They discovered that many—often all—of the women present had had similar experiences.

For Suits, "it was just an explosion! I don't think there was one woman there who didn't feel that she, personally, had been oppressed all her life." What impressed Radican, already a convert, was the atmosphere of the meeting: "A lot of 'I'm not sure I buy that'; a lot of 'I just don't know what to think about that'; and a lot of 'I'm just overwhelmed and numbed at the whole discussion—this whole thing frightens me.' And a whole lot of clicks all mixed in together. . . . I think it was a lot of feeling our way and really enjoying . . . the respect that we had for each other, giving people room to speak. . . . The whole different atmosphere that when I'm in a particular mood, I'll call a 'women's atmosphere.'"

During the meeting, many of the women experienced the proverbial "click" or "revelatory experience." As the evening ended, what had begun as a tentative discussion among a handful of women had metamorphosed into a new cause, immodestly called the Dayton Women's Liberation Movement. In Kathy Kleine's living room, Dayton's first feminist nucleus set for itself no less a goal than that of ending women's oppression and changing the world. For all participants, the meeting marked the beginning of a journey into uncharted territory. They knew they were on to something big, but they had no idea how huge their task would prove to be.

Dayton Women's Liberation (DWL), as the group later called itself, began meeting regularly, holding discussions, rapidly re-baptized "consciousness raising." Simultaneously, members began defining actions. As Radican described, "We planned actions, as well as tried to read a particular article and discuss it to develop theory—everything! . . . It was certainly a consciousness-raising group, but it was also a study group and an action group. I don't think we were capable of separating all those things." Influenced by New Left ideals of participatory democracy— indeed, critical of the Left for not having lived up to those ideals—the group had no designated leaders, functioned by consensus, and encouraged all members to participate. The women examined myriad questions, drawing on their personal experiences and seeking out feminist texts. There supposedly was no specialization: "everyone did everything." However, women would tend to discover specific ideas. Griesinger raised questions of racism. Radican picked up on the issue of abortion. Another woman began to see birth control as a possible weapon for women's liberation. Others examined economics, marriage, and the family. Nancy Galehouse, who did not come from radical circles or the sexual revolution whirlwind that had drawn in most of the new liberationists, was the brave one to introduce crucial discussions on sexuality.

As seasoned political activists and new converts, these women felt compelled to get the word out. The logical channel was the *Minority Report,* where their input was welcomed. In December 1969, an issue on women's liberation appeared in which different positions were stitched together in a patchwork of ideas, illustrating both the infancy of the movement and its openness to many ideas. Revolutionary and liberal philosophies coexisted, sometimes in the same sentence. The style was as eclectic as the content, varying from guidebook language to literary style to New Left rhetoric. A striking absence was that of personal experience; only one woman used the first person. The authors, many of whom had never penned an article in the *Minority Report,* lacked the self-confidence to put into writing the reflections that had begun in the privacy of the consciousness-raising groups.

DWL knew it was but one of hundreds of unaffiliated organizations across the country that made up a whole. The Dayton movement was to be an autonomous but integral part of the overall revolutionary movement from which it had emerged. As such, it was dedicated not only to women's liberation but also to the elimination of capitalism, imperialism, and racism. Dayton's women's liberation movement, it declared, would be another "assault on a society which requires for its existence a dominant class of white males and an oppressed class which includes black men and all women."[5]

The organization's first statement of purpose—printed in the women's liberation issue of the *Minority Report*—targeted the system, not men, as the enemy: "Women's Liberation realizes that men are oppressed by the system too, although not to the degree that women are, and that it is the phony masculinity image imposed on the male which makes him oppress women." The editorial continued: "Freedom of choice is denied both sexes, but women more than men. Women, who traditionally perform service functions—housekeeper, nurse, teacher, child-raiser, etc.—keep the present system functioning. Therefore, neither sex can be free until women are."[6]

[margin note: Did not believe individ. men originated the oppression]

Men would benefit from a new society in which both sexes could "enjoy full development of their potentialities," in contrast to a capitalist world that "has run rampant to destroy, exploit, the great majority of Americans, the great majority of the world's population for the benefit of a very few."[7] In the statement of purpose, "society," or "the system" was at fault; however, elsewhere in the issue it was men, male chauvinism, or "white men in power" that were to blame. Who or what was the enemy remained one of DWL's most glaring, unresolved issues.

The women's liberation issue included articles on birth control, abortion (with a "guideline to illegal abortions"), working women (including a breakdown of salaries by race to show the double oppression of black women), housewives or "unpaid domestic workers," and women as consumers. In this first attempt to elaborate theory, women often appeared as victims—poorly paid workers, passive exploited wives, mindless consumers—who were "economically superfluous" and lacked a cultural heritage. Yet documenting and exposing the dismal situation served as a tool in an active process. Radical women, like participants in national minority and third world struggles, would forge new identities and transform social relationships. Women's liberationists were "pioneers [who would] build consciousness and free all women" in what was "perhaps the most revolutionary of all movement goals."[8]

From the start the writers drew an analogy between the situations of blacks and women: "[T]he history of female oppression throughout the world closely duplicates the oppression of black and other third world peoples."[9] White feminists were borrowing legitimacy from black liberation in a plea to be taken seriously. While it has been demonstrated that the analogy negates overlapping systems of oppression, thus making black women invisible, nevertheless it had tremendous power. In Dayton, as was true nationally, it was essential to white women's consciousness-raising.[10]

DWL's immediate objectives were breathtaking, reminiscent of the magnitude of the 1848 Seneca Falls declaration that marked the beginning of feminism's first wave in the nineteenth century: free and legal walk-in abortion clinics, free birth control, twenty-four-hour child-care centers, prison reform, socialized medicine, guaranteed income for all, equality in sexual relations, education reform eliminating racism and sexism, and "full recognition of the processes by which women have been exploited, and a total reversal of those processes." One author added other strategies, including creating women's communes, abandoning "the marriage trap," and reexamining all of history and anthropology.[11]

Prospective members began to contact DWL, thanks to the women's liberation issue, advertisements in the *Minority Report,* and the grapevine. While the group proclaimed that it hoped to expand, there were misgivings. Personal ties were being created, and more important, only by limiting size could the members ensure full participation. Rapid growth of some groups, such as New York Radical Women, apparently was a factor in their demise. Although little had been published on the question, nationally the small group was emerging as a model for the women's liberation movement.

DWL's solution tapped into what was proving to be the most brilliant organizing tool of the movement: the creation of semiautonomous consciousness-raising groups. Dayton's groups provided both content and form for years; they were the basic cells of the movement and the space within which new ideas and new identities were forged. This practice later proved to be effective for all who used it in Dayton, irrespective of age, class, race, or sexual orientation. Early pioneers of feminist consciousness-raising groups evoked various historical inspirations, mostly minority and third world peoples who created discursive liberated zones, translated into women's liberationese as "free space."[12] But no movement had ever put this form of organization into practice on such a large scale.

No one at that first meeting had intended to create a consciousness-raising group. The process of deciding whether women were oppressed and thus needed liberation easily slipped into the recounting of personal experiences. Pooling these experiences came naturally. This first jump from a classic political meeting to a consciousness-raising group was intuitive and theorized only later. But by the end of DWL's first year, the CR group and process had become its heart and soul.

Whereas in some cities feminists advised potential recruits that "the surest way to affiliate with the movement these days is to form your own small group,"[13] DWL took the process in hand. The organization would hold a meeting for interested people, after which members from the original group would help new groups get started. The facilitator would introduce some of the themes DWL had found to be important and encourage participants to speak about their lives, attempting to reproduce the revelatory experience that was the trademark of the CR group. The facilitator was supposed to help place women's liberation in a larger political context, making connections between sexism, racism, and imperialism. She also helped set up ties with the overall organization.

Contrary to what has been written about CR groups elsewhere, no other guidelines or directives were spelled out.[14] Nevertheless, a similar process developed, not unlike that described in Californian Pam Allen's *Free Space*.[15] Many first-timers found an all-women's group odd: "Why are there no men here?" they would ask. By their second meeting, the reason for excluding men was self-evident. Similarly, many women examined other participants, wondering, "Who are those strange characters?" Creating trust among women from different backgrounds constituted a first step. Most groups did so by spending weeks, even months, encouraging each woman to talk about her life. This launched several processes. First, opening up to the others helped establish trust. Second, women learned to speak out and validate their experiences. Simultaneously, women moved beyond the individual and built up a "collage of similar experiences,"[16] a frame through which to view the world, based on their individual and collective experiences. After telling their life stories, women would come to meetings with issues from their past, their present, or from their readings. Some groups chose texts or themes to study; others developed exercises. Some defined specific projects, believing that the CR group was an appropriate base for undertaking action.

The consciousness-raising process was the driving force in Dayton's nascent movement. In each new wave of arrivals, most women experienced the same "explosion" that had occurred in the original group. As women described what they saw as personal problems—whether related to housework, sexuality, or the workplace—they discovered that other women had experienced the same things. This discovery of commonality had far-reaching implications as they sought the roots of the problems not within themselves but in society. The feminism of the CR groups meant seeing women's oppression, identifying with the group "women," and envisioning a changed future—a meeting between awareness and vision, for both the individual and the group. In *Feminism and Its Fictions,* Lisa Maria Hogeland suggested that feminism can be comprehended as a form of literacy, "a set of reading and interpretive strategies that people applied both to texts and to the world around them." She rightly claimed that this helps clarify how membership in the movement "really did exist 'in your mind.'"[17]

Most participants described consciousness-raising in terms of a sudden conversion, revelation, or click. However, while new ideas came out of a collage of personal experiences, applying these perceptions to their own lives did not come easily. The initial realization was often one of the existence of women's oppression, generally that of other women. Most early feminists continued to believe that they had surmounted the situation due to personal strength or luck and were "Exceptional Women." Little by little, they began to realize that they too were oppressed by men. The realization that was the longest in coming was that the men in their lives could be oppressors. The anger and depth of these women's convictions were directly linked to this realization. As feminists realized that sexism was more far-reaching and internalized than any had imagined at first, they began viewing consciousness-raising as a gradual, ongoing process. Several evoked the image of shedding layer after layer of oppression, like peeling an onion.

Consciousness-raising was not another form of 1960s pop psychology.[18] Feminists criticized existing therapy for being sexist and normative and denounced the role of an authority, the therapist. The consciousness-raising process used a collective approach and was political. National texts faithfully reflected the Dayton women's position. Carol Hanisch wrote, "Therapy assumes that someone is sick and that there is a cure, e.g. a personal solution. . . . Women are messed over, not messed up! We need to change the objective conditions, not adjust to them." Ignoring the political nature of CR was deemed sexist. As Irene Peslikis stated, "[W]hen women get together to study and analyze their own experience, it means they are sick, but when Chinese peasants or Guatemalan guerrillas get together and use the identical method, they are revolutionaries."[19]

Seeing the political nature of the CR process constituted one of the most important insights of the women's liberation movement. Summed up in the brilliant, if ambiguous, slogan, "The personal is political," it was the theoretical foundation of the CR group as well as its method. With each click, women reinterpreted their supposedly individual problems as parts of complex historical and political processes. If the personal was the basis for a different understanding of the world, a new approach to experience became necessary. "The effect of those initial consciousness-raising groups was to learn to trust our own experience," Kleine said. "There was a gut reaction that there was validity to [our experience] that we had never before allowed ourselves to give."[20] By no longer imposing theories from "sacred texts," experience became the basic stuff from which DWL elaborated its theory. Thus, issues such as sexuality, reproductive rights, and the family moved to the center of its worldview. Ideas for projects were distilled in the same manner, providing one way in which CR process and political action connected: "[T]he consciousness-raising group provides the impetus, direction and frequently the vehicle for direct participation in societal change."[21] The process was also political, many participants believed, simply because it staked out nonsexist islands where women could forge new identities and create noncompetitive, nonhierarchical, sisterly relationships.

Creating sisterhood was crucial to the CR process. As one member said, "We had all been taught not to trust women, that women were not interesting." But participants rapidly became convinced that "women [are] gems!"[22] Sisterhood differed from friendship, and although rarely theorized in early periods, the distinction was political in nature. "A sister," wrote June Arnold in an early feminist anthology, "can be someone you don't especially like personally or agree with politically. [Sisterhood] is the common bond you feel with another woman because you know you can work with her as a woman for all women."[23] CR groups were not just intimate discussions among women or feminist friends. "Most of us were used to having women as best friends . . . and talking really personally," one DWL member commented. "[CR] was an extension of that. But the novelty was extending it to women who you weren't best friends with . . . and recognizing that we all had things in common."[24] Sisterhood meant going beyond personal affinities and formalizing the process.

The high expectations in the CR groups carried a negative side as well. As New Yorker Roz Baxandall declared, "[W]omen's liberation was love at first sight," but "like romantic love, the movement also generated many illusions."[25] Some participants harbored resentment when their groups were not able to meet their sometimes unreasonable expectations. For example, groups did not always replace the family and provide the long-term support needed to sustain a person through a divorce, a drug problem, or the beginning of a career. Inversely, when less was expected, the intensity of feelings of sisterhood, and probably the commitment to the group, was lower. There were other sources of disappointment. Several individuals felt excluded from the inner circle of DWL. But conflict was surprisingly rare, due perhaps to the personal process used, but also no doubt to the mandatory sisterhood. Personal conflict was relatively taboo, often forcing differences to be repressed or couched in political terms.

Despite reservations, sisterhood was not just an abstract theory. In interviews conducted some ten to fifteen years later, many women said the bonds established in these groups were the strongest they had ever known, calling them "utopian friendships" or alternative families. The CR process remained one of the most important experiences in their lives and the one that most contributed to changing their understanding of the world.

By the middle of the 1970s there were half a dozen CR groups in Dayton. Over the history of DWL, there is written evidence of more than forty—no doubt there were more than that—with six to ten existing at any given time, each consisting of six to fifteen members. Groups met once a week at a member's home, usually in the evening. Those groups that made it past the first few months usually lasted two to three years. Several went on longer, continuing even after the overall organization ceased to exist. As groups multiplied, they adopted names. Some used historical or literary inspiration, giving rise to Sacagawea and Lysistrata. There were a number of "Sisters" (Nora's, Plath's, Elizabeth's, and Wilder Sisters). Others opted for humor, such as Pandora, TNT, and Alpha Xι Tinsel Tarts in a Hot Coma.

Mary Morgan joined an early offshoot group. She described her first meeting: "We went on for three hours, and it was nonstop 'click, click, click.' Once the gate was opened, it wasn't Chewerl [the facilitator] telling us how we were oppressed, but sharing experiences, experiences pouring out." In Morgan's group—comprised of eight women in their thirties and forties, many from affluent South Dayton—the first discovery was that they had been victims of "the *Better Homes and Gardens* housekeeping syndrome of the fifties. . . . We'd all failed miserably at being wives and hostesses," Morgan recalled. As a result, many had questioned their mental health. "At least three of us had been through the period of going to the psychiatrist, and if not crazy, being neurotic. . . . And all of us were crazy over the same thing! We were not able to be the 1950s housewife, . . . and we'd all ended up with psychiatrists helping us adjust to our roles." One group member had even been committed to a mental hospital by her husband. The women in the group uncovered other similarities in their pasts. They realized how, as girls, they had been taught to distrust other women and vie for men's attention. They also discovered that almost all of them had become nurses or schoolteachers. Morgan, herself a teacher, and another woman came to realize that they should have studied engineering.

As a girl in a West Virginia town in the early thirties, Morgan had shown a propensity for dismantling clocks and playing with her brother's Erector set. Her parents, rural schoolteachers as young adults, believed that "education was the key to the good life," but Morgan dismayed family and teachers alike by "doing well in all the wrong things." She linked this to having lost her mother at age five and knowing that consequently she was "not going to be quite normal."

By the end of high school, still enthusiastic about science, Morgan enrolled in the West Virginia Institute of Technology. It was soon made clear to her that she had entered the wrong field; for example, faced with a shortage of microscopes, a professor forbade female students to use them. In the meantime, the United States had entered World War II and the need for workers drew women into the labor force. When recruiters came to Morgan's college in her freshman year, she was hired as an engineer's aide for the Dayton Air Force Base. She remained in the job until the end of the war, when the women were fired. Over the ensuing years, she worked at a number of jobs, got married, and trained to be a teacher.

In the late fifties and early sixties, Morgan, who had been "reared to be a Christian and not to be prejudiced," became active in the Dayton civil rights movement. Her first connection was through the American Civil Liberties Union, where she and fellow Unitarians made up a majority of the dozen or so active members. A "bleeding-heart liberal," as she later described herself, her radicalization began as she encountered black activists within the movement. The next stage in her political education came when she received a fellowship to complete a master's degree at Columbia University in the 1967–68 school year. Columbia was a hotbed of radicalism, and Morgan was witness to what Kirkpatrick Sale dubbed "the most significant student rebellion to date."[26] Over the course of the year, she discovered Marxism, observed police brutality, and heard Mark Rudd, leader of Students for a Democratic Society, speak. Simultaneously, she observed the deterioration of New York and was captivated by liberal mayor John Lindsay's plans to save the city.

Upon her return to Dayton, Morgan decided to run for city commission to help save Dayton from New York's fate. Although she chose to run as a gender-neutral citizen, she was aware that no woman had ever been elected to the commission. The campaign was a painful experience. For the first time Morgan understood the experience of being "invisible," as reporters asked questions about her husband, commented on her looks and her age, and ignored her political platform. Furthermore, sexism melded with racism. With two slots to be filled and three other candidates—two white men and one black—Morgan was portrayed as running against the black man. She finished third in the election, with more than seventeen thousand votes. It was after this that Morgan started asking her acquaintances from the Dayton Left and the Unitarian Church about the new women's group. Feeling battered and "desperate for recovery," she was ripe for a CR group.

Over the years, the various CR groups took on their own personalities. Morgan's first group, for example, was largely made up of women who had tried to adapt to the 1950s housewife role. A later group began with two closet lesbians, and within a short time five of its seven members had come out. Issues related to sexual orientation were prominent in this group. Tolerance was a theme in another group that included not only liberal and radical women but even a Right-to-Life supporter. Some groups were relatively homogenous in terms of age or marital status. In one, all members were young and single; in another, all were married, few worked outside their homes, and by the end of its existence, all but one had children.

DWL members called one group "the epitome of DWL," "the elite," "the powerful." Betty Jean Carroll saw Elizabeth's Sisters as "up on a pedestal" before joining. Barbara Gregg felt jubilation at being "one of the chosen ones." Started in October 1970 after the founding group had begun to disintegrate—several women, including Radican, had left town, and a few had left DWL—the new group was later baptized Elizabeth's Sisters when Kleine gave birth to her daughter Elizabeth. (As member Joan Ediss laughingly recalled, "We all had concentrated very hard on her being a girl!") Elizabeth's Sisters was the first to bypass the usual method for creating new groups. DWL founders had wanted a group with other politicized women, and several friends from the Left and the counterculture were interested. The group originally included Kleine, Griesinger, Morgan, who had rapidly joined the DWL core group, and several new members. Between fifteen and twenty women took part in Elizabeth's Sisters in its more than four years of existence. Most of them were between twenty-five and forty and had experience in other social movements. At one point, eight of the ten women lived in the same area of town.[27]

Members of Elizabeth's Sisters considered experience essential, but as Barbara Gregg recalled, "[T]here was always someone who could abstract from whatever it was that was being said. . . . There was this constant interpretation of someone's personal experience into what I would call a political realm." Between members' political backgrounds and Griesinger's constant push for studying feminist writings, Elizabeth's Sisters became the most intellectual of DWL's groups and the one that most produced theory. Integral to this was the group's utopian vision. "We had a long series of what I would call 'dream sessions': if we could create a perfect society, what would it . . . be like?" Gregg said.

Joan Ediss quickly became part of Elizabeth's Sisters and the DWL activist core. Although this was Ediss's first involvement in the women's movement, her two daughters, young adults, had been involved in DWL nearly since the beginning, and Ediss, an activist in the Left and counterculture, knew Radican and Griesinger well.

Ediss was born in Kentucky in 1930, to an Irish Catholic mother and a Jewish father, and had been raised in Cincinnati. Although benefiting from white, middle-class privilege, she had three strikes against her: being from Kentucky and being a member of two religious minorities.

Ediss began college at a school of music, but got married and dropped out. She later followed her husband to Dayton. "I was a product of the fifties: the nuclear family dream with the wife hidden away," she said. But she also had a rebellious streak. For example, in a presidential election she opted for Eisenhower because her husband voted for Adlai Stevenson.

In the midsixties, Ediss divorced and joined a circle of artists. She became involved with a man who opened her eyes "to the reality of the Vietnam War"; as a result, she campaigned for pacifist presidential candidate Eugene McCarthy. Ediss also got "turned on to Black Power" and began doing Black Panthers support. Although she had contacts with the *Minority Report,* her personal affinities and her anarcho-artistic side meant she sympathized with the faction that split from the paper. She did not sever relations with the Left, but she preferred her work at the countercultural crisis line called Switchboard. In the summer of 1970, when leftist Revolutionary Union organizers came to Dayton, Ediss housed one group. Discussions with the women, who called themselves feminists, helped Ediss "get in touch with other women's oppression— not my own." That, plus her attraction to DWL's nonhierarchical structure, compelled Ediss to join the organization. It rapidly became her "school" and her "home."

Another key member of Elizabeth's Sisters was Barbara Gregg. Gregg grew up in northwest Dayton in a lower-middle-class family in which money was scarce. Her father was a conservative Republican, a domineering man who beat her mother. Her mother nevertheless remained "her own person," a Democrat with a casual personal style that contrasted with the other fifties housewives in her neighborhood. Gregg was a bright, athletic girl, the prom queen at her high school. Like many early DWL members, her goal in life had been to happily marry and have children. Yet she wanted to go to college and fought bitterly with her father to be able to do so. He acquiesced, she said, in the hope that she would marry above their class, but he then siphoned money from her scholarship to help pay for her brother's studies. In Gregg's first year of college, she met her future husband, dropped out to get married, and followed him to New Jersey, where he attended divinity school. Raised Catholic, Gregg had little knowledge of birth control, and her first three children, all girls, were born in rapid succession. Her fourth and only planned child was born to produce the boy that "the whole world wanted," she said. Gregg worked regularly at odd jobs to supplement family income and organized a child-care cooperative with other "discouraged, harried women" at her husband's university.

Gregg returned to Dayton when her husband got a job at a local church. He was, as she put it, "a movement star" who viewed the church as a vehicle for social change. Through him, she was on the periphery of the civil rights movement and the New Left, but she was not active. Her introduction to politics was the issue of abortion.

The founders of DWL used their strategy of expansion by reproduction of small groups to create activist offshoots. It is no coincidence that the first such group, created in February 1970, was Women for Abortion Law Repeal. The abortion issue was mobilizing feminists throughout the Western world.

In 1969, when DWL was created, abortion was illegal or restricted in all fifty states. Over the following year, three states passed "near-repeal" bills on abortion, but Ohio was not among them. From the outset, the issue had been brought to the attention of DWL through national feminist publications and because women who needed abortions had begun calling the organization.

Women for Abortion Law Repeal was filled with members who for the most part never became active in the women's movement. Labeled "latent feminists" by a local newspaper, the *Journal Herald,* they expressed various motivations for working for the cause. One, a medical attendant, had seen victims of botched abortions in local emergency rooms. Two women had tried CR groups but preferred an action-oriented group. The issue of abortion appealed to them because it spoke to the needs of poor women.[28] One member had been in the *Minority Report* circles but had left during the culture-politico split, and although she supported the idea of women's liberation, she undoubtedly did not feel comfortable with DWL.

It was in conjunction with Women for Abortion Law Repeal that DWL made its first public appearance and came face-to-face with the media. In February 1970, with abortion reform legislation pending in the Ohio House of Representatives, some fifteen Dayton women and several children traveled to Columbus and, armed with picket signs and leaflets, marched around the state capitol in freezing weather. The group was heterogeneous, ranging from young women in jeans to one woman who was to become a DWL legend—a platinum blonde in nylons and a mink coat, pushing her twins in a stroller.

The protesters demanded not just reform but repeal of all abortion laws so that all women, regardless of age or financial means, could have safe abortions. The laws, they argued, were due to the failure to separate church and state, and far from preventing abortions, "they merely cheapen[ed] the lives of the women who [sought] them."[29] They pointed out the dangers of eugenics and argued that while women must not be forced to bear unwanted children, neither must they be coerced to abort.

The demonstration attracted reporters from local newspapers, television stations, and even the Associated Press. This was the protesters' first encounter as feminists with the media. With television spotlights on their spokeswoman, the first question came: "How many of you are wearing bras?" Controlling their anger, the demonstrators made reporters stop the cameras, politely stated that their underwear was not anybody's business, and emphasized that they were there to discuss the issue of abortion. Another take began, and again came the same question. At this point, Mary Morgan recalled, the spokeswoman put "her greasy acid finger" on the camera lens and sent the livid journalist "into orbit." On the third take, after fending off questions about their husbands and their makeup, the protesters managed to speak to the issue. The ensuing articles varied; whether overtly hostile or not, most paid little attention to the issue of abortion. One, Radican recalled, described the protestors as "a group of bra-less, make-up-less, militant women."

The myth of the bra-burner was a tenacious one that originated in reports on the demonstration at the 1968 Miss America Pageant in

Atlantic City. Protesting the objectification and mutilation of women's bodies in the name of beauty, demonstrators threw girdles, curlers, high-heeled shoes, and bras into a "freedom trash can."[30] Two years later and more than five hundred miles away, journalists faced with women demonstrating for abortion rights—all wearing bras, most wearing makeup, and one wearing a mink coat—could think of nothing but (missing) underwear. It was one of many indications that feminism—not abortion—was the controversial issue.

For the politically experienced demonstrators, the incident cemented their distrust, inherited from the New Left and civil rights movements, of the mainstream media. Through the early seventies, coverage of social movements was hostile. Not atypical, one article about Kent State the day before the infamous shootings by the National Guard described antiwar demonstrators as "vandals . . . on the rampage." "Students, Blacks Start Most Trouble on Campus" was another telling headline.[31]

Shortly after what Jo Freeman called the "grand press blitz" of January and March of 1970,[32] Dayton's two dailies began to devote space to feminism. Coverage was generally confined to the "women's pages" between Dear Abby and Heloise's helpful household tips, and it was consistently hostile. One particularly virulent wire service article began, "[T]o those who have had their fill of radical movements, the reawakening of a strident women's rights movement is about as welcome as finding out that coffee causes cancer."[33] The nationwide "rash of bra-burnings," the author continued, accounted for the "stigma of silliness [that] has stuck to women's liberation ever since." As late as mid-1972, the *Dayton Daily News* editor referred to abortion (and gay rights) as "faddish causes."[34] The standard image of a feminist was that of a young, extremist, man-hating, single woman. Journalists who refuted the picture did so with surprise, constantly pointing out when a feminist was married, older, or "feminine." In mid-1973, DWL members were still being described in terms of their makeup and hairstyles.[35] Although some changes had occurred by that time—help-wanted ads had been desegregated in 1972, and more respectful coverage was appearing—any article that took feminist ideas seriously long remained the exception.

From DWL's inception, there was no question of the mainstream press's being a partner, or even a viable channel of communication. The press was an adversary that could occasionally be forced to make minor concessions. As Mary Morgan put it, "Established lines of communication simply cannot be used for the women's movement."

While the abortion protest illuminated the movement's relationship with the media, a second demonstration illustrated DWL's changing relationship with the New Left. Robin Suits and another DWL member learned that groups around the country were planning antiwar actions with an anticorporate slant for the spring of 1970. The two believed that the Dayton demonstration should be organized by DWL. Reactions to the proposal varied. Some women in the DWL core group suspected Suits of being manipulated by male leftists, particularly her lover, a controversial leftist leader and hard-liner at the *Minority Report*. Indeed, he supported the idea, but Suits herself hoped to maintain connections with the Left and politicize new women. Some newcomers with no history of radical activism did not see the relationship Suits and others took for granted between feminism and left-wing causes. Although the core group unanimously spoke out against the Vietnam War and multinational corporations, members disagreed on how to relate to the Left and how to politicize the new women. Some promoted confrontation politics; others advocated a more gradual, personal approach in CR groups. DWL finally agreed to organize and sponsor the demonstration, and although there was little discord, this was the first sign of differing conceptions of political activism.

The demonstration, held on April 15, the anniversary of the first mass draft-card burnings, was endorsed by local groups including the Black Panthers. "Who pays for the War?" the DWL leaflet asked. "We do. . . . Who profits from the War? The Corporations." In Dayton, the demonstrators targeted AT&T and the Internal Revenue Service. A feminist slant appeared only in a line in the leaflet: "Women, as the 'creators and preservers of life,' wish to share the feminine ideology with the rest of humanity."[36] This essentialist reasoning was peculiar for DWL and appeared only twice in its history. The demonstration was a success; Suits claimed some 750 people marched, the largest demonstration she had ever seen in the city. In spite of this, the relationship between the Left and the women's movement was becoming strained.

Parallel to the situation throughout the country, DWL was becoming independent of the New Left. Nationally, although antiwar protests were drawing record numbers, New Left organizations were in disarray. Students for a Democratic Society had splintered into numerous factions. And in the month preceding DWL's April demonstration, three Weatherpeople had died and several others had gone underground after their homemade bomb exploded in a New York townhouse, symbolically marking the end of an era. At the same time, the women's liberation movement was dynamic and growing. By 1970, many women believed it necessary to choose allegiance to feminism over the Left. Texts explaining the split had begun to appear as early as 1968, and Dayton feminists were reading them.

The earliest of these texts, Beverly Jones and Judith Brown's "Towards a Female Liberation Movement" (the "Florida Paper"), was one of the first pieces of literature Radican circulated among her friends at the *Minority Report*. Suits remembered it as "undoubtedly the most significant single cause of my political conversion to feminism. . . . [I]ts concepts figured heavily in our budding ideology."[37] The text freely used the women-black analogy, described sexist treatment of women in the Left, and called for women's liberation to strike out on its own. The mixed Left was viewed as an integrationist approach proven erroneous by Black Power. Jones wrote: "One of the best things that ever happened to black militants happened when they got hounded out of the stars-and-stripes, white-controlled Civil Rights Movement, when they started fighting for blacks instead of the American Dream. The best thing that ever happened to potential white radicals in civil rights happened when they got thrown out of SNCC (Student Nonviolent Coordinating Committee) and were forced to face their own oppression in their own world. . . . And the best thing that may yet happen to potentially radical young women is that they will be driven out of both of these groups. That they will be forced to stop fighting for the 'movement' and start fighting primarily for the liberation and independence of women."[38]

In "Women and the Left," Ellen Willis showed how women already were being forced out of the Left. She recounted the infamous incident at the 1969 Washington anti-inaugural rally—witnessed by a contingent of Dayton radicals—when a feminist speaker faced catcalls and cries of "take her off the stage and fuck her." Radical women's initial desire to fight for equality within the Left, Willis contended, had led to the assumption that women's liberation was a branch of the Left. Arguing that patriarchy predated capitalism, she concluded that although feminists may make temporary alliances with the male Left, "we intend to make our own analysis of the system and put our interests first, whether or not it is convenient for the (male-dominated) Left. . . . We do not assume that radical men are our allies or that we want the same kind of revolution they want."[39]

In their second generation, these texts were angrier and full of the self-confidence of the growing women's liberation movement. They examined how leftist men, supposedly dedicated to liberation, had constructed a microcosm of the oppressive society. In January 1970, one month before speaking in Dayton, Robin Morgan published what was probably the strongest of these statements. "Goodbye to All That" appeared in the first issue of the "Women's *Rat*," a New York underground paper that was sprinkled with pornography until it was taken over by its women staffers and a coalition of feminists. The issue had circulated in Dayton. In it, Morgan angrily proclaimed: "Goodbye, goodbye forever, counterfeit Left, counterleft, male-dominated cracked-glass mirror reflection of the Amerikan Nightmare. Women are the real Left."[40]

DWL women did withdraw their energies from the New Left. The split was a no-fault divorce in which the partners agreed to remain friends. In other cities, supporters of an autonomous women's liberation movement told stories of harassment and of being accused of divisiveness and incorrect politics. In Dayton, although aware of these incidents, the small radical community prided itself on remaining aloof from the sectarian battles that were tearing apart left-wing organizations elsewhere. The leadership, which included several strong women, tried to stay in tune with the effervescence of ideas that characterized the sixties, including feminism. Male leaders believed, with attitudes ranging from paternalism to respect, that feminism was progressive. A case in point: whereas feminists at the "Women's *Rat*" had to take over the newspaper, men on the *Minority Report* staff welcomed DWL's proposed for the special issue on women's liberation.

In the feminist-Left split, women's feelings of anger and betrayal may have been proportional to the discrepancies they saw between the revolutionary ideals espoused and the sexism they experienced. Sexism in the Dayton Left took subtle forms. Radican pointed to ways in which men would ignore women in meetings but sometimes use their ideas later. Griesinger realized she was doing all the typing but none of the writing, but even ten years later, she attributed this more to her lack of self-confidence than to any direct imposition by the men. The *Minority Report* contained little outright sexist content. Faced with such subtle sexism, DWL later came to fear manipulation of DWL feminists by men in the Left.

But the lesser degree of antagonism in Dayton perhaps meant that local feminists, even as they were taking their independence, were more aware of their debts to the Left than activists elsewhere were. They acknowledged the numerous skills they had acquired. Many recognized that the movement had been their life, their reason for breaking with old ideas and old communities and discovering new ones—including feminism. For many, left-wing men continued to inhabit their social and political networks.

The amicable split in Dayton questions the universality of the currently authoritative accounts that see the sexism of the Left as the key to the emergence of the women's liberation movement. Rebecca Klatch reported similar findings for a minority of her subjects from SDS, including national leaders. "I expected to hear . . . grievances about sexism in the movement. Instead, I discovered that . . . a minority of them found no differences in treatment based on gender, saying they felt respected by men in the movement. Their feminism grew in relation to women's inequality in society, not out of discontent over women's secondary status in SDS."[41] In Dayton, we find repeatedly that the budding feminists remember a positive heritage in previous social movements.

Along with the feminist-Left split, historical accounts identify another split, this time among women dubbed "feminists" and "politicos." The feminist-politico rift has been portrayed as fundamental in the early women's liberation movement nationally, but in Dayton, no such clear-cut lines can be found. Judith Hole and Ellen Levine wrote, "This politico/feminist division has influenced the organizational development, characterized much of the literature, provided the basis for conflicting theoretical formulations, and caused internal dissension within the movement."[42] A sizable portion of Alice Echols's influential book *Daring to Be Bad* centered around this "near lethal" split. "From the beginning," she wrote, "the women's liberation movement was internally fractured." Echols traced the origins of the conflict among New York leaders and described how it spread to the rest of the country. "[M]ost early women's liberation groups were dominated by 'politicos,'" she wrote, but within two years of its inception, "radical feminism had established itself as the most vital and imaginative force within the women's liberation movement."[43]

The battle lines vary from one account to another. One question was whether the women's liberation movement should be autonomous or a part of the Left. "The politicos took their priorities from the male-led New Left and did not want to separate from it," whereas radical feminists "felt they had to make a clean break with 'male' thought," Rochelle Gatlin wrote. Underlying this decision was a question of priorities: Was the "primary contradiction" that of class or sex? Would women be liberated by a socialist revolution? Echols stated: "Believing that women's oppression derived from capitalism, or 'the system,' as they often called it, politicos maintained that women's liberation groups should remain connected and committed to the larger Movement." She added, "While politicos acknowledged that women needed to meet in separate, all-female groups, they generally thought of women's liberation"—and here Echols quoted Robin Morgan's introduction to *Sisterhood Is Powerful*—"as an 'important' wing" of the Left; as a tool, perhaps, for organizing as-yet apolitical women into . . . the Movement.'" For Gatlin and others, the issues raised by women's liberation groups depended on their position in this split. Politicos stressed class and imperialism and "attacked the radical feminists for ignoring working-class and Third World women." Radical feminists stressed sexuality and consciousness-raising; Barbara Ryan used "CR feminists" as a synonym for radical feminism.[44]

These descriptions may hold true for specific times and places. However, while DWL members held conflicting views on many of these questions, there was no feminist-politico split. It could be argued that women in the DWL core group were both politicos *and* feminists in terms of allegiance and politics—politicos because, although none of them were members of leftist organizations at the time, many identified themselves as revolutionaries and wanted to maintain links with the overall Left, or at least with "something bigger." Most, although not all, had sided with the hard-liners in the counterculture-politico split at the *Minority Report*. Most considered issues of work, working women, imperialism, and third world and minority peoples to be of the utmost importance. On the other hand, they were feminists. All supported an autonomous women's movement, and their primary loyalties were to this movement. None advanced the idea that women would be liberated by socialism. Consciousness-raising was crucial to their philosophy and practice. Sexuality figured among the first issues raised.

Suits, for example—the closest thing to a politico in DWL's core—had indeed pushed for the April antiwar demonstration and supported continued involvement in the *Minority Report*. She identified herself as a revolutionary and was living with a prominent male leftist who was distrusted by other women. But the radical feminist Florida Paper shaped her early ideas about women's liberation. She spoke out for women's control over their sex lives and for setting up women's communes, and she was the first to write that men were the enemy. Another core activist opposed the *Minority Report* hard-liners and distrusted feminists close to the Left, but remained friendly with women from an ultraleftist group. She later came out as a lesbian and identified with Mary Daly's radical feminist writings but categorically rejected the terms "radical" or

25

"cultural" feminist, preferring the label "socio-anarchist" feminist. The same women might in the same breath point to men and the system as the enemy. When DWL was infiltrated by two women from the Marxist-Leninist Revolutionary Union, they were opposed by all, and mostly simply ignored them until they went away.

Radical feminism, according to Echols, remained the "hegemonic tendency within the women's liberation movement" but was later eclipsed by cultural feminism. Again, no such pattern emerged in Dayton. An interesting intersection with the history Echols recounted was the 1971 North American Women's Conference in Toronto, which brought together North American feminists and Vietnamese women. At least partly in response to sectarian battles during the organizational stages of the conference, delegates penned "The Fourth World Manifesto," an "embryonic but highly influential expression of cultural feminism," according to Echols.[45] DWL co-organized the Toronto conference, and the infighting affected Daytonians as well. However, rather than become political, radical, or cultural feminists, members of DWL worked harder at avoiding sectarianism.

In Dayton, most individuals did not adhere to clearly drawn political or feminist lines. Many core members were searching for new political analyses that somehow included sex, class, and race. Most women's positions were in flux as they continually examined new questions, and radical overnight changes were not uncommon. Jo Freeman illustrated the fluidity of the debate. A feminist in Chicago, she realized that she would be situated as a politico in New York. "How substantive is an ideological disagreement if the same views would be on different sides in different places?" she asked. Leslie Cagan, speaking about the situation in Boston, recalled feeling "torn apart" by the description. "It felt like the 'politico-feminist' distinction was not quite accurate, and it certainly did not give people space to really find ways to pull it together. After all, we were all exploring lots of new ideas."[46] The infancy of the movement and lack of political clarity do not explain all. In DWL, the pieces did fit together, and they did so under the banner not of politico or feminist, radical or other, but of liberation. Dayton's history questions the universality of the feminist-politico split.

In the spring of 1970, the *Minority Report* ceased publication. Its collective had been gutted by the departure of several groups, among them the women from DWL. Given the decline of the Left and the rise of the women's liberation movement, it simply seemed logical.

Its demise left DWL with no channel to transmit its ideas. Before founding its own newsletter, the group tried its hand at a special issue of another magazine. Significantly, DWL turned to *Here and Now,* which was edited by Barbara Gregg's husband and whose editorial board included Gregg, Morgan, Kleine, and a who's who of Dayton's progressive theologians. The journal's statement of purpose began, "[C]ivilization as we know it is collapsing, and while the foundations of a new age have already been laid, its structures have yet to be determined." The publication, "in harmony with God," was intended to "chronicle and to serve as a catalyst in that planning."[47]

Some fifteen members of DWL collectively prepared the July/August 1970 issue, called "What Do Women Want, Anyway?" It was a defensive title, dedicated to convincing the skeptical—women, that is, not men. "Helping women become aware of their inferior status in society" was the first part in a process Kathy Kleine spelled out in her article "In Defense of Liberation." Once women reached this stage, Kleine wrote, two other steps were necessary: recognizing and creating space for women's differing philosophies and political analyses without negating the commonality of their oppression, and understanding the necessity to "radically alter society," freeing all peoples. Most articles in the issue argued for militancy to effect radical change, Kleine wrote, "Those who complain that militant tactics are self-defeating are in reality saying, 'If you ask us nicely, maybe we'll give you what you want.' The truth is, of course, that what we want, no one is going to give us. . . . We started over 100 years ago and we began asking nicely. Then we stopped being nice and we struggled, and struggled, and struggled, and whittled away our demands until all that was left was suffrage. We finally got suffrage. So what? . . . Radical? Yes, because there's no other way."[48]

When the writers did call for reform, they took care to incorporate it into their vision of radical change. Abortion and birth control must be safe, with no coercion, not signifying men's "free" access to women's bodies, and accompanied by the means for women to bear and raise children humanely. Equal pay for equal work made sense only if the concept of work was redefined. Child care could not be a tool to improve production, but must "free men, women and children for regular pursuit of their individual interests and needs."[49]

Kleine's reference to the nineteenth-century feminist movement confirmed that DWL members had been doing their homework. From the beginning, they were aware of their historical precedents. The article in the *Minority Report* announcing the creation of the group was subtitled "Rebirth," signifying both individuals' changes in consciousness and the

historical roots of the movement. The special issue of *Here and Now* discussed suffrage, the historical context in which Freud conducted his
research, women and work during World War II, and the mechanisms
used to force them back into the home in the fifties.

Mary Morgan also traced the history of women's suffrage and argued
against electoral politics and liberal reform for women's liberation. "The
democratic process as we know it in this country has not ended social
injustice or economic oppression for either men or women," she wrote.
"If radical changes are to occur in our total society it will require political activism, planned and executed by women, not for 'the good of
mankind,' but for the liberation of ourselves." She was optimistic:
"[T]he present Women's Liberation movement is making a conscious
effort to avoid liberal causes, single issues and minor reforms." DWL's
goal was not equality but liberation, as Morgan proclaimed. "Equality
with men in the existing society means being brutal the way men are; it
means being an oppressor the way men are; and it means being
oppressed the way men are."[50]

In the *Here and Now* articles can be seen the rudiments of a theoretical framework drawing from diverse political philosophies, including
socialism, third world nationalism, and liberal ideology of individual
choice. Women (and many other peoples) were seen as oppressed, with
men as the (more or less willing) agents of that oppression. Society created and maintained this situation, but men benefited from it and were not
ready to give up their power without a struggle. To give women the possibility of "realization of their human potential" and "freedom of choice
in all domains," an autonomous revolutionary feminist movement was
necessary. Most writings portrayed women and men as alike, with a rare
mention of the different "nature" of women as givers of life. The road to
consciousness for women required understanding their own oppression
and that of other women, seeing commonality while accepting differences,
and struggling in sisterhood with other women for their liberation while
maintaining links with other revolutionary movements. Although it was
recognized that attaining the long-term goals of women's liberation was a
"legacy for our children," changes had to begin immediately. Learning
self-defense, setting up a women's commune, and considering abandoning
the institution of marriage had already been suggested in the *Minority
Report*. Articles in *Here and Now* discussed setting up communal systems
for child raising, refusing the traditional gender-determined division of
labor in the workplace, and having men and women share both paid and
unpaid work. These ideas were presented not as distant goals but as a

compelling call to the readers. "A Utopia?" Kleine wrote. "No! It is within our capabilities if we have the will. The difficult part is willing it."[51]

By the summer of 1970 DWL metamorphosed from a small group known within radical circles to a visible public phenomenon, thanks to the August 26 Women's Strike Day, one of the largest feminist demonstrations the country had ever witnessed. The event, originally called by the National Organization for Women and NOW president Betty Friedan to coincide with the fiftieth anniversary of women's suffrage, encouraged women to strike at their workplaces around three demands: twenty-four-hour child-care centers, abortion on demand, and equal opportunity in employment and education. Immediately, groups from the entire spectrum of the movement appropriated the event, each adding its own touch.

DWL organized the local strike day. Although individual Daytonians paid dues to NOW's national office, no Dayton chapter existed. As we have seen, contrary to what historical accounts have described nationally, women's liberation predated liberal feminism in Dayton. During preparations for the Strike Day, DWL decided to set up a local NOW chapter, hoping that the more conservative, action-oriented image of NOW would attract new people. For the first but not the last time, women's liberationists hoped to create the elusive liberal branch of the movement. By the end of the summer, a chapter existed with approximately fifteen members, two-thirds of them new to the movement. However, a few months later the group disbanded without having pulled the new women into the movement. In 1970 and throughout most of the decade, neither NOW nor any other liberal mainstream group took hold in Dayton. Although many feminists had been involved in liberal causes, when they became self-defined radicals and feminists they broke with liberal politics and the liberal, respectable community.

Many people outside of DWL consider August 26, 1970, as the beginning of the women's movement in Dayton. More than two hundred participants attended the Strike Day, held at the United Theological Seminary. Activities included feminist films, skits, and presentations by a neighboring city's women's group, a welfare mother, and a hospital workers' union. A cross-section of women attended—"young and old, rich and poor, black and white." Both women and men staffed the child-care center, "a truly beautiful experience," as one DWL member wrote. "[W]e're not interested in 'dumping' our kids somewhere, but in truly giving all children the love and care they need. [It was] wonderful to see men, young men, holding infants they'd never seen before, feeding them and radiating their pleasure."[52] DWL gave a presentation that led into the most memorable part of the day: about a hundred women participated in a giant consciousness-raising session, discussing their experiences and their problems. Immediately following the event, some twenty-five women joined DWL and several new CR groups were formed.

New members poured in despite hostile media coverage. "Women's Lib Falls Flat on Face Here," proclaimed the title of an article in the liberal *Dayton Daily News*. The "sympathetic" article by the paper's editor promoted Betty Friedan's feminism while criticizing the "outlandishness" of the rest of the movement and lamenting how Simone de Beauvoir "babbled on . . . endlessly" in *The Second Sex*.[53]

After the Strike Day, DWL's membership continued to soar; the mailing list, which doubled as a membership list, rose to nearly three hundred by June 1971 and later peaked at five hundred. Although this method of calculating membership may seem overly optimistic, it is probably less so than methods used by traditionally structured groups such as NOW or the ACLU, which include all those who make a contribution. (Actual participation rate for national NOW, for example, has been estimated at 10–20 percent of its total membership.[54]) With records showing six to ten CR groups at any given period, containing six to fifteen members per group, there probably were a hundred or so women in CR groups at any time. In addition, many others not in CR groups were involved in DWL, and some CR groups continued independently of the organization. Without using the mailing list, I found written evidence of 230 different names, and it can be assumed that several times that many women took part at some time. Probably some twenty-five women made up DWL's activist core, perhaps three times that were relatively active, and several hundred were sympathetic and in touch with the organization, taking part occasionally.

One of the new women to join DWL was Betty Jean Carroll. Carroll had arrived in Dayton only a few weeks earlier for a job at Wright-Patterson Air Force Base. She met Mary Morgan at an ACLU meeting and learned from her about the Strike Day. Up to that point, Carroll had been a feminist without a movement.

Carroll was born in 1930 in San Antonio, Texas. She was raised in a conservative Southern Baptist tradition by poor, working-class parents. Although a product of her era, Carroll had always had a rebellious streak. The first time she took a bus alone, at the age of eleven, she purposely broke a taboo of the segregated South and sat in the back. Racism, she remembered, "contradicted what I was taught in my Sunday school class: that Jesus loved all the little children." When Carroll was twelve, her mother died, her father began to drink heavily, and she was sent to live with an aunt. Sensing that she was not wanted, she dropped out of high school at age fifteen to get married. Five years later, she was pregnant with her fifth child. The marriage was not a happy one; her husband was an alcoholic, refused to let her work despite their poverty, and abused her. Carroll found a job and left him.

Desperate for financial security, Carroll believed that education would be the key. While working late shift as a telephone operator, she attended school in the morning, passed the GED test, and got a scholarship to a local college. Hers was a success story, perhaps, but one that cost her dearly. "For a ten- or fifteen-year period, I was always . . . tired," Carroll said. "The kids raised themselves. When you start the mothering process, nature cuts it off. But nature didn't do it for me—it was aborted by economics."

In college in the early 1950s, Carroll was attracted to a group of left-wing Democrats, as much for social as for political reasons. She was too poor to dress according to the mainstream college standards, and one of the attractions of this milieu, she recalled, was its rejection of a dress code. Through the group, she met and fell in love with a New York union organizer, a socialist who as a seaman had jumped ship to fight in the Spanish Civil War. Carroll was a member of a union, but until then it had merely been a part of her quest for financial security. She married the organizer, followed him from city to city, and was exposed to a new world. Her husband was a cultivated, self-educated intellectual, and Carroll learned about politics, history, and literature. Unfortunately, he also was abusive, and Carroll's children "got on his nerves." Forced to choose between her husband and her children, Carroll got divorced and found herself a single mother again, this time in Fort Wayne, Indiana.

Over the following years, Carroll worked as an office manager—a euphemism for accountant. She had believed that by doing a "man's job" she would earn more money, but she discovered that she was systematically paid less than her male predecessors. Before leaving Fort Wayne in 1970, she had filed two sex-discrimination charges with the Equal Employment Opportunity Commission.

In 1964, Carroll read *The Feminine Mystique* and "lights flashed on" in her brain. The impact Betty Friedan's book had on Carroll drives home an important point. The book clearly addresses middle-class, suburban housewives. Carroll had been desperately poor, to the point of having to water down her babies' milk; she had almost always worked;

31

she did not live in a middle-class suburb; and she had no husband to support her. Nevertheless, she identified with Friedan's housewives, as did many other Dayton feminists who did not fit the stereotype. For Carroll, more important than any specific account in the book, or even any particular book, was the realization that she was not alone. *The Feminine Mystique* did not address women's physical isolation in the suburbs but the psychological isolation of those women not happy with their position in society.

The transformative experience women underwent after reading their first feminist book can be summed up in the comments of one Daytonian: "I realized I was not a misfit." *The Feminine Mystique* was most often cited in this respect, but other writings, such as *The Second Sex,* equally filled the role. The importance of early feminist texts in breaking though women's isolation is confirmed repeatedly. Maren Carden reported that half of her respondents who had read *The Feminine Mystique* at the time of its publication felt "greatly relieved to discover that someone shared their worries." One woman commented, citing *The Second Sex,* "I knew then there were two kooks in the world."[55] Feminist ideas were rarely all new; rather, they resonated with something already inside women. Cheryl Radican had spoken of someone "writing down what was in [her] head." Meredith Tax, later a founder of Boston's Bread and Roses, remembered that upon reading her first women's liberation newspaper, "I recognized the voice. . . . It sounded just like my own voice."[56]

Betty Jean Carroll had been one of the few whites to be involved in the civil rights movement in Fort Wayne. Later, with the rise of black nationalism, black activists made it clear that she was no longer welcome, and she transferred her energies to the antiwar movement. But it was not until the DWL Strike Day that she finally found "her group." It was the "apex of everything up to that point . . . what I was waiting for." She immediately got involved in DWL and in a CR group.

Dayton's early activists differed dramatically from media portrayals and popular representations of feminists, usually described as single white students in their early twenties. The emphasis on youth suggested immaturity and hot-headedness. Scholarly studies come closer, identifying activists' roots in social movements of the sixties, for example. Yet apart from the fact that all active members of DWL were white, differences remained.

Dayton's feminists were somewhat older than had been described elsewhere; most were in their midtwenties to late thirties. A handful were younger, and a small but significant number were in their forties. Virtually none were college students, and those who were often had resumed studies after having dropped out, typically after marriage. For some, college no doubt served as a "free space," and it was upon leaving and entering the "real world" that they confronted their limited prospects. DWL activists, like many feminists across the country, were a well-educated group; almost all had completed at least one year of college, many had undergraduate degrees, and some even more. Their educational level, however, was lower than that of subjects in other studies.[57]

Most of Dayton's early feminists had been young adults in the fifties to early sixties and had grown up with marriage as their goal in life. While not questioning this outright, they married slightly later than average for women of the same socioeconomic status. They did marry, though, and approximately one-third had children. They thus had more to lose than the young, single women described elsewhere, yet they risked it regardless. Most had already broken with respectability by becoming part of the marginal Left community, but this community was based on fairly traditional gender roles, and relationships were threatened by feminism.

By the beginning of the women's movement some of these families had already been shaken. Although divorce was on the rise nationally, a larger number of DWL women were divorced or single than other Dayton women in their age group.[58] Myriad factors might explain this. First, their involvement in the social movements of the sixties may already have served as a disruptive factor, either by drawing them into the public sphere and providing a glimpse of freedom and self-worth, or through the chaotic "nonmonogamy" that reigned. Second, in their milieu there was less stigma attached to divorce and to unmarried couples living together; they may have divorced more, or just remarried less. Third, while many had had aborted university careers, these single or divorced women remained significantly better educated than average. It can be hypothesized that they either held fulfilling jobs or were better prepared to find satisfactory employment than most women. However, this difference is only a relative one, for the majority of DWL members were married.

Feminists were almost always portrayed as middle class, and indeed, nearly all of Dayton's early feminists did consider themselves middle class. However, this identification was oversimplified, because most white Americans at the time called themselves middle class, and because a woman's class was automatically associated with that of her husband. In truth, class origins of DWL members spanned a broader range, and quite a few had working-class roots. Ruth Rosen pointed out that many activists in the first generation out of the working class obtained their middle-class credentials at college.[59] Furthermore, middle-class status, when gained through marriage, proved precarious, as dramatically demonstrated in cases of divorce. Finally, as had been true for the New Left and countercultural movements, there was a process of self-marginalization for feminists that further complicated the issue. It would seem that feminist activism may have been an element not only in the well-known success stories of the career-climbing "superwomen," but also in downward mobility. Despite the fact that class origins varied more than is commonly assumed, neither the poor nor the traditional working class made up a substantial minority in the ranks of DWL.

Most members worked outside the home throughout their involvement in DWL. Professions varied: many held odd jobs; a few had "movement jobs," usually political organizing subsidized by church groups; several were teachers and health-care workers; there was one journalist and a minister. Over the years, a growing number worked in the social services. Early feminists may have worked, but their husbands' careers came first. Many had followed their husbands when they moved to Dayton for jobs.

All DWL members identified themselves as heterosexual at the outset. Beyond that, it is impossible to generalize about their relations with other women. Some had primarily women friends; others preferred the company of men. Some had mothers of exceptional character who served as role models; others had particularly subjugated, even battered mothers. No pattern emerges as to family background.

Polls have shown black women to be at least as favorable as whites to feminist ideas and to the movement,[60] but DWL was all white. Although Kleine and Morgan were talking with a few black women friends, those friends only visited a few meetings and never settled in. The absence of blacks in the group cannot be attributed solely to racism or segregation. It was also due to the logic of black separatism. The DWL core group was deeply affected by Black Power, which excluded whites from civil rights organizations so as to empower blacks. Black Power proponents admonished whites to organize against racism in their own communities. Indeed, Summer in the City, in which several DWL founders had been involved, was a direct response to that call. Black activists, Robin Suits recalled, "certainly didn't want whites coming into the black community in any way, and black women didn't feel it was appropriate for them to be involved in feminist organizing." The "correct" position was to form alliances with black and other groups as an independent part of the broader movement. Ironically, the antiracist stance of DWL women contributed to the group's white identity. In assuming this stance, the women had relied on their contacts with radical black men, taking these men's word for what their sisters wanted. Moreover, establishing a white identity from the start compromised future connections with black women. Finally, the acceptance that the group was white offered later generations, with less commitment to fighting racism, an easy excuse to wash their hands of the issue, as we will see later.

Geopolitics played a role in the networks that pulled women into the movement. A large percentage lived within a few blocks of each other in the Five Oaks and Dayton View areas in the northwest part of the city. A disproportionate number of Dayton's leftists and feminists lived in these areas, undoubtedly because they included most of the city's racially and ethnically mixed neighborhoods, along with being attractive, inexpensive, and in the city proper.

Most of the first activists had been brought up Protestant. Far fewer came from Catholic families, but this changed in the second wave of recruits. Although Jews had been disproportionately present in previous social movements, and feminist activities were concentrated not far from where many of them lived, Jews were surprisingly absent in the first decade of the women's movement.[61]

The role of religion was one of the most surprising characteristics of DWL activists. Although attention has been paid to the influence of feminism on theology and on religious institutions, I know of no study on the influence of religion on feminist consciousness and on the second-wave women's movement. Sociologist Carden made only one short reference to religion: "Institutionalized religion (in the sense of attendance at religious services) rarely plays a significant part in the lives of participants."[62] While it is true that fewer Dayton feminists were churchgoers than in the general population,[63] it is inaccurate to write off even institutional religion as insignificant. Materially, churches contributed more to Dayton's women's movement than any other outside source. The strong church connections of the handful of women who made up DWL's early core is telling: Griesinger was on her way to being ordained, Gregg's husband was a Methodist minister and she had taught Sunday school, Radican had taken theology classes and her husband was studying at a seminary. Nearly all of the DWL women in my sample first became involved in political activism in some way through a church—even Suits, who had been raised an atheist. Most important, time and time again, DWL members evoked religious teachings as a source of their belief in social justice. Taught by parents and clergy to believe in equality, they applied these teachings to oppose racism, imperialism, and sexism.

Only Sara Evans linked religion and feminism when she discussed the religious sources of the egalitarian ideals of the Southern white civil rights activists who later pioneered the women's liberation movement. She also mentioned the importance of the progressive Christian press and youth groups in the developing civil rights movement. But she then skipped over the period between the advent of the New Left and the emergence of the women's liberation movement, mentioning it only in a footnote: "Perhaps because of the cultural expectation that women should be more religious, the student Christian movements had strong female participation. . . . Though religious motivation was far from universal as it was in the south, it remained an important avenue into activism for northern women."[64] The study of Dayton's movement shows that, as in the South, religious teachings weighted heavily in the emergence of feminist consciousness and that religious institutions opened paths into activism.

While many DWL women, including those who had been in the New Left, were still involved in churches at the outset of the women's movement, their affiliations were more often determined by politics than by upbringing. Many had changed from their original affiliations to the more socially progressive Protestant denominations, in particular the Unitarian Church. Unitarian Betty Jean Carroll said the church was "made up of people basically that have been in other churches and have got fed up with their creed or philosophy, and found that there was a religion that had no creed. They could believe or not believe, as they wanted, but yet it gave them fellowship." Involvement in institutional religion did tend to drop during women's first year in the movement. When Carroll became involved in the Unitarian Church in 1970, she found that most of her sisters were already gone or leaving. She added, "Many people that become Unitarians do not stay. They make that transition from some other church through the Unitarian Church to no church." In the case of feminists, sisterhood replaced fellowship: "The women's movement became their church," Carroll said.

The trait that best defined Dayton's early feminists was their political trajectory. They had embraced political ideals that included participatory democracy, distrust of authority and hierarchy, antisectarianism, and autonomous organizing for oppressed peoples. They had begun to develop a sense of their abilities and their strengths, encouraged by the free space that the movements had created. They learned organizing skills: how to make a leaflet, produce a newspaper, and organize a demonstration. They also modified and put to use preexisting communications networks to create their own movement.

In feminist writings on the national scene, authors' anger often blinded them to the positive legacy of previous social movements and the counterculture. Not so in Dayton—no doubt due to a lesser degree of sexism and the tight fabric of the radical community. The sexism in previous movements did not eliminate future feminists' sense of agency, nor did it prevent transformative experiences.[65] Later, as feminists, they recognized their debts to previous movements, even while separating from them.

Contrary to the East Coast and Chicago pioneers described in other literature, Daytonians benefited from a national feminist movement. This movement had defused part of the shock value of feminism. It had also broken ground. Daytonians witnessed and learned from its failures and successes, and they knew they were not alone. They pooled their experiences with those of women near and far to redefine their understanding of politics.

Recent scholarship stresses other influences on early feminists, including the Old Left.[66] For instance, local feminists were reading Eleanor Flexner's *A Century of Struggle* and other works by former Communist activists. However, no early feminists were themselves red-diaper babies; the closest was a granddaughter of a socialist. Unitarians were numerous, however membership in this church was often a result, not a cause, of radical awakenings. Several prominent Quakers were sympathetic to DWL, but they were not the founders or leaders. Early feminists had participated, sometimes simultaneously, in local politics and in liberal organizations such as the ACLU and the League of Women Voters, but their identities were forged in the social movements of the sixties and in opposition to these organizations. Rather than producing a liberal feminism, becoming feminist meant breaking with such groups and the communities around them. Other scholars point to continuity between first-wave (nineteenth century to the vote) and second-wave (sixties onward) feminism via "elite-sustained women's rights organizations." However, if any such group survived the midperiod in Dayton's "doldrums," I was unable to find links to the women's movement as it emerged in 1969.[67]

While Dayton's story in no way invalidates other findings, it does challenge their universality. Observers and participants generally divide the women's movement into two parts (branches, strands, wings, or arms). Some characterize these parts by ideology and some by structural differences, often with interplay between the two. (Many recognize that there is rapid cross-fertilization between them.)

Scholars often define the two parts by their organizational structure. Jo Freeman, in her path-breaking study *The Politics of Women's Liberation,* distinguished them by both the age of their participants and the structures that they created: the younger branch, made up of consciousness-raising and other small groups, and the older branch, with NOW as its most important organization. Myra Marx Ferree and Beth B. Hess spoke of collectivist and bureaucratic strands. Barbara Ryan contrasted the small-group or CR feminism with the mass movement."[68]

In Dayton, the movement combined attributes that scholars identify as being specific to one branch or the other. Made up primarily of collectivist structures—though not averse to creating traditional organizations—it was inhabited by somewhat older women than was typical in the younger branch. And small-group or CR feminism was central to the closest thing to a feminist mass movement that the city had.

Those who present the divisions as ideological separate a liberal, mainstream, or women's rights part from women's liberation.[69] Among liberationists nationally, the term "radical" by itself was apparently used more or less as a euphemism for the political and cultural New Left. However, as the movement developed, "radical feminist" came to mean a particular strain of feminism for which the patriarchy predated capitalism and served as a model for all oppressions. Other currents continue to develop; among the most important was socialist feminism (distinct and separate from earlier politicos).

Although Dayton's feminists saw no contradiction in supporting the NOW campaign to end sex-segregated classified ads, or other liberal feminist demands, they clearly identified with women's liberation and always tried to define an agenda that would transform society. DWL did occasionally use the term radical feminist, but at least until 1973 it meant radical *and* feminist, not a particular current of feminist thought. For instance, DWL's Radical Feminist Collective invited women who had "some commitment to radicalism" to join.[70]

In recent years, scholars have taken to describing the early women's liberation movement with the term "radical feminist." Examples abound. Echols reduced the movement to radicals (used interchangeably with feminist) and politicos (her sympathies were with the former). Nancy Whittier slipped from the cautious "radical women's movement" of the title of her book to "radical feminism" as one of two arms of the movement. Rosalind Rosenberg referred readers to Sara Evans for "the origins of radical feminism," although Evans herself spoke of "women's liberation." Claire Reinelt operated from a liberal-radical feminist divide. Suzanne Staggenborg discussed socialist feminist groups under the subtitle "radical feminist organizations."[71] A case can be made for reclaiming the appellation "radical" to refer to all of women's liberation; however, given the usage as a specific current in the movement, I believe that doing so flattens out the movement. It wittingly or unwittingly takes part in the radical feminist-politico and other such debates and potentially allows supporters of the specific current to lay claim to all that liberationists have done.

Ironically, despite this distinctive situation, DWL members accepted a two-strand movement as a model, as illustrated by their voluntaristic, unsuccessful attempt (the first of several) to create the liberal branch in the form of NOW. Many in the immense pool of potential recruits, they apparently believed, would join the movement only via liberal feminism.

In Dayton, Ohio, supposedly the epitome of Middle America, the search for equality or reform was not the driving force in the women's movement.[72] Liberal feminism was not just incapable of serving as a catalyst—in Dayton, it was nonexistent. The type of women whom Betty Friedan described as having founded NOW were not only absent from Dayton's movement, they often opposed feminism during this period. NOW, formed as a civil rights organization for women, was not "the first and major structure of the modern Women's Movement" in Dayton.[73] The shortcomings, not the strengths, of the civil rights movement most influenced DWL founders, who rejected both an integrationist approach and the idea of working for equality within the system. Few were interested in working in an organization that functioned in a traditional mode and that included men. Black Power and other examples of autonomous organizing set the tone for DWL.

The key to the emergence of Dayton Women's Liberation and organizations to come was the connection between the personal and the political. A vivid illustration of this was the first Ohio Conference on the Status of Women in 1970. For Friedan and others, these conferences, years earlier, had been catalysts for the women's movement. DWL women traveled to Columbus to attend the 1970 gathering—in protest. The conference assembled a slew of experts to testify on questions of employment and legislation, with a break for a fashion show. DWL distributed leaflets through the crowd; all its criticisms centered on the lack of connection between the personal and the political:

> *Why* are there no day care facilities provided here for women with children? Many women with children are not free otherwise to take a Saturday off to consider the status of women.
>
> *Why* is the $3.75 fee charged for registration and lunch? For many working and unemployed women that fee alone excluded their participation. . . .
>
> *Why* is there no opportunity in the program for women here to talk freely to each other? Why is it assumed that "experts" and women who have "made it" are the most qualified speakers? . . .
> The "status of women" is a problem which touches every woman at every point in her life and covers a great deal more territory than the employment picture, although of course that is an important aspect. Every woman, if you scratch the surface a little, is an expert about the status of women. Every woman can tell you about a broad range of things in her daily life that points to the need for the liberation of women—problems in marriage, birth control, abortion, sterilization, childcare, boredom, lack of self-image.[74]

The radical women's liberation movement has often been presented as a marginal phenomenon that could not speak to the masses of women. Issues of work and legal equality supposedly had broader appeal. This was not the case when the movement appeared in such on "unlikely" place as Dayton. It was the radical women's liberation movement—and more particularly, the link between the personal and the political—that sparked a feminist consciousness for the DWL founders and those who joined their ranks. As Evans argued, "[T]he initiation of a mass movement required that the problem be addressed at its core. The pressures on most women were building up, not on the level of public discrimination but at the juncture of public and private . . . where older structures and identities no longer sufficed but could not simply be discarded either . . . [and] required a radical—in the literal sense—response. A new movement would have to transform the privacy and subjectivity of personal life itself into a political issue."[75] DWL activists did just that. They created a movement for themselves, simultaneously discovering sisterhood and, through the consciousness-raising process, learned that their problems, which had been dismissed as individual and personal, were shared and rooted in society.

2

WOMEN'S
LIBERATION—
The Belle Epoque

F OR MORE than four years Dayton Women's Liberation constituted not only the hub of the city's movement, but also the engine and all four wheels. Other groups existed, but most were created by and connected to DWL. That did not mean that the movement was narrow in scope. DWL's ambitious goal of liberating women meant that issues and actions covered a remarkably broad spectrum, a spectrum extended ever further by the group's desire to encourage multiple perspectives on each question. The long-term goal of women's emancipation was coupled with the desire to create a prefigurative organization: a piece of utopia in the here and now. Thus, the search for an appropriate and democratic structure was a creative process and a channel for political debate. This was a period of effervescent thought and action as members constantly sought to extend the movement's boundaries. Debate and even conflict occurred, but the organization's loose structure and tolerant atmosphere usually allowed peaceful, although sometimes contradictory, coexistence. Nevertheless, general lines emerged from this creative jumble.

The most central issues for DWL can be characterized as sexual and personal politics: reproductive freedom, marriage, divorce, sexuality, and so on. The group's first public action was on abortion, and the demand for "free and legal walk-in abortion clinics" appeared on its first platform.[1]

In the intimacy of the consciousness-raising groups, some women had told of having undergone illegal abortions and others of having borne unwanted children. Only in retrospect did they evoke these reasons for supporting the legalization of abortion; initially, abortion was for "other women." As soon as the advertisement for women's liberation appeared (see beginning of chapter 1), calls began coming in from women seeking pregnancy tests and abortions. "Somehow there was that immediate connection . . . in their minds that if anybody would know anything about abortion [we] would," Jan Griesinger said. "Well, at first we didn't!" Chewerl Radican, who had "discovered" the issue, investigated solutions: finding qualified abortionists in other cities and countries and seeking funds. For its first eight months, DWL acted as an underground referral service, made known through word of mouth and, according to DWL, by Planned Parenthood counselors. In mid-1970, Griesinger created a local branch of Clergy Consultation Service on Abortion.

While many DWL women dared not speak openly of their illegal abortions, there was unwavering support for "free abortion on demand."[2] Reform or even repeal of restrictive laws was seen as piecemeal. DWL opposed the myriad restrictions attached to proposed reforms and maintained that abortions had to be free and accessible to all, with no mandatory spousal or parental authorization and no requirements concerning age, marital status, residency, or psychiatric condition. As for most feminists nationally, abortion meant "women having control of their own bodies, and women having control of anything is taboo in our society."[3]

Abortion was not the be-all and end-all of the movement. For DWL, "legalized abortion will certainly bring in the Age of Aquarius."[4] As Griesinger wrote, "[S]ome more basic issues were involved." Safe birth control was one of them. Also, by 1970, DWL members had learned about forced sterilization and coercive birth control measures used against poor and third world women. Discussions of birth control and abortion included opposition to these practices. "Those women who have been most oppressed by our social system rightly fear that abortion may be forced upon them for economic or political reasons," Griesinger wrote. "Strong guarantees must be built into present legislation and practice, protecting women from compulsory abortions which are likely to begin as the laws become more 'liberal.'"[5]

DWL acted on this position. In 1971, for example, state representative Gailbraith, previously seen as an ally, suggested paying welfare mothers three hundred dollars to abort. DWL called for a letter-writing campaign against what the organization termed a racist, genocidal policy.[6]

Contrary to a commonly held belief about social movements, DWL did not grow more conservative or narrow in its focus over time. On abortion, for instance, its analysis moved outward to encompass other issues, because "everything is related to everything else."[7] Aware that safe abortions were available for those who could pay while poor women risked their lives, DWL demanded free abortions, implying socialized medicine. The most comprehensive statement on the subject demanded "guaranteed adequate individual income," equal pay for equal work, recognition of housework and child rearing as socially productive labor, and free child care—all as prerequisites for women to be able to freely choose whether or not to have children.

Developing analyses and providing services were only part of the picture. DWL was instrumental in all local actions concerning abortion, including creating abortion repeal organizations (the overlapping membership was such that they were sometimes confused with DWL). Women for Abortion Law Repeal, created in 1970, was succeeded by the Association for Repeal of Ohio Abortion Law in 1971, the Ohio Abortion Alliance in 1972, and several ad hoc groups. Following the national strategy, these organizations participated in statewide coalitions to pressure the Ohio legislature. In 1971, with two reform bills pending in the House of Representatives, DWL members initiated a letter-writing campaign and attended the hearings with "repeal" signs pinned to their clothing. The bills were shelved because, DWL argued, male professionals were the only experts called upon and "women's testimony was [seen as] irrelevant and not permitted." DWL announced a week of "witchy" actions, including a demonstration to express "Women's Outrage."[8] "We will have a mock hearing exposing the hypocrisy of the official hearings, then women will 'take over' and begin the public hearing that women never got."[9]

Repeal efforts abruptly came to an end on January 22, 1973, when the Supreme Court handed down the *Roe v. Wade* decision, but Dayton feminists did not close up shop. "We must have no illusions that society yet believes that women have the right to control their own bodies," Griesinger wrote. It became clear that area hospitals refused to change their practices. "Lest we be self-satisfied rather than vigilant," she wrote, "we must report that a black sister [on welfare] was recently told by Miami Valley [Hospital] that they would consider doing an abortion after she obtained two psychiatric consultations and if she agreed to be sterilized."[10] Nearly a year passed after the *Roe v. Wade* decision before any elective abortions were performed in local hospitals. While DWL and the other groups investigated ways of forcing hospitals to change their policies, Griesinger and several other women began work on establishing an independent abortion clinic.

Antiabortion activists have accused feminists of being more concerned with abortion than contraception and even of encouraging abortion as a form of contraception. This was not true of DWL. "Free birth control supplies and information to all" was one of the eight demands in DWL's first platform in December 1969: "We must immediately avail ourselves of the latest forms of birth control and make these forms readily available to all our sisters desiring the tools with which to control their own destiny."[11] Knowing that the pill had first been tested on Puerto Rican women, and citing a study in which Chicanas were given placebos for control statistics, DWL added to its demands the condition, "[N]o more use of third world women as guinea pigs for drug companies!" Alongside the call for free, high-quality contraceptives on demand was "More research for safe and effective contraceptives, especially into male contraceptives."[12] DWL's position came from the meeting between two personal itineraries of DWL members, largely depending on their age. For those who had been young adults in the late forties and the fifties, limited access to contraceptives (Dayton had no family planning clinic from 1955 to 1965, and the birth control pill was approved by the FDA in 1960), along with the effects of the "feminine mystique," meant that some had given birth to unplanned or unwanted children. They either had been unfamiliar with contraceptives, had not known how to obtain them, or had used the available methods with high failure rates. Alongside these women were those who had become sexually active during the period of relatively easy access to effective birth control, which was also the period when, as Griesinger put it, "sexual freedom meant that men can enjoy sex anytime, anywhere, leaving the woman to worry about and bear the consequences of conception."[13]

In part because of their support for reproductive freedom, feminists often are seen as opposing family and motherhood. In Dayton, little evidence supports this perception. All concurred that a woman had to go beyond childbearing and rearing to find her selfhood. Some individuals did abandon motherhood, either by refusing to have children or, in cases of divorce, leaving their children with their ex-husbands. But the position consistently defended over the years was that motherhood had to be a free choice: "At every crossroad we are directed by stop signs telling us the only true feminine fulfillment comes from the womb. While no attempt is being made to degrade the experience of motherhood, we must recognize our right to choose the proper time, if ever, in our lives for procreation."[14] For most DWL members this choice meant no longer being coerced to have children, but their opposition to eugenics led them to also demand the freedom to have children. It was with this dual perspective that related actions concentrated on making the material prerequisites available: birth control, abortion, child care, equitable salaries, and a range of political activism to offer children a freer world.

Despite the large number of mothers in DWL, feelings towards motherhood rarely appeared in writing. One image surfaced in 1970 and 1971—that of women producing babies for the Vietnam War: "To breed or not to breed becomes a serious existential question, particularly in the light of the fashionable, profitable and devouring militarism of this country."[15] A full-page drawing of a pregnant woman with a fetus labeled "U.S. Army" appeared on the cover of the women's issue of *Here and Now* in 1970. This was again the theme when Vietnam Veterans Against the War requested a DWL speaker for a demonstration. DWL performed a guerrilla theater skit about fetuses snatched up by Uncle Sam and immediately outfitted for military duty. (Lest it be thought that only male children were seen as victims, the slogan "Your sisters and [their] babies are dying in a man's war" appeared as well.[16])

Some DWL members related their feelings about motherhood in a special issue of the newsletter on children. One wrote an ode to motherhood: "I am intrigued by the creative process that a woman and a man undertake in conceiving children. I dig every minute of pregnancy from the first twinge of morning sickness to the last twinge of the stitches. I fantasize many a night about the looks of my children; I hope for them to have fascinating personalities—all liberated women, all non-MCP's [male chauvinist pigs]. . . . These emotions and experiences I refuse to give up. . . . It is an experience I want more than twice in my life. It is a unique experience that only women can have. I revel in that knowledge and cherish it."[17]

This contrasted dramatically to a piece written by a member of the Nora's Sisters CR group who realized that she had had children because of social pressures. The result: "When I look at how abusive and hateful and unloving my own mother was, then look at my behavior towards my own kids, I see two sick women who act exactly the same." She concluded with a poignant plea for the movement to help make women aware of their options, to support them in their choices, and to be tolerant and understanding of "bad mothers" like her.[18]

DWL members understood, many from experience, that Dayton child-care facilities were grossly inadequate. Most facilities were private, profit-making enterprises. Child care was expensive: "[A] woman working for minimum wage will often have less take-home pay after paying for child care . . . and other work expenses, than if she stayed on welfare."[19] A child-care detail was a constant at all DWL events, and CR groups tried to accommodate mothers by meeting at their homes and sharing baby-sitting expenses. Child care was discussed not only as a way to relieve women of a burden, but as a new way to take care of and raise children. Members supported child care in industry, for example, only if parents got time off work to participate, not if it was "to free women as cheap labor in corporations' factories."[20] When a member, following a suggestion in *Ms.* magazine, wanted to write the (female) owner of a local department store to request child care for Christmas shoppers, radical DWL members denounced the idea as reinforcing women's role as consumers in the capitalist system.[21]

Long-term goals for child care were that it be round-the-clock and free, that it be run communally—including by the children themselves—and that it provide a noncompetitive, creative, antisexist, and antiracist environment. Finally, "the presence of male as well as female models at all times" was necessary. In the history of DWL, this was the sole area in which support for the full participation of men was unanimous: "Without including men in the day care program, the demand for day care runs the risk of contradicting the goals of women's liberation."[22] And men from DWL's entourage did participate.

In late 1970, DWL began a child-care cooperative, declaring: "The socialization process which defines masculine roles for boys and feminine roles for girls begins in infancy and is re-inforced continually by the education system, both in pre-school nurseries and primary educational institutions. If life-styles and values are to be radically altered, there must be some viable options to existing structures."[23] The cooperative later founded a successful free school for children from infancy through elementary school age. DWL women participated in several child-care cooperatives over the course of the organization's history.

The nuclear family as an institution was criticized by all, irrespective of their personal situations; indeed, some of the most violent critics were part of stable nuclear families. "Destruction of the family or even its radical change, Kleine wrote, "will be the first crumbling brick which will bring the rest of the superstructure down." Robin Suits criticized the nuclear family as "a stabilizing force for capitalism which keeps men tied to jobs and women powerless."[24] Only once did an explicit call to spurn marriage appear, aimed particularly at single women in the Left. According to the author, women would thus reject a predefined role and refuse to morally or legally sanction the institution at the expense of alternative life styles.[25]

In practice, however, many DWL women believed that an egalitarian form of marriage was possible, as was shown by a "utopian marriage contract" published in the organization's newsletter[26] and by the time they devoted to reforming their own marriages. One member of the Ovarian Society CR group, who conceded that "the traditional nuclear family must be rated as the most ingenious trap designed by man," went on to ask whether "the bars which are often made of guilt, and economic and psychological dependence can be torn down and replaced with the more flexible barriers of positive values." She was optimistic, and described her personal struggle to change her own family. "Choice" became the key, even for critics of the institution; a 1971 platform demanded "the right to marry or not marry . . . without social ostracism."[27]

In practice, the attitude of the DWL core group was less tolerant. "Premovement" but not postmovement marriages were accepted, and virtually no DWL members wed during the early years. The criticism of those who did marry, particularly radical women, showed a feminist double standard: married women were welcomed as proof of grass-roots support; however, single women, once radicalized, ought to know better.

Marriage was discussed less than divorce. While some women believed that DWL helped save their marriages, it was more common to hear that DWL, particularly the CR groups, gave women the courage to leave their husbands. "We lived through her divorce," CR group members would say, meaning they offered not only emotional but also material aid. One woman resumed her studies thanks to financial support from a member of her group. Another group helped a member evacuate her house while her husband was away.

Divorce was generally viewed as liberating. "Didn't I have a husband! a man! the trimmings! the trappings! the trapped mind, the trapped body, the trapped spirit!" one member wrote. "And now in the present—Good company, pertinent ideas from specially picked people, choice friends from stimulating groups, and any loneliness dissipated by dialing the phone or opening the door or choosing the direction I want to go."[28]

With experience, the problems related to divorce appeared. One woman whose marriage was shaken by her feminist transformation became cautious in DWL, according to a close friend, because of the fear of losing custody of her three children. While DWL was not unaware of the economic problems involved in divorce, such problems were minimized and sometimes even romanticized in this period of selective affluence. The reality of poverty in female-headed households became clear as several women experienced the fall from the middle class firsthand. It drove home a lesson about women and class. As Barbara Gregg wrote:

"Women find themselves armed with their new declaration of independence (their divorce papers) but equipped with neither the educational tools nor skills to allow them to economically survive. . . . Divorced women are generally allotted a token sum in child-support and/or alimony to keep them off the welfare rolls, but are hardly given enough to allow them to gain the knowledge and resources to attain their long forgotten dreams, goals, and aspirations. . . . They have traded one yoke for another. They are freed from the servitude of a marriage and are thrust into a competitive, ruthless man's world where daily survival becomes paramount." Gregg was writing from experience, having recently divorced. "I lived in absolute poverty from the time that I got my divorce until after the kids were grown," she recalled. Her children remembered the gas being turned off, having to heat water on the stove to fill the bathtub, and at times not having enough to eat. Child-support income, Gregg discovered bitterly, was too little to let her go back to school but too much to allow her to qualify for welfare. It often came late, and she had to go through humiliating and expensive court procedures. Her CR group was tremendously supportive. But although she had written that divorce could be liberating, could create "kinship with other women," and could be "the beginning of a perpetual and permanent revolt," she learned that it most often resulted in a struggle to survive. While at first she had more time for her sisters, ultimately the energy she spent on survival was drained from her feminist activities.[29]

Feminists in the early years were seen as being promiscuous, lesbian, or frustrated, and sometimes all three at once. Left and Right, one could hear, "All she needs is a good fuck." While seemingly contradictory, DWL understood that this reduced women to sexual creatures, and in terms set by men. As Nancy Galehouse wrote: "Because women have been for centuries, and still are, economically dependent on men, they believe deeply that they owe men sex. To get a guy, a girl had better use her body—at least if she wants to keep him and not be labeled frigid. Many a promiscuous woman finds the only time she feels real and vital is when she is in the act of sex with a man who worships her body in order to possess it sexually. Even her own orgasm does not belong to her. It is often offered up to men, even demanded by men, who use it as an index of their 'virility.'" She concluded: "A woman's sexual identity, like the rest of her identity, must be claimed as her own before she can enter wholly equally into the kind of mutually satisfying sexual relationship that should be her birthright."[30]

A crucial step for feminists' developing an autonomous sexual identity—although it was never discussed in literature about the movement—was "talking sex" in CR groups. The discussions about "what do you do in bed?" or "what would you like to do?" were among the most memorable. Whether through objectifying men, discovering that some women were aggressive in demanding sexual satisfaction, or learning that others had never had orgasms, breaking through the taboos and talking about sex in graphic terms was an integral part of the consciousness-raising process—and the most enjoyable part for many women.

This sex talk differed in spirit from that of the sexual revolution of the sixties. Like feminists elsewhere, DWL members declared that free love had turned out to be a "royal holiday for some men and a most disillusioning experience for women."[31] Many DWL members had felt a malaise at the time, but had seen it as an individual problem. Suits bitterly recalled the men who saw her as a cock-teaser because she wore miniskirts but would not have sex with them. Gregg recalled, "I felt terribly exploited by it. . . . I was the one who was always waiting . . . and being sad." The women's experiences made them ready not only to work for birth control and abortion, but also to establish the right to say no, be it to a stranger or to one's husband. They encouraged other women to learn self-defense and later organized classes "to put some teeth into our refusal to be pressured or forced into sexual relations."[32]

Gregg's comment points to a paradox that feminists and scholars have glossed over. After reflecting sadly on the sexual exploitation in the sixties, she blurted out, "It was *really* fun! . . . and a step in my learning process!" These women had themselves helped forge the sexual liberation ideology of the sixties; the alienation and anger they later described had not prevented them from feeling like active participants. Braving sexual taboos—rejecting mandatory virginity for the unmarried, elevating sensuality to a positive value, and experimenting with nonmonogamous relationships—remained an important, positive part of their identity. Their bitterness was not about the sex per se, but about a betrayal of their utopian visions for sexuality.

Heterosexuality in DWL was taken for granted until 1973, when some members felt it necessary to justify themselves. The editorial in the newsletter's special issue on lesbianism announced, "[O]ne article, bravely perhaps, deals with heterosexuality, where most of us still are and where many of us will probably remain and from where, therefore, we must figure how to wage a women's revolution with a pure conscience."

This article combined defensiveness with opposition to a "correct line" on sexuality. It began by stating that "most of us, most of our lives, will be relating intimately with a man or wishing we were. . . . So here we are, us heterosexual women. Conditioned to cringe from a homosexual relationship and made aware through years of consciousness raising that we can't trust our heterosexual relationships, yet drawn to them nonetheless. Is that a fatal weakness, the ultimate contradiction in our ideology that will flaw and eventually destroy our movement? Not as long as we can be strong in our relationships with men and close in our relationships with women. . . . To deny a desire to be intimate with a man, to make a political decision, as have some in the women's movement, to repress only sexual feelings for a man and respond only to sexual feelings for a woman, that is a fatal contradiction. It invalidates part of our experience which is an antithesis of our hard won understanding that no part of our experience is invalid."[33]

DWL's defensiveness came in part from the tension between members' involvement in heterosexual relations and their emotional and political investment in women and the movement. The need to justify heterosexuality also stemmed from a national dialogue in which lesbian feminism was depicted as the vanguard of the movement. One month earlier, the DWL newsletter had carried an article by Charlotte Bunch declaring that "a lesbian feminist consciousness is absolutely crucial to the success of the women's liberation movement. . . . Lesbianism is not simply a personal choice: it is a political issue in this society."[34]

Lesbianism was rarely discussed in DWL at first; the word literally did not appear in writing until February 1972. The term "women-identified-women" was used, but it was devoid of sexual meaning—an example of how things took on different meanings in different places. "I didn't realize until I went to Washington how almost everywhere else in the country women used that term to mean lesbians," Robin Suits recalled, as did several other DWL activists.

For the first few years, there were no self-avowed lesbians in DWL. The organization was made up of older women, many in heterosexual relationships or marriages, who had "a lot to lose" by questioning their sexual orientation.[35] Also, women who subsequently came out pointed to Dayton's small size and the homophobia present there. Throughout the 1970s, lesbians feared repercussions, including loss of employment. One DWL core member who came out after leaving town commented, "It's just too frightening, too isolating, and too threatening in Dayton . . . to be a lesbian." As detective novelist Marcia Muller wrote about a character, a native of Dayton: "Phil Collins was one of the legions of homosexuals who had fled the Midwest to find freedom and acceptance in San Francisco. . . . He probably took Valium because he hadn't yet come to terms with emerging from the closet. It was not surprising, given Dayton, Ohio."[36]

Lesbianism as an abstract issue was not unknown to DWL; in fact, the group's first publication in 1969 had carried a piece on the subject.[37] Articles such as "The Woman-Identified-Woman" had circulated in Dayton. Griesinger recalled that while she was working on a World Student Christian Federation project, Charlotte Bunch had given her an issue of *The Furies*. In addition, antifeminists forced DWL to face the issue: in Dayton, as across the country, accusations of "man-hating lesbian" flew freely against outspoken women. Members learned to scoff and to respond in the affirmative at these supposed insults. When a local college audience snickered after a man accused the women's liberation movement of being lesbian-dominated, the DWL speaker answered, "That always gets a laugh, as if [l]esbianism is a joke. . . . There certainly are women in the movement who are lesbian."[38] DWL refused to be lavender baited. Members believed that "if we grew up in a free environment, we'd all be bisexual," and "[i]f anybody was allowed to fall in love with *anybody*, the word 'homosexual' wouldn't be needed."[39]

In June 1972, lesbianism and sisterly love was slated as a topic at a DWL retreat. It was there that Suzanne Wilka and her lover, probably the only lesbians in the group at the time, came out. Wilka, who had moved to Dayton from Columbus the previous year, was acutely aware that some feminist groups in the country had purged lesbians,[40] and she worried that might be her fate. In fact, the general reaction was acceptance. "Everybody felt really touched and moved by it," Griesinger remembered. Suits, who had encountered hostility from lesbian separatists during a stay in Washington, D.C., recalled: "It was very romantic the way they told us they were in love with each other. I liked it a lot."

Wilka had secretly hoped that other women would join them with similar confessions. She was disappointed: "It was a very heterosexual group." While this was true during the following year, when Wilka and her lover left for California, it was an overly hasty judgment. Several women who came out later remembered Wilka's avowal as a transformative experience. "Simply the fact that these were women that we knew made the whole thing an option . . . that kind of revelation, of light coming in," Griesinger said. "It took a long time to go through with it, but I got more intrigued."

By 1972, some women were exploring their sexuality. Even before Wilka's coming out, Jeri Simmons was open about her bisexuality, but nobody seemed to have taken note. Simmons, no doubt DWL's youngest member when she joined in 1970 at fifteen, came from the countercul- ture and the antiwar movement. Her relationship with her parents was conflictual, and when her father discovered her in bed with a man, she left home. A service for runaways sent her to stay with Radican, who invited her to a CR group. Simmons began to attend regularly, and after returning home used baby-sitting jobs for DWL members as a cover to fool her disapproving parents.

Being bisexual came easily in Simmons's countercultural environment. In the spring of 1973, she helped found the cosexual Gay Activist Alliance at local Wright State University, where she was a student. With- in a year, tensions in the group sparked the creation of the all-women Sappho's Army. Defined as a support network and a social group, it brought together students, several nurses, and women from the lesbian subculture.[41] Through Simmons's influence, Sappho's Army affiliated with DWL as a CR group several months later. However, there was lit- tle intermingling. Many members used Sappho's Army for its social func- tions only, and some DWL members had doubts about the group's commitment to feminism. Indeed, feminist issues were rarely discussed. The main link the group maintained with DWL was providing speakers on lesbianism for feminist events.

Although DWL had little to do with Simmons's coming out, the situ- ation was different for women in the Bodicea CR group. Member Sheila Drennen had moved to Dayton in the spring of 1973 to escape from her small southern Ohio hometown. She had recently fallen in love with a woman, and the couple wanted to get away. After some months of iso- lation and loneliness in Dayton, they looked up "women" in the tele- phone book and found DWL. Praying it was not a trendy dress shop, they called late that night. They were so excited to hear DWL's record- ed announcement that they called back over and over just to savor the knowledge that they were no longer alone.

Drennen had never known other lesbians or homosexuals; it had not even occurred to her to look for them. "We were strictly looking for some feminists," she recalled. The two women joined a CR group but kept their sexual orientation a secret. Drennen rapidly realized that "this group was important to me and if it was going to continue to be, they were going to have to know who I was." She was also getting bored with heterocentric discussions. Like Wilka, she feared rejection but found warmth and acceptance. However, unlike Wilka, Drennen assumed she and her partner would remain the sole lesbians in the group. Instead, her announcement turned into "one big coming-out party," she said: within a few months, five of the seven members identified as lesbians. Women in Bodicea rapidly connected with the Gay Activist Alliance, Sappho's Army, and the gay bar scene, but their primary commitment remained to their CR group and to DWL.

DWL's attitude toward lesbianism began as one of intellectual support. Contrary to the national situation, there never was talk of excluding lesbians or of downplaying the issue. As one DWL author wrote in 1972, "A very sad point is that many straight sisters in the women's movement have yet to accept their lesbian sisters."[42] When put to the test, the support proved to be real: for example, when a small foundation gave DWL money after rejecting requests by two other regional organizations—including a lesbian group—DWL shared the money with that group.[43]

As lesbians became more prominent in the movement, DWL began making an implicit but clear distinction between its "own lesbians" and "the others." The few lesbians who were active in DWL, and who were perceived by the others as feminists, remember feeling accepted and supported. The attitude was different toward Sappho's Army. Many of DWL's heterosexuals had never encountered the lesbian subculture, and they were shocked by what they found. Some "bar women" were not committed to the women's movement, they believed, and reflected in their butch/femme roles what DWL opposed in society. Some of DWL's lesbian members shared this critical attitude. As Drennen recalled, women in Bodicea believed that "those lesbians weren't conscious lesbians; they were old-world dykes—hard-drinking, hard people . . . [who] didn't give a hoot for feminism." For Drennen, "That wasn't what I wanted—the CR process was too important for me." Furthermore, since Dayton is the home of a major air force base, some of the bar women had military backgrounds; DWL's antiwar baggage made this hard to accept. Finally, an unstated strain came from the fact that the women were more often working class than were most DWL members.

As lesbians in DWL gained self-confidence, there was a gentle drift toward separatism. Members of Sappho's Army had had relatively little interest in men or straight women from the start. In Bodicea, where Drennen believed there was "never the feeling that we wanted to separate ourselves from heterosexual women," members got "really sick of rape and violence and war, and we thought in our naiveté that if we

53

could just get away from men, then the world would be a better place." But separatism never gained political clout in the Dayton women's movement, and what mild tendencies were discernible contrasted sharply with the violent rifts described in other cities. Some saw this as simply a side effect of small-town feminism, but because wide divides have been reported in university towns, it appears in Dayton to have been an accomplishment of the movement's nonsectarianism, exemplary organizational process and tangible sisterhood.

The opposition between Bodicea and Sappho's Army faded after 1973, and the two groups cooperated on various projects. The lesbian community changed with the arrival of younger women influenced by feminist ideas, and overlapping membership between the two circles increased. When the women's movement later created the Women's Center, offering a physical "free space," many lesbians became active.

Aside from sexual politics, another category of concern was work, paid and unpaid. Contrary to the view that feminists were against housewives, DWL, like groups across the country, promoted analyses of the economic and social value of housework. Housewives, or "unpaid domestic workers," were welcomed into the group. One such woman, Donna Parker, commented, "I did not experience any judgment from women who I came into contact with in DWL; in fact, I felt just the opposite—that they appreciated my involvement, my work." Alix Kate Schulman, writing about her reception as a housewife-mother in New York's Redstockings and WITCH, said she was treated "like a treasured resource instead of the useless has-been I considered myself at thirty-five."[44]

DWL members did condemn "the endless, spirit-breaking routine of housework" composed of "task(s) that a child of eight could perform."[45] Such work, members generally believed, should be shared by men and women, with certain functions collectivized, although some believed that women should be free to choose whether or not to stay at home.

DWL also believed that the importance and the amount of housework had been exaggerated by men for their comfort, by businesses to sell their products, and by the state to keep women at home when it suited its needs. Commenting on advertisements for cleaning products, one author wrote, "[T]he message is clear: a good woman considers her laundry in the same class as her children, and at least two cuts above her own well-being. . . . Frankly, I don't care if things are brighter, shinier, whiter, fresher, etc. I've got more important things to do. If men want to concern themselves with that kind of trivia, that's their business."[46]

DWL also addressed, from a personal point of view, the issue of paid domestic labor. Although they rarely admitted outside their CR groups, several members had "maids." This difficult and painful question combined issues of class and, in particular, race. DWL members were white, and most domestic employees were black. These white feminist employers tried to change their attitudes, first by legitimating the work through a code of standards including decent pay, benefits, and respect for the employee: "When we hire other women to come into our homes and work for low pay with no benefits we are saying something very crucial about ourselves and about all women. We are acceding to the false valuation of homemaking and child care as unimportant and of little real worth."[47] Some DWL members remained unhappy with what Mary Morgan compared to the attitude of a benevolent plantation owner. Morgan was among those who decided that she could no longer "pass on [her] oppression to other women," and she fired her long-time employee. It was, she later reflected, a poor solution to a no-win situation.

Feminism has often been reduced to the fight against inequality in the labor market. This no doubt stems from several factors, such as NOW's and other groups' emphasis on employment and attempts to portray feminism as compatible with the American system. But it also undoubtedly comes from feminists' tendency to fall back on the hard data of discrimination, which is easier than trying to explain the more subtle or less measurable aspects of sexism and more likely to be treated with respect by the media.[48]

Although most DWL members were wage earners, the group, seeking to redefine the nature of work, downplayed equality in employment issues. The protest against the 1970 Ohio Conference on the Status of Women for limiting itself to such issues is a good example of this oppositional stance, as is the disdain for individual women's success stories. DWL proclaimed, as did many feminists nationwide: "Our goal is not to have a woman become president of General Motors. Our goal is to create the kind of society where people have the right to decide if they need General Motors. . . . We don't want to replace a white man's elite society with a white woman's elite society."[49]

Work under capitalism, Pat Rector wrote, unnecessarily "mangles the spirit of millions in meaningless labor." With the optimism of the post–World War II economic boom, Kleine declared: "There is no longer any reason why a lifetime must be spent in a constant struggle to keep nourishing food on the table or a tight roof over our heads or that, once these basics have been attained, we must continue to struggle with meaningless futile attempts to satisfy an ever-growing number of falsely created needs." Work should be redefined as pleasurable and rewarding and determined by individuals' desires and capabilities rather than their class, race, or sex.[50]

DWL's rosy short-term goal was to strive toward a more liberated division of labor, with men and women sharing the responsibilities of taking care of the home and earning money. This goal contrasted sharply with the group's concomitant analysis of job discrimination. Members noted, for example, that the idea of men and women sharing all responsibilities was unrealistic due to women's lower wages. They pointed out how race affected earnings as well: black women were at the bottom of the scale, and while black men earned more than white women, they faced greater unemployment. They argued that most women did not work for pin money, but out of necessity.

As with most employed women then, few DWL members had worked in unionized sectors. In addition to the sexual segregation of the labor force and the exclusionary practices that kept women out the unions, DWL members inherited the New Left's distrust of the labor movement as it had emerged from the repressive 1950s. Betty Jean Carroll was a notable exception; she not only was a union member, she had been married to a union organizer and was from the working class. By 1972 she was a shop steward at Wright-Patterson Air Force Base. Within the union Carroll was ostracized for trying to introduce radical and feminist ideas. An enthusiastic and active participant in DWL, she drew support from her CR group but nevertheless felt different from the other women, particularly those in the core group. These women, she believed, had not experienced the struggle for survival that working-class women did: "I always felt that I had the experience and they had the rhetoric. . . . All of these things that they could look at in the abstract, I had experienced at some gut level."

By the end of 1973, divorces and a deteriorating local and national economy meant that more DWL women had begun to share Carroll's experience of struggling to survive. Work issues assumed a more central place in individual lives. Many DWL members began trying to establish careers. Many—like Carroll, who later organized a women's group at Wright-Patterson Air Force Base—applied the skills and ideas learned in DWL at their workplaces. Rather than reinforcing the organization, this investment in work often drained energy from DWL.

Following her divorce, Barbara Gregg found she cared less for theoretical discussions, and in contrast to Carroll, she was not able to apply her feminist ideas to her work. "Work took on a whole different meaning to me. It made me very aware of the power that the system has [over] whoever is working when that person is responsible for the bread that goes on the table. Because up until that point, if I got tired of a work situation, I could leave. I found myself in a situation where I had to have a job. . . . Keeping that job was probably the most important thing in my life at that stage; I was willing to do whatever was called upon me to do. I was consumed."

Opposing job discrimination was not central to DWL's activism. When members founded the short-lived NOW chapter in 1970, they believed it would relieve them of such issues as equal pay and sex-segregated want ads. DWL did, however, come to the aid of individual women fighting discrimination, including Wright State employee Betty Thomas, who was fired shortly after she sued the university for sex and racial discrimination.

Members reacted differently when local companies and administrations asked for help in their affirmative action efforts. A particularly telling example came in 1970 when DWL was invited to participate in a General Motors conference on discrimination against "minority groups including women." The group rejected the request, stating that while members were qualified to speak on the issue, DWL had "neither the womanpower nor the inclination to provide consultants to General Motors' management." In its response, DWL pointed out that of fifty-six recent promotions at a Dayton-based division of GM, not one had gone to a woman. If the company was sincere about ending discrimination, the group reasoned, it should look no further than among its own female employees—a group of whom had recently filed suit for discrimination. DWL sent out eleven copies of its letter, including to a local member of Congress, the Women's Bureau of the Department of Labor, a union, and newspapers, as well as to the GM employees concerned, asking for more information on their case.[51] GM did not renew its offer.

DWL also backed striking workers when a large number were women and minorities, supporting actions by hospital workers, Bell Telephone employees, and the University of Dayton custodial staff. The support took the form of distributing information, attending demonstrations, and raising money for strike funds. DWL called for boycotts of nonunion lettuce in support of United Farm Workers and of Farah clothes to support unionization efforts of the company's mainly Chicana workers. Yet such support remained distant. DWL did not identify the working class as the agent of revolutionary change, having inherited the common New Left attitude that the American working class had been bought off. As Carroll remembered, "There was the feeling in most of the Left that unions were very conservative, and no good." DWL looked instead toward the lumpen proletariat, women, and blacks as the vanguard.

The absence of black members did not mean that DWL ignored the issue of racism. Taking Black Power leaders at their word, members of the core group believed that "there was a role for white people—to confront other whites and their racism, to confront the oppressor," Robin Suits said. This confrontation started in their own organization. Morgan said: "I remember Jan [Griesinger] many, many times pointing out in meetings or something that what we were about to do was in fact racist," such as considering holding an event in a part of town where no black women would go. The DWL core group stressed consciousness-raising on issues of racism. But the core group's underlying belief was that as women became aware of their own oppression, they would extend their understanding to the oppression of others. Morgan and Kleine, in retrospect, believed they often were unsuccessful in making those connections.

DWL also was careful to point out, in writings and public-speaking engagements, how black women were doubly oppressed. Members tried to see how questions took on different meanings for women of color (as in issues of work and reproductive rights). Yet with no active black members, their information came secondhand. DWL members had learned that it was condescending for whites to think they could "organize blacks." There was no talk of recruiting black women and only little of outreach, but members spoke rather of dialogue. Several actually talked on an individual basis with black women comrades and friends, but this was not common. Griesinger was not alone in feeling that "there was a lot of legwork to be done as far as real contacts with people. . . . It seems to me now that there was a real minimal effort at that kind of thing. . . . I don't recall any discussion of 'instead of worrying about getting *a* black women in here, or *a* black woman to speak at some program, suppose we should find out what black women *are* doing.'"

DWL's limited connections with black women activists, combined with the view that black men were allies, led members to take men's words for women's desires. In the organizations with which DWL had contacts, Griesinger said, "there were not black women allowed to have leadership positions, [who] could see their way clear to doing that, who could get out of the house, or [who had] the time and the energy." Furthermore, DWL's connections rapidly dried up. With the weakening of the black liberation movement, the groups remaining were the more traditional Urban League and the NAACP, not organizations with which radicals identified. In the end, to quote the title of a path-breaking book on black women's studies, all the women were white and all the blacks were men.[52]

In lieu of a direct dialogue, the DWL newsletter reprinted articles from other publications by black women on feminism. The most common idea expressed in these writings was that black women saw the women's liberation movement as "ineffective at best and harmful at worst."[53] This distrust, another article explained, came from their experience of being courted by movements and then used by them, and more important, from the history of racism: "The faces of those white women hovering behind that black girl at the Little Rock school in 1957 do not soon leave the retina of the mind."[54]

DWL members recognized the validity of black women's charges of racism, but they rejected the image of their movement as white, upper-middle-class women defending the interests of their class. "Yes, we confess, we do come out of our own experiences and analysis of what is wrong with things, and perhaps some of our priorities seem wrong to some women," Griesinger wrote in answer to one such accusation. But she emphatically proclaimed: "Every time we speak to women or high school classes or fight local political issues we make it clear that we don't want a piece of the Amerikan fucked up pie. We explain that poor women fear legalized abortion as a political tool which will further remove control over their bodies and lives. We reiterate that black women are the worst paid."[55]

Many radical black women opposed participation in the women's movement; however, as bell hooks wrote: "[F]or every black anti-feminist article written and published, there existed a pro-feminist black female position."[56] DWL's tendency to air critical articles may have served to justify the "whiteness" of the group.

Similarly, the position that whites should not organize blacks, the diminishing of visible black activism, and the arrival of less politically experienced feminists led to the acceptance within DWL that it was an all-white group—a comfortable attitude for many. Indeed, in later periods members paid less attention to confronting white racism. Morgan remembered how, in a new group she was facilitating, no one reacted when a racist remark was made. Racism was never addressed in Sheila Drennen's group, started in 1973. DWL's initial respect for autonomous black organizing later allowed white feminists to wash their hands of problems of racism.

A number of issues were glaringly absent from DWL's political palette. Most were lacunae in the movement nationally: rape, battering, sexual harassment, and pornography were among the topics rarely discussed in those early years, locally or nationally. In some cases, avoidance was linked to DWL's history. "Women's culture," or artistic expression, so important elsewhere, developed slowly in Dayton. Several factors hindered such development. First, women's culture may have emerged more in communities where there was an influential lesbian feminist community. Second, the fairly amicable split from the male Left possibly gave less impetus to creating an autonomous cultural community. Finally, many of the women who founded DWL had been involved in the *Minority Report* and had sided with the politicos who ousted the "culture freaks."

Other absences reflected political stances, notably the disregard for legal rights and specifically for the Equal Rights Amendment. At the beginning of the 1980s, both pro- and antifeminist writers called the Equal Rights Amendment the sum and substance of the movement. For DWL, nothing could have been further from the truth. In the organization's first four years, only one written reference to the ERA appeared. DWL emphasized the importance of liberation over equality: "It isn't equality that the militant female wants. It's liberation for herself and the rest of humanity."[57] In 1973, DWL published two articles and, with the debate on ratification in the Ohio House, held a meeting to define an official stand on the question:[58] "Dayton Women's Liberation supports the Equal Rights Amendment. At its best, the Equal Rights Amendment will provide a constitutional basis for ending legalized discrimination. At its worst, the ERA will be used to strike down those remaining protective laws which benefit women. We believe equality under the law is an essential but small part of liberation. Women's Liberation is different from equal rights movements with which we are frequently confused, because we want a society which maximizes options for everyone."[59] After this brief foray into equal rights, the issue again disappeared from DWL's agenda. Even at the end of the decade, Chewerl Radican referred to the ERA as symbolic but "frivolous."

Electoral politics also were low on the list of DWL's priorities. A few members, not from the core group, expressed admiration for feminist politicians such as Bella Abzug and Shirley Chisholm, but discussions of politics stressed the need to see beyond the sphere of government and political parties. As Mary Morgan proclaimed in a 1972 speech: "[T]here are many of us who know on a 'gut level' that elections are not 'where it's at.'"[60] However, if women wanted to get involved in electoral politics, DWL advised them to run for office rather than educating voters via the League of Women Voters or stuffing envelopes at a campaign headquarters—a familiar experience for many.

DWL's limited direct involvement in electoral politics was noteworthy. Pre–women's movement, Mary Morgan had been a candidate for Dayton's city commission. In spring 1970, after a commissioner resigned, DWL members argued that Morgan should fill the vacancy. After all, they contended, the commission had never had a woman, and Morgan, with some seventeen thousand votes, had been the first runner-up in the earlier election. DWL printed leaflets, organized a rally,[61] and mobilized some 250 women to attend a commission meeting. In an unprecedented move, many were shut out by the police. The commission remained unaffected by the protesters' accusations of sexism and appointed a man. About a year and a half later, another seat was vacated, and the commissioners "spontaneously" decided that "the time was ripe for a woman." They chose a bright, charismatic Republican, Gail Levin, president of the League of Women Voters, who said that she had "no interest in Women's Lib or the 'women's role' because it's no different from anyone else's role."[62]

The process went full circle, though, and in 1975, former Morgan supporter Pat Roach became the first woman elected to the commission. Sympathetic to the women's movement, Roach was on the DWL mailing list and was in a CR group through her church. Her campaign involved many DWL members and other feminists, and explicitly sought "the support of women willing to do battle in male-dominated politics . . . in order to make possible that better society where power is shared by all."[63]

Despite the impressive array of concerns addressed by DWL, "the issues were not the issue," to borrow a New Left slogan. More central to DWL's philosophy was its organizational structure. The *Dayton Daily News* observed, "The lack of formal organization within [DWL] makes the growth all the more surprising."[64] For DWL, success was not in spite of its organization, but because of it. As Barbara Gregg wrote, "Women's Liberation has developed a process and a structure which attempts to maximize input and contributions from individuals and yet function collectively. It is difficult and taxing to operate in this collective manner and sometimes it is slow and tedious and sometimes we fail, but our vision perseveres and we try again. If we sacrifice this process we have sacrificed the principle upon which our movement was built and which is an integral part of the society we are building."[65]

It is precisely because DWL saw itself as prefigurative of a new society that its search for an appropriate structure was a prime form of political activity and debate. Experimentation, including failures, was a creative process, with each new form scrutinized and revised again and again. Having rejected traditional forms of organization, activists were left with few models and had to rely on trial and error. Thus, although harsh self-criticism was constant in those years, the frequent calls for increased participation and structural revision did not represent a crisis situation but rather the striving for an ideal. Many scholars of feminism see internal conflict of this kind as a cause of fragmentation.[66] For DWL, debate and the proliferation of new structures were healthy parts of what member Joan Ediss called its "beautiful and well-oiled" system.

For most of its life, DWL lacked what is often central to organizational structure—physical space. Although the idea of creating a women's space had existed from the start, it was not until 1974, after several unsuccessful attempts, that the Women's Center was founded. Until that time, the group relied on meetings, retreats, and a phone line for operations.

Decision-making occurred in a monthly coordinating meeting, initiated in September 1970 to "maintain communication between . . . members, provide a central clearing house for actions, activities, problems, requests and charting new directions."[67] The agenda was always open, with minutes published in the newsletter. Meetings were open to all, but to ensure democratic functioning and flow of information, at least one person from each CR group was supposed to attend—preferably the newest members, to integrate them into the organization. When a chairperson was necessary, the task was rotated, with at one point a lot system. Attendance fluctuated from a recorded high of twenty-five to a low of six women from the same CR group. While participation was high compared to traditional organizations' decision-making bodies, DWL was invariably dissatisfied. Ironically, calls for increased participation were as common when attendance was high as when it was low.

Frequently there was pressure on DWL to make decisions between the monthly coordinating meetings. For instance, after a television station requested an interview on short notice, DWL decided that "such requests [are] the caller's emergency or deadline to meet and not ours."[68] The issue was debated, and process was deemed more important than expediency.

Ensuring participation of all members was among DWL's highest priorities. The use of consensus as the exclusive mode of decision-making was one means of doing so.[69] Much has been written on the drawbacks of consensual decision-making; for instance, it can give considerable power to an individual who is persuasive or stubborn. In DWL consensus often meant authorizing a person to act upon her own proposal rather than collective decision-making, implemented collectively. Despite these disadvantages, the DWL core group considered the positive aspects of consensus to outweigh the negative. Consensus encouraged participants to listen attentively to others and to express their opinions in understandable ways. It empowered those who were not accustomed to public speaking, for their opinions counted.

Coordinating meetings proved too short to include general political discussions, so monthly citywide meetings, called Fireside Chats, were begun "to respond to [DWL's] urgent need to discuss, in-depth, subjects that are not unanimously agreed upon in Women's Liberation."[70] In late 1972, the Fireside Chats were vested with the power to make policy statements.

Other meeting spaces were less formal but equally as important for organizational cohesion. Occasional weekend retreats, along with other social events such as potlucks, picnics, and dances, were "a deliberate attempt to create a women's space, where we could be together, where we could dance, swim, play, have discussions, or whatever," Jan Griesinger recalled. Although there were several all-women group houses, for most DWL members retreats were the closest they came to their goal of creating women's communes. The sisterhood created there was powerful (it is no coincidence that the first public coming out occurred at a retreat). One woman wrote in the newsletter: "A good time was had by all. . . . Wild, free dancing Friday nite by candlelite; fire in the fireplace giving everything a golden glow; lots of spaghetti being passed from the kitchen to eager hands; sitting in your bag watching the sister 3 inches away drifting into sleep; the clang of pots and pans from the kitchen in the early morning, and then rising for a cup of steaming coffee . . . and finally Sharon Kalkis' car stuck in the mud until about 10 sisters come to her aid and by sheer cooperation with each other free her and the indescribably delicious feeling of accomplishment and POWER."[71] Although some women began the weekends slightly ill at ease with eating, sleeping, and dancing with other women, all later agreed that the retreats were an emotional high.

The multitude of DWL activities made it necessary to find ways to divide labor. DWL was not unconcerned with efficiency, but placed it second to its goals of increasing members' input and avoiding concentration of power in the hands of any individual. With this in mind, the organization experimented, first using open collectives for the various functions. But not enough different people participated, and so tasks were later rotated among CR groups. After a year, DWL decided to return to collectives; members believed they alone could foster the feeling of a movement as women from various CR groups worked together. Permanent collectives performed ongoing tasks: starting new CR groups, producing the newsletter, filling requests for speakers, returning calls, ordering literature, and keeping the books. In addition, ad hoc collectives dealt with the media and organized retreats, demonstrations, and conferences.

Alongside the task-oriented groups, several issue-oriented collectives were established in late 1972. One noteworthy example was the Indochina Peace Campaign Collective, created in the fall of 1972 as a chapter of the national antiwar organization. DWL members, instead of creating a traditional chapter, decided to "work internally in DWL, not just as an extension of the already existing peace group," and "to deal with the war from a feminist point of view."

One of DWL's most important collectives was the speakers group. Consciousness-raising through education was consistently viewed as a means of outreach and of effecting radical change. This coincided with the requests for DWL speakers that poured in from high schools, universities, church groups, government agencies, women's and men's clubs, and social groups. The speakers collective's mission was to get the job done while respecting DWL's organizational principles. One rule was that solo speaking engagements were refused. This was to prevent the media and institutions from singling out "stars" and to help women develop speaking skills.[72] But by 1973, the collective began wondering, "Are we being useful, or are we being used? . . . Who is the person requesting our service? . . . Do we know anything about the group— what they're in to, how they function, their size and sex composition? Shouldn't we also know if any women in the groups have any connection to the women's movement, is there a woman's caucus. . . .[73] Do we want to legitimize the concept of 'good image' (arrive, speak softly, leave) and 'poor image' (organizing, confronting sexists, day by day living and struggle on home grounds)? Is our time, our effort, our knowledge, and experience, valuable or valueless? If valuable, by what exchange or coinage do we demand payment?"[74] Historical context made these questions pertinent. By the end of 1972, professional feminist speakers bureaus had developed nationally. These varied from central bookings of famous personalities to questionably feminist businesses that were "ripping off Women's Liberation."[75]

DWL's awareness that feminism was becoming lucrative also came from experience. By the end of 1972, members were being solicited for in-depth work with institutions. One such request came from officials at Wright-Patterson Air Force Base to help develop an affirmative action pilot program for a laboratory there. The DWL newsletter cynically quipped, "[L]ast year it was racism, this year 'socialization,' which is about as close as the air force will get to sexism."[76]

In response, DWL created the education task force, an active, cohesive group that outlived DWL. The task force prepared skits, speeches, bibliographies, and multimedia shows. In its first months, the group did workshops for the faculty of a private high school about to go coed, for freshman orientation at Antioch College, and for a mothers' group at a public elementary school. Member Donna Parker described one of the presentations:

> We sprayed the room with hair spray or something. We had a table set up with women's grooming aids, which required about two of those long institution-type tables. And then we had another table set up with men's grooming aids. . . . [W]e bent over backwards to be fair. I mean, we got hair spray for men. . . . But the difference was just incredible. And then we had sexist music playing. So they came in and they heard the music, they smelled the smell, and they saw the stuff on the table. We were hitting them in all the senses. . . .
>
> Then we had skits. . . . One was "Adjust." We had a "male" psychologist with a tie, sitting at the desk, played by one of us. . . . [T]he first woman would go sit down and be the patient, and she'd say, "Doctor, I just don't know what's happening to my marriage, but it's just been falling apart lately and I don't know what to do about it." And the doctor says, "Well, my dear, you know it's the woman's responsibility to keep the marriage together. Are you keeping yourself up, keeping your weight down, taking care of your hair, cooking nice meals?" And then the group behind says, "Cope, cope, we hope you learn to cope. . . ." And then we had a problem about sexual preferences, and a whole gamut of problems, and the standard male psychologist's response. And then this chorus in the background: "Adjust, adjust, you must adjust."

Knowing that there was money to be made, the education task force charged substantial fees, ranging from fifty to a hundred dollars. This income was new for DWL, which had operated on a tiny budget and consciously opted for a light structure as a means of safeguarding its independence. No money had ever been requested from mainstream foundations or from government sources. Members wished neither to spend time raising funds nor to accept the restrictions often required. Furthermore, they believed that feminism, like the New Left, was too subversive to be funded. Granted, activists had become accustomed to their marginal status, but as shown elsewhere, the resulting austerity may have reinforced commitment.[77]

DWL never required dues from its members, no doubt to remain accessible. Revenue came from individual donations, literature sales, small radical foundations, and progressive church groups. Interestingly, while there was distrust of private foundations and of the government, this was not true for church groups. A number of women had the necessary contacts, and they knew from experience that the process involved minimal paperwork and compromise. Churches proved to be the most important external source of income for DWL, a phenomenon not reported in other studies.

Maintaining communication networks was among DWL's chief concerns. In addition to the informal communications of meetings and the inevitable friendship networks, DWL's formal network was impressive. The most important means of internal communication was the newsletter. The first issue came out in August 1970 as Kathy Kleine's personal initiative. "Believing that there are now enough of us to require written communication to fill the gaps left in verbal communication," she wrote, "I have arbitrarily decided to put out a newsletter."[78] Although she listed herself as editor on this first issue, by the second the newsletter was a collective endeavor. When Dayton feminists decided to produce a paper, it was launched with record speed; Kleine was an experienced journalist, and other members had produced leaflets and newsletters in previous activism. Several had been on the *Minority Report* staff. The low-budget production, costing around thirty dollars an issue, was nevertheless the group's third largest expenditure. Its eight to thirteen pages were run on a mimeograph machine of mysterious origin, possibly stolen, that was anonymously donated to DWL after having been used for years by left-wing organizations.

The *Dayton Women's Liberation Newsletter* appeared monthly for five years, an accomplishment that reflected group vitality and continuity. Sent free to everyone on the mailing list, it informed them of events, organizational decisions, and activities and provided national news unobtainable through the mainstream media. Most impressive, it operated as a glass house, constantly bringing into the open conflicts, criticisms, and debates and effectively serving as a tribune for members. There was no censorship, and only one accusation of unwelcome editing throughout its existence. Over the five years of publication, more than sixty Daytonians signed writings in the newsletter, and dozens more signed with initials, first names, or as members of a group. Reprints from national publications supplemented the articles. The themes raised spanned the spectrum of women's liberation concerns, in some cases following debates in the organization and in others used deliberately to spark debate.

The newsletter was an effective and exemplary DWL structure. As in all of the group's bodies, trying to involve members fully led to ongoing debate and experimentation with modes of organization. Participation remained high, even later, when responsibility for production rotated among CR groups. The number of different women signing articles and the number of articles per author remained constant. Perhaps the inordinate concern over democratic functioning, and a sense of ethical answerability to the movement—Jane Mansbridge speaks of internal accountability to a discursively created movement—rather than the actual structure used, ensured high participation rates.[79]

DWL also sold feminist periodicals, reprints of articles, and various brochures. Selling literature (and running bookstores) often was a sideline for radical groups. In the days before the Internet and large bookstore chains, obtaining feminist and radical publications was a problem outside big cities and university towns.

The local media were another link in communications, the sole source of information for those outside radical circles. The media's effectiveness in outreach, despite typically unappetizing descriptions of feminism, is one of the great ironies of the women's movement. For example, side by side in one newspaper with a venomous antifeminist article was a "shopping guide" to the area women's movement listing DWL, two DWL offshoot groups, and organizations in neighboring cities.[80] Despite the article's warning of possible man haters, DWL received many calls as a result. Feminist stirrings were so strong that even a distorted, hostile account provoked a click. This shows yet again that breaking through isolation, knowing "other kooks" existed, was a crucial step in consciousness raising.

Relations with the media were problematic. Reporters tended to contact DWL at the last minute, which was difficult to reconcile with the group's lengthy collective functioning. Refusing to bypass its process, DWL formalized guidelines to preventing journalists from singling out leaders.[81] Despite DWL's unruliness, it continued to be sought out. Women's liberation had become good press and an excellent subject for talk shows. Members interpreted the interest as a search for titillating topics and weighed the risks (being ridiculed or used simply to help a show's ratings) against the size of the female audience. The interest in provocative subjects was confirmed repeatedly over the years, as the local media showed a preference for issues such as lesbianism, sexual harassment, and rape.

The most significant television program for DWL was *The Phil Donahue Show*, which originated in Dayton before being syndicated and gaining national fame. Donahue, whose wife and several close friends were sympathetic to feminism, began inviting women's liberation activists almost from the beginning. DWL was invited to do a program, and when national feminist celebrities appeared, the group was expected to provide part of the television audience. "He wanted a few feminists in the audience to liven things up," Griesinger recalled. "He'd give us twenty-four-hour notice. We figured out we were being used after that had happened a few times." Robin Morgan, invited to appear alongside a man from *Playboy*, contacted DWL. They spent the preceding night strategizing, but "it was a case of not having the technology," Griesinger said. "As long as [Donahue] was in control of the microphone, it didn't matter what we did. He would interrupt us, cut off conversation, change the subject. . . . We never could speak adequately to our own point of view." As his fame grew, Donahue became Dayton's "expert on feminism," predictably aggravating DWL.

Of the local media, a cooperative relationship existed only with WYSO, Antioch's FM radio station. A part of the same political culture as DWL, WYSO had long had feminists in its ranks. As early as 1968 or early 1969, Antioch student and future Daytonian Julia Reichert had what was perhaps the first regular feminist radio program in the nation; and in 1971 the station started a women's news broadcast. With the flow of people between Dayton and Yellow Springs, there was overlap in membership. However, before 1973, WYSO's signal was too weak to cover most of Dayton, so the station's impact was limited.[82]

No doubt the most important element in DWL's external communications was the telephone. DWL had first appeared publicly as a telephone number ("Women's Liberation—call Cheryl 278-6271"), and through-out its history this constituted its public face. After a year of using mem-bers' personal numbers, a DWL line and a "recorded answering thing" were installed in a member's basement. The newfangled machine was DWL's largest expenditure during the period, costing $640 plus mainte-nance and taking more than two years to pay off. In 1972, the number was printed in the Dayton telephone directory under "Women's Libera-tion" and in the yellow pages under "Social Services," and announced on radio public service announcements and at DWL speaking engage-ments.

This telephone line made access to the group easy for the first time. Previously, a woman could not readily find DWL unless she was acquainted with members or radical circles or happened upon a public presentation. Once the number appeared in the phone book, the vol-ume of calls doubled. A surprising number of women actually "joined" the women's movement over the phone. Over the first two years, the group received an average of thirty-five calls per week, with seven peo-ple leaving messages. The largest number of calls came from women wanting to attend meetings for prospective members. Callers also requested speakers and made inquiries about DWL's services and activ-ities. Another important category of calls was what one report called "horror stories": tales of job discrimination, unemployment, credit rejections, divorce, health problems, unwanted pregnancies, rape, and domestic violence.[83] These calls provided a means of seeing beyond the immediate group, gauging the needs of women in Dayton, and they subsequently served as impetus for new projects. Finally, a small but noteworthy number of calls were received from individuals and groups from other cities, both long distance and when they happened to be traveling through the area. The telephone was thus one way in which DWL connected with the loose network that was the national women's movement.

DWL considered itself the legitimate local representative of the nation-al movement, although there were no organizational links. This is illus-trated by the group's sentiment that national celebrities passing through town owed it to the movement to contact DWL—out of abstract sister-hood, to help use their influence in Dayton, and to talk shop. In the peri-od from 1969 to 1973, Marlene Dixon, Robin Morgan, members of the Boston group Bread and Roses, Florence Kennedy, Germaine Greer, Glo-ria Steinem, Shirley Chisholm, and Holly Near were among those who came to speak on local television or at area universities. Few contacted

DWL beforehand, but many agreed to meet with the group afterward. DWL members were ambivalent about the presence of these celebrities. While proclaiming that the women's liberation movement had no leaders and that its stars were media creations, DWL did not condemn individual women for speaking. Members did resent it when these women did not contact DWL; letters of complaint were sent at least twice, to *Ms.* magazine and to the Boston Women's Health Collective. (Robin Morgan, who did meet with DWL, gave a glimpse of the other side of the feminist celebrity speakers circuit: "[T]he at-first temptingly homey stay at the local feminist commune was to be avoided." It usually meant, she discovered, being forced to stay up all night talking, "the unstated by equivalent price of room and board"; being fed "gagingly healthy gummy brown rice"; and feeling obliged to do the dishes, so as not to appear "a horrible New-York-type-star-leader."[84])

Other forms of national communications were carryovers from the New Left and underground newspaper networks. The *Minority Report* and other groups had been on scores of mailing lists that were appropriated by the women's movement. At first the underground press diffused information, and DWL rapidly began to receive feminist publications from many other cities, such as "Women's *Rat*," *The Furies, Women, a Journal of Liberation, off our backs, Ms., Notes* (from the First, Second, and Third Years), and *Know-reprints*.

DWL participated in regional and national structures. DWL women cofounded statewide coalitions on abortion rights. The group helped organize several conferences, the most famous being the 1971 Toronto conference. As had been true in the New Left, individuals traveled regularly to conferences in other cities, such as the 1972 socialist feminist conference in Durham, North Carolina. They were members of NOW, the ACLU, and the Congress of Labor Union Women, creating direct lines to people and ideas across the nation. Robin Suits and several others at one point belonged to the national leadership of the socialist New American Movement; Carroll was a steward in the American Federation of Government Employees; and Griesinger was in the leadership of church organizations such as the World Student Christian Federation and Campus Ministry Women. The beginning of a phenomenon can be discerned: many people knew more about what was happening nationally in their realm of interest than in a Dayton CR group meeting down the block. Similarly, a surprising number of Daytonians connected to DWL after having met members at a national conference.

Members also expressed the feeling of being part of an international women's movement. This undoubtedly was abstract for most of Dayton's feminists, who had little knowledge of feminism outside the United States and no direct lines of communication. At first, this feeling of international unity was scarcely distinguishable from anti-imperialist sentiments. It took on more precise meaning thanks to a project of the World Student Christian Federation. At the suggestion of Charlotte Bunch, the federation paid Griesinger to coordinate, compile, and edit a book on international feminism. The goal, Griesinger said, was "for American women to understand that feminism was coming in a number of forms, with different languages and different priorities in different parts of the world, but that it was coming." The book, *Women in the Struggle for Liberation,* was one of the earliest of its kind.[85]

At the same time, Griesinger, several other DWL members, and women from the United Theological Seminary obtained funds from the Methodist Church to study the international women's movement. In June 1974, a small group called Women Here and There was created. The group lasted years, although Griesinger was the only DWL member to remain. It later became involved in the campaign against multinationals' promotion of baby formula in the third world.[86]

DWL's organizational structure and stances were indicative of the founding members' radical aspirations. Having criticized the New Left for not going far enough, these women believed that their movement had replaced it as the cutting edge of a broader movement. Thus, when they spoke of wanting to draw new women into something larger, it was not a form of infiltration by the Left, for they believed that they were at least one if not *the* driving force of that something in Dayton. Because of this, DWL did not restrict its sphere of intervention to "women's issues." While there was disagreement about working in cosexual organizations, there was general agreement with the group's opposition to not only sexism but racism, imperialism, and capitalism. And DWL embraced a number of other causes, such as guaranteed minimum income, socialized medicine, refusing to pay taxes on phone bills used for the war effort, strike support, and the impeachment of Richard Nixon. Members participated in other coalitions, groups, and campaigns.

DWL's core group and the organization as a whole, even as it changed and grew, maintained a radical identity. Although radical members were quick to point out that perhaps half the membership was made up of liberal women, this was not entirely true. The autonomy of the CR groups and lack of formalized membership did mean that diverse women found a place in the organization. Over the years, the decline of the New Left meant that the original recruiting networks were progressively replaced by traditional women's organizations, church groups, and publicity through the media. But although some members identified themselves as liberal, the consciousness-raising process and organizational process radicalized many. Equally as important, their association with a group tainted by subversion usually resulted in a break with the respectable liberal community.

The organization's radical identity did not prevent liberal and radical ideas from coexisting, as Donna Parker's position illustrated. A paid member of national NOW and the Women's Political Caucus and peripherally involved in the Fairborn, Ohio, NOW chapter, Parker viewed these groups as complementary to her primary involvement in DWL. "I saw this as the very strategy. . . . You needed the wild-eyed radical people to make it possible for the milder—viewed as the more reasonable—organizations to make any progress." However, when asked about her personal long-term goals, she admitted that she wanted (figuratively speaking) to "blow this place to smithereens. . . . I don't want to change the rules; I wanted to change the game."

Only once did a member openly contest DWL's leftist identity. At a 1973 meeting, the newsletter reported, "a sister who is relatively new to women's liberation objected that the Dayton movement seemed to embrace 'every Left and liberal cause' that came down the pike, whether or not that cause had to do with women's issues." Her objections were rapidly countered: "It is the contention of the Newsletter collective and of a great many women in women's liberation movements in Dayton and elsewhere, that there is a relationship between the women's movement and other struggles for liberation by other oppressed groups. . . . [W]omen's liberation is a leftist organization."[87]

DWL defended its radicalism, but it steadfastly refused to do so at the expense of its feminism. In 1971, two members of the Marxist-Leninist Revolutionary Union (RU) joined DWL. These women were not prevented from expressing themselves. The issue of the newsletter produced by their CR group, for example, included a review of a ballet about the struggle of a Chinese peasant woman who joins the Red Army, as well as a virulently antifeminist "letter from a welfare mother." The latter stated, "*You murder me, women's liberationist, every bullshit demand you make. . . . Your movement is a farce and a travesty to us, because you uphold the forces that make us beg for our existence. . . . How dare you call yourselves our Sisters?*"[88] DWL members, with no strategizing beforehand, instinctively closed ranks against the RU. DWL's founders had inherited a distrust of sectarian leftist groups, and any doubts they might have had about the RU members' intentions were dispelled when they discovered an RU document describing its strategy of recruiting members from women's liberation groups. The RU women's arguments were refuted when they could not be ignored. Their presence went virtually unnoticed in the organization.

DWL embraced no single feminist philosophy. Members drew on and were influenced by a number of different political philosophies. Although some adopted labels, those labels did not correspond to usage in other places. Even by the end of 1972, for instance, the use of the term "radical feminists" meant feminists who had "some commitment to radicalism."[89] Most individuals in the group also used what at the time were identified as radical, socialist, and liberal feminist ideas. Attacks from the Right brought out members' leftism; attacks from the Left brought out members' radical feminism. Griesinger wrote, in answer to the welfare mother's letter: "Some sisters have claimed that we should be working among working class sisters (a la Marxist-Leninist revolution of the workers) but we say that *all women* (except a very privileged few . . .) *work,* most for little or no pay, and that women must come together as a class since they are oppressed as a class."[90]

While DWL often used negatives to define itself (as being *against* sexism, racism, and imperialism), it did begin to trace the contours of a political philosophy of liberation. First, its structure, diametrically opposed to a vanguard party, incarnated a liberated alternative. Second, its method, based on the politics of experience, brought together the personal and the political to produce theory and guide actions. Finally, DWL's version of human liberation envisioned a genderless society.

DWL hoped to live out their ideals of liberation and create a "microcosm of utopia." The idea of living liberation was not a creation of the women's liberation movement; without going far back in history, the social movements of the sixties had rejected traditional life styles and created concrete alternatives. In Dayton, unmarried couples living together, communal households, and alternative institutions—concentrated in the neighborhood in which most DWL members lived—had become reality. But DWL first introduced many newcomers to this alternative community,[91] and for those already a part of it, DWL pushed beyond the New Left and the counterculture. The institution of marriage had been criticized before, for example, but it was in terms of the meaning of love and the role of the church and the state. The women's liberation movement brought the debate into the kitchen and the bedroom. Living with a man, if social relations remained unchanged, was criticized as the same as or even worse than marriage. Similarly, though few DWL women came out of the closet in the early years, lesbianism became an option for the first time.

While long-term liberation needed to be associated with immediate transformation, DWL's core group was adamant that one could not limit the feminist struggle to changes in individual life styles: "Any decision to begin a new life style *now* must be accompanied by a real struggle to free the majority of people to be able to choose how and with whom they will live. . . . What alternatives we choose are only important in so far as they give us the power to share our own lives as a part of the process of revolution."[92] Nevertheless, the way people chose to live was seen as activism. As Kleine put it, "It is the way we relate to each other that not only determines how we live but also the kind of society we shall have."[93]

In a group that encouraged multiple opinions, contradictions naturally abounded, a result of the ebullition of creative thought. But by the end of 1973, there were signs of trouble. Many DWL members carried on unaware or unconcerned, but for the activist core, contradictions became crevices, separating what had previously been different facets of a whole.

Some of the difficulties stemmed from the growing size of the organization and the change in structure caused by the proliferation of collectives and task forces. Throughout 1973, collectives steadily gained independence and were granted decision-making power. The independence of these groups may have been necessary for smooth functioning, but it contributed to what was perhaps an inevitable fragmentation of the movement.

The smooth incorporation of new members via CR groups also was affected by a change in how the groups were established. Although individual CR groups took on personalities, one of their central principles remained that of finding commonality among participants. As time went on, groups self-consciously formed around particular interests or characteristics. Apparently unnoticed by DWL, this change represented a shift toward affirmation of difference rather than the breaking down of barriers.

The intensity of the bonds of sisterhood created in the CR groups sometimes fostered intergroup barriers, a hindrance to the integration of newcomers. Nowhere was this more noticeable than in the accusations leveled against the core group, personified by Elizabeth's Sisters. A number of DWL members accused Elizabeth's Sisters of being elitist and of controlling the movement. It is undeniable that this CR group contained a higher concentration of the activist core than any other, particularly a small subgroup of about five women. These women were responsible for an inordinate amount of organizational work and writing. They attended almost all important DWL meetings, were in and often initiated numerous collectives, drew up bibliographies, produced a slide show, and filled numerous speaking engagements. Four of them were responsible for writing more than thirty articles in the newsletter, often long theoretical pieces.

Sensitive to these critiques, Elizabeth's Sisters admitted new members. "We would say, 'We've got to expand . . . because we're too elite,'" Barbara Gregg said. The way they did it justified the accusations. Gregg recalled discussing potential candidates in detail and then "beckoning" them majestically. Elizabeth's Sisters also was apparently the only group to have expelled a member. Robin Suits was suspected of being manipulated by her leftist lover and of not respecting the "aura of confidentiality" of the CR group by sharing with him what the members discussed. According to Gregg, Suits was "purged." Suits herself denied the term; she said that because tensions had become unbearable, she precipitated the act by asking the group to vote—unheard-of in the CR groups—on whether she should stay.[94]

Members of Elizabeth's Sisters believed, as Joan Ediss recalled, that their power stemmed from long-term involvement, the amount of time invested, and their desire to preserve what they had created. If this was elitism, they said, it was by default, since other women left the work and decision-making up to them. Kleine argued defensively that such accusations came from women who were insecure, illustrating a contradiction between the notion of empowering women as individuals and seeking a leaderless mode of functioning. Feminists had to be strong, but strength was then equated with elitism.

Another pitfall came from the organizational structuring around consciousness-raising groups. For the core group, consciousness was not a form of nirvana to be attained. It was a contradiction in terms to say, as did some newcomers, that one's consciousness was "raised." However, even the most fervent defenders of the process admitted that there was a progression in one's level of awareness. After several years, long-term members no longer had patience for new people's meetings because there were "no new discoveries with new women anymore," Kleine said. Inversely, some women joining after 1973 felt that their CR groups received little support[95] and had minimal connections with the old guard, resulting in a generational divide. One woman spoke of "mixed feelings about revealing my reactions to my present situation to sisters who have their consciousness raised to the point where the types of questions I'm posing for myself were answered for them long ago."[96]

Newcomers began seeing the CR process and action as separable, that they should "get [their] head[s] together, get [their] rage out, and then go do something," Mary Morgan recalled. This shocked women in the core group. "I couldn't see any action without a CR base," Morgan said. "Almost everything we did that went wrong was because we hadn't worked out the feelings, the strategy, or the sort of things you did in the CR group." A structural development confirmed the trend toward the separation of consciousness-raising and action. As collectives and task forces became new kinds of cells for the organization, it began to be seen as acceptable for a person to join DWL through them rather than through a CR group. Some latter-day recruits merely sought personal support and transformation. To the founders, this was heresy. "It was integral to DWL that CR groups were not support groups, but a base in which you got to know a small group of women well, and then you got involved in larger things," Morgan recalled. "And then in some groups, instead of the whole group participating, you only got one or two people participating in the larger thing, and then maybe they'd drop out." This was the beginning of what Lisa Maria Hogeland dubbed the "softening" of CR. Using Claudia Dreifus's categories "soft " and "hard" to distinguish between CR as sisterly support and CR as a link to broader ideas and collective action, Hogeland critiqued the conflation, increasingly visible over the years, between the former—that is, feminist literacy—and feminism itself.[97]

While different from the intentions of the founders, an emphasis on personal support was not inherently incompatible with political action or the maintenance of the organization, particularly given the structural function of the CR groups. One group, Wilder Sisters, illustrated how for many it was possible to emphasize personal change without abandoning other goals. Formed in July 1972, Wilder Sisters was composed of eight women. With the exception of a pair of (blood) sisters, the women were at first strangers to each other and came from different parts of the city. (By the end of the first year, however, half were living near each other.) They were from twenty to thirty years old and middle class. Only three were married (information on the marital status of one member wasn't available), and one had children. Member Barbara Schroeder described the group as having started out with "a 'real' hippie, a few typical students, two straight school teachers, a 'housewife-mother,' and a social worker." Members expressed similar motivations for joining the group, at least half commenting on having had problems fulfilling their prescribed roles. The feminine mystique was still taking its victims, as one of the "straight schoolteachers" explained; she attended the first meeting because "summer vacation stretched ahead of me full of depression and loneliness because I had no friends, only acquaintances caught up like me in suburban life."[98]

For Wilder Sisters, the personal took precedence over the political; learning to accept oneself was seen as necessary in order to accept others. Accepting oneself included the physical. Members examined how they had been taught to dislike their bodies and how, at the same time, they had learned that they had to make themselves attractive in order to keep a man. They were struck by their inability to be physically close to other women. One woman wrote that she had never hugged or kissed a woman outside of her family. This was a topic for discussion and work in the group; the members held hands during meetings and gave each other massages in the nude to overcome such inhibitions.

Nonjudgmental support of one another was a goal for the group, and initially, everyone seemed to agree about everything. But the women rapidly became aware of a danger of sisterhood—that of avoiding confrontation. They believed that certain issues were taboo and felt pressure to conform to be a "real" feminist. Wilder Sisters worked to prevent this: "[A]cceptance without confrontation can lead to stagnation. . . . It has been hard for us to distinguish between accepting people and supporting everything they do."[99]

Personal transformations did take place in Wilder Sisters, as reports told: "[A]t least fifty percent of our meetings are absolute dynamite," and "no one has regressed . . . all of my sisters grow more beautiful every day." One woman discovered that she didn't need "to keep a man around to support [her], protect [her], or keep [her] dependent in any other way."[100] The self-defined housewife-mother changed the way she socialized her children, improved her family life, and found the strength to get a job. In the workplace, her feminist experience helped her speak out against discrimination.

The most dramatic changes were for one of the teachers, a woman from an affluent suburb. Her CR group, she said, saved her from depression, and she lived from one meeting to the next. She also grew better at "touching, loving, trusting, and telling the truth to other women." When in 1973 her husband needed to relocate for professional reasons, she chose not to follow him but to move into a communal house in Dayton View. Deciding that she did not want to make the sacrifices necessary to have children, she had a tubal ligation. She quit teaching and entered law school.[101]

Wilder Sisters was more than a support group. It extended beyond the individual by holding political debates, participated in group actions, and fulfilled its responsibilities as a DWL cell. Finally, and most difficult to gauge, members of the group believed that they became individual agents of change, carrying their feminism into other spheres of their lives. However, this position revealed another problem with the CR group structure: women drew strength from their groups, but this energy was not reinvested in the mother organization. Transforming a marriage or beginning a career, for example, limited activist involvement.[102]

One of the most serious unresolved dilemmas of DWL's approach to consciousness-raising related to the politics of experience. To what extent was one's experience the basis for change? In some cases, the elevation of experience to the level of the sacred was used as justification for immobility. Gregg and Kleine, in a defense of heterosexuality, argued a point by writing, "[I]t invalidates part of our experience which is an antithesis of our hard won understanding that no part of our experience is invalid."[103] Here, validating an experience seemed to preclude change. Similarly, as pointed out by Wilder Sisters, the need to create an atmosphere of trust and acceptance in the CR group made it difficult for women to challenge or criticize a sister. It might be important, for example, to understand why a woman lived with an oppressive husband, but it could not be done to the point of implicitly encouraging her to put up with abuse. It might be important to understand how an individual may have become racist in this society, but not to reinforce that racism by accepting it. Uncritical sisterhood, rare in the beginning, later increased.

Another glitch in DWL's philosophy became apparent. The core group's theory held that as women came to understand their own oppression, they would understand other people's. "Our method was to begin with the personal, and then hopefully—and I think for the most part unsuccessfully—bring women . . . to an understanding of their personal oppression being related to oppression of [others]," Kleine said. This coexisted, somewhat paradoxically, with the notion that consciousness-raising was largely based not on differences but on similarity of situations and personal experiences. In practice, it was discovered that understanding one's own oppression by no means led automatically to understanding other forms of oppression.

The most flagrant and unresolved contradiction for DWL was that the group's revolutionary aspirations contrasted with a theoretical void on how to make a revolution, how to overthrow patriarchy and capitalism. Members rejected previous theories but found little to replace them. The group often glorified national liberation struggles and armed warfare in the third world, but discounted violent revolution and urban guerrilla warfare in the U.S. as macho fantasies of the male Left. There was no analysis of the role of the working class in the revolution, nor was there any attempt (beyond the analysis of housework) to redefine the notion of the working class. The group expressed some hope regarding the role of the powerless, the lumpen proletariat, but with little thought as to precisely how they were to be empowered. And yet, members often stressed in their theoretical writings that power, be it the state or men, concedes nothing without a fight. The need to struggle for liberation, and not just on an individual level, was repeated over and over. But the means fell far short of the revolutionary goals. DWL's forms of agitation tended to be relatively traditional: lobbying, letter-writing, education, and direct action such as nonviolent protest. The group seemed to believe that a mass movement using education and consciousness-raising, organized according to feminist and revolutionary ethics, would make women's oppression magically wither away.

3

MAKING SPACE
A Women's Center (1974)

THE WOMEN'S movement in Dayton entered a new stage in 1974 when
the Dayton Women's Center opened its doors to the public. The
Center was a creation of Dayton Women's Liberation, as were most feminist initiatives at the time, and it was the local movement's first alternative institution. The Women's Center was a passionate experiment in
creating a utopian institution to carve out free space for women and to
prefigure the society toward which its creators strove. This utopian
experiment, ironically, set the scene for the first major split in Dayton's
movement and marked the beginning of the end for its mother organization. While there was no feminist-politico rift among the first generation of Dayton feminists, conflict did arise as a new activist core of
socialist feminists formed during the creation of the Center. This new
generation contested DWL's organizational principles, and in the ensuing
conflict, DWL was shattered.

From the outset, DWL had wanted to create a women's space and
had made several unsuccessful attempts at starting a center. Housemates
Jan Griesinger and Chewerl Radican turned their front room into a
fledgling women's center, putting out feminist literature and flouting city
law by hanging a sign in the window. In early 1971, DWL met with feminists from neighboring cities in an unsuccessful attempt to create a
southwest Ohio women's center. In the summer of 1971, when a member left on an extended vacation and offered the use of her rented house,
DWL opened its first space, but the experiment was aborted after only
six weeks when the tenant dropped her lease.

Collectives existed on and off to explore potential goals and possibilities for a women's center. The vision for a center progressively expanded. Initially planned to improve internal communications, it began to be

envisioned as a means of outreach, "a neutral place for women to come find out more about Women's Liberation."[1] Various options were contemplated, from housing a center in a member's basement, a storefront, or the YWCA to creating a women's communal house that would offer space.

Money was expected to be the main obstacle, so each time DWL received its tiny grants, the debate was reopened. But because DWL shied away from any commitment that might transform the organization's light structure, it was assumed that a center would need to be self-financed through pledges from members or consciousness-raising groups. When it became clear that outside money would be required, DWL decided to "re-explore [its] reasons for needing a women's center."[2]

In early 1973, however, an event occurred that was to change the face of the women's movement in Dayton. The latest women's center collective, revived in December 1972, discovered that money was available through the Model Cities Program. In a matter of weeks, the collective drafted and submitted a proposal and was granted the substantial sum of fifteen thousand dollars.

DWL member Barbara Roberts, who had joined the Elizabeth's Sisters CR group, was a member of a Model Cities neighborhood board, the Fair River Oaks Area Priority Council (FROC). FROC prioritized proposals for federal Model Cities funding in an area where many DWL members lived. Indeed, DWL had encouraged members to be candidates for these boards, one of only two times the organization pushed for participation in electoral politics: "Why not have a voice in how that 5 million dollars will be used? Day Care Centers, Half-Way House for women, a women's advocate???"[3] But public support for feminism had seemed so unlikely to DWL that when Roberts spoke of the possibility, everyone was taken by surprise.

Written accounts tell how Roberts met with the collective to explain the application procedure. But Barbara Gregg remembered it differently: "[Roberts] called me up one night and said that FROC had this money and that they didn't know what to do with it." Gregg called several other members of her CR group, and they "came up with the idea that FROC should fund a women's center." As she put it, "The idea had been in the air for a long time, and this seemed like an opportune moment to grab at some money."

The collective rapidly drafted a funding proposal. While the emphasis on providing services was new for DWL, the understanding of the specific needs was the result of years of feminist practice. The future center would offer self-help courses. It would provide counseling and advocacy in the areas of job discrimination, unemployment, marital difficulties, rape, unwanted pregnancy, health problems, single parenting, and child care.[4]

Among the proposed main goals was to dispel alienation of women who were isolated, evoking single mothers but also homemakers. Although expressed ostensibly to appeal to FROC authorities, the proposal shows how Dayton feminists considered the feminine mystique to be universal. This view did not come from DWL members' own experience, and it contradicted the trend of increasing numbers of women entering the labor force. Indeed, projects based on the needs of the elusive "other woman" failed; the programs aimed at housewives, such as "clothing construction, food preparation and preservation, . . . slipcovers and drapes," never materialized.

While carefully avoiding any direct mention of feminism, the proposal showed that the center was intended to serve as headquarters to the local women's movement and to draw new women into the movement who would, euphemistically put, "gain strength through community to work to change the situations with which they are faced."[5]

DWL requested more than twenty-three thousand dollars for nine months. Betty Jean Carroll was drafted to give the presentation. (She recalled that she was chosen because she was "older and looked conservative.") After much debate, FROC whittled the budget to fifteen thousand dollars and approved the proposal. DWL members were flabbergasted. Few had actually believed their project would be accepted. Looking back, several commented that it was approved only because there was money to burn. But Griesinger pointed out that the FROC task force was about two-thirds women, and that since many women in DWL had strong roots in the community, they were "not total strangers to other liberals involved in community affairs and less likely to be perceived as the lunatic fringe."[6] DWL members also understood, if only intuitively, that feminism was becoming more respectable and fundable. Increasing numbers of institutions were willing to pay for feminist speakers and programs. While never articulated, DWL sensed that if it didn't seize control of this turf, nonfeminists would.

Not all DWL members agreed with the idea of a women's center. Some were distrustful of possible strings attached to state funding. Others simply felt that given DWL's numerous activities, a center would require more work than the organization could handle. Such concerns were pushed aside in the euphoria of the moment.

Of course, the strings rapidly materialized. First, DWL discovered that final decision-making power lay in the hands of the Dayton city commission. The collective mobilized DWL members to attend commission meetings. There, they learned that for the commission, feminists were still very much the lunatic fringe. "As soon as a women's center was mentioned, there was snickering from the 93% male attended meeting [sic]. The staff of the Model Cities Program . . . recommended that the Women's Center not be funded as Ron Gatton [Dayton Model Cities director] stated, 'It is not well thought out' and that we could not handle it. They also recommended that another project not be funded called 'Adventure Playground.' This gave the commissioners great material in order to ridicule the Women's Center proposal. Like: when both were mentioned one commissioner said 'Aren't they the same project?' and [city commissioner] Kurran said, 'I think I'll send my wife there.' Another replied, 'Where? to the Women's Center or Adventure Playground?'" Another account said that the collective was referred to as a group of "incompetent women."[7]

Veteran activist Carroll, not one to be silenced, castigated the assembly for its sexist reaction. FROC president Michael Means supported her, seeing the proposal as representing not only a women's issue but a struggle between community and city government control. FROC "did not need to be wildly enthusiastic about women's liberation," Griesinger later wrote. "The real issue was whether neighborhood groups can choose their own priorities or whether city hall still maintains control by vetoing those it doesn't like."[8] Finally, the entire slate of FROC recommendations was approved.

Any suspicion that DWL's perception of hostility might have been overblown can be dispelled by reading the subsequent editorial in the *Dayton Daily News:* "It seems only fair that commissioners also make federal money available for a Men's center. That would feature such things as night care, counseling by sympathetic bartenders, bowling, poker and pool. Para-legal services might not be needed, but a combination of para-medical and extra-legal services could produce a mighty fine massage parlor. It would, of course, be fully distaffed."[9]

DWL's victory at the city commission was just one step in the eight months of negotiations that preceded the city's final approval. The heady atmosphere of the times and the collective's lack of experience with bureaucratic institutions made the obstacles seem unbearable. DWL was forced to incorporate and name three trustees, which was contrary to its ideals and only agreed upon as a front. Budgets and contracts had to be negotiated, revised, and renegotiated. A site had to be found that was properly zoned and passed building inspection. In the process, the content of the future center's programs was challenged. For example, the city's law department contended that counseling women about divorce might constitute illegal practice of law and lead to husbands' suing the city for alienation of affection.[10] Despite the red tape, the feminists knew that securing government support for a women's center marked an important victory: "We are feeling all the positive energy that comes from SUCCESS in the best sense. . . . We don't feel our political perspective has been compromised nor have we had to sell out as individuals."[11]

The founders of the Dayton Women's Center had little experience in inflating budgets; their initial request had been for bare essentials. Once the funds were slashed by almost 40 percent, the collective immediately faced the need to raise the rest. A letter to launch the campaign read: "Dayton Women's Liberation has intentionally avoided membership dues and fund-raising events, because women have traditionally been exploited as fund raisers for organizations in which they held no power. But this will be our center. . . . Bake Sales? Ring doorbells? Knit booties? Sell chances? Spaghetti dinners? Good Grief NOOOOOOO!"[12] Instead, DWL requested monthly pledges from members. By the opening of the Women's Center, the organization had received fifty pledges for a total of $410 per month, only 10 percent short of its goal. This fund-raising campaign was the first manifestation of what was to be a permanent feature, and bane, of the Dayton Women's Center.

As soon as DWL learned of possible funding, it became necessary to clarify goals for the proposed center. Writing documents for city and federal officials sparked much debate as real and tactical goals mixed. By the summer of 1973, the differences between the various conceptions of the future center were becoming apparent. Energies were spread thin as another DWL group began working on opening an abortion clinic. The number of active members on the Women's Center collective dwindled from eight to three: Mary Morgan, Robin Suits, and a relative newcomer, Sherrie Holmes.

Holmes, born in 1951, was to become one of the most powerful figures in the movement. Her father, who grew up on an Iowa farm, moved to Dayton to work for General Motors and succeeded in the business world. Her mother was a Christian Scientist who by virtue of her religion, Holmes believed, was more open to different ideas than her conservative father. Holmes and her three siblings grew up in an all-white, affluent suburb of South Dayton. By the time she was in high school,

Holmes's growing sympathies toward the protest movements she watched from afar made her stand out as a hippie. Near the end of her senior year, when her class went to a sex education program at a progressive Catholic center, Holmes fell in love with one of the organizers, an antiwar activist. She began college but dropped out in her first year. She and her boyfriend first lived together, and then, since "everyone was hassling us so much," they got married. Holmes was eighteen at the time. As she described her life a few years later: "I was stuck at feeling strongly pissed off at the way our society and government was run and accepted. I thought the war in Indochina didn't make sense. I could see that blacks and poor people were constantly getting screwed, our environment was becoming a mess, that women were pushed and pushed into an exploited role. I hated our consumer society, and everything about the school system. There seemed no humanness anywhere. My answer to all this was having few possessions, communal living, dropping out of school. . . . In general I tried to have very little to do with the system personally."[13] Because Holmes and her husband were part of the counterculture, she thought she would gain independence by marrying him. Instead, she recalled, "I felt like I became invisible, that I sort of lost my identity. I didn't any longer really try to have my own friends and my own life. Everything just sort of melted into his." The marriage lasted two years.

Holmes tried working for VISTA, but concluded that the volunteer organization could not fundamentally change society. Looking for new horizons, she "somewhat haphazardly" joined an antiwar coalition in the summer of 1972. There, Robin Suits, whom she immediately liked and admired, invited her to a DWL meeting.

Holmes became part of the Wilder Sisters CR group and experienced her click: "It was a very exciting thing. . . . Until I got in that group, I really don't believe I understood how much I had been programmed. . . . I thought, 'Oh, that happens to other women.' Also, I don't think until that time I had really discovered women." She started reading; her first meeting coincided with the first issue of *Ms.* magazine. "I read it cover to cover and was very excited about the ideas." Thanks to her CR group, Holmes reported, she became self-confident and strong, and she began to understand how the pieces of the puzzle fit together. Sexism, war, and the "general mess of this country," she concluded, were caused by the "US government and economic interests [that] are geared entirely toward white male ideology, profit and power."[14]

In the collective, Holmes allied with Suits, who saw the Women's

85

Center as "a tool to reach out to the masses." Morgan, on the other hand, believed that the Center should simply serve women. Suits recalled: "[Morgan] would say things like, 'The Women's Center should be the tool only of the women who come to it.' That if women come in and say—this is one thing she used to say that drove me crazy—they want to have a class on makeup and charm, we will have a class on makeup and charm. And I would say, 'No way! Every time we have a group of classes, they should be one-third political ideology, one-third self-help, and one-third consciousness-raising.' I was trying to get them to have a conscious structure and a conscious strategy for moving these women into the revolution."

In retrospect, Suits and Morgan both ascribe the intensity of their conflict to fatigue. But it was also precipitated by an important development in Dayton's Left. In June 1972, shortly before the Women's Center project took form, a new New Left organization was founded: the New American Movement (NAM). Both Suits and Holmes joined the local NAM chapter, and the group was to play an important role in the history of the Dayton Women's Center and the local feminist movement.

NAM was born at a time when the New Left was in disarray and the women's movement was ascending. Contrary to other New Left organizations, NAM defined itself as socialist and feminist from the start. With influential feminists in its national leadership, NAM incorporated feminist analyses and priorities. Its definition of the working class was broad, including those "who must work without pay in the home." Particularly targeted was the "sexual division of production," which "fragments social life into 'public' work life and 'private' isolated home life'" and which "determines the specific form that sexist social relations have taken under capitalism." Contrary to many ultraleft organizations, NAM unequivocally recognized the need for autonomous women's organizing. Seen as necessary due to women's distrust of the mixed Left as well as the "unique position of women in society," these groups were to struggle for their own liberation and continue to critique the socialist movement.[15] In November 1972, NAM women, several Daytonians included, held a socialist feminist conference in Durham, North Carolina.

Dayton had a large NAM chapter for a city of its size. Although membership probably never exceeded thirty, this was substantial in comparison both to chapters in other cities and to other sixties and seventies left-wing organizations in Dayton.[16] The local chapter had a socialist feminist/women's caucus by the beginning of the Women's Center project. At first, Suits and Holmes were the only DWL members who were in NAM and the caucus. But by the opening of the Center the balance of power was shifting.

In November 1973, a DWL socialist feminist CR group was founded, bringing together NAM members and other socialist feminists. Overlap between this group and the NAM women's caucus was such that there was constant confusion between the two; together they formed a more or less formal group referred to hereafter as the socialist feminists. While socialist feminists never accounted for more than a small segment of DWL membership, they had tremendous impact on the movement for several reasons. First, because they arrived at a crucial moment, they became influential in the Women's Center project. Second, like the old core, they became dedicated, hard-working activists. Finally, they constituted a closely knit, coherent group.

Although there were similarities in the sociological profiles between the socialist feminists and early DWL members—they were, for instance, all white and well educated—there also were differences. The socialist feminists were somewhat younger, in their early twenties, including DWL veterans Suits and Holmes. Most were recent college graduates, and although they had already worked for pay, they were between school and career. They were unmarried, had no children, and had not directly experienced the feminine mystique of the 1950s. They had some experience in the Left and the civil rights movement, but less than the DWL core. While few had been in consciousness-raising groups prior to the socialist feminist group, most were already sympathetic to feminism, and their entrance into a DWL group was much less of a blinding-light experience than for early members. As for many of the women who joined after the first generation, as feminist ideas were more broadly diffused in society, many felt that they were already feminists before becoming active in DWL and that their feminist awakening had been gradual. DWL was no longer *the* movement, but simply an organization within the broader movement to which they owed their allegiance.

Julia Reichert had been a feminist activist since even before the emergence of the women's movement in Dayton. An influential NAM member both in Dayton and nationally, she was a member of the women's caucus and socialist feminist group.

Reichert came from a small New Jersey town. Her father was a butcher in a grocery store and her mother was a nurse. "Where I grew up everyone seemed to be Republicans," she said. "There were no Jews, and blacks all lived in one little part of town." In 1964, Reichert became the first in her family to go to college, and although she was a Republican like her parents, she chose progressive Antioch. "I had really no idea that Antioch was radical or that I was 'conservative,'" she said. During high school, she had written to dozens of colleges in alphabetical order, hence her early interest in Antioch, where she liked the sound of the work-study and travel abroad programs. Then her family, on a trip out West, drove by Yellow Springs; Reichert insisted they stop. "I remember three things: girls with long, straight hair and guitars slung on their backs, my dad looking at the names on the student mailboxes and noting how many were Jews, and the wail of a saxophone coming out of an upper dorm room. That last thing really did it." Within months her political sympathies shifted completely.[17]

It was Reichert's roommate, a New York Jewish red-diaper baby, who "brought women's liberation to Antioch," Reichert said. In late 1967, at a co-op job in Gainesville, Florida, the roommate met Florida Paper coauthor Judy Brown and joined an early CR group. Upon returning to Yellow Springs, she started a CR group with Reichert and others. While Reichert had become sympathetic to, and peripherally involved in, the Left and the civil rights movement, she said, "Nothing made my life make more sense the way the women's movement did." It was through the movement that she "got deeply connected to radical ideas."

Reichert and her friends started other groups. They attended protests, including the demonstration at the 1968 Miss America Pageant, where the violent antifeminist reaction affected her deeply. Atlantic City was home turf to Reichert, and "the folks on the boardwalk were like my family and friends' families." Rather than join in the New York style confrontational politics, Reichert was no doubt among those who, as Jacqui Ceballos remembers, "tried to talk to them person to person."[18]

In late 1968 or early 1969, Reichert started a feminist radio program on Antioch's WYSO that may have been the first ongoing program of its kind in the country. In 1970, she and her partner, Jim Kleine, made *Growing Up Female,* one of the first feminist films to come out of the Second Wave movement. In 1972, they cofounded the feminist film distribution cooperative New Day Films.

Reichert moved to Dayton in 1972 to shoot a film. She knew the city from her days as news director for WYSO, and she had met Dayton radicals, including Suits, at the founding conference of NAM. In 1974, Reichert helped found the Media House, an urban commune in a beautiful rambling home near the edge of Dayton View and Five Oaks. The Media House eventually was home to a number of NAM members and socialist feminists. It became a focal point for the city's Left, a gathering spot for political debates and social events, including frequent showings of radical and feminist films.

Reichert's films made her something of a celebrity, locally and nationally.[19] She traveled extensively to promote her films and also became part of the national leadership of NAM. In an antileadership movement that reputedly devoured its prodigies, one might have expected her position to have been contested. In fact, as had been the attitude toward national personalities, the Dayton movement expected commitment from "stars" but did not condemn them for their position.

Among those who moved to Dayton for the Media House project was Sherry Novick. She had been a member of NAM in Yellow Springs, and she joined the socialist feminist group shortly after her arrival in Dayton in the summer of 1974.

Novick was from a well-to-do, liberal family. She grew up one of the only Jews in a small Mormon town in Idaho where her parents had moved for her father's job as a nuclear engineer. In her teens in the late sixties, she was a part of "a renegade group—you know, straight-A students that held student body offices but also smoked dope and got drunk a lot." Her activities ranged from partying to participating on the debating team to campaigning for Eugene McCarthy and petitioning against antiballistic missiles. In high school, she won a Betty Crocker scholarship, which she used to go to Antioch.

Novick arrived in Yellow Springs shortly after the bombing of Cambodia in 1970 and found the campus a whirlwind of ultraleft activism. She and a group of friends dove right in, doing Black Panther support, strike support, and media work. It was an exciting period, she recalled: "People organizing to take control of their lives," people feeling they were "on the brink of some kind of a revolution." But it was also a time of madness. "A lot of it had to do with being young, naive college women," she said. "We were all just real open and real vulnerable and wanting to get involved. . . . And we were really taken advantage of a lot, in overt and subtle ways." The summer after her freshman year, a comrade raped her. He was black, and Novick knew from her Antioch classes how "rape was a charge used to lynch black men." This contributed to Novick's denial about the rape that lasted for years.

To get away from "the madness of Yellow Springs," Novick used Antioch's work-study program to live in Europe, Mexico, and cities in the U.S. She sought out new forms of activism wherever she went. Her exposure to doctrinaire groups predisposed her to support pragmatic, effective methods. Upon returning to Yellow Springs, she joined NAM, which seemed "really sane," she said. "And because I was in NAM, I was automatically in the socialist feminist group."

Tricia Hart was drawn into a DWL CR group in the summer of 1973, around the same time she joined NAM and its women's group. Hart was raised in Louisville, Kentucky. Her Irish Catholic parents had grown up poor, but her father, who had received scholarships to Yale and Harvard Business School, succeeded in business. Hart's mother "spent from age twenty to forty-one just having kids all the time"—ten children, nine of whom survived—"way too many for what she was capable of doing." After her youngest child was born, she broke down and was in and out of mental institutions for some ten years. During this time, Hart took care of her four younger siblings.

Hart had always been a caring person who felt strongly about injustice and racism. After attending a Catholic retreat in a poor black parish, she got involved in camps for inner-city children. In 1969, she went to the Catholic University of Dayton, where she majored in elementary and special education.

During Hart's freshman year, one of her sisters got divorced and in the process became a feminist. Hart grew close to this sister, who discussed the abortion rights work she was doing and gave Hart feminist literature. The following year Hart accompanied some Louisville friends to an antiwar workshop in Cincinnati. Although she had lived in Dayton for two years, it was at this workshop that she met Daytonian antiwar activists and joined their coalition. There she met DWL members, including Sherrie Holmes. When Holmes invited her to a CR group, she was ready. Hart joined NAM for a brief period, but found the group too abstract and intellectual. Also, as one of the few with a "straight job" (she was teaching special education at an all-black high school), she had little patience with the many late-night meetings. It was the socialist feminist group and, eventually, the Women's Center that became her new political homes.

Like Hart, Barbara Tuss had gone to Catholic schools all her life. She had been born and raised in northwest Dayton, to "pretty much working class" parents. Her mother was a homemaker, and her father did mechanical drawing at a General Motors plant. Tuss inherited a sense of "not wanting to be pushed around by the upper classes" from her Hungarian grandparents, yet her upbringing taught her to respect authority. In 1968, as she was about to leave Dayton to go to a small women's college in Chicago, she was shocked by the letter she received from her future roommate: enclosed was the cover of *Time* magazine showing the roommate's brother demonstrating at the Democratic convention in Chicago. Over the following year, influenced by her roommate and friends, Tuss discovered radical politics and got involved in anti-imperialist and feminist activism. While in Chicago, she purchased a copy of *Women in the Struggle for Liberation,* edited by Jan Griesinger, and discovered to her surprise that it came from her hometown. Upon her return to Dayton in 1973, she sent a card to the post office box listed in the book and was contacted by Griesinger.

Tuss was thrilled to find activism in what she had imagined to be a political desert, and DWL members were excited to learn what was happening in Chicago. She joined a CR group, but found it preoccupied with personal matters. The Women's Center project interested her, and her first DWL function was a painting party for the Center. She dropped out of her original CR group and joined the socialist feminist group and then NAM.

The arrival of a younger generation of socialist feminists—what sociologist Nancy Whittier called a micro-cohort—infused new energy into the movement, but the women also formed a tightly knit social and political group that subsequently triggered the movement's first major split. According to Whittier, the very existence of such a group creates conflict. Writing about Columbus, Ohio, she said: "Each micro-cohort entered the movement at a specific point in its history, engaged in different activities, had a characteristic political culture, and modified feminist collective identity." These differences, Whittier argued, "were a major source of conflicts within the women's movement." Their new ideology, as Carol Mueller pointed out, could confer status on recruits, putting them on equal footing with the old guard.[20]

Socialist feminists had self-consciously organized among themselves according to political allegiance, rather than along the relatively anonymous lines of new people's meetings. They saw each other outside of DWL, in the socialist feminist group and, for most, in NAM meetings. As Sherry Novick recalled, this created opportunities to strategize, sometimes overtly, sometimes developing a hidden agenda. "We decided we wanted a strategy for the women's movement," Suits said. "I wanted the Women's Center to be a tool to reach out to the masses, and I wanted to have a conscious political philosophy, a strategy, and then tactics. [DWL] just had an amorphous idea that CR would make a revolution."

Many socialist feminists placed great importance on defining oneself as socialist, sometimes taking precedence over actual political goals or actions. Indeed, the politics of many other DWL women incorporated Marxist analyses, and some called themselves socialists. It was not the support of socialism that drew the line between the socialist feminists and the others, it was personal allegiance and positions on the organizational structure, the role of the CR group, and utopianism.

For socialist feminists, allegiance determined relations from the start; as Novick recognized, she had "ready-made allies" upon arrival. On the other side, Barbara Gregg, who considered herself a socialist, nevertheless remained aligned with the DWL core. So did Griesinger, who recognized that "politically, I would have had very few differences with them or the kind of analysis NAM was putting out." The prime issue articulated was one of trust—or more accurately, of distrust. Joan Ediss put it bluntly: "The main danger of the socialist feminists was male domination." Certain men were seen as manipulative, and the women involved with them were guilty by association. More generally, sympathy toward a cosexual organization was seen as causing divided loyalties or a drain on energy—or worse, as a way of exploiting the women's movement. "Here were the masses [the men] were waiting for!" Gregg said.

Griesinger, who was often able to span the chasm, believed that "women in NAM were suspected of and showed some evidence of behaving like people in the Left, of trying to snatch people into their own group, to use the women's movement as a recruiting ground for NAM." This was merely the "institutional logic of any group recruiting," she believed. Furthermore, "the fact that they existed in another group, knew each other there, made them already suspicious . . . a kind of a bloc."

These accusations hurt socialist feminists. Contrary to the infiltrators from the sectarian Left or the politicos described in national splits, they were deeply committed to the autonomous women's movement. Those who were members of NAM fought to further feminist ideas within the organization. But despite similarities in long-term goals, there were real political differences.

Many of these differences are made clear in two Chicago texts embraced by Dayton socialist feminists: the Chicago Women's Liberation Union's *Socialist Feminism: A Strategy for the Women's Movement* and Jo Freeman's article "The Tyranny of Structurelessness," both published in 1972.[21] In late 1973 and during the following year, socialist feminists used these texts to challenge what DWL's old guard held most dear.

The Chicago Women's Liberation Union text had already circulated in DWL, and Tuss further promoted it upon her arrival from Chicago. Novick remembered feeling that the Chicago group's strategy "made so much sense. . . . It was just an affirmation of 'yes, we're going to deal in this society as it is now. We're really going to organize and build things and get a lot of women active and bring women who aren't necessarily attracted to a consciousness-raising group.'"

The text criticized much of what was vital to DWL. It held that utopianism led to immobilism and needed to be replaced with winnable goals. Its limited concept of "rap groups"—as appropriate places to deal with experiences and feelings, but often in isolation from direct action—was diametrically opposed to DWL's conception. (Ironically, the critique of CR groups contradicted socialist feminists' own experience. For many, the most memorable aspect of their involvement in DWL was participation in a CR group.) Finally, the text Chicago argued for explicit structure and means of decision-making and leaders who would be responsible to the organization (the term "vanguard" is also used) as prerequisites for organization-building.

The call for explicit structure is the main point in Freeman's "Tyranny of Structurelessness," a classic that marked a turn toward more traditional structures in the movement. The early structurelessness, Freeman argued, was an understandable reaction to an overstructured society and useful for rap groups, but unsuited for organizations and action. Structurelessness itself, she contended, masked an informal structure and informal elite that could not be held responsible to the organization. She pushed for explicit forms of organization, combining methods used in the movement (such as rotation of tasks) with traditional ones (such as delegation of authority and division of labor).[22]

Socialist feminists found Freeman's analyses directly applicable to DWL. Suits said: "People would pretend there were no leaders or chairperson, but there were. . . . They would maintain that we had true democracy, but I would maintain that it was not democracy . . . because there were certain people running things but they were not elected, so they weren't accountable to anybody—and I admitted that I was one."

Socialist feminists added another dimension to this critique: structurelessness permitted a lack of political clarity. DWL was so accepting of diversity that it had allowed its politics to be watered down. In an article entitled "Political Reality and the Women's Movement," Tuss asked: "What happens when the interests of the women under the umbrella of women's liberation clash or are in fact antagonistic? Has our striving for unity, leaderlessness, and structurelessness resulted in just so many 'sacred cows' that serve to hinder and inhibit women from exploring the revolutionary potential of women's liberation?"[23]

DWL initially welcomed such debate. Mary Morgan described the December 1973 Fireside Chat on elitism in the organization as conflictual and painful, but constructive and "one of the necessary struggles to free ourselves from the cobwebs of the past." But by mid-1974 the socialist feminists' critiques had crystallized, pushing some DWL members to adopt radical feminist positions in opposition. Kathy Kleine, for example, who had called herself a socialist, and who only five months earlier had written that DWL was a leftist organization, now wrote, "[DWL women] did not call themselves socialists because they did not develop a class analysis of American society. They developed a feminist analysis. . . . Regardless of race or class all women experience similar kinds of oppression solely because they are women."[24]

Conflict first surfaced over hiring staff for the new Women's Center. The job openings were announced in the DWL newsletter and in classified advertisements in the local newspapers. Forty-five responses came in, seven through the newsletter, including from socialist feminists Suits and Holmes. The Women's Center collective formed an interviewing team that short-listed fourteen women to be interviewed.

Despite underlying tensions, the interviewing process exemplified sisterly hiring practices. Applicant Kathy Ellison remembered being impressed by the friendly atmosphere and the rigor of the interviewing team. Before the interviews, candidates received a description of the Center and were invited to an orientation session to learn more about the project. They were asked about their experience with women's groups, with counseling, and with recruiting and supervising volunteers; their willingness to help raise funds; their knowledge of the community; and their experience "working with races, ages, economic status or lifestyles [sic]" different from their own.[25] The interviewers recommended hiring Holmes and newcomers Roberta Fisher and Ellison.

Kathy Ellison was born in 1946 to a middle-class Jewish family. For Ellison, being Jewish was not about religion, it was about being an outsider in her small Ohio factory town. For instance, knowing that the local swimming pool and the country club excluded Jews sensitized her to questions of discrimination. A bright student and high school valedictorian, Ellison assumed that once she went away to college she would never return to her hometown. She studied sociology at Smith College, then at Antioch, and she earned a master's degree in education at Ohio State. Ellison had worked as a probation officer in Cleveland, as a researcher in Philadelphia, and as a teacher in Memphis, Tennessee.

By 1973, while still in Memphis, Ellison had begun to study law. As she recounted in her application for the Women's Center position: "At age six or thereabouts I noted the bemused stares which met my declaration that 'When I grow up I want to be a lawyer' (The plan has not been abandoned)." When Ellison was laid off, she followed her husband to Dayton, where he had been offered a job. Concomitantly to her application to the Women's Center, the University of Dayton announced the opening of Dayton's first law school, and she determined to apply for the following year.

Ellison had attended demonstrations in support of the civil rights and antiwar movements. By the late sixties, she had also become peripherally involved in the women's movement. Pragmatic and action-oriented, she joined NOW in Tennessee and later in Ohio.

Ellison's personal style was traditional. Her resumé emphasized academic and professional credentials. Her dry wit was hidden behind a deadpan, often monotone delivery. She looked "straight"—a novelty for DWL. Tricia Hart was surprised by Ellison's style: "She just dressed real different and acted real different and came from a much different place than we were all coming from." Ediss was "frightened by [her] straight-lookingness." Style, at the tail end of the sixties, still represented a political stance for some women.[26]

Ellison herself recognized that the women around her were not her peers. "The people who I would have been most likely to have things in common with" or the "kind of NOW people . . . are the people who just weren't there. . . . The kind of people who I always figured I'd have as friends are the people who had the same upbringing as I had . . . , a little more conservative in their personal lives." She added, tongue-in-cheek, "I went through a number of years living with mattresses-on-the-floor kind of stuff . . . but I always figured I wouldn't always live like that." Ellison's commitment to the women's movement overrode such differences.

Roberta Fisher struck people as even straighter than Ellison: she was married, thirty-eight years old, the mother of five children, and an inhabitant of affluent South Dayton. Several DWL members recalled thinking that Fisher was not a feminist, and indeed, she had never been involved in Dayton's movement. But in her circles, she had been a self-conscious feminist for years.

Fisher had grown up poor in Cincinnati. Raised Catholic and the product of parochial schools, she lived out her Catholicism by attending church, rejecting birth control, and believing that "abortion was a great evil." It was in the early sixties, during her fifth pregnancy, that she picked up *The Feminine Mystique* and thought, "This is it!" She recalled: "I just knew I could do other things than have babies." Like some other women, she said to herself "somebody else had going on in her what I had going on in me!" In 1965 Fisher heard Betty Friedan speak as part of a Dayton Junior League lecture series. Subsequently, she got involved with a new circle of friends, among them Maddi Breslin, whom she later drew into the Center project, and Phil and Marge Donahue. "When Watts was burning down was when . . . I learned how to think," she said. She and her friends were reading the critical and progressive Catholic press and discovering the civil rights and antiwar movements. Temporarily quashing her feminist stirrings, Fisher plunged into other forms of activism: "It was easier to . . . identify with other oppressed groups, like black people, than to deal with my own [oppression]." Her actions included fighting a local priest's project to build an expensive replica of a Spanish cathedral, pushing instead for the money to be used in poor parishes. She also supported voluntary busing by sending her children to inner-city Catholic schools.

Fisher and her friends became disillusioned with the Catholic Church and abandoned their efforts to reform it. To fill the void, Fisher decided to resume her nursing career, which had been interrupted by her pregnancies, and got a job in a hospital psychiatric ward. More than any previous experience, she attributed her feminist consciousness to this job. "Most of the patients were women. . . . All the people giving the women shock treatments were men. And most of the things these so-called crazy ladies were saying I agreed with. . . . I just cried inside of me every day at work. . . . To me it was, as soon as [a woman] started thinking, if she had the misfortune to get herself into a state that her family hospitalized her, she was going to get her brain fried so she wouldn't think those thoughts anymore."

Fisher had long had a support group in her female comrades-in-arms. They evolved into a de facto CR group, reading and discussing feminist literature. They realized that in their reform work for the Catholic Church they had been doing the "shit work" while their husbands got the more glamorous tasks, such as meeting with the press.[27] Fisher related her nursing experiences to her friends, and they began to discern the sexism involved. After a year, Fisher began psychotherapy herself and, unusual for the period, started coaching girl's soccer.

When Fisher read the advertisement for the Women's Center staff positions in the newspaper, she had never heard of DWL and hadn't a clue what a collective was, but she called herself a feminist. Her application letter ended, "[M]ostly what I feel I have to offer the Center is that I like being a woman, and enjoy being with and working with women."

The interviewing team decided to hire Fisher, Ellison, and Holmes, but then discovered that the coordinating meeting considered itself the final decision-making body. The coordinating meeting, in one of the few nonconsensual decisions, made by vote, decided to also hire Suits. Mary Morgan, who had invested heavily in the complex interviewing process, remembered the scene bitterly: "The recommendations of the hiring committee were totally ignored. . . . They hired who they wanted." Morgan didn't believe previous participation in DWL was necessary for the jobs, but Suits angrily declared, "People like Mary Morgan wanted Kathy Ellison and Roberta Fisher, who had not been in women's liberation"; they wanted, Suits believed, "anybody except Sherrie Holmes and me." Suits, unemployed at the time, had wanted the job badly: "I did see myself as a full-time revolutionary, and it was the ideal situation: to get paid for the work I'd been doing."

Joan Ediss was unhappy about the decision for a different reason. She believed there "should be some kind of qualification as feminist" but that the group "ended up getting two women who were clearly not feminist . . . and two women who were a political bloc." Ediss and other core group members distrusted NAM.

To Holmes, it seemed as if DWL had gotten "cold feet" and wanted "to hang on to Dayton Women's Liberation as a comfortable place. . . . That's when the fears started developing that a kind of . . . woman would be coming in . . . [who] hadn't been through consciousness-raising groups, . . . and then there's all these kind of control issues: you know, people who had been in control with DWL were not so in control."

Ellison saw the situation as a result of personal questions: "I figured if I would get the job it was because they decided not to hire someone else." But she also rightly saw the tensions as inherent issues of power. "When a group becomes successful enough to have a paid staff, that always entails the alienation of the people who've done all the volunteer work who feel correctly that they have lost power."

As a result of the conflict, many DWL women left the Women's Center collective. The Center officially continued to be a project of DWL: the phone line and equipment were transferred there; the newsletter continued to serve the Center; DWL women, including those who quit the collective, continued paying their pledges; and final decisions remained in the DWL coordinating committee meeting. However, after the Dayton Women's Center opened, many DWL members were never to cross the threshold.

The departure of these women on the eve of the opening decimated the Women's Center collective. It was revived using newcomers. "We had a collective of about twelve or fifteen women, and they were mostly new, very energetic. It was wonderful, very dynamic," Suits said. But it was not a simple matter: "The staff, particularly Sherrie and I, were organizing this collective to be our bosses—we were sort of teaching our bosses to be our bosses!" Socialist feminists encouraged comrades to get involved, and when the Center opened, other women were immediately recruited. The latter had little or no experience with the women's movement, which created ambivalent feelings, but such reservations were offset by the new blood and excitement.[28]

On January 8, 1974, despite tensions and freezing weather, the Dayton Women's Center opened in a euphoric, festive atmosphere. Collective members had worked nonstop to the last minute, fixing up the large old house that they had, with some difficulty, found on North Main Street. The women silk-screened posters and distributed mimeographed leaflets, and the media announced the opening and the following week of events. The response was tremendous. More than a hundred women attended the opening, three-fifths of them new to the movement, and 91 women signed up for the Center's first session of classes. In the first four months alone, more than 2,700 women used the Center. Nearly 150 referrals to other agencies were recorded, in answer to legal, medical, family, and economic problems, and 549 names were added to the mailing list. By the end of the year, the list reached 1,300, from the initial 500 names inherited from DWL.[29]

Coverage of the Center was copious, showing a new rapport with the media. The opening alone was covered by two television stations, two radio stations, and eight area newspapers.[30] Contrary to the hostile and sporadic coverage of DWL and even of the preparatory stages of the Center, the media became an ally. More surprising than the volume of coverage was the change in tone: feminism had become a legitimate news topic. Throughout its existence, the Center was portrayed in the media as a respectable community institution. Relations so improved that at one point, regular monthly meetings were arranged with a staff writer from one of the daily newspapers.[31]

The opening of the Dayton Women's Center ushered in the second stage of the women's liberation movement in Dayton. With federal money, good press, and a physical presence, the movement went public. This was a time of rapid expansion and broad diffusion of feminist ideas. It was a period of accrued self-confidence; as one grant application proclaimed, "[U]nless one is living in a cave or has just come from Mars it is pretty evident what women want."[32] This next stage in Dayton's movement was also a period of interplay between the DWL-style utopianism and institutionalization.

In addition to the movement's expansion and its gain in legitimacy nationwide, there were specific reasons for this development in Dayton. First, the Center had received government funding and was thus seen as an agency or a social service. Furthermore, feminism had also gained an indigenous institution. Dayton was more receptive to a home-grown product than to a national movement. Also, certain characteristics that had previously put off journalists were no longer true: the Center filled a concrete space, an office; there were visible leaders (the staff) to interview, several of whom were "straight-looking"; and there were regular, identifiable services and events about which to write. In addition, Center activists were more favorably inclined toward the media than DWL had been, not having experienced the unfair treatment of the early years and of previous radical movements. "There were always a lot of reporters who were our friends," Ellison said. "I always thought of the press as potential allies. . . . They were nice to us, and we were nice to them." Fisher and new activist Maddi Breslin were close friends with talk-show host Phil Donahue, who was on his way to national fame. Their influence was mutual: they spoke to him about feminism, and he gave them pointers on dealing effectively with the media. Finally, some local reporters were themselves becoming more sympathetic to feminist ideas, and feminists, including at one point a former DWL member, were among new recruits to the papers.

The Center marked the entry of a new generation of feminists, both a new activist core and new followers, and it became the new hub of feminism in Dayton. It offered services including educational workshops, self-help classes, programs for the community, referrals, and therapy. With various levels of commitment possible for the first time—from sending a check or taking a class to volunteering or serving on the collective—far more women became active. The house on Main Street, as one member described, was a busy place: "There were times when that place was really hopping with all kinds of things going on, something in every room. There'd be a counseling session downstairs, . . . kids in the back screaming, and a meeting going on, and a couple of people at the front desk wanting to know about the up-and-coming classes, and the telephone ringing, . . . and somebody walking in off the street and pouring out her whole soul because something had happened to her."[33]

In many respects, the new Center was an extension of DWL's utopian vision. First, it viewed the movement as serving all women and potentially open to all issues of concern. Second, it created a woman's space
for the first time in Dayton's movement. Furthermore, its structure was
far from traditional. Biweekly collective meetings were open to all.
Agendas were open, and the chair was rotated. Although the Center collective advocated more formal means of decision-making than DWL,
Robert's Rules of Order never took hold. Voting was not uncommon,
but as one woman recalled, motions were often tabled until consensus
was reached. No hierarchy existed among staff, salaries were equal, and
when funding ran low, those least in need were taken off the payroll.[34]

Finally, the Center set out with a utopian feminist vision of a city
where women would be free from violence, self-sufficient, and supportive of each other. Many of the Center's classes filled this role. While DWL
had organized classes, the Women's Center was the first to do so on a regular basis, with classes taught by women for women. Among the most
successful were those with a self-help orientation, such as self-defense and
a careers class for women who wanted to reenter the job market.

Another manner in which the Center worked to make a women-
friendly city was by fighting rape. In February 1974, Women Against
Rape (WAR) was created, the first Dayton group ever to address the
issue. Theoretically a task force of DWL, WAR began at the Center with
about fifteen women, including DWL and Center members and Fisher,
her friend Maddi Breslin, and their daughters. Several rape victims later
joined.

One of seven children, Maddi Breslin was the product of a Catholic
education. She married at twenty-two and had three children. When her
last child started school, she became president of the Rosary Altar Society in her affluent white suburban church, raising funds through bridge
parties and fashion shows. But news of the civil rights movement was fil-
tering into Breslin's consciousness, and when her priest announced his
plan to build a replica of a Spanish cathedral, she joined with Fisher, the
Donahues, and a handful of others to urge the Church to use the money
instead to support poorer parishes. They also began working actively for
desegregation. With about a dozen other couples, they sent their children
to a black parochial school, where "old bedraggled nuns," Breslin
quipped, "ministered to the black folk" in what the Church saw as "a
mission outpost."

Thus began Breslin's long involvement in Dayton's black community.
At meeting after meeting, she was "the marshmallow in the hot choco-

late." As Black Power was emerging, she began working as a secretary for her children's school and later became assistant to the prominent black activist Art Thomas. "I was in the black community almost totally," she said. "I dreamt in black. . . . Every day, light bulbs would click. And I'd see things and then I'd piece it together with me as a woman, as an Italian, how much I didn't want to be an Italian." Breslin's involvement rocked her marriage, as was true for many in her circles. "My husband didn't know what was happening to his wife. And the kids, too. My one son, who was in second grade, picked up black dialect. They'd be spouting Black Power slogans!"

Meanwhile, Breslin, Fisher, Marge Donahue, and others were contesting their positions as women. "The women were doing all the work," Breslin said. "We were typing, mimeographing, meeting—plus cooking and doing all the other stuff. . . . [W]e began to read some of *that* literature: *The Second Sex, Feminine Mystique.*" For Breslin, readings on racism and sexism melded: "What rang a bell for me was the similarity of oppression." When Fisher was hired at the Women's Center, Breslin came along as resident adviser and report-writer and enthusiastically joined Women Against Rape.

During its active period of one year, WAR provided self-defense and assertiveness training, public education to expose myths about rape, sensitivity training for people who worked with rape victims, and practical advice about what to do in case of rape. WAR gave approximately twenty-five presentations to groups including schools, hospitals, the Dayton police academy, nurses groups, women's groups, and "hip old dudes" (according to Breslin) from a men's business association.

While some aspects of the Center reflected a utopian vision, others reflected a deradicalization that became increasingly obvious over the years. A division of labor was established: some people learned newsletter production, for example, while others specialized in fund-raising. Structural stability became more important than experimentation. A hierarchy was instituted among paid staff, volunteers, the collective, and those who used the Center, which institutionalized differences in power and in knowledge and resulted in a decline of participatory democracy.[35]

Doing referrals buffeted the Center between collective self-help and acting as a social service agency. "The Women's Center is a feminist institution," an introduction to the Center for volunteers proclaimed. "Through our programs and services, we promote the equality and liberation of women." For women to gain freedom, the text continued, "we do encourage women to stand up for themselves and other women." However, the services the Center offered attracted many women who were overwhelmed by their problems. "We've gotten a number of calls from women who play 'Ain't it awful' and long conversations are not only a waste of time, but can tend to support a woman in avoiding a solution to her problem. . . . Attempt to steer callers who seem to have nothing but problems towards solutions with questions like: 'How do you think the Women's Center can help you?' and 'what are you going to do to change your situation?' Remember, the Women's Center isn't here to 'Rescue' women who oppress themselves by acting helpless. . . . The Women's Center is here to help women who seriously want to solve their problems and change their lives."[36] While this tone clearly grew out of the desire to empower women and to avoid turning the Center into a social service agency, it contrasted starkly with the pro-woman atmosphere of DWL's CR groups. It also reflected an attitude born of feminist therapy, a hallmark of the Center that was to gradually transplant consciousness-raising. Nowhere is the difference between DWL and the Center clearer than in the practice of feminist therapy.

The issue of mental health had been addressed in DWL. The initial position was that women's oppression was the root cause of most mental illness. An early article stated that "[m]ental hospitals, alcoholic wards and doctors' offices are filled with women experiencing the terror of realizing that, 'this is all there is' after being duped by the magical, all fulfilling joys of wifehood and motherhood." Another one suggested that Sylvia Plath might not have committed suicide had there been a feminist movement in her time.[37] Charlotte Holovack wrote: "[I]t is no measure of mental health to be well adjusted in a deeply sick society." Therapists, she said, should "assist individuals in developing their full potential and should provide the knowledge and emotional support to deal with [their] environment, NOT submit or adjust to it."[38] These positions no doubt came from members' experiences of having been pressured by psychiatrists to adjust to a feminine role; at least two women had been forcibly institutionalized by their families. By 1973, this position was being contested by mental health professionals such as Twila Merta, who spoke out against romanticizing madness: "Madness is not romantic, is not fun, not heroic. . . . [It is] suffering . . . painful and incapacitating as hell." Madwomen might "be capable of being aware, but incapable of doing much about it."[39] Irrespective of their positions, DWL members did not see therapy as an alternative to consciousness-raising.

Therapy became a major component of the Center from the start. In the first month alone, forty women were in group or individual counseling; over the first four months, 443 woman-hours were devoted to counseling.[40] This continued throughout most of the Center's history, and many members, socialist feminists included, became involved in feminist therapy.

Staff member Roberta Fisher was largely responsible for the introduction of feminist therapy at the Center. Deeply involved in radical therapy, Fisher believed in using whatever worked, but was particularly influenced by transactional analysis: the victim-persecutor-rescuer triangle seemed relevant to women's position.[41] Fisher, Breslin, and to a lesser extent Holmes, who was in training, ran most of the early counseling. Breslin, who like Fisher had children and was somewhat older than the socialist feminists, believed they were seen as mother figures.

Socialist feminist Tricia Hart was in an early group led by Fisher. "I've made some terrific changes in my life as a result," she enthusiastically wrote at the time. "I can't get away with any of this, 'poor dear, I've experienced this same horrible experience, tell me more.'" She linked the "poor dear" attitude to the CR group: "I think many women, even in . . . consciousness raising groups are into rescuing each other. We must learn to confront our problems and express our feelings, especially anger."[42]

Hart's critique of the CR group is telling. DWL had identified the problem of avoiding confrontation and the need for feminist therapy in addition to CR. But few new Center members joined CR groups, and some groups were phased out. In its growing opposition to DWL, the Center was searching for an alternative to the CR group, which was being criticized as an inappropriate basis for organizational structure and as having become an end in and of itself. Despite the Center's own warnings that therapy "reinforces the concept of individual solutions to problems rather than social solutions" and "serves to maintain the social status quo, attempting to fit the individual in,"[43] feminist therapy supplanted CR little by little.

Financial pressures also pulled the Center further from its utopian beginnings. Rather than settling financial matters, the initial Model Cities money marked the start of an ongoing battle for money. In March 1974, the Center collective learned that the grant would not be renewed.[44] For the first time in the movement, fund-raising became a preoccupation, and a time-consuming one. Breslin, who had gained experience in writing proposals while working with activist Art Thomas, drafted a massive fund-raising proposal.[45] Suits and Holmes, in particular, devoted a large portion of their time to seeking grants. Despite expertise gained over the years, no governmental body ever again subsidized the Center, aside from several positions funded by the Comprehensive Employment and Training Act. Private foundations were only slightly more responsive.[46] The only consistent organizational donors to the Women's Center were church-related groups, such as United Methodist Voluntary Services and Church Women United.

These combined sources made up between a quarter and a half of the Center's monthly budget of one thousand to eighteen hundred dollars.[47] The rest was raised through traditional means. The preferred method was personal pledges to pay the rent; regular campaigns were held, and an optional membership was instituted in 1975. Enrollment fees for classes were raised. But the Center finally gave in and began using the traditional women's fund-raising methods members had reproved: yard sales, raffles, parties, and bake sales (although with a twist: one bake sale, for example, featured only "man-made" food cooked by local male celebrities and politicians).

Despite these efforts, the Center was constantly skirting bankruptcy. Once Model Cities money was exhausted, Fisher and Ellison went off the payroll because they could survive without the income, and Ellison wanted to resume law school. From this point on, while money was always found to ensure some paid staff, the Center began to rely more heavily on volunteer labor.

Fund-raising drained energy, but more important, it made Center programs and politics susceptible to shifts in fashion and in social policy. Requests for money for general operations were repeatedly turned down, with foundation and government officials advising the Center to adopt single-issue projects. As a result, programs were developed that otherwise might not have been priorities. In the rare cases when projects received funding, it was seed money; the funding bodies expected the projects to eventually become self-sufficient. This rarely happened, adding new financial burdens to the Center's load. (Along the same lines, as media relations improved—and as the Center became adept at creating media events—attracting coverage was seen as a criterion for holding an event, which contributed to goal displacement.)

Before giving money, funding bodies often wanted proof of the Center's ability to realize a project. For example, one group refused to subsidize a service directory, citing doubts as to the Center's ability to produce it. When the excellent first edition of the guide was used to justify asking for money for a second, it was seen as evidence that volunteer labor was sufficient.

This process pushed the Center toward professionalism and respectability. But appearing respectable and legitimate, both to funding sources and to clientele, often went against the need and desire to remain on the cutting edge of feminism. It was through raising new and controversial issues and anticipating demands that enthusiasm and creative energy were maintained.

By the time the Center opened, two poles, based on both personal and political allegiance, had emerged in DWL. With most of socialist feminists involved in the Center, most of the old guard staying away, and large numbers of new women pouring in, the Center and DWL had distinct identities from the start. The chasm widened during 1974 and culminated in intense conflict and separation between the two entities.[48] "The Center began to be separate from DWL, with new women in the collective. There were attempts to bridge the gaps, but twelve months later the two groups said good-bye to each other," Mary Morgan recalled.

By the end of 1973, the Women's Center project was plainly the most vital part of the Dayton movement. The participation of a group of socialist feminists in the project was partially coincidental, due to their entry into the movement at this time and their attraction to its most dynamic component.[49] It was also partially due to strategizing within the socialist feminist group. In the Center, the women found a place to test their developing theories, including those being produced nationally.

These developments coincided with the move in DWL toward autonomy of task forces and collectives, a move that accelerated, but that was not created by the Center collective. The renewed self-examination entailed posing pertinent questions—such as, "Will DWL become an umbrella organization . . . with many autonomous Collectives who handle and control their own resources?"[50]—but yielded few concrete results. Although the question was posed of how the organization's structure needed to be revamped in this new era, no real provisions were made for integrating the new Women's Center.

Of common accord, the Center became the office of the movement. The seemingly natural act of installing the DWL telephone line and printing equipment there meant that the Center acted as the clearinghouse for DWL, with some resulting confusion. It often was unclear as to which requests for speakers were intended for the Center and which were for DWL. The staff's job descriptions included "develop[ing] educational programs for the larger community," and in the first three months alone, fifty-nine staff-hours were devoted to community speaking engagements.[51] This popularity sparked debate in DWL, which wanted publicity for the Center and had granted collectives increased autonomy, such as the right to give interviews. But all general requests were supposed to be channeled through DWL's speakers collective and filled by members of a designated CR group. Also, DWL had assumed its long-standing principles, such as not giving solo interviews, would continue to reign. But none of these points were understood by the new collective members or by the Center staff.[52]

As headquarters of the movement, the Center became the point of entry for new women. Many thus considered themselves Center members and knew little of the relationship to DWL. For example, one woman who joined a CR group following a DWL new people's meeting held at the Center apparently was unaware that her group had been started by, and was considered to be part of, DWL.[53] Even when these women knew of the DWL-Center connection, it remained hypothetical. Members of WAR, officially a DWL task force, had no allegiance to its mother organization.

As tensions mounted, new women were less interested in connecting with DWL. The Women's Center collective sent representatives to coordinating meetings, and as Suits recalled, "[W]henever it was anybody new, they would be totally floored by the fighting and screaming and crying." These women, attracted to a pragmatic and concrete Center, were coming in with the ideas and energy of new recruits, and they wanted action and not political debate or conflict. But the oft lamented reinventing of the wheel was not always a bad thing: in some cases it insulated newcomers from debilitating conflict and ensured continued dynamism.[54]

While new women energized the Center, for DWL they had become a burn-out factor. Starting new CR groups became a drain: veteran facilitators who remained involved in new groups spread themselves too thin. If they stayed only for one or two meetings, they had no opportunities to make new discoveries for themselves. The new women, in turn, felt they were on their own and predictably were less effectively integrated into the larger organization. While CR groups had always been considered to be fluid and changing, a fair number now were disbanding.

DWL's core group also was weakening. Many members' lives were in transition as they entered the work force, changed jobs, or began careers. Some were recently divorced, and others were leaving Dayton. Preparatory work for the Center had been exhausting, and several key participants had done the least gratifying work of dealing with bureaucracy but had left before they could be reenergized by the Center's success. For

DWL, maintaining involvement in the overall organization had always required considerable effort, and with the Center cutting off the flow of new blood into DWL, more burden was placed on the core members.

The sides crystallized with the articulation of the socialist feminist critique of DWL. The DWL core had feared a loss of political consciousness and utopian vision with the arrival of new women; here they were faced with a group of politicized new women, but with a different vision. To add insult to injury, the socialist feminist group was intent on politicizing DWL, according to Suits.

While DWL's commitment to self-examination left the group open to attack, the openness had been tempered by a feminist double standard. Criticism was accepted far more easily from a new member who was a political beginner or unaligned than from a person with clear opinions and/or an affiliation to a group. There was far more willingness to calmly discuss the conservative ideas of a novice than the radical, but differing, ideas of a socialist feminist. This cannot be reduced to a question of independence versus affiliation. Indeed, the socialist feminists showed the same tendency toward a double standard, being far more severe in their criticisms of DWL women than they were of new women. It was linked to an implicit theory of outreach and expansion that was based on an unlimited pool of potential, unformed feminists. These women would see the light, becoming feminists or realizing that they had already been so without knowing it. With the passage of time and the diffusion of feminist ideas, more and more women coming in were self-aware feminists and had some set opinions. Whether or not these women who had been involved in the movement previously were "already feminists," the Center and other initiatives merely represented one project of a larger women's movement rather than the movement itself, as had been the case with DWL. Joining an organization differed significantly from entering a movement. The shrinking of virgin territory led to increased sectarianism.

The first serious clashes came in late 1973, particularly with the hiring of the Center's staff. After that, socialist feminists called for a series of meetings to clarify stances and define the relationship between the Center and DWL.[55] Using the Chicago Women's Liberation Union text and "The Tyranny of Structurelessness," they again pushed for the transformation of the coordinating meeting into an elected steering committee: "A representative steering committee, democratically elected, responsible to the CR groups who elect them, would prevent excessive power by any one CR group."[56] They opposed the primacy of consensus. "It was so obvious that you couldn't have consensus when people didn't agree with each other on anything!" Suits said. "But they thought it was one sign of how we were male dominated."

The core members saw these critiques as abandoning women's attempts at self-determination and viewed "political clarity" as the imposition of a correct line. To further exacerbate the antagonisms, a number of male NAM members were heard speaking of the Women's Center as a NAM project. This infuriated the DWL core, some of whom suspected socialist feminists of having promoted the idea. In fact, it angered those socialist feminists who also were DWL veterans; however, some of the newcomers, with little knowledge of Center history, did believe that credit was due if not to NAM, then at least to NAM women. Sherry Novick, for example, commented years later, "From the beginning, the most intense effort came from NAM women."

By mid-1974, the well-oiled system of DWL was grinding to a stop. Rotation of tasks by CR groups was discontinued, several coordinating meetings were cancelled, and an issue of the newsletter was skipped. The Fireside Chats were held only sporadically. New people's meetings continued at the Center and some CR groups apparently were started there, but no new CR groups were listed in the DWL newsletter between January and November. In July, at a meeting on "apathy in DWL," one "neutral" CR group announced its disaffiliation from DWL. The four Fireside Chats held in 1974 addressed the relationship between DWL and the Center. Their titles tell all. The first, in January, was, "What shall we do with the Women's Center?" The "we" is self-evident, referring to DWL, an organization in full control. By September, the Center had assumed the position of strength, and the Chat was ominously entitled, "The future of DWL." The issue was controlling the political direction of the women's liberation movement in Dayton.[57]

On the evening of September 18, 1974, approximately sixty women met at the Women's Center to discuss DWL's future. It was there that "the battle lines were drawn," said Kleine, who remembered it as "that hideous night" when she started smoking again. Many people were shaken up, some cried, as accusations flew. That evening, a personal and political war was fought. Four position papers had been drafted for the meeting, but the lines formed between two camps, the socialist feminists and the old core group, represented by the education task force. All others were forced to choose.

Both sides recognized that problems existed. They agreed, for instance, that DWL had failed to build a mass movement. The old core readily acknowledged that they had not sufficiently involved new women in the overall organization, and that some CR groups had stagnated to the point that they were dealing solely with individual problems. The conflict centered around the causes and cures of these problems: issues of structural reform and of so-called elitism.

"We would like to propose that Dayton Women's Liberation . . . adopt a new structure and statement of purpose and goals."[58] Taken in isolation, the five-page socialist feminist proposal appeared to be a compromise text. Read in context, however, its style departed brutally from the previous sisterly tone of writings. It emphasized areas of disagreement, with confrontation seen as leading to necessary clarification and then unity. Lack of confrontation and of clear political goals supposedly rendered DWL incapable of confronting sexism.

The description in the proposal of DWL's history originated as much in "The Tyranny of Structurelessness" as it did in direct observation—not surprising, since few of its endorsers had much firsthand experience in the group. The text argued that the CR structure may have been appropriate in early stages of the movement when everyone knew each other, but that it had been outgrown. CR groups inevitably broke up, and so new organizational mechanisms were required to build the movement.

Guidelines for the future included defining goals and, as described in the Chicago Women's Liberation Union text, working toward "winning successes," or pieces of the long-term goals in the short run, thus overcoming women's sense of powerlessness. The proposal favored creating an elected steering committee, spelling out responsibilities of CR groups and collectives, and making members sign a statement of purpose and commit to pay dues and attend semiannual organizationwide meetings.[59] The text constituted an attack on the DWL core group; by proposing a more traditional structure and challenging the primacy of the CR group, it questioned the two most important achievements of the organization.

The education task force's proposal defended the status quo, arguing that critics misunderstood the core group's positions. It emphasized the importance of process: "The *process* by which something is done is as important [as] or, sometimes, more important than whether it gets done." This structure was important, it argued, because "oppression is based on hierarchical arrangements." One concession was made: voting by secret ballot was acceptable when consensus could not be reached. But the reactive text pushed the core group further than ever in promoting a politics of experience, contrasting with the group's previous positions against a correct line for personal life or seeing lifestyle changes as sufficient. "We are each a product of our experience and therefore our experience, whatever it may be, is of equal value with another's experience. . . . [A]ny activity pursued in one's personal life either upholds the status quo or is contrary to it."[60]

Two other groups wrote position papers aligned with the socialist feminists. One made a plea in favor of women who were not full-time activists and/or not in CR groups, either because of time constraints (work or children) or involvement elsewhere. This group's concern led it to an extreme position in the elitism debate, a subject that the socialist feminists had originally skirted: "We define the elite as those in DWL for 3 or more years; those serving on one or more collectives for a year or more; those having substantial assertive skills (can you express yourself at a coordinating meeting . . . , do you readily 'chair' meetings?)."[61] All articulate, assertive, and committed women were thus suspect, and egalitarianism could only mean restraining individuals' participation. Accusation of elitism clearly targeted the old core group.

The core's position fluctuated from denying the existence of an elite to recognizing it but considering it justified by the time these women had invested in DWL. The education task force's position paper contended that "influential" members were not elitist because they did not "conspire to prevent other women from functioning in leadership capacities." The problem, the group said, was not one of a faulty structure but of a breakdown in communication. Kleine believed that the very structure that DWL had instituted was intended to overcome elitism by helping women gain assurance. She felt betrayed: "We were being attacked because we were strong females."

With tensions mounting, the debate crystallized over structural reform: signed commitments, dues, and most important, whether an elected steering committee was a liberating prospect, as socialist feminists claimed (speaking for one's group and not oneself), or one that would increase women's passivity ("women should not be 'steering' other women"[62]). The September meeting ended in deadlock.

On October 13, DWL held an all-day meeting in a last-ditch effort to work out a compromise. Griesinger, gifted at mediating, was inducted to chair, and elaborate formal negotiating methods were spelled out. The official decisions represented a compromise between the groups: a modified form of designated representation was adopted; the coordinating meeting became the coordinating committee and not a steering committee; consensus as a mode of decision-making was maintained, but backed up by votes when necessary. The next meeting scheduled was to discuss "ways to evaluate our elitism and process."[63]

But it was far too late for compromise. The DWL core was already weakened, and the conflict over the Center had devastated the mother organization. Many women from the core group had given up, leaving the remainder even more isolated. Looking back, Kleine recalled: "My feeling to this day is that I fought that battle by myself, and when I couldn't fight it any longer, I gave in. . . . I just felt like a voice in the wilderness, and I just said, 'Fuck it! Have it your own way, socialist feminists. Have a steering committee and hierarchy and the whole works.'"

The new structure supposedly went into effect immediately. A new coordinating committee meeting was attended by only a handful of women who continued to discuss problems between DWL and the Center. To aggravate matters, in November the Center was broken into and fifteen hundred dollars' worth of materials stolen. Negotiations over dividing the insurance money between the Center and DWL, whose materials had been transferred there from the start, was the final straw. At the January 1975 coordinating committee meeting, representatives from the socialist feminist group, Women Against Rape, and the Dayton Women's Center formally announced their withdrawal from Dayton Women's Liberation.

Many Dayton feminists did not take part in the conflict or join a camp. Some DWL women, off in their CR groups, knew only vaguely of the problems. As the conflict escalated, they retreated further into isolation, weakening DWL even more. For the Center, however, the repercussions were different. With the fight taking place within DWL, the fact that many Center activists followed only from afar actually preserved the Center. At the same time, however, most allied with the women they knew, that is, the socialist feminists.

Most lesbians in DWL, even the most active participants, were barely affected by the conflict. "The split didn't touch me," Sheila Drennen commented. "I was not friends with any straight women—there were so many lesbians to get to know." Jeri Simmons of Sappho's Army couldn't even recall the issues. Only the hiring process for the Center had attracted attention, because one staff member was suspected of homophobia. For the most part, the lesbian feminists' personal and political allegiance remained with DWL. Paradoxically, however, their activism was physically located at the Center. Throughout its history, virtually all of Dayton's lesbian feminist meetings took place at the Center, and participants consistently supported the project with time and money.

If lesbians were untouched by the conflict, it also was because their movement was ascending. Lesbians had at first been grateful for being accepted in DWL, but by the end of 1974 they had become more self-assured and confrontative. At the November 1974 coordinating committee meeting, only weeks after the fatal October meeting, members of Sappho's Army criticized DWL for its lack of support and interest in issues of lesbianism. They offered to send representatives to each CR group and collective to begin dialogues. Several weeks later, the group produced a special issue of the DWL newsletter on lesbianism with an editorial criticizing DWL members for not responding to Sappho's Army's invitations to coffeehouses and dances. "Are feminists afraid of us or ignoring us or both?" it asked.[64]

The tragically poor timing of this sisterly confrontation, coming at the height of the conflict, meant that DWL proved incapable of responding. While this probably had little effect on the split, the pressure from lesbian women may well have further destabilized the organization. Heterosexual women in DWL, already under pressure due to national developments, particularly the increasingly common position that lesbianism was the vanguard of feminism, were feeling defensive. Accustomed to a position on the cutting edge, they were ill at ease with this idea. And as lesbian women became more assertive in their own backyard, it seemed to add to their feeling of isolation.

The conflict between the Center and DWL can be summed up as a power struggle that nobody won. According to Suits, the socialist feminists wanted to apply their strategy at the Women's Center and maintain involvement in DWL to have a power base in the movement. They were interested in DWL as a central political organization, a complement to the Center, and a means to organize new women. But their victory was only partial: they won the battle, but the war ravaged the territory. With the tensions high and stakes no longer worth fighting for, they withdrew.

It is doubtful whether the socialist feminists' proposed structure would have been more efficient or democratic. It is clear, however, that the group had perceived the dawning of a new era for the women's movement. DWL, in a period of self-examination, had been too introspective to grasp the changes occurring around it. The socialist feminists demonstrated their understanding by raising new and important themes (such as rape and work-related issues). More important, they saw that the movement simultaneously faced diversification and complex co-optative pressures. In a revised proposal published in the October issue of the DWL newsletter, the socialist feminist group wrote: "The idea of women's liberation has come a long way over the past 5 years or so. DWL as an organization has grown with the spreading of these ideas in a society that seeks to co-opt, subvert, exploit and defuse the revolutionary essence of feminism. The growth and development of our movement means a broadening constituency, diversified needs and ever changing forms of organization to unite women in their collective struggle."[65]

The movement's expansion meant that DWL had been reduced to a single organization, rather than the movement itself. The socialist feminists themselves joined in this spirit, and they knew that many other women were also choosing one of several outlets for their preexistent feminism. These women's level of commitment was lower than that of women who had experienced the consciousness-raising process through DWL. As the audience grew more sophisticated, sympathizers situated themselves more in relationship to specific projects and ideas rather than to an amorphous yet united movement.

In February 1975, fourteen DWL women—more than half of whom had been members since the first year—decided that "reactivating the movement, even in a small way was worth a try."[66] They put out a call in the newsletter for a general meeting and to revive the organization, reverting to old DWL structure and practices. For six months, the organization continued in a much reduced form. Only the education task force remained in full swing; indeed, it was active into the 1980s. An alumnae CR group was started and several others continued, most often in the form of irregular reunions. New collectives included the Religious Coalition on Abortion Rights, founded by Griesinger; formalized study groups; and direct political action collectives, with suggested subjects combining the themes of rape and job discrimination with ones aimed at recapturing old-style DWL militantism, such as opposing grand jury abuse.[67] DWL members participated in protests and held several all-women's events. In fact, for the first time, they paid attention to "women's culture," particularly feminist music. The newsletter appeared five more times, with debates on topics including mental health, the roots of feminism, and proposed rape legislation. The organization continued to monitor health-care services and push for full abortion rights. It communicated with the national movement, publishing, for example, accusations from the feminist group Redstockings that Gloria Steinem had CIA connections, along with Steinem's response.[68]

But these projects merely slowed the demise of Dayton Women's Liberation. In the fall of 1975, after a two-month gap, the newsletter appeared with an editorial acknowledging that the organization was in trouble. This was DWL's last newsletter, and without it, the final element of cohesion disappeared and Dayton Women's Liberation as an organization ceased to exist.

It is difficult to evaluate DWL's accomplishments. With sights set so high, it obviously failed in many respects. It did not revolutionize all of American society, nor did it cross racial lines or sufficiently cross class lines to create a broad mass movement. It fell short of its goal of raising consciousness on racism and imperialism. It was unable to create the durable support mechanisms to sustain women through life changes.

But the list of the organization's achievements is impressive. DWL lasted for six years and unified Dayton's women's liberation movement for five. From existing reports, this apparently constituted exceptional continuity and unity for a so-called structureless organization. It served as an informal but effective link between the national and the local movements. The newsletter was produced monthly for five years and consistently provided an open forum for the exchange of information and ideas. The organization was the first to offer feminist classes and services. It was responsible for constant feminist and political agitation. It created more than forty consciousness-raising groups, some of which continued to meet after its demise, and numerous other projects and groups. With some six hundred members (that is, names on the mailing list) at the end, DWL directly touched the lives of thousands of women.

Few DWL activists became prominent in subsequent feminist groups in Dayton, but that did not signify a rejection of feminism. The names of those who remained in the city cropped up on petitions and on lists of donors to women's organizations, and many of them were responsible for antisexist projects in their workplaces. Many, probably a majority, moved from Dayton[69] and became active in other cities. Joan Ediss, who changed her name to Joan Ruth Rose, was active first in California and later at a battered women's shelter in Springfield, Ohio. Griesinger, now campus minister at Ohio University in Athens, continued working in feminist and gay church groups at a national level, and she and Mary Morgan moved to a farm that they later opened to other women. Another woman helped found a group in San Diego that offered support services to victims of sexual assault.

For participants, the most important legacy of DWL, and the most commonly heard evaluation, was "It changed my life." Ediss said: "I went to school in Dayton Women's Liberation. And I learned how to be a feminist and what being a feminist meant. . . . I learned how to do a lot of things. I personally learned how to put together a newsletter, how to do public speaking, I learned how to do some multi-media stuff.

I learned how to be powerful and to be strong. I learned and learned and learned. . . . It was the beginning of really, really strong relationships with women." Griesinger said, "It is a constant thing . . . in my life," one that has given her perspectives that are "real basic to how I see the world, a feminist analysis of reality."[70] For Kleine, "It gave me a sense of purpose I will carry till the end of my days. . . . Whatever I do has something to do with that period, whether I'm acting alone or with other women."

While several outsiders said that former DWL members regretted the changes in their lives, no such reports were confirmed.[71] Some DWL women admitted to reminiscing in moments of weakness about their previous state of blissful ignorance, but none rejected their feminism or the life changes they made as a result.[72] For example, one outside critic, a friend of DWL activist Diane Graham, claimed that a major result of consciousness-raising was divorce, and that "many of them, including Diane, ultimately regretted it."[73] While Graham admitted that perhaps DWL "gave me too much of a pat on the back," she denied having seriously regretted her decision. "Women's liberation gave me the confidence to stand on my own," she said. Suits, who left in open, painful conflict with many of her former sisters, still felt: "I have never experienced anything like the beginning of [Dayton] Women's Liberation." She added, "I was always trying to re-find that feeling."

Many echoed this melancholic desire to recapture the spirit of the early movement. One woman, who had divorced and left custody of her child to her husband, asked, "What have we set ourselves up for?" She lamented, "I don't think I want to live [alone] in an apartment in New York City until I die."[74] This bittersweet feeling was due to the lack of adequate support for the changes they made. It was also because for these women, nothing replaced or renewed the magic of DWL and the intensity of the early years. They knew they were contributing to earth-shaking changes—they were making history, and the relationships they established at that time were among the strongest many were ever to experience. Regrets stemmed, not from their experience in DWL, but rather from what followed.

4

Expansion, Diversification, and Co-optation

BY 1974, the feminist movement in Dayton had entered a new era, not only because of the shift of its locus to the Women's Center, but also because of transformations outside the movement proper. The scope of feminism was widening steadily, the movement's projects were diversifying, and its ideas were penetrating in varying strengths and forms in diverse spheres. The boundaries of the movement began blurring and the fringes started spilling over into the mainstream. The distinctive ability of the American system to incorporate watered-down versions of social movement demands raised questions about the movement's relationship to institutions—or about the tension between, as it was put at the time, victory and co-optation. Moreover, certain projects became potentially profitable. With financial and career incentives in the air, nonfeminists entered the struggle for control. This chapter examines three projects that were offshoots of the movement, but that strictly speaking were neither feminist nor a part of the women's movement: an abortion consultation service, the abortion clinic, and a rape crisis center. Their stories show different ways in which feminists created institutions and affected existing ones and how, in turn, women's lives in Dayton were affected. They also show how the historical context for the women's movement was changing, setting the scene for the second half of the decade.

In mid-1973, as the Women's Center collective was jousting with city bureaucrats, an overlapping group of women was facing similar opposition from Dayton's medical establishment. The January 1973 Supreme Court decision to legalize abortion, they had realized, would not automatically make abortion accessible. Matters had to be taken in hand by the women's liberation movement.

From the start, Dayton's abortion rights movement had two distinct components. One, for political action, was linked to Dayton Women's Liberation. The other, although started by DWL members, was a separate entity for providing services. This division greatly influenced the development of abortion rights organizing in Dayton for years.

As women seeking abortions started to contact DWL, Chewerl Radican and others learned to do referrals. But it was DWL member Jan Griesinger, a seminary student at the time, who was to become the most important abortion rights agitator in the first years of the movement. At a January 1970 church meeting in Milwaukee, Griesinger had heard a woman speaking about the Clergy Consultation Service on Abortion, a nonprofit, national counseling service founded by members of the clergy three years earlier. This and similar groups compiled lists of abortionists who were competent and humane and who charged reasonable fees. The groups' collective action offered some bargaining power and control over the quality of the services. By operating aboveground, they not only provided services but also challenged the laws. When Griesinger learned about Clergy Consultation, she experienced a "real strong 'click'": "Here was something I could do that related to feminism and also [my] seminary background." Back in Dayton, she started working behind the scenes to organize a consultation service. Women from the recently created abortion rights group pitched in to contact local clergy. Response was excellent, and the Dayton Clergy Consultation Service on Abortion went into operation in June 1970.

Nationally, Clergy Consultation was not the only referral service. Unknown to most Daytonians, an informal feminist network also existed. However, Griesinger had many reasons to connect to Clergy Consultation. It made sense for her personally because of her religious connections, and DWL was accustomed to using church resources. Moreover, Clergy Consultation, with groups operating openly in cities in some eighteen states,[1] had more resources than did the feminist network.

Another consideration influenced the decision: it was unclear at the time whether the activity was legal. Counselors had been arrested in some cities—some willingly, in order to provoke test cases in the courts.[2] Dayton activists had no desire to be arrested, perhaps in part because they made up the service branch of a movement that had an action-oriented component. They wanted to work effectively, unhampered by legal problems. They believed that the respectable image of the clergy and the privacy of the confessional would protect both counselors and clients.

For the sake of safety, Griesinger, not yet ordained, downplayed her role. She had done most of the organizational groundwork, but John Gould was chosen as chairperson. A Lutheran pastor from a church in a nearby rural county, Gould was "a very established-looking minister with gray hair," Griesinger described. "He was the press person, and would wear his clerical collar. . . . If we had done it just through a women's liberation group, there would have been a lot more nervousness about repression."

That fear turned out to be unfounded. When purged of its feminist content, the idea of abortion did not overly shock Dayton's citizens. Rarely, if ever, did people express moral opposition. Even advising women how to flout the law to obtain illegal abortions did not seem problematic. When news of Clergy Consultation hit the Dayton press, it was as a legitimate item—contrary to coverage of other social movements of the time. Similarly, participating clergy reported no repercussions in their congregations. As the DWL abortion rights demonstration in Columbus in 1970 had shown, opponents aimed their hostility not at the issue of abortion, but at feminism. The media respectfully reported the views of abortion rights activists, but only after airing their criticisms of the women's movement.

Clergy Consultation Service involved some twenty clergy, including Protestant ministers from various denominations and Reform rabbis. In July 1970, upon ordination from the United Church of Christ, Griesinger became its first woman counselor. Shortly thereafter, she found a job with Dayton Area Campus Ministry that paid her to continue her work at Clergy Consultation.

The service worked to "provide resources to women to enable them to make real whatever their choice might be for dealing with a problem pregnancy in a medically safe, legal, and dignifying way."[3] It had a decentralized structure with four people on call at a time. Women calling the widely publicized number heard a recorded announcement directing them to the counselors. Counselors offered advice not only on abortionists and their fees, but also on logistics—directions from the airport, risk of being cheated by cab drivers, and so on.

Griesinger collected information and dispatched it to the counselors. Among her preoccupations was finding the least expensive solutions. Although the service was free, abortions were expensive, ranging from six hundred to eight hundred dollars for medical and travel expenses. (Although not publicized, the service made some loans.) At first, women traveled to such far-off destinations as Mexico City and Rapid City, South Dakota. Abortion was still illegal in some of these destinations, but having the referral service, the doctor, and the client from different states made prosecution difficult. When in 1970 a "near repeal" bill was passed in New York, travel expenses decreased. One New York clinic was created in connection with Clergy Consultation, and the assured volume of business allowed it to maintain a sliding scale, with $125 as the official price. Local clergy were responsible for determining a woman's ability to pay.

From 1970 to 1973, around twenty-five women, mostly young and unmarried, obtained abortions through the service every week. (Approximately 60 percent of them were single, 20 percent married, and the remainder divorced, separated, widowed, or unknown; the majority were eighteen to twenty-five years old.) Counselors reported varied motivations, with no single pattern emerging; however, many commented on the severe social pressure felt particularly by young single women, as well as the numerous individual "tragic situations."[4]

By 1971, under the influence of the women's movement, Clergy Consultation Service followed the example of other services around the country and opened itself to lay counselors—here "lay" meaning women.[5] The new counselors included feminists, abortion rights activists, social workers, and therapists. Thereafter, women could choose between the two. According to one report, women counselors were contacted most frequently.[6]

Clergy and Lay differed in several ways from its feminist counterparts. More important than the sex of the personnel (most feminist groups were staffed only by women) was the ambiguous role of counseling. For the Dayton group, counseling was a required part of the process. As counselor Anita Wilson put it, "At the time we thought that all abortions were really a very emotional experience, and that the woman needed all this [tender loving care] and that we needed to talk to her about her feelings." Commenting years later, she saw this as a mild form of harassment.[7]

Some feminists supported the idea of counseling. The authors of *Our Bodies, Ourselves* believed that "it is both possible and important to find someone to talk to" about the possibility of aborting and recommended Clergy Consultation as a good resource. Many feminists, however, had criticized Clergy Consultation for its "Lord Bountiful" attitude. During the debates over including lay counselors, one DWL author criticized the "men of the cloth" for being "afraid that women [counselors] would interfere with their special role as representatives of God."[8] For most feminist counselors in Dayton, their job was to dispense information, but they were happy to counsel—or rather, discuss things with women who so desired.

According to Griesinger, the clergy's desire to counsel was one of its main motivations. "The clergymen were just thrilled with the idea. They thought that it was wonderful, that—since people didn't come to them for *anything*—suddenly they were getting calls from women wanting to make an appointment with them right away! . . . They were needed." However, Griesinger believed, "By and large the women needed the information about where to go to get an abortion. They only needed counseling about 20 percent of the time."

If for feminists the service was a step toward reproductive freedom, few clergymen saw abortion as a feminist issue. Many believed that they were dealing with purely personal problems and as such, that counseling was essential. Their role was that of spiritual adviser, not political activist. The Reverend Joe Betch said, "It's not really a decision-making situation, but more like a pastor-to-parishioner relationship." Reverend George Hupp, no doubt an exception, actually refused information to a few women. "I'm not in this to handle abortions," he told reporters, "but to counsel people who are in real deep trouble."[9] The service thus offered women various alternatives, including adoption. But unlike antifeminist referral groups such as the Right to Life Birthright/Woman-line, which discouraged women from getting abortions under the guise of counseling, Clergy Consultation repeatedly made it clear in public statements that helping women find qualified abortionists was its main purpose. Some clergymen began to see abortion as a civil right. Reverend Lawrence Ford summed up what became the group's official stance: "I'm becoming convinced the matter should be between only the woman and her physician." Abortions, the group proclaimed, should be "governed only by the general laws regulating medical practice." It was this line of reasoning that led the Reverend Lawrence Stumme to state that when abortions were made easily accessible, "we would be more than happy to go out of business."[10]

Clergy and Lay—as the service was called after women counselors were added—was one of the Dayton movement's first nonfeminist off-shoots. Practical concerns motivated the decision to relate to the clergy network, and this may have been why the organization got so much press coverage and successfully reached such a broad spectrum of women.[11] However, certain side effects of the decision may have deprived feminists of using the powerful issue of abortion rights to build the movement. First, although women beyond feminist circles became active in Clergy and Lay, it is not clear whether this was due to the group's nonfeminist, respectable image or to the appeal of the issue itself; other, more feminist abortion rights groups also attracted new women. Clergy and Lay did not seem to have provided these women with a feminist consciousness-raising experience, and very few were subsequently drawn into the women's movement. Second, while the group's excellent public relations resulted in considerable press coverage, these articles did not connect abortion to feminism; instead, they made abortion a single issue, a lacunae in social or health services, separate from questions of women's liberation. Despite the considerable feminist political activism on abortion going on simultaneously, little was brought to light in the media. The public also remained unaware of the service's feminist origins or that DWL had done similar work previously. The service came to be regarded as a de facto authority. With the 1973 legalization of abortion, Clergy and Lay counselors (along with doctors and other ministers) were quoted constantly. Feminists, despite their long-term activism, found themselves partially dispossessed of the issue precisely as it was being legitimated.

On January 22, 1973, the *Roe v. Wade* decision seemed to render abortion rights work redundant. However, as an informal Clergy and Lay poll found shortly thereafter, all Dayton-area obstetricians continued applying the old statutes.[12] Several local hospitals were Catholic and had directives from the U.S. Catholic Congress prohibiting intentional termination of pregnancy. Others were extremely cautious at best, invoking difficulty in changing hospital rules.[13] One hospital in a nearby town claimed that there was no demand for abortion because its clientele preferred traveling to another city rather than risk scandal. In a similar vein, Dayton's private Miami Valley Hospital suddenly grew concerned with the opinions of its janitorial staff, attributing its lack of services to moral opposition not only from doctors but also from "the house cleaning lady."[14] It was to be nearly a year before area hospitals offered their first elective abortions, and even then, numbers fell far short of demand. The local Planned Parenthood affiliate made no move to fill the void.[15] Clergy and Lay thus found itself obligated to continue sending women to other cities.

Clergy and Lay, several abortion rights activists, and DWL members began investigating ways of providing abortions locally. Some thought was given to initiating a class action suit, particularly for late abortions that required hospitalization. But because the group hoped to avoid the expense of hospital stays for early abortions, it favored the option of an outpatient clinic. Planning began within weeks of the Supreme Court decision. Griesinger, writing about the future clinic, proclaimed that it would be independent, nonprofit, and woman controlled. In June 1973, incorporation papers were filed for a nonprofit clinic "[t]o establish and operate a medical facility to accommodate women with problem or unwanted pregnancies; to offer high quality, low cost medical treatment, counseling, birth control and family planning information; to provide such facilities and services to women regardless of ability to pay."[16]

The central figures in organizing the clinic were Griesinger and Clergy and Lay counselors Laurie Heindal and Anita Wilson. Neither Wilson nor her close friend Heindal had been involved in the women's movement. Wilson felt hostile toward DWL because she claimed it was judgmental of her staying at home to raise her children. She had come to her commitment to abortion rights from a social service background. More conservative than her left-wing parents, she had nevertheless attended cooperative children's camps and ban-the-bomb marches in her youth. She became involved in the civil rights movement in the midsixties, while in high school and college, and became president of the Student Nonviolent Coordinating Committee chapter at Temple University. After earning a degree in social work, she got married. During the following years she worked in various cities for a welfare department, with women prisoners, and with pregnant teens. In 1969, she followed her husband to Dayton for his job. He later cofounded the Dayton Free Clinic, where she also volunteered.

In 1971, Wilson joined Clergy and Lay. "I had just had a third baby. . . . But I wanted to keep up on my skills in counseling. . . . I decided that counseling women, sending them to New York for abortions, and exercising that freedom of choice was important, and that it fit my needs." While Wilson had originally sought volunteer work that allowed her to stay at home, by 1973 divorce drastically changed her outlook on life. Thus, as she was working to create the clinic, she knew she needed a paid job to support herself and her children.

Griesinger found a female obstetrician-gynecologist who agreed to perform abortions. Wilson and Heindal visited pharmaceutical companies, drew up budgets, and traveled to New York for a workshop on how to start a clinic. Back home, they discovered that opposition to a freestanding clinic was fierce. First, their physician backed out. Second, they discovered that landlords didn't want to rent to what they termed "an abortion mill." Finally, it became clear that the capital would have to be raised through personal loans. It was largely Griesinger, thanks to the respect she commanded, who raised some fifteen thousand dollars in personal loans from feminist and progressive acquaintances.[17] Griesinger also worked on drawing up incorporation papers, applying for tax-exempt status, and setting up a community board for policy decisions. Other feminists helped open the bank account and investigate insurance policies.

Space was finally found from a sympathetic landlord. The major drawback was its location in an all-white, affluent southern suburb not serviced by public transportation. For Wilson, these were minor inconveniences. Indeed, the added expense of taxi fares for the two required appointments paled in comparison to other expenses. Had the clinic expanded as intended to offer general women's health services, however, lack of public transportation would have been a problem. Even more, the choice of a neighborhood inhospitable to women of color did little to relieve those women's ambivalence toward birth control and the abortion movement.[18]

To find physicians, the three women called virtually every obstetrician-gynecologist in the phone book, but even those who were sympathetic to the cause claimed it was unsafe to work outside a hospital. Four finally agreed, but then suddenly pulled out. Dayton's medical community was conservative, and according to Wilson, doctors "were really afraid of what the community [and] what the other physicians in town were going to say." Tired and broke, Wilson and Heindal were close to giving up when, within hours of the final deadline for signing the lease, one doctor gave in. The next day four others joined her.[19]

Doctors were originally offered $50 per abortion performed, more than the fees paid in many clinics. This would have allowed the clinic to charge the same $150 fee as the New York clinics. At the last minute, the doctors demanded $100 per abortion. A compromise solution was reached: abortions would cost $175; physicians would receive $75 and perform 15 percent free.[20] The desire to perform abortions through the sixteenth week, was thwarted by doctors' refusal and the plan to expand services was blocked by the prohibitively high fees the doctors demanded.

Despite the "greed of local physicians," as Griesinger put it, who were "making money off our unwanted pregnancies," the opening of the Dayton Women's Health Center on September 7, 1973, was heralded as a victory for Dayton's women's movement. Griesinger's report to DWL lauded it for providing a "non-profit, women-controlled abortion," and stated, "[T]here is some consolation that the clinic is in our hands—in Columbus, Cincinnati, and Cleveland, the clinics are owned by physicians and businessmen." Once loans were repaid, she said, the price of services would drop.[21]

Located in a sparkling, modern building, the clinic was decorated with plants, paintings, and modern furniture. The staff consisted of Wilson and Heindal as codirectors, two nurses, a lab technician, and a secretary. Among those hired were socialist feminist Sherrie Holmes and DWL activist Barbara Gregg, who had counseled for Clergy and Lay.

A different physician came in every afternoon. His or her sole function was to perform the abortion. First-trimester abortions were performed using the suction method. Patients arrived in the morning with results of their pregnancy tests, filled out forms, and had laboratory tests. The abortion process was explained to the patients in a group; the women also were counseled and, on request, given contraceptives.[22]

In the first few days an abortion took an hour, but it was rapidly reduced to a ten-minute procedure. The caseload rose from eight to ten patients per day to eighteen per day by 1981. Thus, even at the beginning, physicians were earning more than five hundred dollars in an afternoon and about twice that after several years. After deducting doctors' fees, salaries, operating expenses, and depreciation of furniture, the clinic made between five and six thousand dollars in profit in the first two months alone.[23] Contrary to expectations, the personal loans were paid back, with interest, in six months.

For Griesinger and other feminists, the clinic could be seen only in the context of the long struggle for abortion rights. As a product of the women's movement in general, and Clergy and Lay in particular, it was to be nonprofit and community controlled. Clinic directors Wilson and Heindal were seen as sisters who had contributed to the process. Feminists thought the community board, with Griesinger and DWL activist Robin Suits and several others, would be the decision-making body. Indeed, the code of regulations stated: "The Board of Directors shall set policy for the Dayton Women's Health Center, Inc. and shall hire an administrator(s) to implement such policy. The Board shall act in an advocacy role for recipients of the DWHC's services and shall hear any grievances brought to it by its recipients."[24] But when Griesinger proclaimed that the clinic was women controlled, she was right. It was controlled by two women: Wilson and Heindal. As a legal entity, the clinic had incorporated, supposedly a formality, with Wilson, Heindal, and another Clergy and Lay counselor as its trustees. Griesinger, because of her work with the World Student Christian Federation, believed it best she not appear as a trustee.

To Wilson, she and Heindal were the founders of the clinic, had "done all the work and taken all the risks." She agreed that the trustees had been named only to satisfy a legal requirement. But to her, this meant that power was to remain solely with the directors. The board was to provide advice and input, not make decisions. The nonprofit status, Wilson contended, was motivated by her upbringing.

Tensions surfaced rapidly around a number of issues: the role of the doctors, the structural functioning of the clinic, finances, personal dynamics between directors and staff, and treatment of patients. Staff members and part of the board believed the doctors should be paid per hour rather than per case so that they would not work at such a rapid pace.[25] The directors, after the problems they had encountered with the physicians, did not want to rock the boat. Besides, they said, the doctors were technicians who had no control over the clinic. Feminists disagreed: "We all got ripped off by the doctors," Griesinger commented. Chewerl Radican, the first of Dayton feminists to have raised the issue of abortion, and who ran the pregnancy testing for DWL for years, added, "It was totally doctor-centered." Her opinion stemmed from experience as a recipient of the clinic's services: "It was hideous beyond belief. . . . I was six weeks pregnant. I had a doctor come in without introducing himself, stick his hand inside me, and say to the nurse, not to me, 'I can't do her; she's fourteen weeks.' I said, 'Doctor, I'm not,' and went over the history. He talked to me in this attitude of 'you stupid woman, you can't possible know what's going on.' . . . A totally insolent, arrogant, horrible attitude." Clinic staff members were sympathetic but powerless, Radican said, and could only suggest that she return another day and try another doctor.

While Wilson undoubtedly understated the influence of the physicians, most feminist critics had not been present during the long and difficult negotiations and did not understand the problems involved in recruiting medical staff. The fear that the doctors might have pulled out was not unfounded. One report on an Iowa clinic several years later showed that upon the resignation of the sole physician, the clinic was incapable of finding another, not only in that city but even after an extended nationwide effort. This was one element that led to the clinic's bankruptcy.[26]

As abortion proved to be highly lucrative, conflict also developed over how to use excess income. Feminists considered it wrong to make any profit beyond the minimum necessary to assure the future of the clinic. They wanted to lower the price of abortions, which had been agreed to by all, directors included, during the planning stages. The directors, according to various reports, wanted a cushion for the future, child care, attractive furnishings, and/or an increase in staff.[27] According to a member of the board, both directors independently stated that lowering the fees would encourage women to use abortion as a form of birth control.[28]

The debates over finances showed that feminists were siding with the patients, while the administrators were behaving like the directors of a business. While feminists have been notoriously incapable of dealing with financial management of the institutions they create,[29] the administrators had lost sight of the specificity of the service they were selling. This is illustrated by the attitude toward reduced-fee patients. After Medicaid funds for abortion were cut, Wilson complained that "a lot of women who used Medicaid cards now come up with the money" and wondered how many had been "working off the welfare system." No doubt part of Wilson's annoyance resulted from the clinic's being "dumped on"—that is, used as a safety valve for the medical establishment. When a hospital in Dayton finally began offering abortions—at a higher price—it would skim off the wealthy clients and refer poor women to the clinic, apparently a common phenomenon for alternative institutions.[30] Nevertheless, Wilson blamed the victims. Her attitude avoided not only the issue of health care as a right, but also the weighty repercussions of an unwanted pregnancy—sufficient for even a poor woman to scrape up the money for an abortion. Furthermore, because the clinic looked like a fairly traditional business, it is not surprising that patients behaved like customers and bargained for cheaper goods. Wilson also was indignant about how minors lied about their age when parental consent was needed. Taking the patients' point of view, it is hardly surprising that they would lie to procure a safe abortion.

Conflict increased over the structure of the clinic. Staff and board members with background in the women's movement, despite concomitant antagonism toward the Women's Center, closed ranks. Most favored a nonhierarchical organization. But the clinic had been set up in a classic manner, with pay scales and power in accordance to job status and going rates in the city. Staff members found their working conditions to be little different from those in traditional jobs, and several complained of condescending treatment and even a lack of breaks.[31] (They also argued that Heindal, well paid as a director, was rarely at the clinic.) For Wilson, however, there could be no restructuring. "I felt that they wanted to reorganize the clinic as a . . . collective," she declared angrily. "They wanted to do away with the different job positions in terms of titles, . . . and they wanted to pay salaries in terms of people's need, and not have anybody be the ultimate responsible person—sort of like women's liberation was run." While she considered the clinic to be feminist, this was going too far: "I knew enough about politics at that time that I personally labeled that 'radical socialist feminism.'"

Finally, several staff members believed that the treatment of the patients lacked sensitivity. They felt both from patients and from previous counseling that abortion was generally a traumatic experience. They claimed that individual counseling was not presented as a real option. They reported to the board that statements were made in group counseling that shocked them—such as comparing abortion to "vacuuming out the glove compartment of a car" or "pulling a tooth"[32]—and they asked the board to intervene.

Faced with these conflicts, the directors, who were two out of three trustees, changed the statutes and eliminated the power of the board. "They didn't want what the community involvement was going to mean," Holmes stated. In June 1974, four board members and the third trustee answered the directors in kind, filing an injunction against Wilson and Heindal for usurping the power of the board. On the first day of the trial, three staff members received notification that they were fired for reasons ranging from incompetence to gross insubordination.[33] "Essentially, they got rid of anything that was considered the women's movement," Holmes said. The legal process was nasty. Attempts were made to discredit Griesinger as a minister by dredging up irreverent articles she had written in the DWL newsletter. The court, in a decision rendered public several years later, decided in favor of Wilson and Heindal.

Although the clinic was a product of the women's movement, control rapidly slipped through feminists' fingers. The movement had initiated previous organizing for abortion rights and related services. Several feminists had helped start the clinic, and the money had been raised thanks to women's movement networks. But during the organizational stages no decision-making mechanisms were set up. "A lot of us who thought [the clinic] should be run collectively got upset about that, but we were trying to make the change after the fact, after the machinery and the salaries were already in place," Griesinger said. "It happened by default in the sense that it wasn't planned that way, because there was no planning organization."

Feminists had made the false assumption that everyone was playing by the same rules. For instance, they incorrectly assumed that the trustees would never use their power. Overwork—the feminists most involved in the clinic also were setting up the Women's Center at the time—coupled with the belief in community and sisterhood led many to avoid looking too closely at the directors' politics. While Wilson supported abortion rights, she did not see the issue as inextricably linked to women's liberation in general; and while she supported a nonprofit status and decent market wages, she had no commitment to building an exemplary alternative institution.

The separation between political and service work on abortion, institutionalized since the creation of Clergy and Lay, unintentionally prepared the turf for the ousting of the feminists. Keeping a high profile in political work, including after the Supreme Court decision, meant that the feminists maintained authority in that arena. But in service work, even the most important figure in abortion organizing, Jan Griesinger, had downplayed her involvement for reasons of strategy and, no doubt, modesty. Thus, the links between abortion and feminism were rarely made clear. When acts are not signed, anyone can claim credit.[34]

The Dayton Women's Health Center established itself as a viable institution. Medical care was never shown to be lacking. Needy women often received reduced-price abortions. It was long the sole nonprofit clinic in Ohio. As new women entered the movement, antagonisms died down. But a number of feminists in Dayton, when in need of an abortion, preferred going to Cincinnati. Residue of the conflict lingered for years. When the rise of antiabortion forces later endangered the clinic's existence, feminists rose to the challenge, but the bitter taste that remained for many dampened their enthusiasm.

In early 1974, as tensions were mounting at the abortion clinic, feminists in Dayton's movement were raising another issue of which they were to lose control: rape. The women's movement nationally had not dealt with the question until 1971,[35] and Dayton was by no means in the vanguard. "Why didn't we see the importance of violence against women?" Griesinger said, looking back sadly in later years. An implicit analysis was in the making, however. Helping women gain both physical and psychological strength was central to DWL and the Women's Center, manifest in the self-defense courses, consciousness-raising groups, feminist therapy, and interest in girls' sports.

Dayton feminists began addressing the issue of rape openly in 1973. They distributed the handbook *Freedom from Rape*.[36] They lent support to University of Dayton women when they created a short-lived rape crisis center, and the Women's Center temporarily took over its crisis line in the summer of 1974. Most important, in February 1974 feminists created Women Against Rape. WAR members began investigating the crime of rape, studying the de facto and de jure situation in Dayton. They developed the Stop Rape Program to provide crisis services for victims and to work on prevention and education.[37]

By 1974, rape had become a prominent issue nationally, with several hundred crisis centers around the country.[38] In the same year, the Law Enforcement Assistance Administration (LEAA), a funding branch of the Justice Department, began discretionary funding for rape projects. In early 1974, Loraine Reid, a staff member at the Miami Valley Regional Planning Commission, through which LEAA money was channeled locally, wrote a proposal for a victimization center in Dayton. The victims in question were understood to be mainly victims of rape, but also of other violent crimes. The general administrator of LEAA funds asked the Ombudsman's Office, an agency that inquired into citizen complaints, to coordinate the project. He contacted a personal acquaintance, Bonnie Macaulay, the newly hired ombudsman, because as Macaulay admitted, "he was afraid of the Women's Center." Macaulay, "not a flag-waver," was safer; her prime interest was "human rights" and women by extension, because, she said, "women are people." She was concerned with "women's involvement in equality" and had been a member of a study group based on *The Feminine Mystique,* led by a male minister at an Episcopal church.

After learning of the Victimization Project, WAR, the Women's Center, and the University of Dayton crisis center contacted the Ombudsman's Office to protest their exclusion. The author of the initial proposal, they reported, seemed open to cooperation. WAR, having successfully run educational programs, was asked to write a proposal for the educational component of the Victimization Project. WAR agreed hesitantly. "We are suspicious of federally funded programs because so often the grant money that comes into a city never gets to the people it was intended to help," said WAR cofounder and Women's Center staff member Roberta Fisher.[39]

It is unlikely that the organizers of the Victimization Project viewed WAR or any feminists as potential partners. While they acknowledged that they had asked WAR to submit a proposal, they pointed out repeatedly that the educational part of the program was slated for less than 4 percent of its budget.[40] Of the various agencies mentioned in the Project literature, WAR was the only group whose name was always listed incorrectly: it was called the "women's group" or the "Women's Liberation

Center."[41] Later, when the five staff positions for the Victimization Project were being filled, candidates with credentials from the women's movement were rejected. According to WAR cofounder Maddi Breslin, Macaulay stated point-blank that she would never hire a feminist. Women's Center staff member Kathy Ellison, who applied for one of the positions, observed that she was as well as if not better qualified than those hired. As an Ombudsman staff member explained to a mutual acquaintance, even the moderate Ellison was "too tainted with a radical tinge."[42]

Ombudsman staff member Margo Evans, who had worked on the preparatory stages of the Victimization Project, confirmed this hostility to the women's movement. She had attended several meetings of a DWL consciousness-raising group, but she said participants were "scapegoating" their husbands because of their "own personal lack of satisfaction." With a background in the civil rights movement, Evans believed racism was a more serious problem than sexism. Although white herself and a graduate of Smith College, she condemned the women's movement for being middle class. She questioned the ability of the Women's Center to run programs because of its financial difficulties.

Contact with the Women's Center over the Victimization Project, Evans said, "cemented [her] dislike for the women's movement." When she and a male lawyer went to the Center to discuss future relations, they were informed that the Center was not open to men. "They kicked him out! That fixed my mind on that group!" she declared. She described the women who attended the meeting as "self-righteous," "purist," some as "frustrated suburban housewives," and concluded that they were "the most hostile, unreasonable, unpolitical group that you ever wanted to see." The WAR proposal was turned down, but according to both Fisher and Suits, the group's research and ideas were later used by the Victimization Project.[43] With substantial sums of money at stake, personal and political power networks tightened and squeezed out feminists. Unable to compete, WAR abandoned its plans to start a crisis center.[44]

The Victimization Project not only excluded feminists but also a feminist analysis of rape. The Project came out of the increasingly popular "science" of victimology. With crime rates skyrocketing, victimology aimed at modernizing a criminal justice system in which the public was losing faith because, it was contended, the criminals were getting more attention than the victims.[45] While first used as a euphemism for rape, victimization also dealt with all violent crimes, including child abuse and assault and battery, and encouraged witnesses of crimes to testify in court.[46]

Victimology negated the sexual politics involved in rape. Rape became a genderless crime. No interest was expressed in why men rape and why most people raped are women. Clients were "victims" attacked or "victimized" by "aggressors" or "offenders," all of an undetermined sex. Project literature used linguistic contortions to avoid the words "rape," "rapist," "men," and "women." None of these words appeared in the three-page description of the Project first sent to local agencies.[47] Thereafter, on the rare occasions when men were mentioned, it was to stress how they, too, were victims, pointing to the rare reported cases of homosexual rape. The Victimization Project viewed rape as a fact of life, impossible to eliminate. Aggressors were sick and had to be imprisoned.

Like many feminists, workers with the Victimization Project believed women were discouraged from reporting rape because of the low rate of prosecution. However, whereas feminists encouraged women to report rapes to heighten awareness of rape as a violent crime or to get rapists off the streets, the Project's stated goals were to improve the prosecutor's record, modernize the system, and build confidence in the police and the courts.[48] Modernization included serving as "a strong liaison organization to provide information and referral to *existing community resources.*"[49] That existing services might not suffice was constantly downplayed.

The Victimization Project began operations in July 1974. Almost all of its first-year $127,000 budget came from the LEAA.[50] The Project functioned as a rape crisis center, doing crisis intervention, working with the police and the hospitals, and pushing for legislative reform. Once under way, it operated autonomously from the Ombudsman's Office. It began with a paid staff of four women and one man and relied extensively on volunteer labor. An impressive ninety-two volunteers were recruited and trained in the first year, with an average of thirty to thirty-five working during any given period. About one-third were professionals (teachers, nurses, and counselors); one-quarter were college students, often interns; and one-quarter were housewives, some from local women's clubs and organizations such as the Junior League. Nearly all were women; the few men who participated tended to be in the social services. Many volunteers had been rape victims themselves.[51] Volunteers did some casework and crisis intervention at hospitals, but above all they were the backbone of the crisis line, which went into twenty-four-hour operation in October 1974.

The Victimization Project undeniably brought the question of rape before the public eye in Dayton. Media response to the opening of the

Project far exceeded expectations. In the first year, forty-eight television and radio spots and sixty-three newspaper articles covered the Project's activities.[52] At one point, Project staff wrote a weekly column in the *Dayton Daily News*. The abundant media coverage no doubt stemmed from the titillating nature of the crime, but Project staff made sure that articles included publicity for services, individual testimonies, and good medical and legal advice.

Despite the low priority placed on education, in the first year of operation Project staff and volunteers gave more than a hundred lectures to church groups, women's clubs, high schools, universities, and community groups. They wrote and designed posters, brochures, and training manuals and distributed existing educational materials on rape, amounting to a total of nearly eighteen thousand pieces.[53]

By the end of its first year, the Victimization Project had become an efficient social service, praised by the media, by a professional evaluation team, and by recipients of its services. It had served 227 victims of sexual assault, plus 32 victims of general assault.[54] The pattern for crisis intervention was as follows. The police or the hospital (termed "witnesses") reported a rape to the crisis line. (More rarely, the woman herself called, usually to request counseling days, months, or years after the rape.) A volunteer or staff member was dispatched to the hospital. She, or occasionally he, would ensure that all necessary tests were done, evidence properly collected, and appropriate medical advice given. She would offer to stay in the waiting room and during the examination if allowed by the physician. In addition, police records were examined daily for rapes not reported to the Project, and a Project member would try to meet with those victims. The Project's support continued during police interrogation and, if the woman prosecuted, throughout the legal process.

Numerous other problems also arose. When a rape victim who did not have a telephone felt unsafe returning home, the Project paid for a phone to be installed. The need for emergency housing was a common problem, either because the woman feared staying alone or because she was transient. With limited resources available, Project staff actually took such women into their homes on several occasions.

Although relations with the law enforcement agencies were problematic at the outset, they improved rapidly, becoming the envy of rape crisis centers in the region.[55] The Project held educational workshops for the police, addressing awareness of the crime of rape and dealing with techniques to improve evidence collection. The chief of police placed one officer in charge of sexual assault cases for each district, reducing the number of times a woman had to repeat her story and centralizing information about rapists. By the end of 1974, a large proportion of calls to the crisis line came from the police to request aid for victims. By the next spring, the Dayton police department agreed upon a standard procedure whereby all sexual assault complaints received were transmitted to the Project by the following day. Thus, every victim of reported rape was rapidly offered services. At one point, a nearby township further perfected the system: the police dispatcher called the crisis line directly so that a Project staff member or volunteer arrived at the hospital often before the cruiser.[56]

Given the Project's initial goal of restoring confidence in the criminal justice system, it was not surprising that its relationship with the Prosecutor's Office was good. Several major changes were implemented as early as fall 1974, thanks to this collaboration. Preliminary hearings were eliminated, and a single prosecutor was selected to handle all rape cases, further limiting the number of times the woman had to tell her story.

In contrast, the Victimization Project's rapport with the medical establishment remained poor. This is particularly interesting given reports of the opposite experience elsewhere. For example, a Boston rape crisis center suggested that rape victims, in order to be treated humanely, go directly to the hospital and contact the police only afterward.[57] In Dayton, the hospitals were the institutions most resistant to change.

Problems with emergency rooms abounded. Personnel rarely called the crisis line. Rape ranked low on the priority list of medical emergencies, so victims often spent hours in public waiting rooms, only to finally hear a hospital staffer yell, "Where's the rape case?"[58] Evidence was often improperly collected or recorded, destroying what little proof might exist in a crime that usually occurs without witnesses. Information on venereal disease and pregnancy was not systematically offered.[59] Some improvement came after the Project began conducting regular in-service training sessions for emergency room personnel.[60] However, the high rate of turnover at the hospitals—particularly in personnel working nights, when most rapes occur—limited the effectiveness of such programs. Complaints about the insensitive attitudes of various nurses and doctors continued.

For the Project's first coordinator, Patricia Hussey, legislative change was a priority. Although Ohio rape laws had just been modified,[61] many points objectionable to feminists and reformers remained. A woman's reputation and sexual history were admissible evidence; the notion of marital rape was nonexistent even when spouses were legally separated; no provisions were made to pay for evidence collection or other medical expenses; and corroboration was still required in most cases. The Victimization Project worked with state representative Paul Leonard on drafting a proposal to further revise the criminal code. Bill was introduced into the Ohio legislature in early 1975, and as a result, a new version of the sex offenses section of the code was adopted. It included the following provisions: forbidding the use of a woman's sexual history as evidence, unless it involved the offender; no longer requiring proof of physical resistance; restricting the definition of spouse to exclude separated couples; mandatory five-year prison sentences for second-time offenders; the creation of the notion of felonious sexual penetration (by an object); requiring emergency room physicians, with the consent of the patient, to examine the victim and gather relevant evidence according to standards set by the public health council; requiring hospitals to inform victims of the risks of pregnancy and venereal disease, and possibilities of counseling services; and providing public funds for medical expenses incurred in evidence collection if victims prosecuted.[62]

In mid-1975, as the first year of the Victimization Project—and its funding—drew to an end, its future was uncertain. Although personal antagonisms with feminists had died down and a working relationship had been established with the Women's Center, feminists were ambivalent as to whether they should rally to support the Project.

Jan Griesinger encouraged feminists to support county funding to save the Victimization Project. Writing as a part of the short-lived political action collective of DWL, she praised the Project's direct services: "[T]hey assume [the rape victim] is a strong healthy woman who has been imposed on from the outside in a manner over which she had no control. . . . If the woman has a supportive person there to reinforce her strength . . . the whole rape experience is somewhat less traumatic."[63]

Another DWL author argued against support. In an unsigned article subtitled "Is the Women's Movement Being Co-opted?"[64] she expressed suspicion of the Law Enforcement Assistance Administration, because it funded psychosurgery in prisons and research on civilian surveillance techniques, and pointed to evidence of CIA involvement. More to the point, she argued, by excluding feminists while including men, and by fostering policies that encouraged women to curtail their freedom in order to avoid rape, the Project did not work to change women's self-image. Nor did it encourage resistance; to the contrary, it reinforced women's passivity. Evidence supports this criticism. In an interview with a local newspaper the same month, one of the Project's main lecturers questioned the validity of resistance. While telling women to fight their "natural instinct [of] being motherly," she advised, women faced with a rapist to "[g]ain his confidence. If you can, say something nice. . . . Use your sexual parts to keep the 'whipping' from being a killing."[65] This contrasted with the position defended by feminist Susan Brownmiller in her landmark book published the same year. Brownmiller convincingly argued that acquiescent behavior does not necessarily convince the aggressor to stop at rape: "A victim may choose to play by what she assumes are the rules, but a rapist does not necessarily respond with similar civility."[66]

Feminists had many other reasons to criticize the Victimization Project. The primary commitment to making the criminal justice system work better and building community confidence in it had repercussions. For example, the Project pushed women to initiate civil litigation against rapists. While there was a legal rationale for this strategy—such cases are easier to win—this was not the reason advanced. Instead, it was to "provid[e] a means for the payment of restitution by the offender to the victim."[67] Try as they might, Project staff members were unable to find a single rape victim willing to file a civil suit. They chalked this up to the social stigma attached to rape and to the fact that many rapists were not "collectible." So deeply did the Victimization Project believe in the criminal justice system that it was never imagined that a woman might not want financial compensation for rape. Another effect of the legal framework of the Project was that its mandate was limited; as long as marital rape was not recognized in the state of Ohio, for instance, it could not serve such victims.

The Project's generally excellent *Handbook for Victims of Sexual Assault* revealed another aspect of its nonfeminist perspective. The publication was prepared with the assistance of Nurses Concerned for Life—"life," of course, was a euphemism used by antiabortionists. And although the handbook listed abortion as a viable option in the case of unwanted pregnancy, one of the four referral services listed for medical services was Womanline. Unknown to many Daytonians, Womanline was the medical and counseling component of the Right to Life Society. Right to Life, at best, denies that rape can result in pregnancy, as stated in a leaflet distributed locally: "Pregnancy from rape or incest is very rare, especially if the victim goes directly to a hospital. The English law does not even mention rape as a reason for abortion because of the 'difficulty of legal proof.' . . . What is needed is help for the mother, not the strange sort of justice that would kill an innocent child for the crime of its father."[68] Thus pregnant rape victims were potentially exposed to psychological harassment, one illustration of how the lack of feminist analysis limited the Victimization Project's sensitivity to women's needs.

Despite the fact that the overwhelming majority of victims were women and all rapists encountered were men, the Project continued to present rape as but one example of violent crime, negating the relevance of gender. In fact, in the rare discussions of gender, the Project explained how women could be their own worst enemies. For example, female jurors in rape cases were singled out as being unsympathetic. Men, on the other hand, were often portrayed as sympathetic, even fatherly, in coming to the victim's aid.[69] When dealing with rape, this critical view of women and positive view of men, coupled with the male-dominated criminal justice system, discouraged women's autonomy.

Questions of race and class were even more absent from the Project's analysis of rape. Although black women made up approximately one-third of the clients served, and a study overseen by staff members noted that black women report rape less frequently than do white women, the issue of race never arose. Judging from the Project's own descriptions, its education programs served white middle- and upper-middle-class audiences.[70] The Project's genderless and colorblind "humanism" made it miss the obvious conclusions of its own empirical data.

The Project did not successfully realize its goals, most glaringly in its lack of impact on the number of alleged rape cases accepted for prosecution. While the number of rapes reported to the police increased considerably by the second year of Project operation, no such observation can be made for the number of cases accepted for prosecution. Statistics compiled after thirty months of operation showed a 43 percent increase in reports to police, but only about a 10 percent increase in the number of cases accepted for prosecution. The proportion of cases accepted for prosecution thus actually decreased.[71]

For those who used the Project's services, such criticisms mattered little. Clients enthusiastically praised direct services, unanimously rating them "very helpful" in one survey.[72] Letters to the editors of local newspapers confirmed this support. "[The director] and her staff were remarkable in counseling me during the ordeal and at the hospital," one woman wrote. "They have kept in touch since the incident and are always there when I need them."[73] The staff was consistently commended for its effective and sensitive work.

In August 1975, the Project's grant came to an end. But a year of providing efficient, popular services had created community support. Also, the law-and-order zeitgeist and the Project's nonfeminist approach made it palatable to the establishment. As a result, the Montgomery County Prosecutor's Office agreed to incorporate the Project as its Victim/Witness Division. The office moved to the Criminal Justice Complex, which also housed some prisons and courts. An additional, though smaller, LEAA grant was obtained with matching county funds. Budget cuts brought the number of caseworkers down to two. (For fifteen months, each worked more than sixty hours a week and was on call every other night.)

Despite the cuts, the move to the Prosecutor's Office legitimated Victim/Witness and gave it some power within the system. Notably, since the police had to file crime reports with the prosecutor, they were legally required to cooperate with Victim/Witness as well. The division used its clout when at least one hospital's evidence collection got sloppy. Armed with the 1975 revised criminal code that the Project had helped formulate, Victim/Witness sent a memorandum to all local hospitals threatening that "physicians treating rape victims must fill out the medical forms submitted with rape evidence completely and legibly or be subpoenaed for Grand Juries."[74]

Although its goal of increasing citizen faith in the criminal justice system remained, Victim/Witness's perspective on rape began changing. Time and again, contact with rape victims, against the backdrop of an active feminist movement, raised the staff's consciousness and sparked an ongoing transformation. Increased sensitivity toward rape victims and greater militancy resulted in an institution that became progressively more feminist.

First, Victim/Witness recognized that the pressing need for services came from rape victims, and it therefore deemphasized serving victims of other felonious crimes. Goals were not redefined on paper, mainly to meet an official requirement, but when program cuts were made later, services for general assault victims were the first to go. Director Mary Brooks later admitted, "I don't go out of my way to seek other referrals [than rape]."

One example of militancy came during the first year of operations when workers became aware of how pervasive rape of young girls was. At that time approximately 19 percent of reported rape cases concerned girls under the age of fourteen, and another 30 percent occurred in the fourteen through eighteen age bracket.[75] Victim/Witness designed a course on rape prevention for schoolchildren as young as six, disregarding the recent takeover of the Dayton school board by the anti-sex-education New Right.

The staff's ongoing work led it to challenge the shortsightedness of the original Victimization Project. Faced with a one-year grant, an elaborate system for quarterly evaluations had initially been spelled out, and goals that after a few months' operations proved not measurable were supposed to be reformulated. Nevertheless, as they worked with rape victims, staff members came to reject the idea that the only good goal was a short-term one. They realized that attitudes toward rape, in the general public and among officials, had to change. As noted in the first-year final report: "Due to the fact that the change of attitudes to positive and supportive from negative and unsupportive is a somewhat immeasurable commodity, many effects of the project upon the Criminal Justice System are in the short term immeasurable."[76]

At first, the Project maintained a nonthreatening stance toward local authorities, but the staff progressively began to criticize their insensitivity—although they attributed it to ignorance, not sexism. In the beginning, "fear of insensitive treatment," not actual poor treatment, was seen as discouraging rape victims from seeking aid. But workers could not ignore what they were witnessing. By the end of the first year, two of the major problems encountered were the reluctance of the institutions to change and victims' complaints of poor treatment: "Although failure to report this crime can be attributed to fear of scandal or embarrassment, a large percentage of unreported rapes must be attributed to unknowledgeable and insensitive treatment of rape victims by police officers, emergency room personnel, juries, and judges."[77] To counter male dominance in local institutions, Brooks, who preferred the label "humanist" to feminist, argued for an all-women staff. After years of working with rape victims, she said, "my feeling is that there is an over-amount of men in the system. The odds are it's going to be a male doctor and a male officer. I think there needs to be that female support person there, too."

With a distinctly feminist flavor, Victim/Witness began contesting rape laws, particularly those that permitted spousal rape. "We have encountered wives who have been beaten and raped by their husbands, but who were legally restricted from filing rape charges," Victim/Witness coordinator Patricia Hussey said in an article in the local press. She attributed this to "the historical view of the woman as property owned by her husband."[78] The staff was again forced to remove their gender blinders when a man accused of rape admitted that his victim had resisted but argued that the resistance had been feigned. He passed a lie detector test, making it unlikely that the prosecutor would accept the case.[79] With an implicit understanding of the sexual politics involved—that is, that some rapists believe that a woman "really wants it" no matter what she says or does—staff contested the use of polygraph tests in cases of rape, choosing to believe the woman. Even when the police or prosecutor deemed a rape charge unfounded, Victim/Witness did not. It supported women in "difficult cases," including even those who falsified testimony to cover up circumstances that might discredit them, such as the fact that they had been hitchhiking or drinking.[80]

All reports concur that Victim/Witness staff members showed sensitivity in their work, and their respect for the victims increased with experience. Victim/Witness consistently emphasized that the rapist, not the victim, was guilty: "It is YOUR body that has been assaulted, and YOUR life that has been threatened. There is no shame in what has happened to you. The only shame is if your assailant is allowed to go free to attack again."[81]

Concern for the victims of rape even took precedence over the goal of increasing prosecution rates. Prosecution was encouraged, but "if any woman is reluctant to do that, we are more than willing to back off." When a woman chose to prosecute, her feelings regarding the sentence were respected and transmitted to the judge, Brooks said. "If she wants blood, we'll make sure that's related to the judge. . . . With some, there's some pity for the offender." Similarly, staff supported victims regardless of how they reacted in the rape situation. "If you can fight back, fine; if you just lie back, we can understand that," Brooks insisted. Criticized for not encouraging women to resist, she pointed out the perverse effect of seeing resistance as the "correct" response: "It seems like people are promoting the idea that women should fight back. There are still a lot of women who just cannot do it. And they end up feeling guilty."

During the planning stages of the Victimization Project, feminists questioned whether organizers had women's best interests at heart. Would working within the criminal justice system help liberate women? Bureaucratic and conceptual constraints did limit the program's scope and in some cases worked against the liberation of women. However, if the Project did not always have women's interests as a group at heart, it did so on a case-by-case basis. In the context of a strong feminist movement transforming the ambient culture, staff reproduced the feminist method of grouping individuals' experiences and forging theory from them. Sensitivity and commitment to clients resulted in Victim/Witness's transformation to a more feminist institution. The conflict with the women's movement ceased; by 1978, Victim/Witness even hired a self-proclaimed feminist, Maggie Reck, who had taught classes at the Women's Center.

The Dayton movement's loss of influence on the issues of rape and abortion and its inability to control related resources is fairly typical of what has been reported nationally. By the mid-1970s, power and money were at stake in certain feminist issues. While some minor victories were won in Dayton—the initial (small) funding of the Center, for example—when substantial amounts of money were involved feminists always lost out.[82] The relatively marginal status of the women's movement is often attributed to feminists' choice not to relate to mainstream institutions, but this was not the case in Dayton. Feminists tried to launch initiatives themselves, and when they failed, they tried to cooperate with the new institutions. For instance, feminists applied for jobs—almost always unsuccessfully—with all of the parafeminist projects over the decade. Feminists were not too purist to cooperate; they were systematically rejected.

Paradoxically, the development and sustenance of these projects depended on the existence of a women's movement. The women's movement broke ground by bringing the issues of rape and abortion to light. Furthermore, without the women's movement, the abortion clinic would not have found its seed money and might later have been shut down with the rise of the New Right. Without the women's movement in the background, day-to-day contact with rape victims might have resulted in a paternalistic social service rather than in the raising of consciousness, as it did in Victim/Witness. The future of these projects remains linked to the health of the movement, to feminist and community support.

Some co-opted initiatives resulted in projects of no redeeming value to the women's movement, but in most cases, including those of the abortion clinic and Victim/Witness, things were far more complex. Most obviously, these projects provided vital services to women in Dayton. The Dayton Women's Health Center was long the sole provider of abortions in the area, and director Anita Wilson later became active in the fight to maintain abortion rights. Victim/Witness not only served rape victims remarkably well, it also underwent a gradual transformation and became decidedly more feminist. Since these expanded horizons were not incorporated into the Victimization Project's official goals, they depended on the influence of individual participants and thus on a world transformed by the women's movement. In the meantime, treatment of rape victims improved, laws and attitudes changed, and rape was recognized as a crime in Dayton, Ohio.

The most perceptive evaluation of parafeminist institutions came from socialist feminist and Women's Center activist Sherry Novick. Her comments carried all the more weight because they came from firsthand experience. Novick, who had been raped before feminists raised consciousness on the issue, was again raped in 1980. "I really felt that I was the recipient of what the women's movement had won in this city, because I was not treated like shit," she said.[83] Police had known immediately which hospital had the best services for rape victims and sent her there. Novick recalled, "[T]he hospital was prepared to deal with rape victims, and . . . Victim/Witness was at the police station the very next morning to go through the process with me. . . . It made me aware, in spite of the sell-outs, of the level of institutional change that has happened."

Victim/Witness was simultaneously an example of co-optation and a victory for the women's movement. "It's a defeat in terms of our losing control," Novick said, but "it's a victory that the city of Dayton took rape very seriously. . . . It's a victory in the sense of the women's movement forcing the institutions of society to speak to these needs."

5

THE DAYTON WOMEN'S CENTER (1975–80)

THE DAYTON Women's Center ushered in a new era for the women's movement in Dayton. In a period of broad diffusion of feminist ideas, the Center drew new blood into the movement and increased its audience. Despite this expansion, the movement remained unified for several years. The Center itself, with its classes, referral services, and therapy program, remained the movement's nucleus, even as it spun off other activities and groups. The nature of the Center was very different from that of the preceding movement hub, Dayton Women's Liberation, most notably because it provided physical space and a community center for feminists. Although members worked to maintain a feminist self-help perspective, there was a constant tug toward becoming an alternative social service agency.

The Center was not a political organization, and after the demise of DWL in 1975, attempts were made to fill this void. Thus, the Center started a local chapter of the National Organization for Women. The creation of the NOW chapter, subsequently midwife to the group that was to eclipse the Center, reflected a political shift taking place both internally and externally. The liberal shift at the Center, the diffusion of feminist ideas and activities in mainstream institutions, and the rise of the Right all contributed to the Center's decline after 1978. When it closed in 1980, the movement, for the first time since its outset, was left without a nucleus.

The Dayton Women's Center provided the movement with its first physical, visible space. The large old house was centrally located on North Main Street, on a bus line, a little more than a mile from downtown Dayton. A hand-painted wooden sign hung out front. The house was furnished with comfortable upholstered sofas and other secondhand furniture and decorated with colorful political posters. It was open for classes and meetings seven days a week, and to the public Mondays through Fridays and often on Saturdays. Visitors could have free tea and coffee while consulting the community bulletin board plastered with announcements. They could leaf through information-packed files or borrow books from the library. They could purchase feminist literature (and later, music) not available anywhere else in Dayton.

During the life of the Dayton Women's Center, thousands of women, perhaps tens of thousands, used its services, and hundreds of women were actively involved. Different levels of commitment became possible, from being recipients of services to participating in activities to assuring the Center's daily operations. At the core was the staff—approximately sixteen different people between 1974 and 1978—and the Center collective, which fluctuated in size from eight to twenty members and involved more than fifty different people in its first three years alone. Many hundreds of women took classes or were involved in therapy. The mailing list grew to nearly two thousand people, and far more used the phone service. Incalculable numbers benefited from the Center's public programs and actions.[1]

This new generation of activists in Dayton's movement had begun with socialist feminists such as Tricia Hart, Barbara Tuss, Sherry Novick, and staff members Robin Suits and Sherrie Holmes, along with the newly hired Roberta Fisher and Kathy Ellison. Other recruits rapidly joined them.

Center organizers successfully fulfilled their goal of reaching women new to the movement.[2] Women came to the Center through several channels: the New American Movement and the radical community, friendship networks, and off the street. Many women heard about the Center through local media: television news, public service radio announcements, or newspaper articles. Others, as had happened in DWL, simply looked in the phone book.

One woman, a recent arrival to the area, was searching for community involvement and volunteer work. She found the Center's number in the phone book and called, not because she considered herself a feminist, but because, she said, "there's a woman's center, and I'm a woman." Another, a "feminist sympathizer from afar," wanted to do some volunteering following the birth of a child and a leave from her job. She, too, found the number in the phone book.[3]

Among the Center's most committed members was Pat Russell-Campbell. She had learned of the Center from a poster at a local record store, a counterculture hangout, and her husband-to-be encouraged her to join. The night of her first meeting, a violent tornado hit the nearby city of Xenia. "It was like the tornado hit me!" Russell-Campbell jokingly recalled. "[It was] almost a religious experience!" She joined the collective and remained until nearly the end.

Russell-Campbell was a native of Dayton. Her mother had been a factory worker and a union activist before becoming a saleswoman, and her father was an automobile mechanic. In high school she opposed the war, seeing Vietnam as a far-off land where Americans were dying unnecessarily, but she became active only upon her arrival at the Women's Center. Twenty-four years old at the time, she had worked at various jobs since graduating from high school. In her most recent job at a credit bureau, she had witnessed discriminatory practices against women.

Shortly after joining the Center, Russell-Campbell got married. Although she and her husband saw their marriage as a partnership of equals, she felt that other feminists were critical. "At first people were pretty weird about loving a man. . . . Like it wasn't a feminist thing to do." She scoffed at this attitude: after all, her husband supported the movement, and rejecting men "shut out a base of support that is helpful," she said. Her position converged with that of many socialist feminists who believed that men could be feminists. As NAM proclaimed from the start, "[M]en are not auxiliary to the struggle against sexism."[4]

Russell-Campbell's revelatory experience, reminiscent of the early DWL years, was atypical for this wave of recruits. Although most looked back to their early involvement as a golden era and enthusiastically described their feeling of belonging, they less often described a sudden conversion. Even if most were new to the women's movement, they arrived sympathetic to feminist ideas. Their involvement at the Center was the result, not the cause, of their feminist consciousness. Consequently, the level of commitment differed.

As the years went by, fewer women had prior experience in radical social movements, particularly in the civil rights movement. Although an overwhelming majority situated themselves in the liberal to left end of the political spectrum, there was, in comparison to DWL, a liberal drift.[5] In one 1976 survey, an open-ended question asked the participants to describe their politics: 44 percent said liberal, liberal Democrat, slightly left of center; 17 percent answered left-wing, radical, socialist, or anarchist; another 9.5 percent said in-between (liberal to radical, liberal to socialist, left-liberal); and 12.5 percent placed themselves in the center or slightly to the right (moderate, conservative, conservative and for change, middle of the road).[6] For some activists, this shift was the sign of a much feared depolitization. For others, it was proof of effective outreach.

A large proportion of Center activists were raised Catholic—three times more than in a DWL sample. Contrary to Protestants, who often moved into the more progressive denominations, most of the Catholics had lapsed. Some identified culturally as Catholic, but none agreed with the positions of the Church on, for instance, abortion and birth control. However, as with DWL, a significant number of Center activists, Protestant and Catholic alike, connected religious institutions and religious education to their political awakening and/or activism.[7]

The new Center activists (like most "utilizers") were white and mostly heterosexual. Despite the significant minority whose parents were working class, they generally described themselves and each other as middle class. They were well educated: almost all had attended college. Nearly all worked outside of the home, some in alternative workplaces that they saw as temporary. In comparison to DWL members, Center activists, somewhat younger, were less often married and even fewer were mothers. Many lived in group houses, some as unmarried couples. Most lived in the same neighborhoods as did DWL members.[8]

While no one type of woman dominated among the Center's clientele, staff and activists described them as middle class and young.[9] Several reports claimed that most utilizers were under thirty, but this was exaggerated. Available surveys show that about half were between thirty and fifty-eight. As with DWL, the term "middle class" obscures the reality. Most established, middle- to upper-class Daytonians steered clear of the Center, at the most sending occasional contributions. For them, Kathy Ellison quipped, the Women's Center was "low rent." Conversely, while few of the utilizers were welfare mothers, interviews reveal working-class roots for many Center activists. Disparaging media reports about the middle-class bias of the movement proved somewhat skewed, but often because of activists' self-portrayals.

Center organizers had anticipated a clientele of victims of isolation and the feminine mystique. Indeed, poignant letters and calls did come in over the years, such as from the woman in Troy, Ohio, who wrote in January 1974: "Ladies, I'm thirty-three and find myself full of doubts . . . after marrying at age sixteen, raising four children to school age, and asking questions like, 'what do I do now?'"

However, most of the women (two-thirds according to one report) were in the labor force, and many of the homemakers came to the Center for help reentering the job market.[10] While the "underrepresentation of housewives"[11] was raised as a concern, the shift to issues of work was inexorable.

Concern was expressed, rightly so, about including black women. The Center's utilizers were overwhelmingly white. A handful of black women sent financial contributions. Some attended classes, in particular one described as "Afro-culture—learning about African traditions through sewing African garments." After a local newspaper ran a feature article on the class, calls poured into the Center and it was repeated at least twice. In the otherwise laissez-faire atmosphere, the class sparked controversy, no doubt because the facilitator's activist husband was reputedly polygamous.[12] The class's feminist content was admittedly debatable, but certainly no less so than that of the pottery class or the "well-plant" clinic. The Afro-culture sewing class attracted some black women to the Center, but none became active. It wasn't until three years later that black women got involved.

Some Center members believed that more should be done to involve lesbians. A principled position of advocating gay rights existed, but it remained a passive one. Sappho's Army and subsequent lesbian groups used the Center regularly for their meetings, but few got involved in the collective or on staff until 1977. Lesbians did not always feel accepted; some blamed staff member Ellison's attitudes. Ellison explained, "I just felt like we didn't need to be saddled with that on top of everything else all the time."[13] An early collective meeting posed the question: "Do lesbians hurt the Women's Center image?" but the issue was glossed over.[14]

Recipients of services expressed concern about the future of the Center even if they rarely became involved in everyday operations. One typical letter stated, "I appreciate having a Women's Center in Dayton, even though I have not taken full advantage of it. Keep me on your mailing list." These passive supporters often responded to calls for contributions: "[M]y connection with the Women's Center has been mostly financial and at a distance, but I believe in what the Center stands for and want to see it open and accessible." Another woman wrote that while she did not contribute time to the Center, as a result of her experience there she had "celebrated a year of growth and learning" and started a women's group in a neighboring town.[15]

The original project for a drop-in center functioned well, but not for the community at large. For activists and the extended feminist community, Russell-Campbell recalled, "the Women's Center was our second home." Its hominess reinforced a sense of community, but with a double-edged effect. "We could come in our grungiest clothes possible, with no bras on," Russell-Campbell said. This scared off some visitors, she believed, and confirmed outsiders' prejudices. Indeed, with the notable exception of many lesbians, for whom the Center rapidly became a meeting place and an alternative to the bars, outsiders rarely dropped in except to avail themselves of specific services.

Part of the rationale for a community center was that the Women's Center was located in a neighborhood that supposedly included "old and young, black and white, poor, working and so-called middle-class women."[16] In fact, the immediate neighborhood, though not far from racially integrated Dayton View, was all white and a hindrance to black women's participation. On the other hand, some middle-class and affluent Daytonians avoided this working-class, declining business zone.

The Center served as a clearinghouse for the extended feminist community. Lesbians called seeking peers. Feminists passing through from other parts of the country called or visited. As feminism became popular, high school and college students came to find information for term papers. Women wrote from neighboring towns, asking for advice on how to get involved in the movement. If no feminist organizations existed in their towns, staff members would encourage them start their own, as they did a Greenville woman who wrote: "As I listen to Mr. Nixon's comment this evening, my desire to reach others in my community becomes imperative! His hypocrisies delegate a need to establish myself and my sisters in a more consistent environment. For this reason, I am writing regarding my desire to become more involved and imbued in Our Movement. I would appreciate hearing from you in forms of Literature, suggested readings, and possible organization format."[17]

In addition to its role as a community center, the Women's Center ran a tripartite program of services: an educational component with classes and public events, feminist therapy, and referrals.

The Center was the first institution in Dayton to offer regularly scheduled classes on a variety of subjects, taught by women for women. From the outset, this was one of its most successful activities. Anyone could offer a class provided enough women enrolled; inversely, anyone interested in taking a class could find a facilitator and set it up. At first, staff members' interests heavily influenced content. Later, as fund-raising grew more urgent and because classes generated revenue, the previous success of a class became a prime criterion.

The most successful classes, offered regularly, had a self-help orientation, such as those on careers or job reentry, assertiveness training, auto mechanics, and self-defense. After a feature article about the careers class appeared in the *Dayton Daily News* and Phil Donahue mentioned it on his then-local talk show, the Center was inundated with calls. The class gave "emotional support as well as tips on writing resumes, etc." to women who wished to enter the job market. According to staff member Ellison, it drew "older, less well-educated women who, out of financial or emotional necessity find they must make changes in their lives."[18]

The self-defense class—a classic of the women's liberation movement—was also popular in the early years. Taught by a woman, it maintained high enrollment despite the free self-defense courses taught by a policeman at the Victimization Project. However, when the YWCA began courses taught by a woman, there was a drop in demand at the Center.

The Center's most consistently popular classes were on assertiveness, designed to teach behavior "by which a person stands up for her legitimate rights in such a way that the rights of others are not violated . . . an honest, direct and appropriate expression of your feelings, beliefs, and opinions."[19] Field assignments included going to a shoe store, trying on five pairs of shoes, and not buying any, thus illustrating a woman's "right to say 'no' without feeling guilty."[20]

Other classes and workshops included arts and crafts, such as macramé, carpentry, poster-making, and photography of working women; support groups for overweight women, divorced women, and so on; physical awareness, such as yoga, dance, and sexual awareness; media, such as women in radio; women's legal rights, such as retaining one's name after marriage, divorce laws, job and credit discrimination; and health. Noted failures were those with academic or historical content; early feminists developed their own theory and research collectively within their consciousness-raising groups. Later, with the development and legitimization of women's studies, interested women wanted university credit for their work. Surprisingly, despite demand and repeated efforts, classes aimed at women with small children also failed.

Reading the list of course offerings, one might conclude that many of them had a business orientation, such as the proposed "Women in Management." However, these classes were almost always cancelled for lack of enrollment. Robin Suits remembered, "Usually, the business or credit or housing thing would be there as a sop to Kathy Ellison's position. . . . I didn't like it, but . . . we did work on the basis of compromise, . . . and since she was ready to do a lot of work for it, we'd let it be in the newspaper. But I always knew it was going to fall through." Listing business classes in course offerings may have projected a distorted image to outsiders. One outsider claimed the Center "[bought] into the corporate bullshit." Jeri Simmons called it "a place for career women to meet and hobnob." Ironically, the career women were not convinced. As a latter-day movement participant, commented that she and many proponents of women's rights thought the Center was "a place for radical lesbian women."[21]

Classes were not the only educational component of the Center; part of the staff's duties was to "develop educational programs for the larger community."[22] Staff and Center activists regularly gave talks to high school and university classes, women's and other clubs, church groups, and the like.

The second component of the Center's program was feminist therapy. Consciousness-raising groups had been casualties in the conflict with DWL. The Center did hold at least five meetings between 1975 and 1977 to help set up groups, but they were different in nature. The groups "offer personal support for women going through changes and developing self awareness," the Center newsletter announced, as well as being great places to make friends.[23] This form of CR, emptied of its activist content and structural function, resembled Lisa Maria Hogeland's "soft CR"; most of these groups struck out on their own and lost touch with the Center.

The deemphasis on CR resulted in a fertile terrain for the development of feminist therapy. There was tremendous response to individual and group counseling and to classes such as those on anger and creative awareness and the "gestalt dream workshop." Therapy helped "women going through or recovering from divorce, mothers whose frustrations have the potential of escalating to the point of causing them to abandon or abuse their children, rape and assault victims (including women who were molested as children), and lesbians trying to function within a society which rejects their life-styles." In addition, "non-crisis" women's counseling groups "encouraged many women to explore their own psychological responses to the people and the world around them in order to become healthier and more fully aware human beings."[24] For many years, the Center was the only Dayton institution to offer feminist therapy.

Initially Fisher, Holmes, Suits, and Maddi Breslin ran the counseling activity. Local feminist therapists subsequently were invited to work out of the Center. Suits helped organize the feminist therapy collective in 1976 for present and future therapists to share experiences, support each other, and contribute to ongoing reflection. These women, according to Suits, were "trying to figure out ways to make what they were doing meaningful, and answer the question: 'How do I make other women be stronger.'" The collective, which lasted about eighteen months, included Suits, two other NAM women, Fisher, Breslin, a lesbian-feminist thera-pist who was a professor at a local college, an "Old Left Quaker" psy-chologist who was working on a Ph.D., a Freudian from a radical family, and Maggie Reck.

Reck was in her early thirties and the mother of an infant daughter at the time of the Center's opening. She realized that "the same discrimi-nation that exists across the board was rampant in therapy," but she dis-trusted feminists "because of their bad rep as crazies. . . . I was having enough trouble with being a crazy in my own right. . . : too aggressive, too strong, too independent." Reck joined the Center to work there as a counselor. Through discussions with the staff, she recalled, "I started getting the idea that maybe my ideas weren't so weird after all. . . . They helped me to see that these were political issues, and . . . so my political awareness began to grow and blossom in that environment." She went on to facilitate classes and join the Center collective and later became the Victimization Project's first "staff feminist."

Therapists with university connections sent students to do practicums at the Center. One remembered, "They grilled me: . . . How do you feel about lesbianism? What do you feel about abortion?—because some of those topics related to women's bodies and sex were going to come up in the groups. . . . [T]hey were trying to get to know me, because they didn't want me involved in the organization if I was antifeminist."

The Center charged according to a sliding scale, a common practice. However, contrary to other institutions, there was no screening system. Women could, and usually did, claim that they couldn't pay. The Center began serving Dayton's poorest clients: mainstream institutions dumped their undesirables on the alternative institution.

The third and perhaps the most important function of the Center was doing referrals. Such requests accounted for between a quarter and a half of the ten to twenty-five daily calls. A steady stream of queries came in on abortion, birth control, job reentry, divorce, and child custody. Calls paralleled national trends, as the women's movement named and defined women's problems and made them visible for the first time. Thus, the logs showed an increase in calls related to rape around 1976, to battering in 1977, and to sexual harassment in 1978–79. Perhaps the most striking change was the multiplication of "horror stories" over time. In addition to rape, battering, and incest came economic problems: women who needed jobs, housing, money for heating bills, and even food for their children. There also was a small increase in requests for aid in personal advancement.[25]

Staff and volunteers had considerable knowledge to help them respond to these queries. Some had had connections to the late-sixties Community Switchboard. Others had experience from DWL, notably on birth control and abortion. Many activists worked in the social services and in health care.

Staff members filled the file cabinets with information and stocked the library with directories and self-help books such as *Our Bodies, Ourselves,* which the Center sold along with other feminist literature. Members investigated the quality of services. "When a woman asks for a referral," volunteers were instructed, "[t]ell her that none of the people we refer her to have perfect records, some are friendly, non-sexist, and thorough, but regrettably most only meet one or two of these criteria." Callers seeking an attorney for a divorce case might be informed that a particular person "will handle divorces for women who have no money (by getting the fee from the husband), has done good work with lesbians, and seems to be sharp and friendly," or "although she is not enthusiastic about dissolution, she is the best lawyer we know for women who need a fighter on their side."[26] Center utilizers filled out evaluation forms each time they consulted a local lawyer, therapist, or gynecologist, and these dossiers were open for consultation. The Center conducted surveys, such as on area day-care centers (fees charged; racial composition, training, and sex of staff; racial mixture of the children).[27] Another survey focused on physicians' breast cancer procedures; it reported that in the Dayton area, "[the patient] has little or no alternatives to the doctor deciding, *while she is still under anesthetic,* whether or not to remove her breast."[28] Callers were referred to clinics in other cities.

This expertise allowed the Center to produce a women's service directory in 1975. The fifty-three-page booklet was packed with practical advice on discrimination, health care, educational opportunities, legal services, counseling, child care, rape prevention, welfare and emergency services, consumer rights, and women's organizations.[29] Prefaces to each section provided a feminist framework. The directory sold for a dollar and was financed by advertisements ranging from those for radical community projects to one claiming that "the confident woman driver today is a AAA member!"[30] The use of advertising marked a change in the movement—all the more so in the directory's second edition in 1977, when the printing bill was paid by the Playboy Foundation. Accepting Playboy money caused surprisingly little debate, and although the foundation was supposed to be credited in the directory, its name is nowhere to be found.[31]

The Center also sponsored special events—conferences, fairs, and socials—to build community, do outreach, and raise funds. Contrary to the all-women's DWL events, men were encouraged to attend. The first potluck dinners and open houses gave way to more elaborate and professional events.

The first was the Women's Equality Day Festival, held in downtown Dayton on August 26, 1975, the fifty-fifth anniversary of the ratification of the women's suffrage amendment and five years after DWL's first major public event. It included a speaker from national NOW, skits by a women's theater group, readings of nonsexist children's stories, and booths for feminist organizations from the area. The festival became an annual event and, as with most Center productions, attracted sympathetic media coverage that increased the Center's visibility.

The Center's annual birthday party, delayed slightly to correspond to Susan B. Anthony's birth date, became another ritual event. The first, with entertainment and dancing, drew some two hundred people. A panel granted Susan B. Awards for fighting sexism. The first ones went to the Fair River Oaks Area Priority Council for funding the Center, a task force of Fairborn NOW, a woman on the Ohio Civil Rights Commission, a group of ten striking nurses, and the Center's own rape prevention group.[32] The second category of awards, the Porky Awards for "those who cling to chauvinism (a social disease of the past)," went to a city commissioner who laughed at the idea of Model City funding for the Center, two establishments that refused to grant credit to women, clubs and bars with male-only policies, and a state auditor who blocked funds for abortions. With provocative good humor, these social events provided the extended feminist and cosexual radical community with binding, commitment-building alternative rituals.

In the summer of 1975, Center staff and collective members co-organized the national Socialist Feminist Conference in neighboring Yellow Springs. Although not a Center-sponsored event, the conference deserves mention here because of its historical significance and because of the role Center activists played. Suits, for example, while on the Center staff, spent several months working almost full time on preparations for the conference.

The idea for the conference originated in the Dayton NAM women's caucus, and given the overlap in membership, the Center was drawn into the process. Several Daytonians drafted a proposal that was presented at the national NAM convention in the summer of 1974. The convention approved the idea, allocated about five hundred dollars in seed money, and delegated the Dayton group to organize a national steering committee.[33] Nine organizations participated: Berkeley-Oakland Women's Union, Chicago Women's Liberation Union, New York City Women's Union, Twin Cities Women's Union (Minneapolis, St. Paul), Valley Women's Union (Northampton, Massachusetts), Boston Socialist/Feminist Women's Organization, Lexington (Kentucky) Socialist/Feminist Union, Radical Women (Seattle), and the NAM women's caucus (with one vote shared between Dayton and the Chapel Hill Charlotte Perkins Gilman all-women's NAM chapter). Antioch College was chosen as the site, and Dayton coordinated the event.

The conference was intended to discuss theory, strategy, and current practices of socialist feminism and to establish communications networks for the future. The steering committee spelled out the following "points of unity"—largely to head off sectarian groups:

1. We recognize the need for and support the existence of the autonomous women's movement throughout the revolutionary process;

2. We agree that all oppression, whether based on race, class, sex or lesbianism, is inter-related and the fights for liberation from oppression must be simultaneous and cooperative; and

3. We agree that socialist feminism is a strategy for revolution.[34]

The conference stirred up tremendous interest. Organizers initially expected three hundred participants, but between 2,000 and 2,500 people preregistered, and organizers had to reject all but fifteen hundred. In the end, sixteen hundred women[35] participated in the conference over the three-day July 4th weekend. Around thirty-five attended from Dayton, including women from the socialist feminist group, the Women's Center, and DWL. Daytonian Julia Reichert delivered one of the welcoming speeches. Sherry Novick facilitated a workshop on socialist women in radio, and Roberta Fisher headed one on "revolutionary relationships."[36] Panel topics included theory, economy, third world women, lesbianism, workplace organizing, community organizing, and building the socialist feminist movement.

The conference was "like a hundred different conferences happening at the same time," Tuss recalled. "It was exhilarating; it was wonderful; it was terrible."[37] Daytonians were enthusiastic about having participated in a meeting of so many women and learning about diverse experiences from around the country. Communications networks and several new organizations were created in the aftermath.[38] Although the conference drained energy from Women's Center activities, Dayton organizers believed that it generated interest in socialist feminism and increased women's political consciousness.

The diversity of the assembly created problems. Organizers had encouraged the participation of all women "interested in" socialist feminism. "We were trying to develop a theory of socialist feminism," Tuss remembered, "but we invited this ridiculous conglomeration who couldn't possibly have agreed on theory." Despite the points of unity, vocal opponents to the autonomous women's movement attended, many from ultra-left parties, according to Novick. The conference offered them a platform and increased their impact on the movement. These and other divisions at the conference weakened many socialist feminist groups. One Berkeley socialist feminist wrote that the conference resulted in "a growing confusion rather than clarity and unity about what socialist-feminism is."[39] By 1977, all of the groups that had made up the steering committee had folded.[40]

The divisions and sectarianism found little echo in Dayton. If anything, the conference made Daytonians more timorous. Novick pointed out: "In a way, we moved to the right after that conference. . . . Our goal was to bring in people from the feminist movement and help make them into socialists and help build the socialist feminist movement. . . . But what happened nationally, overall, was that it was a forum for the farther Left to go about its self-destructive behavior. . . . I think it led us, in Dayton, to be a lot more careful about when and how we used the word 'socialist' . . . because the reality is that when you identify yourself as Left, you are more interesting to sectarian groups . . . than you are to people in the middle."

The Socialist Feminist Conference accelerated a shift that was already in motion in Dayton. DWL's demise had left the women's movement with no structural channel for political action, although, because socialist feminists had other outlets for their activism (such as NAM's community organizing projects[41]), they did not immediately realize this. Many Center activists feared that taking political stances would endanger their tax-exempt status—a must for donations and public subsidies. Ellison remembered, "We wanted to be a little more conservative. We felt the Women's Center should be more a social service agency, and that if we were going to do political things we should do them under another guise . . . so that we could get funding for the Women's Center without being saddled with the political part." Others believed that the radical image of the Center alienated some women and institutions.

This was the rationale for creating a chapter of the National Organization for Women in early 1975. For the second time in the history of the Dayton movement, it was women's liberationists who attempted to create the elusive other branch of the movement. NOW's slogan—"Now that your consciousness has been raised, are you ready for a little action?"—was diametrically opposed to the DWL conception of praxis and fit far better at the Center.

The precipitating event occurred when Sherrie Holmes became the first of several Daytonians to attend the Chicago Midwest Academy's organizing school. The Midwest Academy, founded by Heather Booth of Chicago Women's Liberation Union, taught organizing methods adapted from those of Saul Alinsky, a successful community organizer in the 1930s. Alinsky had been rehabilitated by the latter-day New Left, NAM in particular, in the early 1970s. As one historian wrote: "Alinsky's basic premise was that the residents of a community needed to inform and educate themselves as they created their own local action institutions. Participation would create, and continued participation would reinforce, faith in the residents' ability to solve problems." In the process, they would discover the limits of their community's power to shape its destiny, and they would learn to identify "those major destructive forces which pervade the entire social order." Once a local organization existed, it could become "a springboard for the development of other People's Organizations throughout the nation."[42]

The two-week training period deeply affected Holmes, who embraced the methods wholeheartedly. "I felt like I started understanding . . . the importance of organizing people more where they're at," she said. This training session coincided with the DWL-Center split. Holmes found the apparent efficiency and clarity of the Midwest Academy's organizing principles a welcome change to the unending meetings on process and the idea that experimentation was more important than stability. "It was the first time that I had gone through classes that considered it a goal to have a productive meeting . . . and had this whole approach towards organizing that [it] wasn't a mystery, [that] there are these steps on how you do it," she said.[43]

Another tenet of the academy's philosophy was that an organizer's role was to identify and cultivate potential leaders. Targeting individuals for leadership positions represented a dramatic departure from previous collectivist ethics of nonspecialization of tasks and the spreading out of leadership, sacrificing efficiency when necessary.

At the academy, Holmes met activists from around the country, including NOW members. She attended a convention of Chicago Women Employed, an organization cofounded by a member of Chicago Women's Liberation Union and NAM. There, she met activists from Boston's 9 to 5. "Working women's" groups such as Women Employed and 9 to 5 focused on organizing clerical workers, had been created in several cities and were beginning to reach the critical mass of a national movement. Holmes was an instant convert: "I had been really trying to figure out the most effective way that women could organize to influence any change . . . and I started to think about really organizing women around their jobs—and most women are in office jobs." On her return to Dayton, Holmes raised the issue with the Dayton socialist feminist group. To kill two birds with one stone, the group decided to create a NOW chapter and within it, a task force on working women.[44] This task force later metamorphosed into the group that eclipsed the Center.

"We knew socialist women were organizing NOW chapters," Suits pointed out. "I liked the mass politics. . . . I liked the fact that NOW had a national name. It attracted women without being threatening." Novick remembered it as part of a national socialist feminist and NAM strategy, "part of the factions of NAM that wanted to put NAM people in the mainstream."[45] Socialist feminists also hoped that the national dimension of NOW would add clout to their actions locally.

The first public meeting of the new NOW chapter was held at the Center and was a tremendous success, with some forty to sixty persons in attendance. However, when the dust settled, leaving an actual group of paid, active members, only socialist feminists and Center activists remained. Few other women joined, and they were members in name and money only.[46]

The new chapter immediately set up task forces: one on employment, one on rape, a credit task force, and an education task force. The success of the latter two groups rested on the dedication of two individuals.

The credit task force was Pat Russell-Campbell's baby. Russell-Campbell had worked in a credit bureau where observing discriminatory treatment of women had raised her consciousness. Single women were often denied credit cards and loans. Married women's credit was commonly in their husbands' names, and their salaries were not considered secure enough to be taken into account for loans. Upon divorce women lost their credit rating.[47] The previous year, the Equal Credit Opportunity Act had outlawed discrimination on the basis of sex or marital status in credit transactions, but many companies were resisting the change.

As information about the credit task force spread, women called with complaints. "I was a good resource person . . . because I knew the workings of a credit bureau inside and out," Russell-Campbell said. "I would call up the store and say, 'I'm NOW chairperson for the credit task force, and I hear that you are doing unfair credit practices . . . and you could be up for charges. . . .' [T]hey usually fell all over themselves, because at that time suits were happening and the women's movement was finally getting some recognition."

Russell-Campbell later contributed to statewide changes in credit laws. Since federal law did not cover all local businesses, she helped a legislator's assistant write an Ohio bill to fill the gaps. In the name of NOW, she attended the public hearings at the state capitol, arguing in favor of reform using the numerous concrete examples she had collected in the task force.

Roberta Fisher coordinated the new NOW education task force. Like many others, she had been a paid member of national NOW for years but had no contact with other Dayton members. She had worked for equality in the educational system, specifically for equal opportunity in girls' sports. Before her arrival at the Center, she coached girls' soccer to encourage girls to become physically strong.

Fisher rapidly unearthed inequalities in the school system. In her suburban community of Centerville, the school board allotted nearly ten times more money for boys' coaches than for girls' coaches. Ticket sales funded athletic equipment, but no admission fees were charged for girls' sports.[48]

In the fall of 1974, Fisher, with her characteristic passion, confronted the school board. When the members refused to budge on the matter of funding, she declared to the press, "I am going to dog the Centerville school board on this matter until the budget for 1975–1976 is prepared next spring. . . . If they don't allot equal funding for young men and women at that time, I am going to make a court issue out of it."[49]

With the birth of the new NOW chapter, Fisher was ready for action. NOW offered her a structure in which to fit her work and the name of a national organization to back her up. In addition, she and other antidiscrimination crusaders were waiting to add another weapon to their arsenal: guidelines for implementation of Title IX of the education amendments of 1972 that were to go into effect on July 21, 1975. Title IX states, "No person in the United States shall, on the basis of sex, be

excluded from participation in, be denied the benefits of, or be subjected to discrimination under any education program or activity receiving
Federal financial assistance."⁵⁰ It provided a valuable tool in the fight for
equality in hiring and admissions practices, and it covered all public and
most postsecondary institutions. However, as Fisher declared to the
press, the guidelines sold women's rights down the river as far as girls'
sports were concerned: they required "equal athletic opportunity for
both sexes" but not equal funding.⁵¹

Fisher, backed by Maddi Breslin, went to bat for Title IX enforcement
on behalf of the NOW education task force. Joining them were teachers
from the public school system, some of whom had filed individual
employment discrimination complaints, and a woman who had filed sex
discrimination charges over her daughter's treatment in kindergarten.

Among Title IX obligations was the requirement that within one year
following the effective date, all recipients of federal aid carry out a self-
evaluation and make necessary changes.⁵² The education task force continued haranguing the school systems. By 1976, Centerville schools had
complied, but Dayton's hadn't.⁵³ Dayton Public Schools' noncompliance
did not stem from lack of information: a women's rights committee,
established under liberal superintendent Wayne Carle, had existed for
more than a year and had published two reports on sexism in Dayton
schools, complete with recommendations for improvement. By the effective date for Title IX, Carle had been ousted by the right-wing majority
on the school board and replaced by John Maxwell, who immediately
disbanded the committee. Breslin reported that "a local superintendent"
stated publicly, "We wouldn't be doing any of this Title IX crap if the
federal government wasn't making us."⁵⁴

In November 1976, the task force submitted a dossier on illegal discriminatory practices in the school system, including individual cases and
systemic charges. Under steady pressure from Fisher, the Department of
Health, Education, and Welfare began investigations of the Dayton Public Schools in early 1977, citing the complaint filed by Dayton NOW.⁵⁵
Local media coverage was copious, including an investigatory series on
discrimination in local schools with interviews with Fisher.⁵⁶ The school
system was ordered to fill out forms certifying nondiscrimination or risk
losing its $10.7 million in federal funds, 13 percent of its budget.⁵⁷ In the
midst of negotiations, the assistant superintendent declared, "If it were up
to me, boys and girls would go to different schools. Schools are female-
oriented. You take a boy as rough and tough as the devil and then you
restrict him in a comatose, female oriented environment."⁵⁸

Officials' tunes changed in July 1977, when HEW announced that it was withholding $3 million in escrow from the Dayton Public Schools because it was unable to find adequate information showing nondiscrimination according to sex and race. On September 5, 1978, Maxwell was informed that the complaint filed by Roberta Fisher was deemed founded: Dayton schools were in violation of Title IX.[59] As a result, the Dayton school system was forced to make all classes coeducational, including home economics, industrial arts, and physical education. It hired new coaches and opened new sports to girls. Bias-free achievement tests were purchased, and workshops on sex stereotyping were conducted for school counselors.[60] The saga initiated by Fisher and the NOW task force resulted in concrete changes and demonstrated how constant pressure from a social movement organization could translate law into practice.[61]

The most successful of NOW's task forces was the one for clerical workers. For some socialist feminists, this task force had been the raison d'être for the new NOW chapter. Sherrie Holmes was its main mover, joined by another NAM member and Kathy Ellison.

Within several months, the group had taken its independence from NOW. In April 1975 it adopted a new name, Dayton Women Working. From then on, although it was still theoretically a part of NOW, all mention of the mother organization was avoided, and the split was later formalized when the group began meeting at the YWCA. Dayton Women Working was to become so important to the Dayton movement that it rivaled the Women's Center as the pole for feminist activity in the city.

Holmes's perception that the employment issue could mobilize Dayton women was thus shown to be accurate, and her ability to organize was proven beyond a doubt. Ellison said: "She wasn't one of those leaders who everything that came out was her best effort. . . . She'd make other people do it; that was her amazing quality. . . . Nobody else had that skill of envisioning a project. And she was almost always right, in terms of picking something that would sell. She had real good marketing instincts—what would be the right thing to do now, to get media attention . . . and then she would get people, people who could do things she couldn't do." This ability made Holmes the most controversial figure in the movement, detested and accused of manipulation by some and adored by others who credit her for having drawn out their best abilities.

Holmes made the decision to separate from NOW, both to target a single issue and to clear it of its feminist connotations. By 1976 she had transferred most of her energy into Dayton Women Working. Some Center activists bitterly concluded that the group had abandoned NOW and even had used it for strategic purposes. Holmes saw these criticisms as a cross between sour grapes and purism: "It was like the thing was working and growing and being successful, then the parent organization started being critical and . . . thought we should be right out there with all the issues: abortion, lesbian rights. . . . And that somehow, by us just talking about job rights, that we were perhaps somehow misleading people and also being wrong because we should stand strong for all of them."

Beyond the task forces, NOW had little life of its own. The chapter initiated a few scattered actions, such as protesting a policy forbidding women to play pool in a local bar in November 1975,[62] and organizing a group to go to an ERA rally in Illinois the following May. General meetings were held for a couple of years, and a handful of Daytonians became active at a state and national level.

However, a new branch of the movement was not created, nor were new women drawn into the movement. Ellison summed it up well: "If our ideal was to have a place where women who didn't like the Women's Center would go, we hadn't done that because it was the same people. If they didn't like us when we called ourselves the Women's Center, they would hardly like us when we called ourselves NOW. NOW was difficult to distinguish from the Women's Center and the socialist feminist group. As Russell-Campbell recalls, "Sometimes, you'd walk in, . . . and think, 'Hey, what day is this? What meeting is this supposed to be?'"

Not only did the elusive liberal branch again fail to materialize, but organizers did not create a radically different NOW. Robin Suits had been a partisan of "moving NOW to the Left." "Why organize the fucking thing if it was going to be like every other NOW chapter in the country?" she said. "I wanted us to be real open about the fact that we were socialists, and we did have educational meetings where we'd describe socialist feminism and stuff. But Sherrie [Holmes] was really moving away from all that—not even wanting to reveal that." Holmes was disappointed at how the NOW chapter had developed: "I don't think we totally realized how much its national image really would shape our local effort. . . . I ended up feeling like it was a mistake to have thought we could . . . have our own type of NOW chapter." Sherry Novick, who was pleased with what the task forces had accomplished, pointed out that they "were successful in the sense of what NOW is good at, which is making reforms." Barbara Tuss, on the other hand, felt vindicated. She had opposed the project, arguing that "we weren't working out of our own position in society, our own needs, our own circumstances," but rather, "we were working out of an idea about what we wanted to see happen, or a theory about what needed to be done." Another "feminist double standard" can be discerned: members of the Center's activist core credited the movement's emphasis on personal politics as having been essential for themselves, but believed traditional politics was more appropriate for the other women they were trying to reach.

A recent arrival from Columbus and a long-time officer in national NOW, was surprised at what she discovered in Dayton. "Generally, it's a group like Dayton Women's Liberation or the Women's Center who cuts the wake, and there are other groups who come along in the wake," she said. "And each group that successively follows is a little more socially acceptable. . . . [T]his sort of natural bridge develops, and then pretty soon you have women in the League of Women Voters and other places involved in feminist activities. But [in Dayton] . . . there was this sort of more avant-garde group and then nothing followed in behind. They were just out there cutting the wake and NOW wasn't there."[63]

Thus, it was liberationists who over the years filled the role of creating and sustaining a liberal and reform-oriented strand of the Dayton movement.[64] They did this with some success, as demonstrated by the changes effected by the task forces. However, in doing so, they also contributed to a shift in orientation of the Dayton women's liberation movement. Equality—a bad word for DWL—became a major preoccupation for Center activists. DWL saw politics as extending into personal life, surpassing the realm of government, laws, and elections to such an extent that it tended to disdain legal action and reform. The Center's implicit definition of politics accepted a separation of the public (albeit a broadened view of the public) and the private domains. Many informants from later periods of the movement assumed that questions pertaining to politics referred to electoral politics. This more traditional concept—based on the hard data of laws, policy, and so on, with more clear-cut, measurable results—indicates a narrowing perspective in the women's movement. While DWL somewhat sloppily saw politics everywhere, for the Center, politics represented deliberate, separable actions. And as one socialist feminist contended, the Center no longer needed to engage in political action once it had NOW.[65]

After an initial honeymoon period, the apparent shared vision for the Women's Center began to weaken. Tensions surfaced among the staff throughout 1975, particularly between Holmes and Suits. Many observers attributed this to a personal conflict: Holmes had become involved with Suit's ex-lover. Others saw it as a power struggle. Holmes, previously seen as Suits's political apprentice, had become one of Dayton's most successful feminist organizers. But against the backdrop of complex personal relations, the clash between the two women also was political, with consequences for the movement as Center activists allied with one or the other.

While Holmes had drawn closer to NAM, Suits was moving away from the organization. She had always sensed tensions between her role in the women's movement and in a cosexual organization, but she had reconciled this through the socialist feminist group and its efforts to get NAM support for feminist issues. However, when men in NAM embraced their sisters' work too enthusiastically, it seemed to Suits that they were claiming credit for it. After the Socialist Feminist Conference, Suits began to invest her energy in feminist therapy. By June 1976, she had dropped out of NAM.

Suits disliked the tangent taken by Holmes. She was reticent about Alinsky-style organizing, and she disagreed with Holmes's separating of work issues from other feminist issues. Finally, she believed that Holmes's primary allegiance had shifted to Dayton Women Working. "What she did was bring in a lot of women who would have been dynamite for the women's movement, but she didn't even try to encourage them to join the Women's Center collective," Suits said. Holmes feared that linking Dayton Women Working to other feminist issues might exclude a potential constituency. Furthermore, as a very pragmatic person, she sensed that the Center was on the wane, while Dayton Women Working was gaining momentum.

Parallel to the conflicts among the staff, the distance between the staff and the Center collective was widening a classic situation for students of alternative institutions. While at first Suits and Holmes had been responsible for setting up the collective (and "organizing their bosses"), the group had rapidly gained experience and become its own entity.

The two bodies intervened in clearly different spheres. The staff was responsible for daily operations, which involved a tremendous amount of work, but with it came pay (albeit minimal) and the gratification of coming into contact with participants and of seeing projects realized.

Being in the collective required a considerable investment of energy. The group met in the evenings and included many women who could not spend time at the Center during the days; they were thus less familiar with the vital functions of the Center.

The collective supposedly made policy decisions for the staff to implement. But the atmosphere of the movement did not lend itself to a employer-employee relationship. When the collective asserted its power and criticized the staff, the staff retorted that collective members were not sufficiently involved in operations and that their expectations were excessive. "The collective created the seeds of its own destruction," Ellison said. "By hiring staff, it removed itself from the day-to-day work and placed itself in a position to criticize."

These inevitable tensions grew as the thankless work for survival occupied more time. The need for fund-raising grew to such proportions that it dominated all the collective meetings. Beyond the brief time for "criticism-self-criticism," there was little space for discussion of the mounting problems. This took place only in friendship and parallel networks, which exacerbated tensions rather than defusing them.

Differences appeared around one wildly successful project, the parents' day-care cooperative. This cooperative, founded by a socialist feminist, was having housing problems. Holmes proposed that it move to the Center, which would help pay the rent, bring in new women, and counter what she saw as people being "judgmental of women in traditional roles."

The proposal was greeted favorably at a collective meeting in late 1975, although no decision was recorded.[66] Ellison, for one, remembered the situation as being temporary, but others recalled it as long term. Tuss saw this as typical of Center process: "Even though we would set up methods for decision-making, those methods were always circumvented at various points in time. And it didn't seem like a bad thing when it happened, but at some point further down the road, something would come up, and you'd say, 'Oh, wait a minute! Who made that decision?'"

The day-care cooperative was one of the most dynamic activities housed at the Center. The workers cared for an interracial group of children in an educational setting with activities ranging from field trips to antisexist storytelling. However, it was also the noisiest of the Center's programs, and it rapidly antagonized Suits, whose main interest was feminist therapy and self-awareness groups. "Women would come there to get away from their woes, and there would be thirty screaming kids on the other side of the door. When someone would do counseling, they'd actually go into the room where the babies were sleeping, and the woman would have to talk softly." Holmes's role in the decision further embittered Suits.

Other Center members were divided along personal rather than political lines. Ellison, who was notorious for having made antichildren statements (something about boiling them in oil), was not favorable to the cooperative. In reaction to Ellison's excessive positions, Novick, on the other hand, supported it. She and Hart believed that because few of them were mothers, it was pleasurable to be exposed to children. Tuss, a collective member and volunteer, was opposed because "people treated the Women's Center like their own private space," and because she felt the collective had been placed before a fait accompli.

The cooperative grew during the first half of 1976. In late summer, Roberta Fisher returned to the Women's Center staff after a temporary leave to work on other projects. She had grown suspicious of NAM. Through her counseling, she had adopted a pro-woman line, believing that the essential goal of the Center was to bring women together and provide a women's space. "I was dreaming impossible dreams: women's retreats . . . no kids, no men, a place." Upon her return, she felt that the Center had been invaded. "What we would hear from women traveling around the country was that usually in women's centers, gay women would take over. I'd say, 'Great! Come on in! That's women, but not kids, for God's sake!'" As a mother of five, Fisher saw the Center as a refuge, whereas the younger generation of feminists was only just starting to think about having children. As another woman confirmed in a letter to the collective: "Women of my age—40 and up—have mentioned that the Women's Center is not for them—for a number of reasons, including their own hang-ups. . . . Add a covey of kids to the scene, and those of us who have been through that will probably flee to other environs."[67] In late 1976, the day-care cooperative moved to a building next door. Fisher energetically painted over the children's drawings, but the tensions weren't so easily erased.

Simultaneously, another disagreement was brewing. Holmes announced in late 1975 that the Center could finance another staff position through a Department of Labor job training program, CETA. She already had a candidate, Barbara Scalia, a mother of four whose husband was unemployed. The proposal was adopted unanimously, even before others had met Scalia. According to Suits, Holmes railroaded the collective so she could maintain influence even though she was phasing out Center activities.[68]

When a no-fault divorce law passed in Ohio, some Center activists, in search of more militant actions, decided to create a do-it-yourself divorce kit. In the summer of 1976, Scalia and others created a packet of materials and began counseling. Almost immediately, the Dayton Bar Association declared publicly that the Center was guilty of unauthorized practice of law. Center members consulted their lawyer, who advised them that although highly unlikely, it was possible that Scalia could be convicted and even sentenced to prison.[69] Scalia and Holmes wanted to abandon the project. Ellison, on her way to becoming a lawyer, was interested in the potential test case. Suits, who was fiercely in favor of continuing, saw this as a perfect opportunity to instigate militant action, and she was prepared to do the counseling herself and face the consequences. Holmes maintained her opposition on the grounds that Scalia might still be prosecuted.

The project was dropped, and Scalia left the staff for another job shortly thereafter, but the incident left Suits embittered. "I wanted to do something political, and Sherrie wanted to keep away from anything controversial because of her involvement with DWW. . . . I felt I was working for the welfare department or the YWCA." It was into this conflict-ridden atmosphere that Donna Crawl, the first black woman to become a truly active member of the Center, was hired on staff.

At an August 1976 discussion on the decrease in activism at the Center, the Women's Center collective began brainstorming possible ideas for action. Each new idea, however, ran up against the problem of the homogeneous, white, middle-class composition of the Center's activist core. The collective decided that NOW should try to contact black women's organizations. Shortly thereafter, Scalia left, opening a CETA slot. Fisher, who claimed Holmes wanted to hire a man for day care, moved to head her off. Tired of talk about getting black women involved, Fisher telephoned black women whom she knew from her civil rights activism and her NOW antidiscrimination work. "I would just call up and say, 'Do you know any young black women who you think would like working at the Women's Center?'" she recalled. She found several candidates. In October 1976, the collective interviewed and chose Donna Crawl.

When a neighbor told Crawl about the Center opening, she was ripe for feminism. Unemployed at the time, she had just been fired from a job that had opened her eyes to sexism. When she had started the job—as the only female employee in an insurance agency—a Black Muslim colleague warned her that her predecessor had been harassed into sexual relationships. Crawl was subject to similar pressures. She recalled: "I started looking at the world a little differently," realizing that "women were probably treated like this all the time. Where had I been?" On the other hand, the lot of the Black Muslim women did not appeal to her: "They didn't have a voice. . . . I wanted to speak out for myself."

Crawl, twenty-three at the time, was the oldest daughter of a beautician and a civil servant at the Air Force base. Her parents had moved to Dayton from Georgia after World War II, seeking opportunities like many others from the South and Appalachia. "Everyone I know came from somewhere in the South," she said. Crawl was a native Daytonian, but "when you have a southern family, that's always considered your home."

Crawl was an outspoken youth. Her parents, like many others in the sixties, reacted with ambivalence. "My parents brought us up to always speak our mind . . . but they always put little stops: 'Don't talk too much.'" Her mother had always worked outside the home, but, Crawl said, "she brought us up to believe that women are to be in the kitchen" and above all to be "ladies." When her mother visited her school one day and found Crawl in the hall rather than in class, she had her transferred to a predominantly white, all-girl's Catholic high school (even though the family was Presbyterian). Crawl did not regret the experience: "Until then, I was living behind a fence in my backyard. I thought the whole world was nice . . . and that I was going have a knight in shining armor come." Her new school "woke [her] up to the real world" through experiences such as having a locker next to a white girl who for three years refused to speak to her.

As the sixties drew to an end, Crawl had come to understand herself "as a black person": she wore her hair in an Afro and became active in the civil rights movement. She had to hide her radical activities from her parents, who thought she was becoming "too black" and that she should "slow down." After years in a white environment, Crawl chose to go to an all-black college in Atlanta in 1970.

After a couple of years in college, Crawl got pregnant and returned to live at home. She spent some time depressed, fighting guilt about her brutal departure from her family's traditional expectations. When she later was fired from the insurance company, the material problems of being a jobless single mother compounded the psychological ones. Ironically, Crawl recalled, "it was the luckiest break I ever had." Through working the system she learned how to take advantage of unemployment and welfare benefits, from free child care and health care to free schooling. She savored that summer, the strength of success, and the time to get her head together. During her civil rights years, Crawl had accepted the idea of fighting for black men first, but she saw how women got stepped on along the way. When she heard of the Center job, she was angry about women's exploitation and knew that she could teach welfare mothers about the system.

Crawl dove in with the energy of a new recruit. In less than two weeks, she was already on the speakers circuit, had announced the creation of CR groups for black women, and had begun seeking out third world women's groups as a part of an outreach program that she had elaborated. After years of discussion in the Dayton women's movement about how to cross racial lines, it seemed that it might finally become reality. At first, Center activists responded enthusiastically.

The consciousness-raising group for black women began rapidly, and Crawl attended not as a facilitator but as a participant. "That was fantastic," she commented. "I was told that you could not get five women to sit down together and talk to each other. The first thing five black women do is criticize each other and then talk about their men." To the contrary, the group was successful and met weekly during the entire time Crawl was on staff.

As Crawl got the word out, through interviews with local newspapers, speaking engagements, and television appearances, other black women contacted the Center. By January 1977, several CR groups for black women existed. Crawl described one: "We had an older woman. We had a woman who was an engineer—she wouldn't sit on the floor with us. She thought she was a lot better than us. Eventually she sat down. . . . There was a woman who was forty-five or fifty, and her husband was an alcoholic, and she'd wanted to leave him for twenty years, and the group supported her enough that she divorced him. . . . We supported each other into school, supported each other off of welfare, supported each other into marriage or out of marriage. And talked about everything but men. . . . My life changed; everybody's lives changed."

Crawl also tried to find other black facilitators, but most women she asked rejected the movement as a white women's struggle. Then she read an article in a local paper about two women who had organized discussions titled "Black Women Moving towards the Twenty-first Century" and invited them to do similar sessions at the Center. One of them, Michele Roberts, was an acquaintance from high school.

Roberts was not unaware of the Dayton women's movement. One of her brothers had been married to a member of Dayton Women's Liberation, but Roberts had never considered it an option for black women. It was while doing public relations and assessments of community needs for a local hospital that she initiated a parents group and started becoming aware of the specific needs of black women. Existing women's clubs, Roberts believed, were for the "haves," not "everyday people." That motivated her and an acquaintance to organize discussion groups for black women at the Center.

Each of the three group facilitators had a list of interested women who had contacted her in the past. In addition, a leaflet was printed and distributed, particularly through churches. The facilitators chose to recruit black women from the area rather than from Dayton's West Side, believing that the local women were more likely to come to the Center. While the neighborhood may have been considered integrated by Center organizers, blacks saw it as all-white. "[It was] probably not your most feared [neighborhood], but it wasn't one that you had the general impression that you were going to be welcomed into," Roberts recalled.

Roberts and her partner thus started another session of discussions. She described the process in terms similar to those of previous feminists. "I think they really enjoyed having that experience. It was probably something that none of them had ever had before: to just sit down with other black women who they really didn't know, and to talk about what they had in common, to talk about some things that were going on with black women in general." While the group "had some therapeutic value," Roberts saw it as a consciousness-raising group. "We made it clear when we would start the group that we were facilitators, that we were not the authorities, that we shared things in common with them."

While Crawl had become a part of the day-to-day life of the Center, Roberts felt she was in borrowed space. She had no contact with other Center members, and even arrangements for the use of the meeting room were, as she termed it, "negotiated" by Crawl. Roberts believed that black women were admitted to the Center but not offered a share of the power. Not once in her memory did a Center activist try to engage her in discussion about either the Center itself or about the work she was doing.

After her first successful experiment with a discussion group, Roberts intended to hold a second session at the Center. Simultaneously, money was drying up, and Roberts was apparently asked if her group was willing to contribute financially. This was standard procedure for classes but not discussion groups: class participants were asked to pay a nominal fee, part of which was given to the facilitators and part to the Center. But Roberts's previous discussion groups had been free of charge, and facilitators were unpaid. She interpreted the request as a rental fee required of an outside group. Since local churches offered her space for free, her group left the Center.

Crawl, on the other hand, loved the Center. Working there represented a period of freedom that allowed her to be herself, perhaps for the first time in her life. She had good relations with the women who came into the Center, and thanks to their mutual support, "I viewed myself and was accepted totally as a woman." In addition, she learned numerous skills, including organizing skills at the Midwest Academy. She continued working on groups for black women, and one of her early creations metamorphosed into the Black Women's Information Exchange, a discussion group that invited speakers from the community. Later, she created a support group for teenage girls, most of whom were pregnant.

Crawl became close friends with the other staff members, Suits and Fisher. Their varied philosophies on feminism converged, and they agreed that the Center should be oriented toward teaching survival skills for women. This shared perspective and personal affinity provided staff cohesiveness, but, in the context, gave Crawl a negative view of the Women's Center collective. This was immediately reinforced: her first two collective meetings were dominated by the heated and final debates on the day-care cooperative and on staff/collective relations. Furthermore, although she had been specifically hired to do outreach, she rapidly discovered that staff responsibilities were far greater, although poorly defined. In early 1977, as tensions peaked, Crawl automatically became the ally of her sister workers.

In an atmosphere of decaying relations, overwork, and insufficient funds, a final incident alienated Roberta Fisher from the Center. The infamous mimeograph machine—apparently "liberated" by a male leftist years before and later donated to DWL—was housed at the Center. To the NAM members who knew the machine's history, it belonged to the cosexual "movement" in the largest sense of the word. NAM was one of the groups that were allowed access to the equipment. On several occasions, the machine was damaged and women's groups were interrupted.

For Fisher, after having evicted children from her "women's space," finding men there was too much. She viewed NAM men and women, responsible for both of these intrusions, as the source of the Center's ills. In January 1977 Fisher resigned from the staff and sent the NAM women's caucus a soon-to-be-infamous letter, with copies to the Women's Center collective and members of NOW. NAM, Fisher wrote, used the Center as a front, cooperating only in order to recruit, and was a negative force in NOW. Going further, she implied that the organization was totalitarian: "I can only imagine what plans you have for those people in the country who do not agree with you." Caucus members, "baffled, then insulted, then frightened," denied Fisher's charges, pointing out that NAM women had been vital to the creation and maintenance of the Center. They made a plea for open debate and feminist unity.[70]

The following meeting was the time to choose sides. Suits called it the "key confrontation between pro- and anti-NAM forces."[71] Tuss, for one, shared some of Suits's criticisms but "didn't want to be in the anticommunist camp." Discussion centered on the relationship between the staff and the Women's Center collective. Several months previously, in an attempt to bridge the gap, a collective member had been chosen by mutual agreement to serve as liaison to the staff. The attempt backfired: the ambiguities between the roles of sister and forewoman were too great. Both the liaison and the staff members were feeling resentful. Suits, near burnout and supported by Crawl, asked the collective to aid, not supervise the staff. They distributed a proposal reminiscent of DWL, stressing, for instance, the need for consensual decision-making and for strengthening the CR component.[72] The meeting ended on a conciliatory note, but the damage was great. Shortly thereafter, Suits left not only the Center but also the women's movement for years to come. Commenting on splits in the movement, Julia Reichert wondered whether feminists' commitments were so integral to their identity, and so passionate, that irrespective of their personal motivations they could sever the ties only through a political split.

Crawl stayed another five months, but with little to sustain her commitment to the Center. Her two friends were gone; the conflict had left a residue of bad feelings; and her most gratifying activities were in black CR groups composed of new women. Furthermore, all along she had been contending with negative pressure from her black entourage. She recalled being dogged by a black male journalist who said she "had no right to follow that white women's movement." She frequently heard contentions that "these women were a front for a male organization, only put here . . . to take the spotlight off the civil rights movement [and to get] all the money." Although she scoffed at these attitudes—attitudes she said disappeared in the following years—they added to her discomfort.

The Women's Center collective did little to improve the situation. Given the Center's financial straits, money had become an essential consideration in all decisions. According to Crawl, her proposed programs to draw in welfare mothers were rejected in favor of more lucrative programs. On one hand, Crawl, who had never done fund-raising, did not understand the constant struggle to pay the bills. On the other, the obsession with finances prevented some Center members from setting political priorities. This was all the more unfortunate because income from classes accounted for only a minute fraction of the budget.

Crawl's feeling of alienation increased. When the collective inquired about the projects she had started, it felt like an interrogation. Similarly, Crawl's relationship with this new coworker was skewed: CETA required Crawl's supervisor to submit regular reports, a mere formality while Suits and Fisher were on staff. However, the requirement took on new meaning—a common dynamic in alternative institutions—after the new staff member assumed the role. At best, it was an awkward situation, mixing bureaucratic stipulations with actual policy and human relations. At worst, it was a traditional attitude of an employer with racist overtones. It became painful for Crawl to go to the Center. "I was put in a bubble," she said. "The only reason the collective wanted me was [because] I was a black face and it looked good when you went to fund-raise." Crawl, who remembered feeling like "a woman first," was reminded that she was a *black* woman.

Crawl could no longer fulfill the high expectations of a hybrid activist-employee situation. She missed several meetings and occasionally closed the Center during office hours. The collective responded as an employer, keeping close tabs on staff for the first time ever and reprimanding Crawl. In September 1977 Crawl left the Center, moving to a job with the Quaker American Friends Service Committee where she could continue her work with pregnant teens. What remained of the black women's groups left with her.

The period of Crawl's involvement was the only one during which black women came to the Center. Crawl was hired in part through a power play and continued to be fit into different strategies. Center activist Maddi Breslin, who later became a friend and coworker of Crawl's, described her as "the fly in the buttermilk." Breslin contended that while racism undoubtedly was involved, the accusation of racism "was a way to drag Donna in and to get her to choose sides."

This story tends to leave one skeptical of the Center activists' contentions that they tried to get black women involved. Most attempts amounted to talking about why black women were not involved or trying to bring them into the Center, rather than trying to understand their needs or to establish cooperative relations with existing groups. When finally presented with an opportunity, little effort was devoted to establishing communications with black feminists. When Crawl took positions in a polarized group, the other side allowed what some saw as the defense of socialism to override the issue of race. However, more damning than white activists' relationship with Crawl was their lack of contact with Roberts and her recruits. Center activists did not make these women feel welcome or encourage any meaningful dialogue.

The short period of black women's involvement with the Center did make several interesting points. It showed that, at least during this time, white activists' antiracist discourse and practices were grossly inadequate. However, it also pointed to the effectiveness of the consciousness-raising group. The black women's groups stressed slightly different issues than others at times, notably a concern with strengthening the family, but the basic method sparked revelatory experiences and led to life changes for the participants. Despite whites' tendency, feminists included, to view black women as an established, coherent group, Roberts's and Crawl's experience confirmed that for them, the issue was overcoming barriers among black women and building sisterhood. In a country where, as Breslin put it, "racism is our national heritage," this sisterhood did not cross race lines. However, given the diminished status of CR groups during this period of the movement, it is not clear that the method was at fault.

These internal conflicts did not entirely disrupt the life of the Center. Some collective members had written off tensions as personal, and the lack of public forums for debate kept the subgroups relatively separate and insulated from the conflicts. Nevertheless, over less than a year the Center had lost three of its four staff members (Holmes had quit the collective to devote herself to Dayton Women Working). With them went knowledge of Center operations, excellent fund-raising skills, and numerous personal contacts. By the end of 1977, several other long-time activists had also phased themselves out, invoking personal reasons.

While the Center's foundation was weakened, little impact was felt in the short term. Most classes in mid-1977 were canceled, but by the fall a wave of new people arrived. These women were ostensibly unaffected by previous conflicts. Although vaguely aware that something had occurred, rather than stir up old problems they remained ignorant by choice. A common pattern in Dayton's movement, this resulted in a lack of understanding of the Center's history: for example, only months after Crawl left, the debate began anew about how to draw in women of color, with no reference to what had just happened. Similarly, each of the successive teachers of the assertiveness classes developed their own, new material. Activists and historians alike bemoan such collective amnesia and its obvious drawbacks. What is rarely noted is that it can also limit the debilitating impact of conflict and allow newcomers to infuse a group with fresh vigor.

Fall 1977 marked a new departure for the Center. The collective, with more than a third of its members new, organized a new session of class-es, and in November, following six months' preparation, the Center held a day-long conference at Wright State University called "The Needs of Women in the Miami Valley." This conference, held one week before the Houston International Women's Year Conference, showed a new empha-sis on a certain kind of coalition-building that seemed to parallel devel-opments in other parts of the country. The Needs of Women conference highlighted changes in the Center's politics. Whereas activists previous-ly had feared that the Center would become a social service agency, now they hoped to assert their position as an important or even the main player in a new coalition of service providers. After having seen Center work co-opted by nonfeminist groups, they hoped to "increas[e] the public visibility of the Center" so that "if action results, we will share the credit" (including by "overcoming the political isolation which has cut the Center off from effective sources of funding").[73]

Under media spotlights, some 150 people listened to a who's who of prominent Dayton women: a county commissioner, the director of the human services department, and officials from Planned Parenthood, the women's services division of the Ohio Bureau of Employment Services, and many other agencies. Reports were given on eight local projects.[74]

Evaluations of the conference were mixed. Contrary to claims made, it did not incite the creation of new groups, although it may have ener-gized preexisting ones. It did, however, lay the groundwork for the Cen-ter to play a crucial role in coalition-building on women's issues, to be fully realized only upon creation of a reproductive rights group. It also, like similar public events, drew new people into the movement.

One such woman was twenty-seven-year-old Leslie Lizak, who had just moved back to the wealthy, all-white suburb of Centerville after eight years in Florida. Lizak came from a "very nuclear" Catholic fam-ily: her mother was a homemaker and her father an engineer at a divi-sion of General Motors. Lizak had left Centerville in 1968 to go to college in Florida. There, she lived with relatives and became involved in their Baptist church. After two years of school, she dropped out and "fell into" drug rehabilitation work.

Something then occurred that changed her life: she fell in love with a woman. Their two-year relationship did not make a feminist of Lizak. Then her lover "freaked out" when her parents discovered their relationship, and she admonished Lizak to get psychiatric help. Instead, Lizak decided to go back to school and got a full scholarship in theology at a conservative Baptist liberal arts college, a school so conservative that its speaker for Women's Equality Week was homophobic, right-wing Anita Bryant.

Lizak tried to get back on the straight and narrow; she even became engaged to a preacher. But she continued having affairs with women and was coming to accept that she was a lesbian. Lizak knew nothing about feminism, but as one of only two female theology majors, she grew angry at the condescending attitudes of her male classmates, some of them already ministers, toward her and women in general. Lizak started reading feminist books such as *Sisterhood Is Powerful*. This was her sole, tenuous link with the movement.

Upon her return to Dayton, Lizak was looking for a supportive women's atmosphere when she went to the Needs of Women conference. "I was real pleased to be there and very excited by what was going on. . . . It was like coming from nothing, being all isolated, and then—all this stuff!" Many things resonated, such as the woman who said, quoting Ntozake Shange, "I found God in myself and I loved her fiercely," and the courage of an older woman who spoke about her experience in a mental institution. Lizak met Center activists who invited her to their meetings. She remembered hesitating for what seemed a long time in that heady period: "I waited a week, and then I went."

Lizak became one of the Center's core activists. She joined the collective, participated in a new theater group, and taught assertiveness classes. She also joined a lesbian group later dubbed Lesbians United. LU held discussion meetings on organizational questions, bisexuality, fantasies, coming-out stories, and so on, and organized social events: coffeehouses, softball games, and barbecues. Some members considered themselves feminists, but as Lizak recalled, "the majority of the women were there to meet other women, to have somebody to talk to, to just be in a space where they were around other lesbians and have a good time." Only Lizak and two other LU members were actively involved in the Women's Center.

In its 1977–78 heyday, LU meetings included some twenty women drawn from a pool of around forty. Most members were in their twenties and thirties, with a few younger and several older women. All but a few were white, although there apparently was a broader range of class origins and educational levels than at the Center. Given the size of the group, it had disproportionately little impact on the Center's orientation. This was partially due to its lack of feminist identity, but probably more to the fact that many of its members were still in the closet. Some apparently were uncomfortable with having heterosexual women know that they were lesbians, which curtailed their ability to make themselves heard. On the other side, straight women found it difficult to keep a discreet, respectful distance without appearing unconcerned.

Another new arrival at this time was Maggie Mescher. Like Lizak, Mescher, born in 1949, was a native Daytonian who had recently moved back to town.

Mescher's parents had come to Dayton from a nearby German Catholic farming community. Her father was a factory worker at a local division of General Motors, and her mother, after working as a domestic, married late and devoted her life to raising her nine children and to the Catholic Church.

Mescher wanted to become a nun until she became disillusioned with her authoritarian convent school. She believed that her religious ideals implied working for social justice, but school officials thought differently, forbidding newspapers and television news in the school. Mescher dropped out, but she remained a practicing Catholic. Trying to "act like a Christian," she recalled, later got her involved in the antiwar movement and in the women's movement—"because you look around and you say, 'Hey, this is not just!'"

Mescher wanted to go to college, and so, throughout her high school years, she worked twenty to thirty hours at a local department store. In the late 1960s she entered the Catholic University of Dayton. Her high school guidance counselor had given her three professional options: nursing, clerical work, or teaching, and she chose the latter. While in college, Mescher became involved in the antiwar movement on campus.

Shortly after graduation, with Dayton schools finally complying with mandatory racial integration, Mescher—who agreed with the policy—found she was the "wrong color to get a job." She worked for several years in Pittsburgh, where she joined a progressive church, started hearing about feminism, and began her long-term activism in a teachers union. Upon her return to Dayton, she joined a statewide union caucus on women's rights. Caucus members quizzed her about the movement in Dayton, and because she wanted new friends, she went to check out the Center. "It was all very odd to me," she recalled. "I guess I expected a more businesslike environment, and it was certainly was more of a home than anything. . . . I started going to the meetings. . . . I would just go and sit . . . and leave right away. I would never talk to anybody. I would just go and find out what was going on." She eventually found her niche. Because she had begun a degree in mental health counseling and needed a place for her student practicum, she joined Lizak in teaching assertiveness classes.

This modest surge in activism—illustrated by the Needs of Women conference, Lesbians United, and Lizak and Mescher's activities—was situated in a new and unfavorable context: movement services were going mainstream. By the late 1970s, many Dayton institutions offered services that ostensibly resembled those previously offered only by the Center. Assertiveness training, for example, had become a business. The Center's first teachers ran for-pay workshops in rented conference rooms as well as classes at the YWCA. Mescher remembered her surprise upon learning that her younger sister, an accounting major, had college classes similar to those she taught at the Center.

The YWCA also had begun offering several classes from the Center's repertoire, such as those on careers and self-defense. The Family Services Association ran women's therapy groups and offered counseling in divorce. Jewish Family Services advertised counseling for single parenting. A local church announced a lifework planning workshop. Local universities offered continuing education programs and courses in women's studies, such as Wright State's "Liberation through Literature" and "Women and Management." As a result, class attendance at the Center dropped until there was no longer a demand. Mescher realized, "It doesn't need to be available on the 'black market,' because it's right up there in the institutions."

Another form of mainstreaming was the creation of marginally feminist or nonfeminist institutions to address issues raised by the women's movement. The two earliest such developments were the Dayton Women's Health Center and the Victim/Witness Division of the Prosecutor's Office.

Two other institutions of a similar nature were founded in the mid-seventies. The Career Development Center, begun in 1976, was a counseling service for displaced homemakers. Its goal was to communicate "available career, volunteer, and educational opportunities to the unemployed, underemployed, and turned off worker who happens to be a woman." The center stressed connecting to existing institutions and exploring "each person's realistic goals for learning and work."[75]

Co-organizer Gail Levin remembered becoming aware of the issue of displaced homemakers while serving on the city commission: women seeking to return to the labor force complained that they could find no "access point." Levin's friend and fellow Junior League member Sallie Collins learned that federal funding was available for such projects. The two women approached the president of Wright State University, who was amenable because the university was facing two discrimination suits by female employees and because the women brought with them the promise of Junior League funding and a slew of volunteers. As Levin put it, "Who's going to say no to you when you bring in the money?" The project was funded with fifty to sixty thousand dollars from CETA for its first nine months and the balance from the Junior League. During one of the center's six years of existence, staff reached twenty-five and its budget nearly six hundred thousand dollars.

Not only did the Career Development Center draw clients away from the Women's Center, it also represented the loss of control over an issue identified and addressed by the Center. More than five months before the Career Development Center concept paper was written, the Women's Center had unsuccessfully applied to the same source for funds for a "women in employment and careers" project after five sessions of their popular "Careers" class. The Center's scope was far wider than that of the Junior League project: it aimed to fight job discrimination and help young women break out of the sexual division of labor. The future project was to be housed in the Center.[76] The project was submitted on February 15, 1975, by the official deadline, and Center members awaited the decision that state officials promised for June. Center activists grew angry and suspicious when they later learned that the competing project had been selected since the application form was dated July 31, well after the deadline.

The Battered Women's Shelter was another initiative offering services similar to some offered by the Women's Center. Sue Gasper, resident director of Dayton's central YWCA, had become aware of the need for a shelter as more and more women using the Y's temporary housing said they were fleeing a violent spouse. In 1976, Gasper called several meetings with representatives of Victim/Witness (where calls from battered women were coming in daily), the Women's Center, and social service organizations. The next summer the Battered Women's Shelter began twenty-four-hour service, with four rooms, a full-time director, twenty volunteers, and thirty-six thousand dollars in funding. Overwhelmed with demand, the shelter expanded to ten rooms and four staff members by 1979, and to a six-figure budget by the early eighties.[77]

Contrary to most parafeminist initiatives, the shelter acknowledged its roots in the feminist movement. "The recent recognition of the battering of women as a major social problem in this country has been stimulated by the women's movement," an official statement began.[78] Feminists were part of the planning process and joined the organization's board and staff. Ironically, this sympathetic attitude did not mean that the shelter took a feminist approach to the problem. Rather than use a self-help model, it opted for a social service approach. Although enthusiastic about her work, Nancy Grigsby, a feminist staff member, pointed out, "There's no political objective. There's a social objective to find housing—which is a real Band-Aid approach to life."[79]

These mainstream services were not identical to those offered at the Women's Center. Victim/Witness avoided issues of gender. The Career Development Center, aimed at helping people who happened to be women, set "realistic goals" within the system. This was compounded by the organizers' class bias: according to Collins, they were unhappy at being forced by CETA requirements to serve low-income clients rather than the upwardly mobile. The Battered Women's Shelter did not deal with root causes of battering or use a self-help approach to counseling. The Women's Center, even when separating issues, always tried to make theoretical and political connections to the women's movement. "When we did those things, we did them, I think, with a little political consciousness," Kathy Ellison declared to the press. "When these things have been picked up [by other organizations], they've always been done with the idea that, 'Oh, I'm not a feminist, I'm just trying to help women who get beat up.' They act like there's no connection between women getting beaten up and any other problems that they have."[80] However, the new sponsors, invariably better known, more respectable, and with more resources at their command, took control of the issues.

Parallel to the diffusion of feminist ideas in mainstream institutions, the politics of the Women's Center were toned down. Caution about taking political stances, at first a strategic concern for financing, was rapidly internalized. "We did more risky things in the beginning," Ellison said. "I think we retreated from controversial things over time." The radical posters on the Center walls were not removed intentionally, but as they grew tattered, they were not replaced. With the successive waves of new women who had no background in other protest movements, the Center, as Ellison said, moved "toward less political views—not toward anything else, just away from politics." By the last years this had become paralyzing, Lizak said. "The Women's Center tried, I think, to be too mainstream. . . . We didn't want to piss off any group because we needed the support of everybody to stay open. . . . We tried to be everything to everybody, to every woman. We were trying . . . to do an effective job—and I'm not sure if any of us ever knew what that was or how to do that."

This depoliticization, compounded by the socialist feminist strategy of using reform, produced a classic liberal egalitarian philosophy. The heady terms "liberation" and "oppression" disappeared from Center vocabulary, replaced by "equality" and "discrimination." Even the word "sexism" started to give way to "chauvinism." Supposedly used as non-threatening synonyms for the previous terms, these words reflected a profound shift in political philosophy and goals. This was illustrated repeatedly in the creation of NOW and its projects, in the occasional inclusion of men in Center functions, and in the traditional structure and forms of action used. If any perspective of "something larger" was provided through the personal convictions and strategies of socialist feminists, the tenuous link was broken when they left. Thus, to observers in the late 1970s, the Center was left with few distinguishable features and few compelling reasons to get involved.

The loss of clientele was only one aspect of the Center's increasing problems. The chronic financial woes had increased over the years. In addition to the loss of class fees and the departure of the best fund-raisers, support from the feminist community was dwindling. At the outset, supporters had pledged more than $400 of the Center's $1,000 to $2,000 monthly operating expenses. In 1975, monthly pledges were approximately $185. This dropped to around $150 in 1976 and to $83 in 1977.[81]

Grants from foundations continued to make up a substantial chunk of operating money, with one small Left foundation and several church groups being the most faithful donors. With the departure of the most skilled proposal writers, this form of income had decreased. But this means of raising money had been double-edged from the start. Grants generally were for seed money, that is, for creating new projects but not for maintaining them. Thus, the Center was constantly seeking new ideas, but when funding was found it meant the added responsibility of a new component without the money for general operations. After the initial Model Cities award, the grants were rarely in the four-figure range, while competing, nonfeminist groups won five- and six-figure grants.

Programs began to be judged by their profitability. The feminist service directory started to be called the "ad book." Despite original contentions that traditional "women's methods" would not be used, the

Center held regular yard sales and gave thought to such projects as collecting trading stamps, running bingo games, raffling an evening out with a male celebrity, and even selling blood. Minutes of meetings systematically recorded income but neglected to mention attendance or content. Collective meetings began to be devoted almost solely to discussion of the budget, demoralizing participants. Tricia Hart remembered meetings as having become "90 percent fund-raising and 10 percent hassles."

In the spring of 1978, the Center could no longer afford the $210 rent for its Main Street home. The search for new space began. The collective wanted a location on a bus line and in an integrated neighborhood, and—the most difficult—one where the lesbian group would be allowed to meet. The YWCA, union halls, and churches were contacted. In October 1978, the Dayton Women's Center moved into a room on the second floor of St. Andrew's Episcopal Church in Dayton View.

The revived Dayton Women's Center lasted for two years, with increasingly slick mailings and public relations efforts, a second Needs of Women conference, art fairs, the regular birthday party festivities, and reduced class listings and referral services. In retrospect, many activists believed that the move marked the beginning of the end.

Because the Center no longer paid one full-time employee, it was not eligible for a matching CETA position. Without an adequate staff, regular hours were never maintained at the new location. The housing was not visible from the street and did not have the homelike atmosphere of the previous location. The space was not the Center's own. The minister of the church was supportive, often lending additional space for meetings. However, he dropped in from time to time, checking that doors were locked and lights were turned off, and his presence, along with rules prohibiting alcohol on the premises, inhibited the lesbian group's social gatherings, and its following dropped by about half.

At the time of the move, the Center was no longer the only feminist group in town. Dayton Women Working, born of the Center's NOW chapter, had become a new pole for the movement. While Sherrie Holmes was the only Center activist to have transferred her energy to the new organization, many other new women had been recruited, via the Center, directly into DWW. In early 1978, the Center was also instrumental in starting a new abortion rights coalition, and a large number of dedicated Center activists became involved. By 1978, the Center was no longer the driving force in the Dayton movement.

The political zeitgeist was part of the problem. On one hand, many people were proclaiming that the women's movement had outlived its usefulness; on the other, the New Right had begun its frontal attack on feminism. To aggravate matters, as the country's economic situation deteriorated the Center began receiving requests for aid that went beyond its scope of action. "We started getting things that we didn't know what to do with," Lizak said. "We'd get calls from women . . . with real serious, survival kind of problems: money, food . . . and fear—a lot of women who were afraid their husbands were going to beat them up." (The YWCA shelter could not accept women on the basis of "unsubstantiated" fear.)

While burnout was recurrent, in the last years of the Center it became chronic. Suits, Fisher, Crawl, and each subsequent Center staff member left seriously singed. Shortly before the move, Sue Mumpower, one of the last staff members, resigned, saying staff desperately needed more support. "Burning people out," she wrote, "is not a very good example of women taking care of themselves."[82] Long-time collective members held out, even though, as Tricia Hart said, "the Women's Center meetings were not energy-giving." Hart stayed only because she feared no one would replace her.

The period also was one of life changes for many of the women. The deteriorating economy meant that subsistence-level jobs often no longer sufficed. Activists began thinking in terms of careers, and some were returning to school. Age, and perhaps a political void, contributed to a marriage and baby boom among the women in their thirties.

As volunteers and collective members took leaves of absences, they were not replaced. Joann Kleinehenz, one of the few new women in 1980, remembered only four highly active women at that time, and no new arrivals in the last six months of the Center's existence. Lizak, who stayed to the bitter end, recalled, "The last two years, after we moved, it just wasn't the same. . . . The night of the collective meeting would come, and I was just racking my brain for excuses not to go: Was I sick tonight? Did I have to work late? It was like that commitment of going to that dead thing was just terrible."

It was women from the lesbian group who ensured the Center's last stand. At the end, Lizak recalled, "they were the most supportive group at the Women's Center of any of the groups—they really didn't want to see it close." However, their support took the form of donations and some time, but not of taking on the responsibilities that weighed so heavily on the diminished core group. In November 1980, the remaining activists decided to close the Center.

The causes of the Dayton Women's Center's death were multiple. One simple reason was that, in contrast to DWL, the Center's structure required more money and energy to keep going. The feminist community was able to sustain it for several years, but ceased to do so.

No unifying concept of the community base for the Center was ever elaborated. Some spoke of drawing in housewives. For others, it seemed necessary to attract black women or working-class women. But as Barbara Tuss said, "Nobody made that happen anywhere; there was no reason to think that we could have. . . . The Center was satisfying to us early on because it satisfied our needs as a community, but when we started to stretch beyond it, we didn't have any concrete links to those people we wanted to expand out to. [Not many people could] get through the things we put out as middle-class college people. . . . Just the procedure of our meetings, how we spoke, all those things, I think, continued to separate us from people who we wanted to serve."

Others wanted to attract upper-middle-class women and upper-level businesswomen. However, many women in this target group, who were just gaining access to previously closed spheres, wanted little to do with what would be for them a downwardly mobile move. Many were hostile to the Center. Gail Levin, the first female city commissioner, voted against Center funding; she and her friend Sallie Collins were the ones who created the competing career counseling proposal, and they were close to the women who excluded the Center from the Victimization Project.[83] When money and power became available for women's issues, the powerful—women included—closed ranks and squeezed out the women's movement.

Of the women who did avail themselves of Center services, few became activists. This is not surprising given the service orientation, particularly as a social service approach took precedence over self-help, fostering a passive attitude. This was illustrated by a flow of letters from women who thanked the Center for its help but explained that they could not get involved.

While the Center failed to draw in the targeted categories of women, activists neglected their own. Seeking to serve the elusive "other women"—a strategy that almost always failed—they felt guilty about creating programs to fill their own needs. Few support mechanisms existed in the Center's structure, and there was little space for discussion and defusing conflict. The damage done by internal conflict was difficult to repair.

The Center's attempt to become mainstream and respectable accelerated the loss of dynamism and weakened the women's movement. Nearly every tantalizing overture by other institutions proved to be a mirage, and one that masked quicksand. Activists spent hours researching issues, writing proposals, and trying to raise money, only to see projects slip through their fingers. Available funds dictated program content. But the major successes of the Center were those projects chosen through feminists' pooled experience, not those designed to attract funding. Attempts to be mainstream did not result in maintaining control of the initiatives sparked by the Center; they did result in a loss of vision. This weakened the Center's appeal and decreased the commitment and the potential constituency. In the wave of mass-consumption feminism symbolized by the 1975 International Women's Year and spurred on by the 1977 Houston conference, diluted versions of many feminist issues had become acceptable. Shortly after this breach opened at one end, absorbing and defusing certain demands of the movement, the repressive reaction of the radical Right cracked down at the other end. The Dayton Women's Center was caught in the middle—not respectable enough to control what it had started, no longer radical enough to spearhead new resistance.[84]

The Dayton Women's Center lasted for over seven years, an impressive record. It touched the lives of thousands—perhaps tens of thousands—of women in the Dayton area. Center activists were greatly enriched by their experiences there. As for DWL, no confirmed reports exist of dedicated participants who, upon leaving, did so in rejection of feminism, or even of the movement. Many, to the contrary, testify to the life-changing effect of their involvement. Even those who left in bitterness, such as Crawl and Fisher, looked back to their time there as one of the most important experiences in their lives. Ellison, the sole person to remain active over the full seven years of the Center's existence, said it was thanks to the Center that she later established her reputation as a feminist attorney. Even Kleinehenz, who was at the Center for only its final depressing months, remembered thinking, "[F]inally, I've found someplace where people were talking about the things that really interest me." Long-time activist Hart asserted, "[I]f it hadn't been for the Women's Center, I would not be a strong, independent, assertive woman right now. It was through classes there, counseling there, through the process of the collective, through all those CR [and] support groups that I am who I am."

Over the 1974–80 period, most of the projects related to women's issues in Dayton, Ohio, can be traced back to the Center. In this respect, the Center made a major impact on the city, and it did not die without leaving successors. But its overall vision of a society where women would be liberated was not evident in any of them. If this vision was transmitted, it was through the hearts and minds of the women who were involved.

6

DAYTON WOMEN
WORKING (1975–80)

IN EARLY 1977, the former employment task force of NOW, rebaptised Dayton Women Working, left a Women's Center torn by conflict. DWW's move into new quarters at the downtown Dayton YWCA consummated a separation that had been in the making since the organization's creation two years earlier. While other groups also had organized around specific single issues, DWW was the first to separate from the rest of the movement; clearly, the subject "woman" was no longer one. The separation reflected not only local tensions but also strategies of the working women's movement and of socialist feminism nationally. Throughout its history, DWW was a laboratory for these two movements, due to the influence of its most influential leader, Sherrie Holmes. In fact, the two extremes assumed by DWW's organizational structure—an early nonformalized structure with an enlightened ruler and the later hierarchical structure—represented a dramatic departure from earlier feminist groups. More than any previous organization in the history of Dayton's women's movement, DWW was the local correspondent of a national movement, and similarities in form and content were tremendous.

The working women's movement did not challenge the overall organization of work or, as one might have expected, link issues of race, gender, and class. However, through its educational campaigns, and by monitoring business practices and federal antidiscrimination agencies, it went a long way toward improving the status of clerical workers and raising consciousness about working women's problems in general. The movement attracted working-class women and was influential in democratizing the labor movement and in bridging the gap between feminism and labor.

The women's liberation movement nationally had raised the issue of clerical work early on. After all, it was the occupation that employed the largest number of women, and also the major job category with the highest proportion of women.[1] Early feminist writings included such telling titles as "Drowning in the Steno Pool" and "The Secretarial Proletariat."[2] The latter, written in response to leftist and labor views equating the proletariat solely with the industrial working class, argued for an analysis that included clericals: "Although we work at desks instead of on assembly lines, female clerical work is very much like factory labor in its exploitative nature. But unlike factory workers, we don't have unions. The Bosses make a false separation between 'blue collar' and 'white collar' workers, because it's in their interest to keep us clerical workers from organizing to demand better wages, better working conditions, day-care for our children—or maybe even a revolution."[3]

These writings concurred that the role of secretaries—as work-site servants, mothers, and wives—was an extension of their subservient position in society. The work itself, however, was portrayed as mindless, as contributing to an exploitative economic system, or—and this position later dominated—as skilled, dignified, and vital to the operations of a company.

Clericals were the largest group of nonunionized wageworkers,[4] but feminists had low expectations of existing unions, deemed "racist and sexist institutions."[5] By 1970, feminists called for clerical workers—in proper consciousness-raising fashion—to start talking to other women in their offices and to begin organizing. Women's caucuses appeared across the country, some organized by feminists.[6] Several elements converged to make the time right. In the labor movement, rank and file militancy gave birth to new unions and to the challenging of established leadership, as evidenced by the United Farm Workers and the movement that culminated in Teamsters for a Democratic Union. The women's movement raised other concerns by eroding the notions of male superiority and of man as breadwinner, by redefining work, and by providing new models for organizing.

In 1971, Union WAGE started in San Francisco "to fight for job equality for women and equality within the unions."[7] The group subsequently organized campaigns related to clerical workers. In 1974, thirty-two hundred women from fifty-eight different unions met to form the Congress of Labor Union Women (CLUW).[8] These groups were secondary organizations, intended to coexist alongside labor unions.[9] At the same time, other primary organizations emerged.

In 1973, a year after the issue was raised at the New American Movement's Socialist Feminist Conference in Durham, North Carolina, NAM member Day Creamer (Piercy) and Heather Booth created Chicago Women Employed, drawing on their experiences with Chicago Women's Liberation Union, organizing for farm workers, and discussions with working-class women at the YWCA where Creamer worked. 9 to 5 was founded at about the same time as an outgrowth of a group of Boston clerical workers, including antiwar activists and feminists, who had been meeting to discuss personal problems.[10] By the mid-1970s, working women's groups also existed in New York, San Francisco, Cleveland, and—the smallest of the cities—Dayton. Like many cities in the northeastern part of the nation, Dayton had lost thousands of jobs in the industrial sector and was struggling to attract service-sector jobs, ones that disproportionately employed women.

Sherrie Holmes converted to the idea of organizing clerical workers with great enthusiasm. While at the Chicago Midwest Academy in September 1974, she had met activists from 9 to 5 and attended the first Chicago Women Employed convention. Other Dayton socialist feminists, in accord with national strategy, supported the ideas Holmes proposed. Part of their rationale for creating the NOW chapter in 1975 was to launch the employment task force, although reactions were mixed when the group became an autonomous organization only months after the NOW chapter's birth.

From the start and throughout most of DWW's history, Sherrie Holmes was the central figure to the group, marking the first time in the Dayton movement that a single individual dominated an organization. Although Holmes had become a highly contested personality at the Women's Center, at DWW she apparently was admired by all. Noreen Willhelm, second director of DWW, observed fondly, "Sherrie's a force of nature. She was very charismatic. And when she's passionate, it's easy for her to take a whole world with her." Claudia Kinder, Willhelm's successor, said Holmes was "a very, very exceptional person—and charismatic in getting people to do work for her. . . . [Members] never mistrusted her in any way, shape, or form." Kinder quipped, only half in jest, "Sherrie was our mother. [We were] her little duckies."

The first two years of DWW's existence was a time of germination. After only several months as a task force of NOW, in April 1975 it had become an independent organization with a name of its own. By June, DWW's communications no longer depended on the Women's Center's publications; Holmes, Ellison, and several others produced the group's first newsletter. The publication appeared on average three times a year throughout the organization's existence. This newsletter had more in common with those of other working women's organizations around the country than with previous Dayton feminist publications. Printed professionally and sprinkled with drawings and photographs, it contained four to six pages of unsigned, informative articles. With the exception of what internal reports condescendingly dubbed "Ain't It Awful" articles, most content was upbeat. The newsletter covered the situation of women workers, discrimination and possible recourse, news of relevant legislation, and developments in the working women's movement in Dayton and around the country. First intended for outreach, it later worked at solidifying members' commitment. Photos mostly featured members, and a regular column, "Spotlight on Area Working Women," painted flattering portraits of selected members. Most of the three thousand to five thousand copies were distributed in public places.

Aside from the newsletter, little structure existed other than that provided by Holmes. Despite a few experiments with feminist methods (rotating chair, ad hoc task forces, and so on), Holmes *was* Dayton Women Working for several years. As she explained at a 1976 NAM convention, "I have served as coordinator of the group and have offered leadership to the group for its first . . . year." Dayton's group apparently was not the only one that did not formalize structure. A later internal agreement among groups stipulated that no boards would be elected until an organization had seventy-five paid members, and that in the interim, members were to be selected to serve on ad hoc committees.[11] A peculiar mix of socialist feminist critique of early groups' supposed structurelessness and Alinsky and Midwest Academy promotion of leadership made way for an organization dominated by one individual.

Two overlapping forces provided the context for the nascent organization: socialist feminism and the working women's movement. Organizing working women was an important theme at the July 1975 Socialist Feminist Conference in Yellow Springs. Members of Chicago Women Employed held a workshop on using sex discrimination laws to organize working women. Discussions were slated on "organizing the unorganized" and on CLUW. Although initially excited by the model offered by CLUW, by the time of the Yellow Springs conference many socialist feminists nationally found the year-old group too tightly under the control of union bureaucracies.[12] This no doubt confirmed Daytonians' preference for the Boston and Chicago models.

NAM served as a communications network and as a space for strategizing, both nationally and locally. Women in the national leadership had promoted involvement in NOW and in the working women's movement. Socialist feminists and NAM women were joining NOW and even creating chapters in some cities. In turn, Holmes held workshops on clerical organizing at NAM's conventions and sent copies of monthly progress reports to Judy MacLean and Holly Graff of the national NAM leadership.[13]

Although the socialist movement was crucial to the creation of DWW, one would be hard-pressed to find any anticapitalist stances taken by the organization—either on fundamental economic change or on reorganizing the workplace to change the nature of clerical work. Here, NAM's cautious public face and its efforts to appear nonsectarian no doubt combined with the aftermath of the Socialist Feminist Conference. The prominence of sectarian leftist groups at the conference had made many socialist feminists, including Daytonians, cautious in publicly espousing radical views. From the start, DWW sought recognition for office workers within the existing economy.

The other overlapping force was the national working women's movement. Holmes developed strong contacts with the other organizations. She spent several weeks training with 9 to 5, and the Boston group provided her with ongoing advice, including a step-by-step formula for starting a group,[14] which she immediately applied to Dayton. (First, draft a questionnaire and conduct a survey on the condition of office workers in the city. Next, release the results inevitably showing poor pay and discrimination, sparking publicity and attracting members. Finally, hold a public hearing—reminiscent of feminist "speak-outs.")

In April 1975, a handful of DWW activists distributed some two thousand questionnaires at office buildings in downtown Dayton. Kathy Ellison, an early DWW activist, described what was to be part of the group's stock in trade: "We'd make a big to-do about passing [the surveys] out downtown and in front of some companies, with the implication that we thought they were really bad." The small number of surveys returned were used as the basis for "statistics." The first survey showed: "Slightly over $2/3$ (68%) of the women surveyed said that they aren't paid enough for their work. The same number reported that they don't receive cost-of-living increases, and nearly $3/4$ (73%) agreed that women typically earn less than men in their offices."[15] This survey method provided results that had no scientific value, although many of the conclusions were true. As Ellison described with her usual dry humor, "We could pass out a thousand [questionnaires] and we'd get our usual thirteen back [in fact, return rates reached 10–20 percent]. But they never quiz you on that, so you can come up with great statistics based on your thirteen returns." Questionnaires were designed to attract potential members: respondents filled in their names and addresses, and DWW later invited them to meetings. On this questionnaire, DWW announced its first public event, a "Rights and Respect" program for the 1975 National Secretaries Week.

This observance week, established by the Department of Commerce in 1952 and previously distinguished by florists' advertisements encouraging employers to give flowers to their secretaries, gave rise to a new type of working women's holiday with a new slogan: "Raises, not Roses." In 1974, Chicago Women Employed and 9 to 5 used the week to hold rallies and publicize their Bill of Rights for Office Workers. In Dayton, one year later, some fifty women attended DWW's first such program.[16]

The women who joined DWW were described as new to politics. Holmes reported to NAM in 1976: "Every person who has gotten involved came to the group totally inexperienced and [has] developed immensely."[17] Willhelm later said, "To a person, they did not come out of a political background. They came out of a frustration with work." She added: "They were exactly what we were looking for." Yet, several important activists did not fit the profile. Holmes and Willhelm were politically savvy, and at least two socialist feminists were involved, as was Women's Center stalwart Kathy Ellison. Barbara Scalia, whom Holmes had recruited to the Center, became a paid DWW staff member.

Gloria Koch joined DWW at its beginning and stayed with it throughout. While she had never been politically active, she was open to feminist ideas. Koch, in her early twenties at the time, had recently moved to Dayton to join her future husband. Searching for involvement, she had looked in the phone book and discovered the Women's Center. "It was a perfect setting to me, so nice and homey," she recalled. The first night she visited, the NOW employment task force was meeting in the basement. Koch, at the time a clerical worker at the Veterans' Administration Hospital, remembered, "I went downstairs, and Sherrie got me involved immediately."

Koch had grown up in a small Wisconsin mill town. Her father died when she was young, and her mother, an office worker at the paper mill, was the only working woman on the block. Koch's mother lived in fear of accusations of child neglect. "If they think that I'm not taking good care of you, they will take you away!" Koch recalled hearing repeatedly. The issue of women and work thus touched a chord with her. "My mother worked . . . , my grandmother worked . . . , so I always knew, even as a small child, that I had to depend on myself."

Koch, raised Catholic in a small, all-white community, had attended parochial schools. An irregular student who excelled only in what she loved, she was told: "Don't go to college; you'll never make it." By age eighteen, Koch just wanted a job. She first worked as a secretary in the Department of Defense in Washington, D.C., where she was appalled at the conditions. "You were a secretary who worked for another secretary . . . and you had your main boss and all his workers to work for. And you had to get coffee! And wash their cups! . . . I saw women getting jobs through sexual favors. . . . There was something wrong. . . . But I didn't have any place to put it in my mind."

Koch helped compile the results of the first DWW survey. It was an eye-opener. "I was amazed. . . . I had no idea that [a secretary for a lawyer] didn't get paid good and didn't have good benefits," she said. DWW made that "place" in her mind to analyze working women's conditions.

Claudia Kinder, who became the third and last president of DWW, also came to the group via the Women's Center. Kinder, in her early twenties when she joined, had grown up in a white, middle-class suburb east of Dayton. Her mother was an office worker and her father managed a building complex along with other activities. Raised in a Catholic family, Kinder had only two siblings because her mother "thought progressively—to herself." (Years later, she told her daughter that "if the Pope wanted to come and baby-sit all these babies, she would have had as many as he wanted, but she could only afford three.")

Kinder recalled having been politically motivated since the age of five and unwaveringly supported the underdog. Her rebelliousness led to her question the Church: "They wanted me to take things just on faith, and I wanted the answers." At the age of thirteen, she opened the priest's door while at confession and demanded, "Please come out and talk to me!" After their discussion, she told him she was leaving the Church.

In Kinder's conservative parochial schools, little filtered through about protests. Then in high school, a friend "converted" her to feminism. As their first statement, they dropped out of the cheerleading squad. When called at a banquet to accept their letters, they took the media obsession with lingerie literally and went up braless. "I didn't burn it," she said. "I would just take it off when I wanted to make a statement!"

Kinder left Dayton for college at Ohio State University, but she dropped out after a quarter to help put her new husband through school. For the next eight years she worked in various office jobs, seeking out nonprofit and social service organizations. Upon returning to Dayton, she began volunteering at the Women's Center, where Holmes recruited her into DWW.

In fall 1976, Holmes won a commitment from a progressive foundation to provide a thousand dollars in matching funds contingent on local grass-roots fund-raising. As with the Women's Center, fund-raising became an ongoing component of DWW, allowing Holmes to hone her already impressive skills. A membership campaign recruited some sixty paid members who contributed a minimum of three dollars each. Other fund-raising methods included selling notepads with the slogan, "More Rank, Less File." After DWW survived for its first two years on volunteer labor and a few hundred dollars, its budget jumped to eleven thousand dollars in 1977 and sixteen thousand dollars thereafter, not counting staff positions funded by CETA and VISTA.[18]

Holmes quit the Women's Center staff and began receiving minimal part-time pay as director of DWW. Shortly thereafter, two other part-time staff members were hired: Scalia and Billie Sowers, who had been fired from her former job after filing sex discrimination charges. In January 1977, the organization opened its office at the YWCA.[19]

Holmes's departure from the Women's Center came at a propitious moment. The day-care cooperative that she had supported had just been forced to move next door. The debate over the do-it-yourself divorce kit, involving both Holmes and Scalia, had just ended acrimoniously. Suits's and Fisher's anger at NAM was heating up. But Holmes saw the move as strategic, to establish DWW as independent from the women's movement.

As DWW's December 1976 progress report stated, "This move should increase accessibility and help establish our image as less overtly feminist . . . and more legitimate."[20] Over the years, DWW members separated work issues from other feminist issues, even though many of the activists had themselves been drawn into DWW via the Women's Center. Koch asserted, "You'd call people up and talk about job-related problems. . . . You'd say, 'We're a task force of the National Organization of Women,' and they'd say, 'Oh, oh! You're for abortion, and things like that!' And it wasn't a good relationship to have." Kinder agreed: "We realized we had to have our autonomy. . . . We [wouldn't] take any kind of public stand on any other issue than employment. And even personally, we [had] to be careful of talking about our own feelings about issues." DWW began as a radical project borrowing legitimacy from NOW, to an independent organization working out of the Women's Center, to an organization that downplayed any connections to feminist and non-work issues.

This position was accepted with no debate. Like many decisions, it was reached easily because the group deciding was small (active members numbered one or two dozen, only two of whom were "beginning to take on more leadership responsibilities"[21]) and because Holmes had personally recruited and trained most of the organization's leaders. Willhelm recognized that on many occasions, "virtually everything I knew was through Sherrie's eyes." With growth, the organization did adopt a formal structure. General meetings were held monthly. Members elected officers to a new executive committee. All DWW meetings were held after work or at the lunch hour; they were short, efficient, and used *Robert's Rules of Order.* Little or no time was allowed for any general or political discussion. Decisions were made in the executive committee and submitted to the general membership for approval. But even the new structure did little to decrease Holmes's influence.

As several socialist feminists commented, DWW organizers believed that although working-class women were feminist "deep down in their hearts," they were not yet ready for feminism or socialism. "There were all these philosophical discussions about how women weren't really ready to be linking their work stuff with feminism," Willhelm said. Kinder argued, "Most women are not [politically motivated] and they are turned off by that [bra-burner] image—unfortunately." She added, "It takes a couple of years for them to get to the point where they realize that women have been kept down by men."

This attitude resembled that observed among other organizers of working women. One study of four working women's organizations asserted that although all the leaders interviewed considered themselves feminists, they "are sensitive to the fact that the majority of their members—as well as their enormous untapped potential constituencies—do not. . . . Other feminist concerns . . . have no place on their agendas."[22] Jean Tepperman, after interviewing feminist union organizers, observed: "[O]rganizers I spoke to were quite anxious to concentrate on unionism and avoid being 'sidetracked' by other radical or women's issues."[23]

With little data to back them up, authors have disseminated the idea that the women's movement was middle class, and that working-class women distrusted the movement.[24] We have already seen that this assumption is inaccurate in the case of Dayton's movement. The backgrounds of Dayton feminists were far more diverse than commonly assumed, and DWW cut across class lines even more than previous organizations.

But even if this distrust was common for women in the industrial working class, the assumption that it would apply to clerical workers misses a point. Clerical work, because of the sexual segregation of the labor force and women's limited job opportunities, draws women from a broad range of class and educational backgrounds (clerical workers are typically "overeducated"). It is so pervasive that many Dayton feminists had worked as clericals or assumed they would someday, and all had friends or relatives who were clerical workers. The notion that feminists had to hide their political views flowed from the idea of organizing the mythical "other woman" rather than from working from their own experience.

A significant number of DWW's participants were both working class and sympathetic to feminism. Koch, the granddaughter of a mill worker and daughter of a widowed working mother, loved the Women's Center and the consciousness-raising process of "get[ting] people together to talk and discuss their problems and to openly find out that other people had the same problems."

Noreen Willhelm, daughter of a teamster, grew up with her five siblings in the working-class Norh End of Toledo. She was annoyed by the attitude she described as, "'We'll take care of you, little lady, and then when you get to the right point we'll show you the next stage, we'll open the next door for you.' . . . It's crap! I never agreed with it then, and I did think it came from a real patronizing attitude toward working-class people."

Willhelm's father, a cement truck driver, had an eighth-grade education and her mother had finished tenth grade, but Willhelm loved learning. She described herself as a sponge, soaking up knowledge, but at least one teacher saw the steel in her and nicknamed her "Scrap Iron."

The turning point for Willhelm was "being thirteen in 1968 . . . and having a television on in our living room all the time." She watched coverage of the assassinations of Martin Luther King Jr. and Robert Kennedy, the Democratic National Convention, and the student riots in Paris. "I understood that there was something really momentous happening, that the world was beginning to shake beneath our feet," she said. Although she had grown up a "good union girl," and knew that "you never cross a picket line," there was little political discussion in her home. Television news, magazines, books, and music spoke to her.

At the University of Toledo Willhelm started to make sense of the ideas swirling around her. She earned her way by waitressing at a dough-nut shop, until in her sophomore year she got pregnant and had to leave her job. Shortly thereafter, Willhelm went to work for the United Farm Workers, living with, and sharing subsistence wages with the other organizers. She also made her first trip to Dayton, for a farm workers conference. While there, she joined a picket and experienced Dayton hospitality—in jail after local police charged the group, arrested her (seven and a half months pregnant), and some twenty others.

Willhelm returned to college after the birth of her daughter. She did research on a 1934 Toledo strike, a key event in the history of the Unit-ed Automobile Workers, and as a result the regional director of the UAW sent her to the union's education center for training. Back at the university, when a beloved women's studies teacher was refused tenure Willhelm joined the protests and ended up quitting.

By this time, Willhelm had befriended Daytonians through involve-ment in the statewide campaign to increase public control over utilities. One after another, they told her, "Sherrie Holmes could use somebody like you for Dayton Women Working." She met Sherrie, and they became fast friends. When a friend took her to the Women's Center day-care cooperative, that clinched it. "There was this huge community of single mothers," she recalled. "There were lots of folks just like me." When funding became available, Willhelm joined DWW's staff. Fresh out of UAW training and United Farm Workers organizing, Willhelm's labor connections were unique in DWW.

DWW organizers established the group independently not only from feminist issues but also from the labor movement. Even though Dayton was a union town and unionization was on the rise among white-collar workers nationally,[25] DWW devoted little thought to creating a union or encouraging members to join individually. Several factors contributed to this stance. Holmes had discounted the option of working within a union: "The unions had not been organizing women. . . . And also, unions have such a male-dominated kind of image." It was more than just an image. Historical examples abound of women and minorities being shut out of trades and unions. In 1972, of the 177 trade unions that provided the Labor Department with statistics, 149 had no female officials.[26] During the period of DWW's creation, 25 percent of all mem-bers of affiliated unions of the AFL-CIO were women, but women held only 7 percent of key elected and appointed posts. The federation had no women on its executive council.[27] As Willhelm proclaimed in a speech,

"Labor has been very negligent and at times quite loathe to organize women for a wide number of reasons. Probably the most basic . . . is simple sexism."[28]

For most women workers at the time, union membership and unionized sectors of the economy were not a part of their universe. Most DWW members expressed little interest in or familiarity with unions. At a national working women's meeting in 1978, groups from other cities listed local unions one by one, discussing their track records on women workers and clericals. When it came to Dayton, Holmes could only report vaguely that DWW members were "pretty pro-union."[29] DWW did not make efforts to draw in union women. For example, feminist union leader Betty Jean Carroll attended some meetings but apparently was never encouraged to participate. Billie Sowers moved from the DWW staff to a job with the United Electrical, Radio, and Machine Workers; she reported that the union offered DWW use of its facilities, but DWW apparently did not respond.

Strategically, Holmes and national leaders wanted to build an autonomous power base and only then choose a union. Working women's groups did not want to be auxiliaries. When a Dayton union asked for names of potentially organizable women, DWW refused. Cleveland organizers, who had reacted similarly, explained in a national meeting, "These unions are after members (. . . instead of building a progressive movement to organize office workers)."[30]

Unions had begun making overtures to working women's groups in many cities. During DWW's first year, Boston's 9 to 5, after shopping around, had created Local 925 of the Service Employees International Union. The success of this experiment led in 1981 to the founding of a national union, District 925, with Karen Nussbaum as its head. Despite her satisfaction with the 925 model, even Nussbaum believed that the younger groups were not ready for a union.[31]

It is hardly surprising that once DWW had established itself separately from the feminist and labor movements, it attracted less politicized women. (Furthermore, as the first of the city's feminist groups to be located downtown, its members were less concentrated in northwest Dayton's "radical ghetto.") Most of DWW's grass-roots members had no previous experience in the women's movement. Holmes and others proclaimed proudly that these were women who would say, "I'm not a feminist, but . . . " followed by a blatantly feminist idea. Many, Kinder said, had been repulsed by "the image of the bra-burner" and did not see DWW as an outgrowth of the feminist movement. More generally, she added, "for a lot of women, this [was] the first time [they had] ever taken a stand in their lives."

Around 100 women paid dues to DWW, although some 250 filled out membership cards by the end of the decade. Membership figures represented a pool of supporters supplemented by the radical community. "The thing that NAM did was to provide that secondary support," Willhelm said. "So if we held events . . . we could always count on the NAM folks and the Five Oaks community to come and support us." Regular, active participants in DWW's meetings and activities stabilized at around 25.[32]

Kinder described most grass-roots members as young, in their midtwenties through early thirties. Despite a membership campaign targeting older women, the handful of older recruits remained passive supporters. This trend apparently was not specific to Dayton. Jean Tepperman wrote, "Most people who initiate and lead organizing efforts are in their twenties. They tend to have fewer family responsibilities, to be less loyal to the company, more confident about finding jobs (therefore less scared of being fired) and more open to feminist ideas."[33]

Holmes recalled that members were mostly low paid, but had drive: "I think we tended to involve people who wanted to advance in their careers and felt frustrated, but with some amount of confidence in themselves."[34] Willhelm described them as women with "a higher degree of consciousness . . . [about] women being exploited" than society at large.

Contrary to Tepperman's description, many DWW members did have children, including a number of single mothers. As in Dayton Women's Liberation, these women had a lot to lose. Kinder was struck by how many women came into DWW following a divorce, seeking a support group as well as a work-related organization.

While estimates of the number of women of color in the membership vary, none were in the activist core until a black woman came on staff in January 1979. As an electrocardiogram technician at a local hospital, Debra Walker had been denied training and promotion. Angry, and convinced she was the victim of sex and race discrimination, she contacted DWW. Hundreds of women had made use of the group's counseling service to help them through "the bureaucratic maze that comprises equal employment opportunity."[35] (DWW also viewed counseling as a way to recruit.[36]) Walker did not file a complaint. Looking back later after gaining experience in the field, she believed she could have won, but that DWW had discouraged her with accounts of the interminable red tape involved. Walker did find a new job, however. DWW director Willhelm encouraged her to use her anger constructively on the organization's staff.

After Walker's arrival, the number of black women in DWW rose to about 10–15 percent in 1979, according to Willhelm.[37] Kinder thought the number was higher; however, nobody could cite names of active black women other than Walker. Walker reported having difficulty reaching other black women, not because of hostility to feminist ideas, but "because the working women's movement already has this personality that black women see as being a white women's movement."

Walker herself had mixed feelings toward the women's movement. While still on staff, she reflected: "I feel ambivalent. . . . What I'm doing is good, but I'm not reaching black women. . . . And whatever I do, I've got to dedicate myself to helping black folks in some area." Before working at DWW, she believed that the women's movement, while proclaiming across-the-board female solidarity, did not address black women's needs. At DWW, she came to see a commonality in black and white women's experiences, but she thought that many white women in the working women's movement did not understand the specific problems black women faced.

DWW devoted little attention to issues of race. Some discussion occurred among the executive board members on the need to include black women, but it was in terms of recruiting and "developing" them. "We need to work on developing the membership of women of color and their leadership skills," Kinder stated while still president. "We do have some members who are interested and active. . . . We need to bring them along, get them a little more committed." No trace exists, however, of discussion on the specific needs and interests of black women. The problem went beyond a local one; according to Walker at the time: "I've talked to some of the organizers [in the region], and they've all got the aloof attitude that 'we've got the answer; you should do this and this and this.'"

DWW's development cannot be understood in isolation from the other working women's groups around the country. In addition to DWW's connections to the Chicago and Boston groups, it had established strong ties to the new Cleveland Women Working.

National cooperation first took the form of a coalition to defend affirmative action. In September 1976, in the last months of Gerald Ford's administration, the Department of Labor proposed revisions to "rationalize" the bureaucratic affirmative action guidelines, changes that would have narrowed their scope and weakened enforcement.[38] Working women's groups forged a coalition with women's groups, unions, civil rights organizations, and church groups to block the new regulations. Banking on Ford's defeat in the upcoming election, the coalition tried delaying tactics. In Ohio, DWW and Cleveland Women Working, supported by myriad groups (among them, the YWCA, NOW, the Urban League, officials of the Ohio Civil Rights Commission, Federally Employed Women, and the Household Workers Association), organized a meeting with the regional director of the Office of Federal Contract Compliance Programs (OFCCP).[39] The coalition held a "Speak-out to Save Affirmative Action" in Cleveland, prepared testimonies for the regional hearings, coordinated a letter-writing campaign to the Department of Labor, and collected more than twenty thousand signatures on a petition.[40] The strategy paid off. After Jimmy Carter took office, most of the proposed revisions were scrapped.

The affirmative action campaign was one of several examples of impressive cooperation between DWW and civil rights groups. But again, nothing was done to capitalize on the connections to link issues of gender and race. In part, this was due to race blindness; in part, it was characteristic of an organization that favored pragmatism and efficiency and left little time for reflection. The affirmative action campaign offered an untapped opportunity to forge stronger coalitions across race lines.

Although almost no mention is made of DWW in historical accounts,[41] it was one of the founders of the first national organization to come out of the new working women's movement. In November 1976, DWW hosted the first National Conference of Working Women in nearby Germantown, Ohio. Participants agreed to hold regional conferences in February 1977;[42] DWW and Cleveland Women Working jointly organized the Midwest Working Women's Conference in the latter group's hometown.[43]

By May 1977, with an initial grant of twenty-five thousand dollars from the Rockefeller Family Fund, six organizations joined to create the National Women's Employment Project (NWEP), "a research, monitoring, and advocacy project to work for national administrative and policy changes needed to make equal employment opportunity [laws] a reality in the office for millions of women and minorities." In addition to DWW, members included 9 to 5, New York's Women Office Workers, San Francisco's Women Organized for Employment, Cleveland Women Working, and Chicago Women Employed (which subsequently withdrew). A national office was opened in Washington, D.C., to lobby, network with other Washington groups, and work with the appropriate government agencies. The NWEP defined national campaigns and raised funds, which were redistributed to local affiliates (accounting for between 23 and 42 percent of DWW's budget).[44]

The following year, NWEP began discussions on consolidating national working women's organizations. As a result, in 1979 NWEP merged with Working Women: National Association of Office Workers, an organization of similar, mostly more recent groups. The new Working Women, with offices in Boston, Cleveland, and later Washington, began with member organizations in thirteen cities—three on the west coast, three in Ohio, and the remainder on the east coast.[45]

DWW's program and structure were greatly affected by the other groups. The flow of people and ideas was constant. Meetings of the NWEP steering committee and then of the Working Women board were held several times a year. Holmes, Willhelm, and others spent time observing sister organizations, and several leaders of other groups came to Dayton. Dozens of Daytonians participated in national "leadership workshops," grass-roots funding workshops, and Working Women's summer schools. Several were trained at the Midwest Academy, which later became policy for staff paid through the national organization.

These exchanges produced considerable homogeneity from one city to another, both in content and form. Newsletters were strikingly similar. Many special events originated in Boston before being used in Dayton. Questionnaires were modified versions of ones used in Chicago. Public hearings were widespread. National Secretaries Week was celebrated by all affiliates, and slogans such as "Raises, not Roses" were national. Working women's organizations took on a characteristic style, one that mixed research, direct action, and skilled public relations.

Homogeneity came first from informal influences. It became a structural phenomenon as the national organizations developed and highly detailed, strict organizing principles were defined. Contracts were signed between affiliates and NWEP and then Working Women, translating the tried practices of working women's organizations into organizational rules. The money distributed through NWEP, for example, was dependent on the organizations' carrying out specific programs, producing results for the quarterly evaluations, and gaining the approbation of a majority of affiliates. Contracts specified numbers and types of actions to be held and measurable goals for recruitment and leadership development.[46] Working Women even spelled out a month-by-month program for new groups.

The influence of the national organization on Dayton was reciprocated. Holmes, in particular, helped elaborate national strategies. DWW sponsored meetings and conventions and took its turn coordinating NWEP. DWW exchanged ideas continually with the Cleveland group. The two later chipped in to pay 9 to 5's Karen Nussbaum as a "traveler"; together, they helped start new groups in the region, such as Cincinnati Women Working, get started.

Despite this relationship, DWW remained a country cousin. As Holmes wrote in a memo on fund-raising, experience had shown that Dayton was "viewed as fairly small and insignificant,"[47] and this proved to be a tendency also in the national working women's organizations. As the smallest group in the smallest NWEP affiliate city, DWW was constantly needing to justify its role as a symbolic gateway to America: "This movement began as many other movements for social justice began. It has its roots in the larger, more cosmopolitan cities. . . . But in order for the movement to be successful, it must sink roots in middle-America; for without this base, the movement can neither be national nor sustain itself."[48] Willhelm recalled, "We were always given short shrift. . . . When I think about the national leaders, like Karen Nussbaum, Ellen Cassedy, Helen Williams . . . We were their good news and bad news. We were kind of a thorn in their side because we were so small. . . . I mean, they had banking districts and insurance districts. . . . We didn't have that. . . . [DWW] was given a large measure of respect for two reasons: one is Sherrie . . . the other is 'Dayton as the average American city.' You know, 'Oh, well if they can do it in Dayton, then perhaps we could replicate it in Peoria!'"

In the beginning of national consolidation, affiliate organizations were fairly autonomous, with some flexibility in content and structure. One important difference was that DWW's focus extended beyond office work. The assumption that DWW was an organization for clerical workers appeared at all levels. It targeted office buildings for leafleting, it celebrated National Secretaries Week, and its internal reports spoke of clerical organizing. Its affiliation with the national organizations reinforced this assumption. However, one would be hard-pressed to find any such restrictions in DWW literature. The only description in the newsletter said that DWW was started "by a group of working women concerned about problems on our jobs." One leaflet proclaimed: "[M]embership in Dayton Women Working is open to any interested person concerned with job equality for women."[49] Even in 1979, when DWW incorporated, two goals were spelled out: "[T]o promote the equal rights of women who work, and particularly those . . . in clerical . . . positions," and more broadly, "to end the discrimination against women in the workplace."

Dayton leaders attributed the broader scope to size: a small group from a small town couldn't afford to have a narrow focus. But it was also because organizers were willing to address issues as they arose, and many members, perhaps half, were not clerical workers. They included waitresses, health-care workers, insurance saleswomen, and department store personnel.

DWW supported organizing drives by women and minority workers. In 1977 it helped launch the Dayton consumer boycott of J. P. Stevens, notorious for its poor working conditions and attempts to stop its workers, mainly women, from unionizing.[50] Three large stores canceled their orders with the company. In the same year, DWW actively supported the Retail Clerks Union drive to organize Rike's, Dayton's largest department store. Also in 1977, DWW helped campaign for unionization when Wright State University employees, mainly clericals, were choosing between one of two unions, or no union at all. DWW established positive relations with several Dayton unions through such actions. One union offered DWW the use of its hall, and several placed ads in DWW's services directory.[51] One asked DWW for a list of potential candidates for its organizing drives; this same union had previously called a local labor reporter to, as Holmes said, "find out if we were 'all right'—not communists or anything."[52]

Another indication of DWW's broader focus was its position on women in the skilled trades. At a 1978 NWEP meeting it was argued— apparently without dissent—that working women's and other women's groups should steer clear of the issue, deemed "very dangerous since it bolsters the claim that women take jobs from men and minorities."[53] DWW had already participated in a coalition of groups on women in the construction industry. And despite the NWEP position, DWW again joined with civil rights groups in a coalition that resulted in Mayor James McGee's declaring a Women in Construction Week.

Nevertheless, most of DWW's activities, like those of other affiliates, did concentrate on office workers. The group's program had three parts: educating the public, investigating employers, and monitoring antidiscrimination agencies.

DWW activists invested heavily in public education. The group disseminated research, such as a report on automation of the office that was released simultaneously around the country. Both local papers relayed the information, one stating, "Offices are fast becoming factories of paperwork for the 18 million clerical workers in the United States."[54] DWW produced fact sheets and leaflets on pregnancy discrimination, disability guidelines, and equal opportunity laws and enforcement. The organization ran workshops on job discrimination and on how to get raises, and, in conjunction with other working women's groups, presented a career counseling program that more than two hundred office workers attended.[55]

DWW's most spectacular success was in reaching the public through the media. No other feminist group had ever received such copious and favorable media coverage. Significantly, at the 1977 opening festivities for the downtown office, journalists outnumbered prospective members.[56] DWW actions were announced by the media beforehand and well covered afterward, not only by the press but also by television and radio stations.

It is not surprising that DWW attracted so much attention. Feminism was becoming respectable, and sympathetic reporters were not uncommon. DWW viewed the media as an ally and meticulously cultivated contacts. Furthermore, DWW had everything the media could desire: it raised clear issues, backed by hard data and laws, and the organizational structure provided identifiable spokespersons. Above all, DWW's actions were perfect feminist media events, combining humor and flamboyant style. Even the fund-raisers were presented with an eye to the media. For instance, an auction at the 1977 Hardworkers Holiday Party featured one of congresswoman Bella Abzug's trademark hats. Feminist singer Holly Near and activist/actress Jane Fonda were crowd-getters at the 1979 Working Women's Cocktail Hour. One of the annual family barbecues, intended to build community, consolidated media contacts by inviting a local radio station's all-male softball team to play against DWW's team (DWW lost, 18-11).

The ultimate media event was the National Secretaries Week celebration, held annually beginning in 1975 and proclaimed Women Office Workers' Week in 1979 by Dayton's mayor. Like Women's Equality Day (the new name for the anniversary of women's suffrage) and the Women's Center's birthday parties, National Secretaries Week became a new cultural holiday.

Every year, DWW made an appearance in downtown Dayton for the event, with a flurry of leaflets, surveys, and public speakers. The most successful attention-getters were the contests, in particular the "Pettiest Office Procedures" contest. The competition was stiff. The fifty entries in 1978 included a boss who expected help with his manicure; one who wanted his assistant to feed his dog; and another who asked his employee to balance his personal checkbook. The second-place winner was a boss who insisted that his secretary ensure he was properly dressed every morning: she had to see to it that his socks matched and sniff his shirt to be certain it was clean. Several women scribbled "sexual favors" on their entry forms and submitted them anonymously; DWW mentioned this to journalists, but they buried it under the more amusing examples. First prize went to a local physician whose bookkeeper's list of duties included moving the lawn sprinkler regularly and unclogging the toilet. He good-naturedly received his just reward when DWW members appeared at his office to present him with a rose—attached to a toilet plunger.[57]

The media had a heyday with the contest. Surprisingly, the coverage extended to the underlying questions. Even the financial editor of the conservative daily paper pointed out, "Women Working sees its job as helping female workers understand their rights . . . and at the same time [making] the business world more sensitive to the need for treating female workers as workers—not errand girls, valets, servants and sex objects."[58]

Dayton Women Working's second program component was investigating businesses. In 1977 a "Put Your Employer on the Spot" contest was aimed at identifying the city's most sexist employers. The winner, E. F. MacDonald, received a bouquet of weeds and became the target of a DWW campaign. Activists distributed leaflets announcing the results of the contest at the entrance to the company, along with several hundred questionnaires on women's working conditions. More than fifty responses came back, half with names and addresses. DWW invited these women to a meeting and produced a leaflet based on survey results and interviews with employees. "From this kind of response, it looks like unrest is rampant. . . . [S]oon there will be a DWW within EFM," the group concluded."[59]

The company fought back. An E. F. MacDonald representative called the YWCA, to which the company was a donor, to ask about its relationship to DWW. Later, when DWW members returned to leaflet the company, another incident occurred: "Strangely enough, within 10 minutes after DWW distributed the results of our job survey, EFM reported a bomb threat and evacuated the building for the day."[60]

From its inception, the NWEP saw itself as a watchdog of the federal government. Despite impressive federal antidiscrimination measures,[61] poor enforcement limited the impact of such measures. For example, in 1977, the Equal Employment Opportunity Commission (EEOC) had a backlog of more than one hundred twenty thousand cases, and only around 11 percent culminated in a settlement.[62]

DWW had already embraced this cause, as stated in a proposal written with the Cleveland group: "Our projects are based on the recognition that there are laws which exist that prohibit sex and race discrimination in employment. . . . Systematic compliance with these laws by employers and strict enforcement by the appropriate agencies would go a long way toward eliminating sex and race discrimination on the job. This is precisely why we have chosen these existing laws as a framework to work within to begin to make the public policy commitment of equal employment opportunity a reality."[63]

At the 1977 Midwest Working Women's Conference, participants agreed on a plan that included researching local agencies, educating women about their rights, and pressuring the Carter administration to act.[64] DWW held workshops, and activists, armed with a list of questions from Chicago Women Employed, began investigating local compliance agencies. Meanwhile, the Carter administration had decided to reorganize the equal opportunity agencies.[65] Carter appointed feminist civil rights lawyer (and Antioch alumnus) Eleanor Holmes Norton to head the EEOC.[66]

With change in the air, national Women Working and its Ohio affiliates launched an Ohio Equal Employment campaign. Scores of other women's and civil rights organizations endorsed the campaign. In Dayton, the Women's Center, the NAACP, and the Black Political Assembly joined DWW's search for testimonies from people who had filed discrimination complaints.[67] DWW interviewed these people and met with local officials.[68] In 1979, DWW joined the other affiliates in Washington to meet with Norton. That summer the EEOC opened a Dayton office, due at least in part to pressures from DWW.[69] By the beginning of 1980, the Ohio campaign issued recommendations to the EEOC and the Ohio Civil Rights Commission, and the national organization used this and the other reports for its national campaign. However, by 1980 the political climate had changed dramatically.

Combining its work investigating federal agencies and companies, in 1977 DWW began what was to be its greatest success: the bank study. The banking industry had come under scrutiny from the working women's movement from the outset. As early as 1972, Union WAGE had issued a report on banking that found "a statistical pattern of employment discrimination against minorities and women"—a pattern that federal agencies left unchecked.[70] Chicago Women Employed had produced a pamphlet in 1974 on discrimination in the banks, and both Women Employed and 9 to 5 had published results of local investigations in 1976.[71]

With advice from Chicago and Boston, DWW joined the national effort in spring 1977. Members began surveying bank employees for firsthand accounts of discrimination. Their survey, a revised form of one used in other cities, asked: "Do you have a written job description? Do you think you are paid adequately for the work that you do? Is overtime really voluntary? Are all job openings posted and circulated through each department?"[72]

DWW members also investigated the banks' power structures. They discovered that of the sixty-three directors of the city's three largest banks, only two were women and none were from minorities. They traced the interlocking directorates of the banks and other corporate boards. (The corporation with the most overlap in its board of directors was Dayton Power and Light, long a target of local radicals and subsequently the object of a class action suit filed by DWW for sex and race discrimination.) DWW concluded: "[A] substantial amount of power is concentrated in the hands of a few white men, who neither represent nor share the concerns of most of this community."[73]

Through the Freedom of Information Act, DWW ordered copies of the banks' mandatory affirmative action programs and the Equal Employment Opportunity forms that gave statistics on racial and sexual breakdown of personnel. From the moment DWW received the first document, it knew it was on to something big. Although required to give annual updates and periodic reviews of goals and timetables, two of the three banks had not done so since 1971. One bank had submitted a program that was only twenty pages long and handwritten. It was not surprising that despite requirements that equal opportunity policies be publicized, a bank official told DWW, "We don't just wave these [affirmative action plans] around for *anyone* to see!"[74]

Statistics in the banks' own reports showed a pattern of discrimination that was even more blatant than national averages. Although white males made up only 28.2 percent of employees in the three major banks, they held 81.9 percent of the jobs as officials and managers (compared to 31.7 percent and 75 percent respectively in the nation); 89.3 percent of the office and clerical workers were women (82.6 percent nationally), accounting for 90.1 percent of all women employed by these banks (88.6

percent nationally).[75] One bank's affirmative action program showed that the already small number of women and minorities in managerial positions had dropped in preceding years. The bank proclaimed its intention to improve the situation, but gave none of the required goals or timetables. Another bank set goals for minority recruitment and training, but without even paying lip service to creating opportunities for women.

On July 10, 1978, after a year-long investigation, DWW issued a thirty-eight-page report entitled "Banks: Discrimination in Employment." The group organized a public meeting to present its findings to the associate director of the Office of Federal Contract Compliance Programs, who had come from Washington, D.C., for the occasion. Before an audience of some eighty-five women bank employees, journalists, representatives from minority organizations, and local enforcement agency officials, DWW members challenged the banks "to re-examine their own policies and commitments, in light of their responsibilities to their employees and to the community as a whole." However, DWW laid the major responsibility before the enforcement agency: "We demand that the Department of Labor, under the auspices of the OFCCP, intercede and immediately begin a review of the employment practices of each of Dayton's major commercial banks. . . . We recommend that in addition to the obligatory desk audit, the OFCCP begin an on-site review, receiving testimony and input from affected employees, at times and places removed from their place of work."[76]

The results of the meeting surpassed DWW's hopes. The OFCCP official immediately promised audits and on-site reviews, and pointed out that in a similar case in Chicago (a result of the Women Employed campaign), the government was asking for millions of dollars in back pay.[77] With hard data at hand, high-level officials present, and large sums of money at stake, Dayton's media coverage of the event was unprecedented.

In November 1978, nine investigators came to Dayton to conduct reviews at the banks, and officials again met with DWW. The ensuing process was not without snags. For five months, DWW battled with the federal bureaucracies to ensure a thorough investigation. It discovered, for instance, that although it had provided the review teams with the names of bank workers willing to testify, none had been contacted.[78]

In May 1980, the OFCCP, finding DWW's allegations *too* conservative, publicly declared that Third National Bank discriminated against women and minorities. "[A]pproximately 110 of the total affected class members are deserving of nearly $1 million in back pay plus prospective remedial actions such as training, promotions and employment benefits," the report concluded.[79] As a result of DWW's actions, the banks were required to develop new affirmative action plans. Bank employees reported to DWW that they received cost-of-living raises for the first time in many years, and that there was "a flurry of hiring and promotional activity directed at women and minorities."[80]

When the banking decision came through, it fell into the hands of an organization that was floundering. Despite a new slogan proclaiming itself "the movement of the '80s," despite its slick public face, despite excellent national connections, DWW had become an empty shell. Contracts were signed with the national organization to pursue other campaigns, but with no success. By the end of 1980, the organization had ceased publication of its newsletter and closed its office.

Several factors precipitated this seemingly sudden demise. The election of Ronald Reagan meant that numerous laws that gave the group direction were under attack. It became clear that a focus on federal antidiscrimination law and agencies no longer sufficed. At the same time, with the rise of unemployment, with added competition for work, and with the increase of divorce and female-headed families, fewer women were ready to take the risk of losing even a poor job. DWW was too small to offer protection from retaliation. It could not compare with the collective strength of a union.

What most weakened DWW, however, was Sherrie Holmes's departure from Dayton in March 1979. Having created a group largely due to and dependent on her leadership, she was in many ways irreplaceable. She had become a Dayton personality. She had shaken hands with the president at a White House conference on unemployment; she had been named an Ohio Woman of the Year; and upon her decision to leave the city, she was the subject of a profile in a Dayton newspaper.[81] Noreen Willhelm, perhaps the second most influential member of DWW, took over in her place, but she resigned in early 1980.

The final president, Claudia Kinder, noted that many women phased out their involvement in DWW after Holmes departed. "[A] number of people who had been very active for a number of years slowly became inactive, . . . and I noticed that they were all people who Sherrie had recruited. . . . I think that they were more committed to Sherrie than to the organization," she said.

Holmes's departure meant that links with the national working women's movement suffered. Her successors never assumed the status of partner to the other strong personalities in the national leadership. DWW's weaker position meant less input into national decisions. Previously, members seemed not to have resented the rigid framework of the contracts signed with the national organization, no doubt because their group, via Holmes, had played an active role in defining them. Later, as the movement grew and with the bureaucratization of Working Women, DWW had less input into the policy it was expected to follow.

The weakening relationship with national, the failure of nationally sponsored campaigns in Dayton, and the departure of Holmes also led to a decrease in DWW's funds. The burden of fund-raising, although time consuming, had never weighed as heavily on DWW as on the Women's Center, particularly because a big chunk of the budget came from national.[82] Holmes had convinced other national leaders that Dayton had political and symbolic importance to the national movement. Her successors were less convincing. Holmes also had years of fund-raising experience and an impressive network of contacts. Her successors lacked these skills and connections. Concomitantly, the deteriorating economic situation meant funds were drying up.[83] "Equal rights couldn't compare," the argument went, "as long as there were people who weren't eating."[84]

DWW, despite its discourse on outreach and cultivating leadership, never created a large, dedicated membership. Personality accounted for part of this. Above all, the organizational philosophy fostered passivity among members. Critics of DWL and the Women's Center had argued that a more traditional structure would give members greater control. In DWW the opposite was true, producing a hierarchical, undemocratic process and a passive following. For example, when an executive committee was created, a nominating committee made up of three persons, all designated by the president, prepared the slate of candidates.[85] When Willhelm resigned, the job opening was distributed via the national organization and publicized solely among the leadership. The slot was not even announced to DWW's general membership, Kinder said. Holmes handpicked her successors; Willhelm remembered no formal election process. Kinder recalled that the last thing Holmes said to her before leaving was, "I want you to run for president."

DWW's concept of leadership was profoundly different from that of previous movement organizations. The earlier feminists, former New Left activists, rejected the notion of the professional organizer. They warned of the (male) leader, seen as manipulative. Dayton Women's Liberation argued that leaders reinforced women's socialization to be passive; they thus sought a structure that would spread power as broadly as possible. Similarly, as the media began picking feminist stars, DWL, like groups around the country, resisted, never giving individual interviews and refusing to have designated spokeswomen. Women's Center activists promoted a more explicit and traditional structure to allow for account-ability of the leadership. Votes on issues sometimes occurred. But no officers were elected, work was done in task forces or collectives, and the highest decision-making body was always an open collective. For earlier feminists, the notion of leadership as an individual characteristic was taboo. When it did come up, it was attributed to a person's devotion of time and energy, and in some cases it was repressed.

DWW consciously sought to develop leaders and targeted people who possessed skills and were in positions to influence others. Leadership roles included "speaking for the group of women office workers in pub-lic"; "strategizing"; "providing order"; "raising funds"; and "develop-ing" other leaders. Potential leaders should "represent others"; leaders "must have followers," it was pointed out.[86] Holmes's organizing method went further than that of her teachers at the Midwest Academy. In Saul Alinsky's method, a group's staff cultivated other leaders and then stepped back. Holmes called this unrealistic: the staff and the lead-ership were often one and the same. This perhaps contradicted the prin-ciples of her teachers, but it also was a logical result of their approach.

The working women's movement nationally promoted the idea of professional organizers. It began, like unions and certain leftist organi-zations, to plant "inside organizers" in targeted places to create internal networks."[87] Working Women later required all of its employees "to dress approximately like the people we are organizing"[88] (a policy rem-iniscent of that adopted by the sixties ultraleft for its envoys to facto-ries). In this movement that started nationally as grass roots, a process of division developed between the organizers and the organized.

From being a feminist taboo, leadership had been recast as a quality. Holmes explained, "I felt like I was in the leadership roles for good rea-sons. I don't feel like I led people astray. I feel like I did try to promote things that I thought would benefit most people. I think people recog-nized that." Holmes's evaluation was correct: DWW's members trusted her entirely. Several participants believed she allowed them to maintain a minimal commitment without being guilt-tripped into doing more. "Most people didn't feel as though they had time for leadership," Holmes said. "A lot of times they had just never done anything with an organization before, so it wasn't like they thought they should be the ones to come up with all the ideas. They were looking for direction."[89]

DWW was an effective, pragmatic organization. However, effectiveness—through the division of labor, a simplified decision-making process, and direction provided by a small group—resulted in a passive membership. In previous organizations, political and personal differences were played out in passionate, conflictual debates, often on organizational structure. In DWW, the least democratic of the groups, the grass roots seemed uninterested in the question and no conflict was noted. Indeed, on this question, as on most others, there were fewer tensions in DWW than in any previous group. "One of the things that makes this organization so good is that we do get along so well," Gloria Koch commented at the time. Nonetheless, when deprived of its leaders, there was no one to take over.

DWW's exclusive focus on work also may have contributed to its demise. Having downplayed feminist issues, having created a tight organization with little room for discussion, DWW did not provide a basis from which members could build a general feminist framework. DWW's leaders may have been feminist and radical "deep down in their hearts," Kinder said, but in their efforts not to "alienate any potential members," their hidden agendas often got buried. As Jean Tepperman had predicted, radicals in the movement faced "a constant danger of forgetting their larger goals."[90]

DWW's history indicated that the divorce of work issues from feminist and radical ideas limited the group's impact. If, as DWW argued, women's socialization fostered passivity and trained them to fit the role of clericals, then understanding male domination would help them stand up for their rights. While many women came to DWW looking for support (i.e., single mothers or recently divorced women), their needs went beyond work issues. If new members were more aware of that than the average woman, they were no doubt ripe for feminism.

One example shows how avoiding overtly feminist analysis limited the organization: DWW did not challenge the organization of work. In the tension between seeing clerical work as either mindless labor or unacknowledged but dignified work, DWW opted for the latter. Virtually all the organization's attention was focused on improving the material conditions of, and attitudes toward, clerical workers. Contrary to previous organizations, DWW did not target the sexual segregation of the work force or the capitalist system.[91]

At the national level, the distance from feminist stances was even more flagrant. NWEP warned groups not to get involved in issues such as nontraditional work and sexual harassment.[92] DWW ignored this advice on the former issue, but not on the latter. Notes from the 1978

NWEP meeting recounted: "Problems of sexual harassment are too often portrayed as anti-male, not anti-boss." Furthermore, harassment was "more narrow than most people's experience and so is not a good organizing tool, and is issue-oriented, not member oriented."[93] Just days after this meeting, a Dayton newspaper reporter called DWW for a statement on the question. Willhelm, caught off guard, parroted the national position. The article that followed began, "'Fight on-the-job sexual harassment!' exhorts the latest banner hoisted over women's lib ramparts. But with no noticeable rallying of Dayton feminists to the cause." Willhelm, the article said, "expressed alarm that 'the overwhelming play given sexual harassment' diverts attention from matters of 'real' concern to female breadwinners." The article concluded with Willhelm saying that sexual harassment was "'encountered so infrequently, and [is] so borderline hard to define,' that recent emphasis on the issue 'is sort of a detriment to our organization. Since it's difficult to show the woman wasn't an accomplice, it's the most impossible kind of discrimination to deal with.'"[94] "I have never in my life regretted any words out of my mouth more than every single thing I said to that woman," Willhelm said of her off-the-cuff remarks. "We wanted to avoid titillation. We wanted to say, women need to be addressed as a serious piece of the work force." Yet DWW had received several complaints about demands for sexual favors. As a waitress, Willhelm had experienced unwanted attention, which she "knew had nothing to do with me, Noreen. It had everything to do with me as a woman, as chattel." A feminist consciousness-raising approach could have allowed DWW members to pool their experiences and redefine these individual problems as collective, political issues.[95]

Another example surfaced with the slogan "Raises, not Roses" for National Secretaries Week. Before this observance day was appropriated by the working women's movement, florists encouraged employers to give their secretaries flowers. The working women's movement built upon the feminist insight that acts of chivalry created a smokescreen to mask women's subordination. However, the slogan was also an obvious reference to the 1912 "Bread and Roses" strike in Lawrence, Massachusetts, and those roses, as the poem of the same name explained, stood for "art and love and beauty" to nourish the soul as bread did the body.[96] In Dayton, after several years, the slogan metamorphosed into "Raises and Roses"—not to reclaim the past, a past unknown to most DWW members, but, according to Kinder, because florists complained, and women protested that they liked receiving flowers. Both points made by the slogan were thus lost.

While proclaiming itself to be "the movement of the 80s," DWW's retreat from nonwork issues prevented it from fully comprehending the movement on the rise: the New Right. However, DWW was not unaware of this phenomenon. By early 1977, an internal report to affiliates warned of the New Right's use of the International Women's Year forum to oppose abortion and the Equal Rights Amendment, witnessed by several Daytonians firsthand at a Columbus preparatory conference. According to Willhelm, one antiabortion activist joined DWW to ensure that the organization steered clear of the issue. When DWW suggested that working women's organizations "consider a more explicit strategy of support for the ERA," it stressed that it was only "in order to defend antidiscrimination laws."[97] The organization argued that groups must debunk the Right's campaign to associate the ERA with abortion and gay rights, but again reiterated DWW's single-issue focus.[98] The rising opposition had no such qualms: abortion, the ERA, and homosexuality were only the first targets in a broad assault on all feminist issues. As the New Right gained strength, DWW's approach became increasingly inadequate. Perhaps the most eloquent criticism came inadvertently from a speech made by Willhelm: "[A]nother kind of approach must be utilized in organizing women. And the manner indicated is holistic. One must incorporate all aspects of a woman's life. A job is just one dimension of a vastly more important whole."[99]

Although born of the women's movement and distrustful of the unions, DWW and the working women's movement can be viewed more as a step in labor history than in feminism. As the Congress of Industrial Organizations attempted to democratize the labor movement by organizing previously excluded workers, so did DWW by organizing women workers who had been snubbed by the unions. In the early 1970s, it was still unthinkable for most Dayton women to hope for a job in unionized industry or to imagine organizing in the sexually segregated world where most worked. By the end of the decade—thanks to DWW, the working women's movement, and feminist labor activism—labor organizing had become a possibility in a way that it had never been to most women. At its inception, few members of DWW were active in, or even familiar with, the existing unions. By the time of its demise, the situation had changed. Relations with the unions had improved, and signs of local unions' courting DWW appeared, as was occurring nationwide. Several important DWW members became active in unions. DWW supported improved status for office workers, but always within a context of collective action, not as tokenism or getting "a piece of the pie." "Obviously (at least I hope it's obvious) our intention is not to create more women bosses," Willhelm wrote.[100]

DWW cut across class lines and had black sympathizers, both among women workers and within civil rights organizations. Within the organization, openness to feminist ideas was apparently high. Members were becoming more involved in unions. Relations with labor were good, and the unions seemed finally to be realizing the gendered meaning of the local economy's increasing dependence on the service sector. The time was ripe for a permanent organization to advocate for women workers, and even if stability need not be an overarching goal for all social movement organizations, the demise of DWW was unfortunate.

When DWW closed its office in Dayton, it did not do so without leaving its mark. The group helped create a national working women's movement. Among the accomplishments of the local and national movements was the translation of laws and bureaucratic procedures into accessible issues, demands, and political campaigns. "We turned federal regulations and procedures into things which had direct impact on women's daily work," said an NWEP report.[101] The movement later catapulted one of its national leaders, Karen Nussbaum, to the head of the Women's Bureau of the Department of Labor. Locally, its activists carried their vision into their places of work. DWW contributed to the growing consciousness that the low salaries and status of clericals and other women workers were due not to inferiority, but to sexism.

7

COALITION
BUILDING
Freedom of Choice (1975–80)

I n EARLY 1978, an antiabortion law was introduced in Akron, Ohio, some two hundred miles northeast of Dayton. "The unborn child is a human life from the moment of conception," the so-called Akron ordinance proclaimed.[1] Other provisions included "informed consent," requiring abortion providers to give the patient a full description of the fetus. It also obligated doctors to notify parents of unmarried pregnant minors before performing an abortion.[2] Rumors began circulating that Dayton was next on the antiabortionists' hit list.

The Akron ordinance was by no means the first sign of antiabortion activism. The second half of the 1970s saw the rise of a New Right in the United States. While some of its leaders were from the old radical Right, the movement was new in its issues and its mobilization of a mass base. Although often against a backdrop of anticommunist, anti-social welfare, and racist old right-wing politics, its new spearhead, "defense of the family," was antifeminism.[3] Specifically, it met the women's movement on its own turf, contesting its monopoly on direct-action protest and its role as a cultural vanguard. It countered feminists' key issues: the Equal Rights Amendment, child care, rights of homosexuals, sex education, and even battered women's shelters. Of all the issues addressed, none so effectively and durably mobilized and linked diverse components as abortion.[4]

To oppose these groups, activists from Dayton's women's movement joined with liberal women and men to form the Freedom of Choice coalition, the most obvious organizational heir to the city's movement at the time. Freedom of Choice differed from previous organizations in both form and content, attesting to shifts in the women's movement and presaging developments in the 1980s. The new group marked the entry of liberal women into the movement, far later than the literature suggests in other cities. As a coalition, it assumed a new kind of organizational structure much in vogue across the nation. It was pragmatic and single-issue, going even further in this respect than Dayton Women Working had. As a defensive, reactive initiative, it warned of the rough times ahead, times of right-wing ascension and rising antifeminism.

The coalition, called Freedom of Choice, Miami Valley, continued throughout the eighties, well after the period studied here. It proved effective at accomplishing what it set out to do: opposing local antiabortion legislation. However, as the largest, most visible feminist organization of its time, it illustrated how, in the ten years since the beginning of the movement, the subject "woman" had become too vast to be contained in one organization and how fragmented that movement was becoming. Ironically, as the women's movement specialized and its subject splintered, antifeminists linked the diverse questions far more effectively than did feminists.

Nationally and locally, attacks against abortion rights followed on the heels of the 1973 Supreme Court ruling that legalized abortion across the nation. In Ohio, only a few weeks after the decision, a Right to Life activist tried to prevent the state laws from being struck down in the "Mary Doe" test case by establishing a trust fund for "Doe's" fetus (or "unborn baby," as he put it). "Civil Rights had been struck down," he explained. "I thought maybe property rights would be considered."[5] Local antiabortion groups picketed Dayton's abortion clinic and staged protests, including the burial of a fetus on the anniversary of *Roe v. Wade* in 1976. Nationally, the first serious restriction to the Supreme Court decision came in late 1976 when Congress passed the Hyde Amendment to the 1977 Labor/HEW budget, allowing states to refuse Medicaid funds for elective abortions.

Dayton feminists, contrary to a commonly held opinion, had not abandoned the issue of abortion after *Roe v. Wade*.[6] The difficulties of obtaining an abortion locally had kept them on their toes—as evidenced by the creation of the abortion clinic. Dayton Women's Liberation had continued to monitor the situation and put out three calls in 1974 alone for letter-writing campaigns to head off restrictive bills being discussed in the state legislature. But after DWL's demise in 1975, the issue faded into the background. Dayton Women Working, the most active movement component by the time the Akron ordinance was adopted, avoided it intentionally.

Although the Women's Center expressed concern to the press about threats to abortion rights,[7] Robin Suits recalled that her attempts to mobilize against the Hyde Amendment met with little response. The Center was handicapped by its service orientation, its ambivalence toward political action, bad feelings about the abortion clinic,[8] and, no doubt, class and race bias. The Center did support reproductive freedom, however, through services (abortion referrals and collecting money to help women pay for abortions) and public education, such as its classes on women's health.

Before 1977, if Dayton feminists expected problems, it was from the government or from the medical establishment. No one imagined the emergence of a new social movement that would meet them on their own turf of radical protest. The year 1977 marked a turning point in antiabortion agitation. In February, a Planned Parenthood clinic in St. Paul, Minnesota, was the victim of arson, and six months later, an abortion clinic in Omaha, Nebraska, was firebombed.[9]

Daytonians awoke to the growing strength of antiabortion and other antifeminist forces at the May 1977 Ohio conference to choose delegates for the International Women's Year Conference in Houston. Dayton feminists from all horizons were roused: pioneers Mary Morgan, Kathy Kleine, Jan Griesinger, and Betty Jean Carroll; Women's Center activist Kathy Ellison; and Dayton Women Working's Sherrie Holmes and Noreen Willhelm were among those who attended. They had heard about antifeminist mobilization for the event, but they were unprepared for what they encountered at the state fairgrounds in Columbus: "[T]hese buses pull up. And these men . . . jump off the buses with clipboards, and women follow them. And they start going, 'You, that way! You, that way!' And they're assigning women to the various conference workshops, plenary sessions," Willhelm recounted. Although a poll of the women who attended the Columbus conference showed that they backed both the ERA and abortion rights by about two to one,[10] divisions among feminists prevented them from blocking the opposition.[11] Ohio joined ten other states in which right-wing coalitions won more than half the slates.[12] "Be forewarned!" said a report from DWW. "Right to Life and the Eagle Forum (Pres. Phyllis Schafly) are putting an incredible amount of money and organizational effort into these statewide conference[s]. . . . They are using the [International Women's Year] forum to oppose abortion and the ERA. They managed to get 45 Right to Lifers out of 56 Ohio delegates elected."[13] Feminists realized that the days when the right wing shunned protest and direct action had come to an end. Willhelm, new to abortion politics, said, "We couldn't hold a candle to that kind of organization.

And we certainly couldn't hold a candle to the kind of venom they had."

By the time of the Akron ordinance, two elements had gelled at the Women's Center. First, members had become interested in coalition-building, thanks to the success of the 1977 Needs of Women conference, and to coalitions formed for the International Women's Year Conference that same month. Searching for a unifying issue, some suggested repro-ductive health. Although another issue was chosen, clearly the topic was present in people's minds.[14] When external events—the Akron ordinance, attacks on clinics, and new restrictive Supreme Court rulings[15]—pushed abortion to the forefront, the group rapidly and readily diverted its ener-gies to abortion rights.

The Women's Center reacted before any other Dayton group to the threat posed by the Akron ordinance. Alerted by feminist contacts, members traveled to Akron to protest the ordinance and to collect infor-mation. On February 8, 1978, the Center collective decided to form a coalition on the issue.[16] Several days later, a clinic in Cleveland fell vic-tim to an arsonist.

Pat Russell-Campbell, active in both the Women's Center and the statewide NOW, first spoke with abortion clinic director Anita Wilson, who had been closely following the situation across the state. The two women were next-door neighbors and had previously discussed the growing threat of the antiabortion movement. The Center decided to contact Anne Saunier, a recent arrival to Dayton and, as she herself put it, a feminist mini-celebrity.

Days before her arrival in Dayton, the previously unknown Saunier had captured the public eye as a chairperson at the IWY conference in Houston. An expert in parliamentary procedure, she had commanded the respect of feminists and antifeminists alike for her handling of even the most controversial sessions. "Delegates on both sides were captivat-ed by her," Gail Sheehy wrote in *Redbook*. National publications from *Time, Elle,* and the *New York Times* to the radical feminist *off our backs* joined in their praise of Saunier. Her arrival in Dayton as a top execu-tive for the Mead Corporation was heralded with long eulogistic articles in the local press.[17]

Dayton feminists were ambivalent about Saunier's blazing entry onto the Dayton scene. Some resented her media stardom and feared her cor-porate connections. Nevertheless, they had always avoided dogmatic antileadership positions, and Saunier's solid feminist credentials and straightforward attitude quickly put their qualms to rest. Indeed, despite

Saunier's mainstream profile, her outspoken and unequivocal feminism commanded the respect of the feminist community.

Saunier came from an old American family that, as she liked to tell, included a Salem woman who had been put to death for witchcraft. Saunier, born in 1946, grew up in a rural Ohio college town. Her father was an attorney, and her mother was a homemaker who became the first woman president of the school board and the first female elder of their Presbyterian church. Despite having this positive role model, Saunier suffered from low self-esteem throughout her teens. It was only when she left her hometown at age twenty-two to go to graduate school in Columbus that she resolved the problem through marriage and feminism. "On one hand, the marriage put to rest the issue of male approval, . . . and the women's movement helped me to realize that that isn't the right measuring stick to use, anyway!" she said.

As an undergraduate, Saunier had majored in public address and rhetoric, which later proved invaluable in her career and her feminist activism. Her minor in philosophy and religion helped her understand her disagreement with her church. She joined a Unitarian congregation in Columbus, and there she encountered NOW.

Saunier became active in NOW and was elected president of the local chapter. Through NOW, she testified in hearings on a gay rights bill, worked on employment issues, and became one of the key persons behind the Ohio ERA ratification campaign. Although consciousness-raising groups had not been part of Saunier's experience and initial awareness, she later felt the need to join one, specifically on issues of sexuality. This group, composed of both heterosexual and lesbian women, was intended to provide a free environment for participants to explore their own sexuality and to understand each other's. "All of us at that time who were leaders in the women's movement [and] who were straight took a lot of pummeling in the public about the homosexual aspects of the movement," Saunier said. "I felt that unity in the movement was extraordinarily important and that we should not allow any outside force to divide gay women from straight women—and sometimes, one's own ignorance becomes that divisive element."

The Women's Center was not the only group that turned to Saunier for help. She recalled: "Several different women in the community came to me and said, 'We need a coalition on reproductive freedom and . . . we have never been able to have a successful coalition in this community. . . . We think that you're the right person because you're corporate and you're going to be trusted by these more conservative groups; and because you have good feminist credentials in your history, you will probably be able to be trusted by the Women's Center people.'" Among those to approach Saunier was Faye Wattleton, the thirty-four-year-old president of Planned Parenthood of Miami Valley. Wattleton, after eight years as head of the Dayton affiliate, had just been selected to head national Planned Parenthood, the first African American ever to hold the position and the first woman since Margaret Sanger had founded the American Birth Control League.

At the national level, Planned Parenthood had supported legalized abortion since 1970.[18] In Dayton, where other groups provided services, the organization downplayed the issue; as one board member put it, "Planned Parenthood has a lot of conservative money behind it."[19] Planned Parenthood made referrals to the Clergy and Lay consultation service and later to the abortion clinic, but until the mid-1970s little mention of abortion was made in its newsletters.

Since its rebirth in 1964 (the first Dayton birth control clinic, founded in 1935, had disbanded in 1955), most important board members and donors to the local Planned Parenthood had indeed been conservative. However, upon closer examination, one can discern radical influences. Cofounder Konrad Reisner, who first invited Faye Wattleton onto the board and who later encouraged her to apply for the position of local executive director, was known in Dayton as the head of the country's Family Services. Less known to the community was that he had been an antifascist and radical pacifist in Germany in the 1930s. Elsa Reisner, also active in creating Planned Parenthood, had been a left-wing Social Democrat and had fought Nazi antihomosexual and antiabortion policies before swimming the Rhine to escape arrest. At least one other early member had been an active socialist in her youth in New York.

As director of the Dayton Planned Parenthood, Wattleton, a public health nurse who had witnessed the distress of pregnant teens, had eased the organization out of some of its conservative positions, such as its initial policy against dispensing birth control to minors.[20] By the midseventies, the organization had moved away from its timid beginnings thanks to new arrivals who joined the ranks of progressives and feminist sympathizers.

Most important in Planned Parenthood's transformation was its response to conservative attacks. The growing antiabortion movement had begun targeting the birth control and sex education services offered by Planned Parenthood. As a Right to Life Society paper distributed in Dayton put it: "[T]he IUD and certain drugs taken before or after intercourse do not prevent the union of sperm and ovum. . . . A new human life does begin, but this tiny, tiny boy or girl dies at or before one week of life because he or she cannot implant into the nutrient lining of the mother's womb. The IUD and these drugs really at times cause very early abortions."[21] As the antiabortion forces gained momentum, Planned Parenthood rose to the top of their enemy list. Among other ludicrous accusations, the organization was accused of handing out diaphragms without fitting them in order to drum up business for its abortion clinics, and of having a "big barrel" of contraceptives in the lobby so that "anybody who wants to can just stick their hands in and pull them out."[22] Dayton Right to Life president Ginny Folsom wrote to each member of the chamber of commerce to urge them to withdraw their support for Planned Parenthood. Folsom cited the organization's "immoral" sex education programs, such as the one that "condones such practices as abortion, masturbation, and pre-marital sex—and seemingly encourages homosexual acts," and another that emphasized "the unwholesome prurient aspects of human sexual behavior."[23]

As the Right's attacks escalated, the scope of Dayton Planned Parenthood expanded. From 1976, its newsletter addressed the issue of abortion regularly, speaking out against the restrictive measures being taken. When Wattleton became the new president of the Planned Parenthood Federation of America in 1978, she proved to be a fervent defender of abortion rights. In one of her first public statements Wattleton announced her intention to aggressively oppose Right to Life, characterized as a minority group trying to impose its personal and religious dogmas on the population.[24]

On the home front, Wattleton threw her weight behind the coalition project. As with the Women's Center, coalition-building had been on Planned Parenthood's agenda; by late 1975, the national federation's five-year plan identified it as a priority, particularly in order to keep abortion legal.[25] When Planned Parenthood entered the fray, it carried with it a broad base of support.

On February 28, 1978, the Akron city council voted seven to six in favor of the antiabortion ordinance. The next day, Akron's abortion clinic joined the growing list of victims of attacks by antiabortionists. In Dayton, feminists learned that Right to Life supporters had approached city commissioners to push for a similar ordinance.

On March 6, the Women's Center convened a group to brainstorm plans for action. Ten people attended the meeting, including Saunier, Wilson, representatives of Planned Parenthood and of the Free Clinic, and feminist activist Sherry Novick and three other women involved in the Center, the New American Movement, Dayton Women Working, and Lesbians United.[26] One week later, a second meeting drew a much larger crowd, with, in addition to the above mentioned groups, representatives from local NOW chapters, the Urban League, and the YWCA's Battered Women's Shelter. Russell-Campbell remembered her pleasure and surprise at the group's diversity—along with "a bunch of men," there were women "dressed up in suits, hose, and heels," in contrast to her peers, "sitting there in jeans and bib overalls, T-shirts, and jogging shoes."

The assembly adopted a statement of purpose[27] and discussed a new statewide coalition called Freedom of Choice-Ohio that had been founded several days previously at a NOW-sponsored meeting that Russell-Campbell had helped organize. Then the Planned Parenthood representative interjected that her organization was convening a meeting the following week to form a larger coalition. She "extended the invitation to the group to join forces at the first meeting," that is, to step back and merge with the "new" coalition.[28] Saunier supported the decision and at Wattleton's request discussed it with representatives of the Women's Center. "The Women's Center had started a little effort at coalition," Saunier said, "and of course what [happened was] that . . . they [were] able to get NAM and the socialist groups and lesbian groups, and so on. But they [couldn't] get Planned Parenthood [and other groups]. So I kind of nuzzled in on their coalition. . . . But they seemed willing to accept my leadership."

Center activists did go along, both in the spirit of unity and to keep themselves "as low-key as possible at the beginning."[29] "It was such a hot issue," Russell-Campbell said, recalling talks about who should be visible. "Everybody knew we were going to get hit with [accusations] that [we were] 'baby-killers' and all that stuff. So we needed somebody that looked real sane and normal, and real monied." Wilson was out of the question; her position at the abortion clinic could lead to accusations of a profit motivation, and many feminists still distrusted her. Wattleton was preparing to leave the city. The Center agreed on Saunier. "We wanted to come across as being real professional," Russell-Campbell said. "Anne could do that. She carried herself well; she was also an up-and-coming businesswoman, she was known in the community, . . . she was 'somebody.'"

On March 20, 1978, a large community meeting was held in the Planned Parenthood offices. The letter calling the meeting, signed by

Wattleton, went to the pooled mailing lists of all the organizations represented at the first meetings. Perhaps a hundred people attended. The agenda, prepared by the Women's Center and Planned Parenthood, began with an opening address by Wattleton. "I don't think that in the entire, almost ten years I have worked with Planned Parenthood, that I have seen a group such as this convene around a common concern," she began. Her concerns converged with those of local feminists: that is, to prevent the coalition from being too narrowly focused. "I think that, even though abortion has [brought] us together, we must recognize that there are signs that there are . . . forces within our society that would tend to limit our reproductive freedoms in many areas, so that your coming together tonight, I think, really symbolizes, not only a concern around the maintenance of choice for abortion, but around the maintenance . . . of reproductive rights in general." This meeting officially marked the founding of Freedom of Choice, Miami Valley.

The most striking aspect of FOC was its composition: it was the most heterogeneous of all of Dayton's feminist organizations. In particular, FOC marked Dayton's first alliance between the liberal and feminist communities and probably the first major liberal/left-wing coalition since the early civil rights movement.

Motivations for joining FOC were diverse. Sherry Novick recalled: "[T]wo people came out because they [ran] the abortion clinic in town; other people came out because they [believed] in population control; other people came out because they were really pissed at the right wing; . . . other people came out because they [were] young and potentially [needed] the services." Many who worked in the social services were undoubtedly responding to the anti–social welfare concerns of the New Right. As the Right's strength increased, particularly after Ronald Reagan became president, FOC's appeal spread.

The organizational members of the coalition, seventeen on average, illustrated this broad span. The feminist Women's Center and Fairborn NOW coexisted with the traditional American Association of University Women. Socialist NAM and the radical National Lawyers' Guild chapters joined, along with the liberal American Civil Liberties Union. At first, "women's groups" (that is, groups either composed of women or solely addressing women's issues) accounted for more than half of the organizations, although fewer than a quarter were explicitly feminist. Between a third and a half of the groups had religious affiliations, including the Unitarian Fellowship, Episcopal Church Women, the reform synagogue's board of directors, and the National Council of Jewish Women.

Other organizational members were Planned Parenthood, the Free Clinic, the abortion clinic, the National Alliance for Optional Parenthood, the campus-based Women's Action Coalition, the Dayton Area Religious Coalition for Abortion Rights, and, in 1980, the new local chapter of NARAL, the National Abortion Rights Action League. Many other groups, not officially members, later endorsed FOC's goals and activities, including the National Council of Negro Women, the Miami Presbytery's Committee on Women and the Church, the Quaker American Friends Service Committee, Catholics for Free Choice, a new University of Dayton Women's Law Caucus, and the Springfield battered women's shelter.

Individual membership grew from about 100 in the first months to around 150 by 1980. More than 500 people were on the mailing list by 1981.[30] The assembly of individuals was as heterogeneous as the patchwork of organizations. Members were drawn in through the mailing lists of numerous feminist, liberal, and left-wing groups, as well as through the largest community and friendship network to be put to work for a feminist cause.

The group was cosexual. Consensus on including men was such that it was not even discussed. However, while men made up a majority in some of the organizational member groups, only a small fraction became individual members or actively involved in FOC.[31]

Membership was geographically dispersed, far more so than for any other feminist organization. Sign-up sheets from general membership meetings showed a substantially larger segment of members from suburban communities than from the Dayton View/Five Oaks area, including many from affluent South Dayton.

There was one limit to the group's diversity: it was predominantly white. Despite the overwhelming support among blacks for abortion rights,[32] and despite the fact that one of the movement's public figurehead, Wattleton, was black, few black women got involved in the grass roots. The handful who did participate actively did so as organizational members, notably from the YWCA or the Urban League. The presence of black women in the leadership of reproductive rights groups in the 1970s, in contrast to their absence at the grass-roots level, has been noted elsewhere; Loretta Ross called them visionaries without a constituency.[33] Neither Wattleton's leadership, nor the liberals' ties to civil rights, nor the radicals' antiracist rhetoric sufficed to dispel the white image of the group. In part, this image derived from association with the women's movement, but blacks also had to contend with ambivalence linked to the eugenicist past of the birth control movement. "It is extremely likely that the racism of the birth control organizers [of the 1930s], coupled with the genocidal assumptions of eugenics supporters . . . has fueled Black opposition to family planning up to the present time," Ross wrote.[34] Black women, like the early liberationists, had developed a dual analysis that required both bodily self-determination and freedom from coercive measures. Whereas both Dayton Women's Liberation and the Women's Center offered pregnancy tests and many services and actions geared to pregnant women and mothers, and the former campaigned against eugenicist measures (such as the bill offering welfare mothers financial incentives to have abortions), FOC's broad discourse on reproductive freedom rarely translated into practice. Furthermore, the city's abortion clinic was situated in the heart of an all-white southern suburb, and its directors never expanded services to offer women's health care, as originally planned.

FOC membership signified a financial and moral contribution to a cause—in some cases even "liberal credentials"—rather than a commitment to activism. Many of the new recruits were people who "would be supportive on paper and give money, but . . . just weren't activist women," Sherry Novick said. Sybil Silverman described how she joined FOC and then NARAL: "Just like I belong to NOW nationally, I guess my name is on mailing lists you wouldn't believe—from whales to seals to gun control, and every liberal movement. . . . We got information from NARAL and make our contribution to that."[35] Even in the activist core of ten to twenty people, some women rejected direct action because they were not, as they put it, flag-wavers.

Two forces drove Freedom of Choice. On one hand, feminists from earlier movement groups were instrumental in the creation of the organization and remained an important force throughout. The other major force, new to the women's movement, was the liberals, particularly those who called themselves "the old Dayton View liberals."[36]

The Dayton View liberals had worked together in community and civil rights actions in the mid-1960s. Although many no longer lived in Dayton View, the neighborhood had been the site for much of their activism and was vital to their political and social identity. As FOC began, most of these activists were in their late thirties to late fifties. The word "old" in their label referred not to age but to a bygone era.

Dayton View, a pleasant residential area with old houses and tree-lined streets, was the city's only racially integrated neighborhood in the 1960s. Much of the predominantly white Dayton View liberal group had chosen to live in the neighborhood as a commitment to integration. As Noel Vaughn, president of FOC in 1980, said: "I had a baby at that point, and I wanted him to have the experience of knowing different kinds of people." Like many others, Vaughn had been active on the Dayton View Neighborhood Council, serving on its executive committee and chairing its neighborhood stabilization committee. Stabilization meant discouraging white flight as blacks moved into an area. "This was the time of block-busting," Vaughn said. "You'd wake up one morning and there would be fifteen for-sale signs on the block. And then the neighbors would just go crazy. And we would sit in people's kitchens and try to calm them down. We would hold block meetings. . . . And we would sit and talk and try to keep them from fleeing. And a lot of people fled."

Although not Jewish herself, Vaughn attributed much of her political development to contacts with the progressive Jewish community in Chicago.[37] Jews congregated in Dayton View, the site of the city's three synagogues, in part because real estate agents refused to rent or sell to Jews in many parts of the city (particularly south of town) well into the 1960s.

Vaughn was from a highly educated, conservative Republican family from Chicago. After graduating from college, she followed her then husband to Dayton. As the daughter and granddaughter of working women, she assumed that she too would have a career. Over the years, she worked for the YWCA, at a Dayton-based foundation in a high-level public relations position, and as a teacher in public and private high schools as well as at a local university. The beginning period of FOC found Vaughn in the midst of law school. After completing her undergraduate studies in 1959 she had considered becoming a lawyer, but was discouraged by her professors. "We didn't fight then. If someone said, 'Women don't go to law school,' then women didn't go to law school." Seventeen years later, at age thirty-eight, she decided to prove that they could.[38]

Finding law school tedious, Vaughn began volunteering at Planned Parenthood, and there, friends from her Dayton View days drew her into FOC. Vaughn had considered herself a feminist for years. She had long been a member of national NOW and had taught a high school women's studies class in a private school. She had been aware of the Dayton women's movement, sending occasional contributions to the Women's Center. But it was not until she joined FOC that she saw a feminist issue as truly being on the cutting edge. "I think [abortion] may be a more crucial issue to women's rights than anything else now," she said.

"We've got to be able to control our own bodies, if we're going to be able to control our careers and our lives."

Sybil Silverman, another Dayton View inhabitant, had also been sympathetic to the women's movement for some time. A member of national NOW, Silverman agreed with some feminist demands but believed that "all the fringe issues about bra-burning—that was nonsense." She had once been asked to teach a class at the Women's Center, but was turned off by the members' refusal, she said, to place being a human before being a woman. "I consider myself a feminist because I consider myself a humanist first who happens to be female," she said.

Silverman had also been involved in community and civil rights work in Dayton View, but this had by no means been her initiation into politics. She was born in 1921 and reared in a Brooklyn Jewish ghetto. Her Menshevik father had fled Russia to escape conscription in the czar's army, and her mother had left because of the limited educational opportunities for women. In America, both parents became active socialists and got involved in the Jewish Labor movement. Silverman, an "atheist Jew," became a member of the Young People's Socialist League. (She was not the only former socialist among her Dayton friends. Although buried under the weight of 1950s conformism and repression, many of her peers had been radicals in their youth.) Silverman attended school with children from the nearby black ghetto, and she believes that this was one reason why she became a lifelong supporter of civil rights.

Silverman became a war bride in 1942 and followed her husband to military bases around the country, including in Texas and Florida. When the war came to an end, Silverman, who had developed the unpopular habit of breaking segregation laws, suggested to her husband that they either move north or start a bail fund for her. Over the following years, the couple lived in St. Louis and Chicago. Silverman continued her work for civil rights and progressive causes as an early member of CORE (Congress of Racial Equality), the ACLU (American Civil Liberties Union), the Independent Voters of Illinois, and later, the National Council of Jewish Women. Concomitantly, she began a career in the social services.

Silverman settled in Dayton in the early 1960s when her husband became director of the reform Jewish temple. She distinguished herself by not conforming to expectations. She did not attend religious services, women's clubs meetings, or social events, and did not unquestioningly support Israel. Silverman invested most of her energy in social service work, including projects specifically serving women. As part of the

National Council of Jewish Women, she helped found a program to help young women escape poverty by offering tutoring, scholarships, and day care. She was a cofounder of the first Planned Parenthood group in 1965. Thirteen years later, the Planned Parenthood alert network drew Silverman into FOC.

Silverman and Vaughn, despite their strikingly different backgrounds and a difference in age of nearly two decades, approached feminism similarly. Many of their attitudes were echoed among liberal women.

First, these women did not perceive themselves personally as victims of discrimination. "It was the rare and remote issue that I would have been denied anything as a woman," Silverman declared. "I didn't have any problem entering into school, into work, into any area, so that my consciousness as a woman who was oppressed didn't make sense, because I wasn't oppressed." Vaughn agreed, despite her anecdotes of receiving unequal pay, of being asked at job interviews about her method of contraception, and of being expected to do her own typing while male colleagues were not. "It never occurred to me that I wasn't equal to anything I knew. . . . I have never fought to be recognized," Vaughn said. "I just always assumed that I would be, and I think because that was my attitude, I've met very little discrimination."

For these women, feminism represented a personal awareness of their equality with men. Their consciousness, whether attributed to personal initiative, luck, or class privileges, tended to be that of being the exceptional woman. For example, whereas for early feminists the experience of reading *The Feminine Mystique* was one of breaking through isolation, for Silverman it was "the consciousness that other women were not like me." As Marie Ferguson, another FOC endorser and old Dayton View activist looked back, "I come from a family where women I knew all my life were lawyers, doctors, professors. . . . I was brought up to think that women could do anything and everything, and I find it hard to relate to the women's movement."[39] Vaughn explained that she did not contest the unequal pay she received at one job because she was the highest paid woman in the company, hence among the elite of female workers.

If to these women feminism meant an individual consciousness of equality, inversely, they saw oppression or discrimination as the result of women internalizing their "role." Discrimination, they believed, had little or no material basis. The women of the feminine mystique, at least those of their own class, were considered responsible for their lot. Silverman said of women at her temple socials: "I did not sense that I had

to convince these women, because they made their own choices. . . . They were not locked into anything that kept them down
except themselves." Only in the case of women of color or, in some
cases, poor women did the liberals acknowledge material oppression.
However, if these women needed help to overcome their role, it was
because of racial discrimination or economics, not sexism.

Vaughn and Silverman came to their feminism with no blinding-light
conversion experiences. Vaughn believed she had "always been a feminist." For Silverman, it was "a natural propulsion" that "flowed with
the principles that I held before." Many of the liberal FOC supporters,
who shared these attitudes toward feminism, called themselves human-
ists and rejected the label "feminist." Vaughn, Silverman, and a handful
of others, however, came to identify themselves as feminists, and this,
despite the different meaning given to the term, constituted a public
commitment to the women's movement.

Women from the liberal contingent of FOC shared a number of characteristics. They were white, well educated, heterosexual, and for the
most part married or divorced. They had a history of community and
volunteer activities. A significant minority were homemakers, but most
had careers. They were older than the socialist feminist contingent of the
FOC, but not older than DWL's early core group.[40]

Despite similarities to previous feminist activists, a number of differences existed. First, there were both real and perceived class differences
between the two groups. The liberal group apparently saw itself as higher class than previous activists. Silverman described the Center clientele
as women who "for the most part were lower middle class, were caught
in the trap of childbearing, were not conscious of their choices." On the
other end, Sherry Novick said FOC attracted a lot of "society women—
upper-middle-class women." Pat Russell-Campbell remembered, "Somehow, the abortion issue was an issue that all the upper-upper middle
class could get involved with."

The paths of these two groups of women had separated in the 1960s.
While both had been involved in civil rights and community activism,
the liberals' sympathies had stopped with the advent of Black Power. For
instance, Silverman, with her Jewish consciousness of pogroms and ghet-
tos, rejected all forms of separatism. Marie Ferguson said, "I was
brought up [to believe] that integration was the thing to accomplish, and
I found it very difficult to relate to Black Pride." Consequently, these
women's sexual politics also was based on the model of integration,
rather than separatism or autonomy.

As the golden era of the integrationist civil rights movement drew to an end, many Dayton liberals had found a new focus: fair funding, innovative educational programs, and supporting racial integration in the public schools. They rapidly faced the backlash of a right-wing, segregationist group called Save Our Schools, which later won control of the school board and ousted the liberal superintendent[41] and creative programs in the schools. The new Right of the late 1970s, supposedly dedicated to saving children, spurred memories of past struggles.

While the early feminists-to-be poured their energies into antiwar activism, the liberals, while few were hawks, never did. Similarly, the liberals remained distant from the counterculture.

These liberal women did not get involved in the new women's movement, although some sent dues to national NOW.[42] They stayed in traditional organizations—and apparently infused them with diluted feminist vision. For example, as Saunier noted with surprise, the elite philanthropic Junior League supported relatively progressive projects.

The liberals described their feminist consciousness as a gradual process. Some earlier activists also recounted a process with no revelatory experience—generally because they "grew up with feminism"—but once in the movement they developed strong feelings of sisterhood and of belonging to the group "women." The liberal women, even those who called themselves feminists, did not identify with women as a group. They saw no conflicting interests with men as a group. To the contrary, their husbands and men of their class were seen as allies. (While male allies were considered to exist in all classes, authoritarian men were considered to be more common among lower classes.[43]) The other feminists, they claimed, were either misdirecting their hostility or had married the wrong men.

Most of the liberal women took a social service approach to feminism (helping "other women"), and abortion was no exception. Vaughn recalled, "One of the most interesting things about this movement is that the majority of the women, if we're being honest . . . I don't know very many women who have had abortions. Most of the women who are involved in it have an intellectual commitment rather than a personal one. . . . It may never affect them or their daughters or anybody they particularly know."

This contrasted drastically with the feminists' attitude that feminism should and did serve their interests as part of the group "women." They were convinced that abortion was an issue that deeply affected all women, and that a large part of support stemmed from personal experience.[44] As later FOC vice president Betty Jean Carroll said, "What woman hasn't been pregnant and wanted an abortion, or had somebody [who had]?" Russell-Campbell believed many FOC activists had had abortions themselves: "There'd be women who would say that in strict confidence— you know, 'I had an abortion.' . . . There were women who didn't want anything else to do with the women's movement. They'd say, 'I'm not a feminist, but they can't take away abortion, 'cause I've had one.' [There were] women who'd had illegal abortions and went through holy hell and [who] wanted to make sure it didn't go back to that." Even in the movement, according to Russell-Campbell, some women spoke openly of their experience with abortion only after the beginning of FOC.

One long-time feminist and FOC activist confirmed this. Feminists, she believed, may have talked about abortion in CR groups but not publicly before FOC. She, too, evoked personal reasons for her commitment to reproductive freedom: "During the period when abortion was illegal . . . all of my daughters had illegal abortions and I nearly lost one. . . . I had five children, and three were unwanted. The women in my own family needed to be protected."

Several women bridged the gap between the liberals and the feminists in FOC. Saunier was one, as was Maureen Lynch. Lynch, who was thirty at the time of FOC's beginning, grew up in a Catholic family of five children. Her parents owned a small business in Akron. Having gone to Catholic schools throughout her youth, Lynch moved to Dayton in 1965 to attend the Catholic University of Dayton, where she majored in education. Lynch's Catholic education shielded her from the growing political activism of the time. "I was very traditional and [was] still thinking that I would teach for a few years and then get married and have children," she recalled. After graduation, she volunteered for VISTA and started a preschool program in Missouri. VISTA was her "graduate school," she explained: "It exposed me to people with different kinds of ideas and different cultural and economic backgrounds." She learned about feminism from her housemate, but there were no revelations: "It seemed absolutely natural to me. I don't perceive a big change in my thinking, except . . . going from thinking of myself in a pretty traditional mother-type role to knowing that there were other options." Lynch returned to Dayton, taught school, and lived in a group house in Dayton View. Her housemates included progressive journalists from the local newspapers and, for a brief time, Sherrie Holmes. Lynch and two of her housemates, including her future husband, eventually decided to go to the Caribbean, where they spent several years sailing and working in the Virgin Islands. She returned to Dayton in 1976.

Lynch was aware of the local women's movement and had even attended a meeting at the Women's Center, but she remembered the Center as "a place just for radical women, maybe just for radical lesbian women." When FOC was in its planning stages, an old friend from Lynch's group house got her involved, and she later served on the organization's board. Lynch knew women from both the feminist and liberal poles, and although closer to the liberal crowd, she had sympathies with both. She found FOC's tone—"real white, middle-class, nice ladies"—too conservative for her tastes and wanted to move the group "a smidgen to the left." The abortion issue, she believed, required more aggressive action, including in electoral politics. To act upon this, in late 1980 she helped create the local chapter of NARAL.[45]

FOC's heterogeneous membership and the diversity of its members' approach to abortion resulted in a broad, inclusive position rather than a narrow one of the lowest common denominator. The strong role feminists played contributed to this, as did the nature of the opposition.

The consensual name Freedom of Choice was particularly fitting. On one hand, it was (although this was not discussed) a hybrid of the liberationist term "reproductive freedom" and the liberal "right to choose"; on the other, it was sufficiently vague to cover varying stances. The vagueness about what one should be free to choose did not mean that the word "abortion" was taboo: the group consistently named names in all of its public statements. "Choice" was of course used to refute accusations of promoting abortion. "We absolutely reject the idea that because we oppose the so-called 'Right to Life' organization we are pro-abortion," a position statement said.[46] This terminology also allowed people to separate personal positions from their support for FOC; legislators, Catholics, and others could state that they were personally opposed to abortion but favored choice. Finally, this open-endedness allowed the group to extend beyond a single-issue approach.

For most feminists in Dayton's movement, abortion was inseparable from a multitude of other issues, not only access to contraceptives and opposition to forced sterilization but also support for quality child care, greater sexual freedom, and fundamental economic changes. Feminists' influence helped ensure this relatively broad perspective. But the multi-issue approach coincided with the concerns of many other members of the coalition. Arguments included opposition to government interference in private life, support for expanded social services and for a physician's right to make a medical decision, and defense of the separation of church and state. Planned Parenthood's scope also included contraception and sex education. Other organizations, such as the Free Clinic, were concerned with women's health. Interests of both supporters and opponents of population control also extended beyond abortion.

The most important element that prevented the group from adopting a narrow approach to abortion was the nature of its opponents. Liberals and feminists had begun to realize that the seemingly single-issue approach of the antiabortionists was illusory. At the Ohio IWY conference and elsewhere, feminists had witnessed how attacks also were waged against the ERA and a full slate of feminist issues. Liberals noted similarities between the new movement and their old enemies in the fight over education. They observed how criticism of Planned Parenthood was coming from fundamentalist Christians as well as antiabortionists. FOC relayed to the public research that had started to appear on the interlocking directorates of the right-wing organizations.[47] At first, as Silverman remembered, "Right to Life was something in the woodwork, some crazy Catholic-sponsored thing, and nothing to be very worried about. Then there [became] a national consciousness on how the Right to Life group [was] becoming part of the conservative movement."[48]

For all these reasons, FOC adopted a broad stance on abortion not far from the utopian, ultraminority position advocated by Dayton's first feminists. As the coalition's first editorial stated, "The choice of when or whether to have children should be freely made. There is no freedom if we choose to have children because we cannot get safe contraceptives or abortion. At the same time, we are not free in our choice if we choose *not* to have children because of poverty or lack of adequate childcare." The statement went on to demand that contraceptives be readily available and safe and that sterilization be a free choice, never coerced. It concluded that "[t]hese are choices we believe all people should have: women and men, regardless of race or income level."[49]

While the organization was fairly radical in theory, in form it was thoroughly traditional. Saunier, a staunch partisan and master of parliamentary procedure, drew up the proposal for the organizational structure. Her approach converged with that of the liberal women for whom there was no other way. The feminists also concurred: three of the four active in the early stages were members of the New American Movement and opponents of "the tyranny of structurelessness."

FOC established itself as a coalition of organizations and individuals. Fearing infiltration by Right to Life, in the beginning new members had to sign a prochoice statement and have a sponsor in the coalition. The board of directors included representatives of the organizations and at-large delegates for the individual members. Saunier served as the first chairperson. Monthly board meetings, though held in a member's home with refreshments served, were businesslike events. General membership meetings were convened as necessary, once or twice yearly during dormant periods and more frequently during major actions. *Robert's Rule of Order* set procedure when necessary.

After much debate, the coalition decided not to incorporate or to apply for nonprofit tax status. This kept structure light but meant that the group could not hire staff or seek funding. Membership dues were the main source of income, and financial needs were kept to a minimum. Work was done by a handful of activists in small committees. Few options existed for an intermediary level of involvement between participating in the core and remaining on the sidelines.

With no office or telephone—only a post office box—communications went through friendship networks and board meetings (information was then diffused though the organizational members' communications networks). FOC also had a newsletter, produced by socialist feminist media expert Sherry Novick and backed by a small, fluctuating group of individuals. Issued three times a year at most, it went from being a two-page mimeographed sheet to a full-fledged newsletter: six pages on average, attractively laid out and illustrated, and printed professionally on bright-colored paper. The newsletter served internal communications and monitored reproductive rights in the state and across the nation.

The coalition's first task was to head off an Akron-type ordinance in Dayton. Shortly after FOC's creation, the president of national Right to Life visited Dayton and confirmed her organization's intentions to target the city.[50] FOC quickly contacted city commissioners and learned that abortion was, for them, "too hot to handle." Most commissioners declared that while they were "personally opposed to abortion," they would not sponsor an ordinance. Some supported the right (for others) to choose. Some deemed local control inappropriate. Others awaited the outcome of Akron litigation.[51] The immediate threat of a local ordinance was rapidly dispelled.

Created as a defensive response to a specific event—apparently common for coalitions of the time[52]—FOC shifted with difficulty into an offensive mode. While other issues related to reproduction abounded, none easily united the groups. The coalition thus maintained little ongoing activity but rather tended to flare up in response to renewed threats to abortion rights. FOC monitored antiabortion bills and organized letter-writing campaigns. To counterbalance the highly effective right-wing campaigns, the group tried to keep a steady flow of pro-choice letters going to legislators and the press. The Right's ability to produce a tremendous volume of antiabortion letters was such that one local newspaper, a proponent of choice, actually contacted FOC to solicit letters to the editor.[53] Similarly, as abortion became the litmus test for political candidates, FOC tried to counter antiabortion pressures. The coalition assembled an impressive educational packet on reproductive issues with more than fifty pages of articles and original material. FOC sent the packets to political candidates and later contacted them to arrange meetings to brief them on the issue.

The most visible, ongoing FOC action was a petition campaign to commemorate the 1973 Supreme Court decision and to oppose "compulsory pregnancy." First published on the sixth anniversary of the ruling, it took up a full page in each of Dayton's two daily newspapers. The 1979 petition included eight organizations, fourteen members of the clergy, and nearly three hundred names plus more than a hundred anonymous supporters. All endorsers made donations to finance the ad. Such activism reflects the ultimate shift away from joining a movement. Not only did paying dues to FOC mean supporting one group and one issue among many, not only did it merely mean contributing to a cause, but for some, it had come to mean purchasing and publicizing liberal credentials.

Despite the relative respectability of FOC, signing the petition was a risky proposition. No actual attacks had been made against abortion rights activists or the local abortion clinic.[54] However, vandals had set fire to the clinic director's car, and both she and Saunier felt sufficiently threatened to keep their addresses and phone numbers confidential.

Professionally, the risks were great. Vaughn remembered a court reporter telling her, after seeing her speak on television, that she could never be elected to a public office. Saunier, as chair of the coalition, became the object of an aggressive letter-writing campaign. In one of the many letters sent to her employer, the Mead Corporation, a trustee of the Greater Dayton Pro-Life Education Foundation denounced Saunier's activities in FOC as well as at "the Bella Abzug and lesbian dominated" Houston conference. "Most people assume when corporate key level personnel become prominent activists in national social issues, they have at least tacit approval of the corporate hierarchy," the author admonished.[55] While Saunier experienced no fallout, the attack showed the risks in publicly supporting reproductive freedom.

Although hundreds of people endorsed the petition, far fewer were prepared to demonstrate. For feminists, schooled in direct action, this was bewildering. Novick said, "We tried to organize people to go to a march in Akron when [the ordinance] was going up before the courts, and very few people would go. There was a big march in Cincinnati . . . and very few people from Freedom of Choice went." The latter was organized to protest the June 1979 Right to Life national convention. Sponsored by a Cincinnati group and the Reproductive Rights National Network, the demonstration gathered more than forty endorsers, including FOC. Some fifteen hundred people marched—"the largest pro-choice gathering Ohio has seen in years"—but FOC provided only a part of the forty-five-person Dayton contingent.[56] "It was a real frustrating situation," Novick recalled. Radical women "wanted to be a lot more activist."

Resistance to direct action appeared again during the 1979 Abortion Rights Action Week, cosponsored by the coalition, the Women's Center, NAM, the National Lawyers Guild, and the new Radical Women United (RWU). FOC agreed to pay for publicity and took charge of two out of four activities: ongoing petitioning and a twilight vigil for choice conducted by diverse religious leaders (the latter was organized by Betty Jean Carroll, the former DWL member and the Unitarian Church's representative to FOC). FOC's name is notably absent, however, from the list of endorsers of the March for Abortion Rights. FOC decided not to support this demonstration, initiated by RWU to counter Right to Life plans. "The general consensus seemed to be that we do not want to be 'anti' any group or person, i.e.[,] Right to Life," the board decided. "Thus, as a group, we will not support a picket against anyone."[57] The truth was that FOC's had been created in opposition to the antiabortion movement. Their refusal to endorse the demonstration came from its appraisal of RWU.

RWU was a short-lived feminist group organized during one of FOC's dormant periods. Central to its creation was Connie Coker, a former DWL activist and member of the local International Socialist Organization, a recent splinter from the Trotskyite International Socialists, which had attracted several former NAM members. (Dayton ISO leaders, in contrast to those from previous far-left organizations, consisted of longtime community activists who were integral parts of the city's radical community.) Founders of RWU originally considered creating a group on reproductive freedom and had contacted the Reproductive Rights National Network, but they ultimately decided to form a multi-issue women's group. Most members were new to Dayton's women's movement, and many were young. Several were sympathetic toward Far Left political organizations, giving the group a distinctly more radical and confrontative image than FOC. In addition, tensions existed between RWU and the socialist contingent of FOC. The former group criticized NAM for being overly timid, while NAM members found RWU too sectarian. Furthermore, Coker had been one of the five feminists to file an injunction against the abortion clinic directors, and clinic representatives were central to FOC, with one serving as president at the time.

Undoubtedly these factors prevented the coalition from supporting the march. As a result, the turnout was small, despite backing by the Women's Center and the National Lawyers Guild. Demonstrators numbered around thirty, according to the press (and from fifty to seventy-five in one participant's memory), and the antiabortion demonstrators greatly outnumbered them. The coalition's apprehensions were justified when the event turned out to be, as Novick put it, a "yippie and Far Left" kind of protest. FOC activists, concerned with their respectable image, were particularly jarred by one incident: a protester carrying a sign reading "Abort the Pope" appeared on the front page of the *Dayton Daily News*.[58] "Everybody at Freedom of Choice was pretty upset about that picture," Novick said, although the action did draw in some new women and brought back a few feminists who had withdrawn from the movement. The coalition's position on the demonstration and on RWU showed that the liberal-radical alliance came about not only because of liberals' increased sympathy for feminism but also because some feminists, socialist feminists among them, had become more mainstream in style.

After another slow period, an anti–Right to Life action again infused the coalition with energy. In 1981, when Right to Life announced that it would hold its Ohio convention in Dayton, FOC organized a successful demonstration. After the experience with RWU, FOC decided to carefully control the assembly, forbidding "unauthorized" banners and slogans and instructing participants to dress in blue and white. Small American flags were distributed. Former Daytonian and DWL activist Joan Ediss, who had returned for the occasion, was appalled at the difference between the movement she had known and what she observed at the march. "You can't do that! You can't get us people out on the streets and tell us how to march . . . ! It was totally sterile." One incident particularly shocked her: a FOC marshal asked a group of women to take down their banner proclaiming themselves to be lesbians for choice. (They refused.) The presence of this contingent—as well as Lesbians United's initial, although unofficial, endorsement of the march—showed that local lesbian groups understood the need for unity and viewed reproductive freedom as integral to women's liberation. Not all members of FOC had so broad a view.

Maureen Lynch explained the group's concern with appearances: "I guess because of the nature of this issue and the moral righteousness that's arrayed against FOC, there may be an added need to cloak ourselves in respectability at all times and to stress the fact that we're good citizens and many women with children and grandchildren, church members and that sort of thing." Nevertheless, she understood the lesbian contingent's reaction: "I assume they told [the marshal] to shove it—and it was okay." She was not the only organizer to find the demonstration overly controlled: "If [respectability] becomes your overriding concern, then you sort of cripple yourself."

Freedom of Choice, Miami Valley, with its active and dormant periods, continued throughout the 1980s, far beyond the period studied here. It presaged the times to come in several ways. First, it announced the rise of the Right, the centrality of abortion to the upcoming period, and the way in which abortion was emblematic of a broader antifeminist campaign. FOC also illustrated, even more than previous groups, the expansion and fragmentation of the women's movement. Simultaneously, as the first ongoing coalition and one in which feminists made their voices heard, it successfully brought together some of those pieces. Most important, the entry of liberals into the movement ten years after its birth says a lot about the state of the movement at the time.

One reason for the entry of liberal women was the nature of the abortion issue. First, as has been shown at several points in the history of the women's movement in Dayton, it had extraordinarily broad appeal. Nationally, the movement unified around its support of abortion rights, including even the more cautious groups that initially had opposed "abortion on demand." More generally, despite the rise of the opposition, polls consistently showed that the vast majority of Americans opposed a ban on abortion. A poll conducted by Dayton's conservative daily paper during the period of FOC's creation found that only 5 percent of Montgomery County's voters believed that abortion should be illegal under all circumstances, 52 percent said that the woman should have free reign in making the decision, and 41 percent favored allowing legal abortions if the woman's life or health was in danger.[59]

At the same time, by the beginning of Freedom of Choice, many feminist ideas were widely accepted. A 1980 national poll showed 64 percent of all women favoring efforts to change and strengthen the status of women, as opposed to 40 percent in 1970.[60] One study of leaders of traditional women's clubs and organizations—no doubt similar to the Dayton liberal population—showed that three-quarters were in favor of "most of the efforts to strengthen and change women's status in society," and more than 97 percent agreed with a paraphrase of the ERA.[61] While far fewer women identified with or supported the women's movement on the whole, in the FOC constituency feminism had ceased to be a dirty word.

By the late 1970s it had become socially acceptable to be a feminist. While the identification as feminist represented an act of affiliation, the flip side of this development was an increased drain on the content of the word. For example, in the early 1980s, rather than hearing the classical, "I'm not a feminist, but . . . ," followed by *pro*-feminist attitudes, it had become common to hear from women, particularly liberal women, "I *am* a feminist, but . . . ," followed by *anti*-feminist statements.

In Dayton, parafeminist institutions and services had emerged as both direct and indirect products of the women's movement. Preexisting institutions such as universities, the YWCA, and Planned Parenthood had incorporated feminist ideas and programs. These developments created a category of (more or less) feminist social workers and professionals, and against the backdrop of generally increased sympathies for feminist ideas, translated feminist issues into socially acceptable concerns. The combination of this category of feminist professionals and the influence of feminism on traditional women's organizations and clubs provided a parallel track of consciousness-raising through which these new liberal women were brought into the movement.

The key precipitant that brought them to the forefront and into the Coalition was the rise of the Right. This "new" Right seemed familiar to many. Its population indeed overlapped with their old foes, who, after taking control of the school board, opposed desegregation and sex education. For one couple, opposition to abortion and birth control brought back memories of Nazi Germany. Many of these women worked in the social services, and most had been advocates of social welfare, which the

Right was attacking along with abortion. The revived Right threatened their vision of a tolerant, liberal society.

The nature of the pro-choice movement made it a particularly accessible anteroom to the movement. "Choice" was an issue that did not require separation from men. Second, it isolated one area of feminist concern, and one which touched women personally, while not requiring changes in personal lifestyle or commitment to personal politics. Finally, involvement in FOC potentially left social and class relations intact: the antiabortionists were not a part of their social circles, and were assumed to be lower class. As Center activist Kathy Ellison explained, the liberals felt that whereas antifeminism may have been present at all levels of society, opponents to abortion were from the lower classes. Ellison believed that the liberal women "want to keep their upper-middle class, or lower-upper class credentials, and won't do anything to thwart that. . . . Any women's movement issue which they could support that allows them to ally themselves with the monied classes would be fine. And abortion is that kind of issue."[62] However, while lifestyle and social status remained basically untouched, facing harassment and violence of the anti-choice activism implied taking real risks that served as mechanisms in reinforcing commitment.

When liberal women and feminists joined forces in FOC, neither group showed any desire of ousting the other. Feminists' got frustrated with the liberals' individualistic style, in contrast to their years in collectives, and with their rejection of direct action; nevertheless, the two groups respected each other. In the same way that the emergence of the New Right pushed some liberals to ally with radicals, it seemed, as one woman put it, to make radicals "more patient with liberal politics." Although the two groups approached FOC with fundamentally different perspectives, their goals converged. Furthermore, each group had skills and resources that the other lacked. For example, the feminists knew how to produce a newsletter and organize a protest, whereas the liberals knew more about electoral campaigns, and were better acquainted with local politicians. Contrary to earlier experiences, such as the Victimization Project or the Career Development Center, FOC did not involve vying for funding or for the control of an institution. There was no money and little power at stake. A balance of power was maintained between the two poles, with relations further cemented by the women who were social and political intermediaries. Feminists' strength within the Coalition resulted in a broad, radical analysis of reproductive rights even if actions did not always follow.

Yet FOC could not replace the other organizations. The group did not offer sustenance or even impetus for personal transformation. Race and class lines not only were not crossed, they were rarely even questioned. The coalition did what it set out to do—no more, no less. Had it been but one organization among many, these critiques would be less important. But as the main heir to the women's movement, the arena in which activist energy was concentrated, FOC illustrated what so many lamented in early 1980s feminism: a lack of connections.

Conclusion
Watching the Stars:
A View from the Heartland

THE WOMEN'S movement in a medium-sized, "typical" American city was neither a miniature nor a toned-down version of so-called national feminism. Dayton's dynamic, distinctive movement challenges dominant narratives, including those extrapolating from what occurred in a few big cities to a national movement.

The story of Dayton cracks open the apparent historiographic consensus around a universal, two-part movement, one in which liberal feminism is the earliest, most durable, and hence for many most important part of the movement. In contrast to the two-branch pattern so often described, a single strand of feminism emerged in Dayton, drawing inspiration from diverse philosophies but most closely resembling in scope and structure what various scholars have called the women's liberation, radical, or collectivist branch. Liberal or equal rights feminism and bureaucratic, hierarchical organizations came along years later and did not have the same appeal for or impact on women's lives.[1]

Dayton's story counters the commonly held view that equates Middle America with conservatism. To the contrary, demands for equal rights did not give birth to or sustain feminism. Equal rights were a minor concern, as illustrated by the virtual invisibility of the Equal Rights Amendment until the late 1970s. This is further demonstrated by the repeated unsuccessful attempts to create a local chapter of NOW. The first chapter, founded in 1970 by DWL liberationists, lasted only several months. The second, started by socialist feminists and Women's Center activists in 1975, offered the clout of its name to projects that either existed already or were sustained by the efforts of a single individual. A third unsuccessful attempt to organize was made in 1979. Locally, NOW had little organizational life of its own and never drew new women into the movement. The successes in the Dayton movement came from its most radical ideas and practices. Repeatedly, when those ideas and practices were limited, the movement suffered.

The force of the early movement stemmed from the consciousness-raising group. Consciousness-raising provided both method and content, validating individual experience while using it as the basis for building theory and defining actions within a broad vision for a transformed society. Throughout the decade, the CR process worked repeatedly for those who tried it, regardless of class, age, or race. These women emerged changed for life. The CR group also gave structure to the early movement. As a movement cell, it built a nonhierarchical organizational structure that was to be prefigurative of future social relations.

Dayton Women's Liberation's most fatal flaws lay in its grossly inadequate means of attaining its extravagant goals and the overlapping question of its limited audience. Although the feminist population extended far beyond representations in the media and even in other scholarly studies, DWL and its successors still reached only a small minority of the female population and failed to include black women and large numbers of working-class women. The second generation of feminists, particularly the socialist feminists, zeroed in on these shortcomings. However, in socialist feminists' analyses, the culprits were DWL's organizational structure and the role of the CR group—precisely the early movement's most dynamic, inspirational characteristics. Socialist feminists nationally have commented on this. Writing on the development of socialist feminist organizations, members of one collective observed: "In moving from consciousness-raising and service work to more of a focus on political action, we had taken a step forward but had also left something behind. We lost the vehicle which, through its intensity, had created much theory and solidified our collectivity: CR groups. . . . Women now coming into the movement lose the unique experience of support, building a movement from immediate ideas and feelings."[2] Thus it was women under the banner of socialist feminism and in the name of radicalism who suppressed this most compelling aspect of the early movement.

The second major feminist group, the Dayton Women's Center, placed more emphasis on equal rights and was in some respects less utopian than DWL. However, in creating an autonomous women's space, the Center did partially meet the goal of a prefigurative structure. It functioned cooperatively, and its services grew out of a self-help perspective. It filled the role of a general feminist organization by monitoring developments that affected women and by raising whatever issues it deemed appropriate. Indeed, the Center constantly spawned innovative ideas and projects. With its physical space, it broadened its audience by making feminism visible and apparently indigenous.

However, over the following years the most compelling aspects of the Center were sacrificed. In order to raise money and to maintain control of the free spaces that it had carved out, the Center fell under the influence of shifting fashions and mainstream institutions. If, for example, the federal government announced funding for an issue, the members would redirect their energies into writing proposals. Concomitantly, the Center attempted to become more professional in order to command the respect of the funding bodies. But efforts to appear respectable failed miserably. The Center lost control of major initiatives, such as the rape crisis project and the career counseling center, to its mainstream competitors. Meanwhile, the projects inspired by feminists' individual and collective experiences—and even intuition—succeeded far better. Striving for legitimacy shackled the Center's creativity and ability to remain on the cutting edge—precisely that which had been responsible for its dynamism and which had attracted new women. The Center ceased to be the radical wing that sociologist David Bouchier argued is essential in preserving a movement from "a gentle slide into the prevailing hegemony" through "constantly raising unresolved issues and generating new ones."[3]

Most scholarly literature on the women's movement criticizes its so-called structureless organizational forms. Radical as those forms may be, the story goes, they render groups inefficient and ineffective in making policy changes. Structureless groups ruled by unacknowledged *éminences grises* are supposedly predisposed to burnout and early death. They fail at their primary goal of being all-inclusive.[4]

In Dayton, what some called structurelessness was clearly a sophisticated, fluid, collectivist structure, as demonstrated by the constant debate and experimentation with innovative but explicit forms. The two core organizations through the 1970s, Dayton Women's Liberation and the Dayton Women's Center, were magnificent examples of successful radical collectivist organizations. Furthermore, various indicators (the number of different women who wrote articles in the groups' publications, the size of the core group, and so on) suggest that the two groups were more democratic than groups that adopted traditional and bureaucratic organizational forms. Finally, collectivist organizations inspired stronger commitment. They never depended on a single leader and thus survived successive departures, nor were they reactive and contingent on outside threats, as was Freedom of Choice.

The shift of the movement's focal point and the creation of Dayton Women Working again exemplifies the identification of a cutting-edge issue. DWW was a brilliant example of organizing and an important step in raising the status of women's work and bridging the gap between feminism and the labor movement. But gone were all attempts at creating prefigurative structures, and this, along with the intentional separation of work from other women's issues, did the movement a disservice. It rendered DWW incapable of forming necessary alliances to counter the Right and actually hindered the entry of its activists into the broader movement.

The single-issue approach of DWW also revealed a condescending belief that only working-class women responded to bread and butter issues and that they were alienated by other feminist issues. Socialist feminists and liberal feminists believed that, as sociologist Maren Carden reported, working-class women in the movement "were attracted by the 'equal rights' aspect of the ideology" because of discrimination encountered on the job.

Examination of the Dayton movement does not reveal a tendency among working-class women to support only equal rights issues. Even at DWW, women were drawn to the group for far more complex reasons than job discrimination. Lesbian groups had perhaps the largest number of working-class women in their midst, and bread and butter issues clearly were not their main concern. Socialist feminists' assumptions made them "unable to identify with or capture the imagination of working-class women," Wendy Luttrell wrote. Reflecting on her experience working in a Philadelphia settlement house, she wrote: "It is important to emphasize . . . that the concerns and needs that I heard described by the women I met were not simple 'bread and butter' or 'survival' issues."[5]

The critiques formulated by Dayton liberationists, and by radical and socialist feminists nationally, bore witness to a retreat from personal politics. Barbara Haber criticized other socialist feminists for their belief that their "personal experience is so out of the ordinary that it is irrelevant to the lives of most women." In her 1979 plea for another round of consciousness-raising, Haber wrote: "Instead of treating ourselves as members of an oppressed group of people seeking change out of our own self-interest, we view ourselves as privileged people, voluntarily throwing in our lot with the masses. . . . So when we confront the issue of personal life crisis we do not engage it as something that comes from personal urgency, but rather as a strategic question of meeting the alleged needs and desires of our fantasized working class."[6] In the same vein, Linda Gordon and Allen Hunter argued that many socialist feminists, by stressing issues of work and avoiding those of sexuality and family, missed out on the "two strengths of the women's liberation movement: the understanding that the 'personal is political' and the development of organizational forms that prefigure socialist social relations."[7]

One of the paradoxes of the movement is how in time it simultaneously expanded and contracted. It expanded in size and scope as feminists ventured outward into new arenas of thought and action, but contracted as movement organizations specialized, often raising single issues. In 1969, a group of women got together in Dayton to discuss what they originally thought was a single idea, the liberation of women. Over the following decade, feminists continually uncovered the myriad repercussions of sexism, requiring a broadened outlook on the world and political responses to new questions. But the actions and programs that accompanied these perceptions grew progressively narrower. The movement's first major coalition, Freedom of Choice, illustrates this. As a project of a broader movement, like the various abortion rights groups in the early years, it was an exemplary feminist group. However, as the main organizational heir to the movement in the early 1980s, it marked a setback.

The movement's tendency to single out issues was due to many factors. Early liberationists' view that everything was related to everything was a difficult vantage point from which to organize. The actions on abortion and rape were probably so successful because these issues made the connections between the personal and the political and yet were definable.

The awareness of the interrelationship of everything undoubtedly was overwhelming for most women. It required total commitment. As Julia Reichert commented: "We put an awful lot of demands on each other: to work really hard, to be real open with each other, to make our first commitment as dedicated revolutionaries." Women not able to live up to such expectations perhaps framed conflict in political terms in order to split off without losing faith. An alternative method—single-issue organizing—represented a more manageable way to remain active.

To prepare for the long haul of working for such sweeping changes required considerable sustenance. The consciousness-raising group was one answer to this need. But the CR group was particularly successful in the phase of the movement when women were discovering commonality. It was far less successful in helping women understand the oppression of others and, rather than to affirm differences, to build sisterhood across their differences. When CR groups were phased out, another mechanism for maintaining connections vanished.

Finally, the move toward isolating issues was sometimes created by and always reinforced by the media and the state. The hard data of discrimination and the raising of specific demands were easier to deal with because they were more definable and often less radical.

As 1980 drew to a close, DWL had faded from most Daytonians' memory. The Women's Center and Dayton Women Working were foundering, about to shut down. FOC was no replacement for the broad feminist organizations that had lasted through the previous decade. The period was a somber one for feminists, with the rise of the New Right, the ERA on its way to defeat, attacks on legalized abortion, and the election of Ronald Reagan. Only a year or two earlier, one frequently heard that feminism was obsolete because the war against inequality had been won. With the setbacks at the turn of the decade, the music was changing and many began whistling the tune of prefeminist values.

Nevertheless, the demise of several feminist organizations in Dayton can by no means be construed as the death of feminism. Organizational stability was not the overriding goal of all these groups. For DWL, experimentation ranked higher than stability: the goals of women's liberation mattered more than the maintenance of its organizations. Even most of those DWL activists who opposed the socialist feminists believed that the shift of the focal point to the Women's Center heralded a new era of the movement and not its demise. When the Center closed, some activists thought that the need for it had lessened because enough of its services had become redundant—and that this was a victory for the women's movement. Freedom of Choice, originally designed to combat a specific ordinance, successfully fulfilled its purpose and managed to continue beyond the initial threat, a testimonial to the movement's vitality.

The women's movement was not dead in Dayton in 1980, nor is it today. Freedom of Choice continued throughout the eighties and into the nineties, flaring up in reaction to threats to reproductive freedom. Numerous initiatives have emerged during the last few decades, some ephemeral others enduring: NOW chapters, a women's bookstore, women's studies programs in the universities, and several prochoice organizations. Many institutional offshoots of the movement continued, such as the Victim/Witness Division and the Battered Women's Shelter. The city has never been without an abortion clinic, and Planned Parenthood and the YWCA have remained active in the fray.[8]

No doubt the most important legacy of the 1970s, and the most difficult one to measure, was the change in consciousness and the transformation of women's lives. All the feminists interviewed for this book believed that the movement had been instrumental in forging their identities, and not one of them regretted the resulting changes. Not one had renounced her feminist ideas and goals, including those who left the movement in anger. Nearly all were proud that they had integrated their feminism into their lives.

Betty Jean Carroll, commenting on a DWL reunion held some ten years after the organization's demise, summed up the general feeling: "We've gone our own ways; we're . . . applying a lot of the theory that we talked about at that time and pretty much have incorporated it into our life styles. I don't think that any of us have really deviated from our feminist philosophy and life style." But Carroll concluded, "We don't have that strong connection that we had at that time."

In the 1970s, scholarly and *engagé* writings on the women's movement were triumphalist, portraying the future as bright. In the eighties, against the backdrop of a strong radical Right, they often were fatalistic, emphasizing the movement's internal conflicts and flaws to explain its supposed "failure." With a supposed third wave born in the late eighties and the nineties, debates appeared over whether the eighties was a period of demobilization, deradicalization, or unobtrusive mobilization in institutions. I suggest that at the end of the 1970s, the salient characteristic of the movement was fragmentation, or as Carroll observed, lack of connection. Although it has been argued that the sense of oneness in the 1970s was based on blindness to the homogeneity of the movement, the sisterhood and unity were real and an inestimable force in transforming society. Indeed, the demise of core "all-purpose" feminist organizations in Dayton was symptomatic of the dissipation of the movement. Perhaps the feminist community was not capable of maintaining a core, but perhaps also the movement had simply become too vast, too nebulous, to be contained in one structure or under one roof. Perhaps the subject "women" had exploded and expanded beyond any conceivable single structure.

Another sign of disconnection was the lack of progress in finding an ongoing meeting ground for black and white women to address common concerns and to create all-inclusive sisterhood.[9] DWL's core group began with a strong antiracist commitment, but also with the model of Black Power, or separate and autonomous organizing. Rarely pointed out in histories of the movement, the absence of black women was a direct result of antiracist white women's respect for black activists' positions. The initial absence of black women is as much a paradox of Black Power ideology and black nationalist strategies as it is a critique of early women's liberation. However, as time went by, this became a comfortable position for those with less commitment to fighting racism. Subsequent groups often devoted energy to including black women only after the formation of a white core group and identity. These groups also tended to expect black women to join them, rather than trying to understand what black women themselves were doing.[10]

The successful experience of the black consciousness-raising groups at the Women's Center showed that this method of creating sisterhood and linking the personal and the political worked for blacks as well as whites. However, a combination of the Center's internal conflicts and racism stood between black-white sisterhood. Tragically, when black separatist influences were on the wane, when a new black feminism was germinating, most white feminists were not receptive. Dayton Women Working did attract a handful of black women around work issues and through the presence of a black staff member. But these women did not become actively involved in the organization or in the women's movement as a whole. The single-issue approach undermined the group's ability to make broader connections, as much for white as for black women.

However, for black women nationally the 1980s opened encouragingly—with the publication of a landmark book by women of color, *This Bridge Called My Back*—and drew to a close with the Anita Hill–Clarence Thomas affair, inspiring *Black Women in Defense of Ourselves*. In Dayton, the early eighties saw the creation of two black women's groups, although not feminist in name.

In response to the lack of connections among Dayton's feminists at the end of the 1970s, a spate of women's support groups began. Carroll founded a group at her workplace that concentrated on consciousness-raising, participated in several feminist programs on women and work for WYSO, and supported at least one woman in a discrimination case. Another group was initiated by an activist in the campaign for reproductive freedom. An apprentice carpenter, she created a group for discussion and mutual support with other women in the trades.

But one such group, the Women's Network, was the early feminists' nightmare: a female president of General Motors, the antithesis of DWL's goals, would have been warmly welcomed into this network. The group wanted to use its connections—in the worst sense of the word. A few of the women were feminists, including Anne Saunier and one

Planned Parenthood official. But the nucleus of the group included women who had opposed and competed against the Dayton movement.

The Network's stated purpose was "[t]o create a communications network for women executives and leaders providing new contacts across professional lines, mutual support and advice, and access to information to promote personal achievement as well as increased opportunities for women."[11] The Network began in the early eighties with a group of friends and expanded by invitation only.[12] A group that some members compared to the "old boys networks," it included "the kind of people [members] have met on boards.[13] Several women described it as a place where they could let their hair down and shed their burden of being role models. "These were women," one member recalled, "who had some position of power—I'm not talking about real power, but who could make things happen, who had some clout. . . . The idea [was] to be the top person in your company."[14] The Network represented the tightening up and formalizing of a Dayton female elite.

> Ideals are like the stars. You can never reach them but you need them to chart your course.

This 1848 quote from a German socialist[15] sums up the most important lesson in this study of feminism in the Heartland. Demands for equal rights, single issues, or survival issues are not enough to create and sustain a women's movement. Social movement activists must keep their eyes on the stars. Feminists must work to maintain connections, both through the creation of sisterhood and the maintenance of overall feminist organizations. Long-term goals must not be lost. An essential insight of the women's liberation movement must continue to guide feminists: The importance of the personal in the redefinition of politics.

This concern is not just one of principle but of effectiveness. The women's movement is constantly faced with opposition, and when it retreats and restricts itself in scope or depth, the opposition expands to fill the abandoned space. The success of the New Right's mobilization around family issues offers a spectacular illustration of this. In the U.S., where the state has shown a remarkable ability to channel the aspirations of social movements into reform, movement demands are diluted and a certain number are indeed absorbed. But watered-down visions do not raise consciousness; they cannot bring women to take the risks involved in becoming a feminist. They cannot maintain the high level of commitment needed to keep the movement going. They will not liberate women. The argument for radical, utopian visions is thus not just one of principle, but of effectiveness. Without this vision, the Career Development Center could not inspire community support, and it folded. The lack of a feminist approach left the abortion clinic vulnerable to right-wing attacks. The diminished vision at the Women's Center's made it indistinguishable from the outside world and led to its collapse.

Keeping one's sights high does not mean never singling out specific issues, nor does it preclude compromise. It does not mean that all change equals co-optation. Working in the mainstream has won many concrete gains. The Victim/Witness Division continues to provide humane services to victims of rape. It has politicized the issue and changed attitudes in the Dayton police force. The application of Title IX in the Dayton schools eliminated sex-segregated industrial arts and home economics classes. The $1 million decision on back pay to women bank workers has made employers think twice about applying sexist criteria in hiring and promotion. These are but a few examples.

But what are the long-term results of such gains? When these victories are part of a campaign for a single issue, they can be demobilizing. Dayton Women Working vanished after its successful campaign, and bank work is still a female, low-status, poorly paid job. The group that sued the Dayton Board of Education disappeared, and subtle sexism still abounds in the school system. The fear of rape still hovers over women whenever they go out alone at night. In isolation, striving for small victories is like swimming up the mainstream: you must have very good muscles to get anywhere, and when you tire, you are swept back downstream. It is only when maintained in the context of long-term feminist goals that these victories move women further along.

Watered-down visions are not enough to inspire women to brave the departure from familiar and seemingly secure life styles. Nor do they provide sustenance. When right-wing groups argue that "choice" does not hold up against "life," it represents a debatable definition of the word "life." When foundations refuse money to feminist projects by claiming that feeding the poor is more important than equal rights, it may be to mask their antifeminism.

And yet these critics are right. Equal rights and choice do not carry enough weight. On the other hand, goals of freedom and liberation do. If we truly want to aim for the stars, we need to restore the "liberation" to the women's movement.

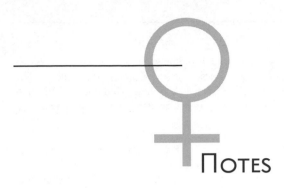

NOTES

PREFACE

1. John Baskin, "On the Way to Nowhere Dayton Became Middle America to People, Businesses," *Dayton Daily News* (hereafter cited as *DDN*), *Dayton Leisure* section, 20 July 1980, 6–7; Kurt Vonnegut, *Slaughterhouse 5,* 1969 (London: Triad, 1979), 9.

2. Wattenberg and Scammon, *Real Majority.* "But Will SHE Go Along?" *Life,* 30 October 1970, 30–32; Lowrey initially looked askance at the changes in America, but later found that her own family was touched by the chaotic sixties; for instance, she discovered that her son and sister smoked marijuana. William Greider, "We're Becoming a More Tolerant Society; Americans Are Turning Tolerant," *Washington Post,* 25 November 1979. Noam Chomsky, "What Makes Mainstream Media Mainstream," talk at Z Media Institute, June 1997: www.zmag.org/chomsky/articles/z9710-mainstream-media.html.

3. Josette Alia, "Du Porte jarretelles à la navette spatiale," *Nouvel Observateur,* 1045 hs *Les Vingt ans,* 52.

4. Hole and Levine, *Rebirth of Feminism,* 135; Echols, *Daring to Be Bad,* 20–21.

5. Ferree and Martin, eds., *Feminist Organizations.* Carden did more than half her interviews in the Boston area and most of the others in big bicoastal cities, but she also did research on Cleveland and Pittsburgh and consulted publications from other places. Carden, *New Feminist Movement.* Jo Freeman, no doubt due to her emphasis on changes in social policy, also maintained a national perspective. Freeman, *Politics of Women's Liberation.* Barbara Ryan's interviews were fairly broad; she covered the St. Louis to Chicago area, Washington, D.C., and beyond by attending national conferences. Ryan, *Feminism and the Women's Movement,* 6–7.

6. Baxandall and Gordon, eds., *Dear Sisters,* 2.

7. Bouchier, *Feminist Challenge,* 227. Nancy Whittier, in her study of nearby Columbus, Ohio, has also shown the importance of radicalism, but because she singled out the radical women's movement as her object, we cannot make conclusions about the movement in general. Whittier, *Feminist Generations.*

8. The "click" was the "the parenthesis of truth around a little thing" that came after women "suddenly and shockingly perceived the basic disorder in what has been believed to be the natural order of things." O'Reilly, "Housewife's Moment of

253

Truth," 12. After O'Reilly's article appeared in the preview issue of *Ms., Newsweek* further popularized the term by quoting her in the cover story of a special issue of "The American Woman": "Where She Is and Where She's Going," *Newsweek,* 20 March 1972, 22. The term "click" became part of Dayton feminists' everyday vocabulary.

iNTRODUCTiON

1. It was not until 1965 that a local chapter of Planned Parenthood was founded.

2. Sanders, *Dayton, Gem City of Ohio,* 46.

3. Long-time community activist Mary Morgan believed that a first step in Daytonians' consciousness-raising came with the construction of the interstate highways that tore through the city to route affluent suburbanites straight to the downtown department store. Several beautiful areas—a black, middle-class neighborhood and a stable, white, ethnic neighborhood—were destroyed. "You're not supposed to tear up the center of town; you're supposed to do a bypass," Morgan said. "But Rikes [department store] had it run right through the center with seven bridges, so that people could get off two blocks from the store. . . . Everyone was outraged. . . . There was a sense that people had never had before, that they were powerless." (All quotes credited in the text to Daytonians are from interviews with the author, unless otherwise specified. For full details on interviews, see Research Methods and Sources.)

4. Daley, "City Manager Government," 52. Although segregation had weakened by the time of my research, the economic divide remained. In 1995, the median household income in the black West Side was $12,480, in contrast to more than $60,000 in the city's predominantly white, wealthiest suburb. Median household value on the West Side was $28,400, the lowest of the fourteen areas described ($172,100 in the highest). "Dayton by the Numbers," *Dayton Monthly,* January–February 1995, 45–49.

5. Article in the Dayton NAACP files, n.a., n.d.

6. Mary Morgan, letter to the author, July 1985.

7. In 1968, the president of the Area Progress Committee also was president of the chamber of commerce. Seven members of the APC were on the chamber's board of directors; twenty-two of the thirty were registered Republicans; seventeen served on boards of the city's major banks; and the APC included the editors of both daily newspapers. Daley, "City Manager Government, 71–75, 82, 119–20.

8. City of Dayton Human Relations Council, "Your Rights Are Protected by Law," brochure, n.d.

9. Robin Small, "Tax Revolt Hits Dunbar," *Minority Report* (hereafter cited as *MR*), 10 April 1969, 1. The staff gradually expanded over the years to thirteen in 1976.

10. This parallels national experience. Philadelphian Reggie Schell, who was to become defense captain of that city's Black Panthers in the late sixties, recalled watching televised reports of police beating women and children in the 1963 voter registration drives in Selma, Alabama, and how "it did something to me inside." "An Interview with Reggie Schell," in Cluster, ed., *They Should Have Served That Cup of Coffee,* 49. Stokely Carmichael wrote that each time blacks "saw Martin Luther King get slapped, they became angry; when they saw four little black girls bombed to death, they were angrier; and when nothing happened they were steaming." Carmichael, "Power and Racism," in Barbour, *Black Power Revolt,* 63.

11. Daley, "City Manager Government," 53.

12. The 1968 busing was supposedly to relieve overcrowding, but clearly was organized to integrate. I was part of the first wave, one of the only white students in my group, bused to an all-white school. Racially motivated busing in Dayton predates desegregation: well into the 1950s, black orphans were bused out of the white neighborhood in which one "children's home" was located. Tom Price, "History Became Big Ally of Segregation Fighters," *DDN and Journal-Herald* (hereafter cited as *JH*), supplement, n.d. (Summer 1986), 2.

13. The ensuing series of court battles between the NAACP and the Dayton school board finally ended with a Supreme Court decision in 1979 that upheld busing to integrate. Desegregation of staff had begun in 1971, but districtwide desegregation of the student body wasn't carried out until 1976. Price, "Dayton Bus Trip Began in Topeka," 3.

14. Much of the transition to Black Power was to be played out in the Student Nonviolent Coordinating Committee, a racially mixed, nonviolent but militant organization in the South. From the black-led, interracial "beloved community" of its early years, SNCC went on to ban white membership in 1966. Among the books that cover this part of the civil rights movement are Zinn, *SNCC*; Carson, *In Struggle*; and King, *Freedom Song*.

15. Carmichael, "Power and Racism," 72.

16. Ibid., 73, 74.

17. Another example was the interracial, church-related Malachi, which focused on raising whites' consciousness about their own racism. Whites also organized autonomously in support groups for black organizations. For example, after attending a Saul Alinsky organizing seminar in Chicago in 1967, a mixed group of Daytonians returned to create the predominantly black Force and a white counterpart, Force Associates.

18. Breines, *Community and Organization in the New Left*; Burns, *Social Movements of the 1960s*; Gitlin, *The Sixties*; Miller, *Democracy Is in the Streets*; Sayres et al., eds., *60s without Apology*. Two interesting historiographic critiques by feminists are Echols, "'We Gotta Get Out of This Place,'" and Breines, "Whose New Left." In recent years, attention has been paid to the formation of another part of this generation: the future activists of the New Right. In particular, see Klatch, *Generation Divided*.

19. Charles Radican, "Report to Ichthys," *MR*, November 1969, 4.

20. This attitude was due in part to the much publicized patriotic demonstrations of the "hard hats" and their clash with antiwar protesters. In fact, polls showed more opposition to the war among rank and file workers than among the upper middle class. Support for withdrawal from Vietnam was the highest in groups of lower socioeconomic status and among people with a grade school education as opposed to the college-educated. Carroll, *It Seemed like Nothing Happened*, 59; Zinn, *People's History of the United States*, 482.

21. Sale, *SDS*. In recent years there has been a tendency to romanticize and exaggerate the importance of the New Left's numerical strength. The New Left did represent a significant minority and had impact beyond its numbers in American culture and politics, but only a small minority even of that generation got involved.

22. Priscilla Long, an Antioch student in the early sixties and later a founder of Boston's Bread and Roses, remembered that only one of her forty classes was taught

by a woman, and she remembered hearing on campus disparaging comments about bluestockings. "We Called Ourselves Sisters," 325.

23. Kathy Kleine interview, July 1985.

24. Mike Ezekiel, "On to Greener Pastures," *Phoenix*, 13 January 1969, 18.

25. The paper printed around five thousand issues and had a few hundred subscribers.

26. On the culture-politico rift in underground papers nationally, see Peck, *Uncovering the Sixties*. Conflict in Dayton's New Left, however, was far milder that what was occuring nationally. There was consensus at the *Minority Report* around the need for political independence from the sectarian Left, and members prided themselves on not getting bogged down in the splits that were tearing apart the New Left elsewhere.

CHAPTER I

1. *motive* 29 (March–April 1969). Most of the articles are reprinted in Cooke et al., eds., *New Women*.

2. Cooke, "Editorial," 4–5.

3. On the conference and accounts of feminist developments in the underground press, see Lewis, *Outlaws of America*, 33; Peck, *Uncovering the Sixties*, 207–17.

4. "Group Forms: Rebirth," *MR: Women's Issue*, 18 December 1969 to 1970, 5.

5. Ibid.

6. Ibid.

7. "Up against the Wall, Betty Crocker," *MR: Women's Issue*, 6.

8. Pat Rector, "Woman as Guru," *MR: Women's Issue*, 5; Robin Suits, "Rebellion," *MR: Women's Issue*, 18.

9. "Group Forms," 5.

10. On the black women analogy, see hooks, *Ain't I a Woman*, 138–45; Hogeland, *Feminism and Its Fictions*, 129–48; Ferree and Hess, *Controversy and Coalition*, 37–40.

11. "Group Forms," 5; Suits, "Rebellion," 7+.

12. Celestine Ware cites T-groups of industrial psychologists and the Human Potential Movement. Ware, *Woman Power*. Hanisch and Amatniek both recount that while working in the civil rights movement in the South, they had been impressed by the revival-style mass meetings where blacks would testify on their personal experiences of oppression. Brownmiller, "Sisterhood Is Powerful," 144–45.
Hanisch and Bunch-Weeks refer to the process of "speaking bitterness" used in Mao's China. Bunch-Weeks, "Asian Women in Revolution," 351. Others spoke of the "Guatemalan guerrilla approach" of the SDS. Evans, *Personal Politics*, 175, 214.

13. Brownmiller, "Sisterhood Is Powerful," 148.

14. Dayton's groups thus differed from what Anita Shreve described: "Almost all successful CR groups followed a format . . . that had been finely tuned as the process passed from the New York Radical Women, to the New York Radical Feminists, to the Redstockings, and on to NOW. A topic from a prepared list was selected for each meeting." *Women Together, Women Alone*, 13.

15. Allen's booklet, based on her San Francisco group's experience, came closest to describing the CR process as it was used in Dayton. She identified four group processes: opening up, sharing, analyzing, and abstracting. Allen, *Free Space*, 24–31.

By early 1972 at the latest, this text was being discussed by DWL members. Shirley Varga, "Much literature . . . ," *DWL News,* April 1972, 8.

16. Allen, *Free Space,* 26.

17. Hogeland, *Feminism and Its Fictions,* 3–4, 13.

18. While CR and therapy were not seen as synonymous, DWL recognized that the CR process included the therapeutic experience of "momentarily relieving the individual of all responsibility for her situation." Allen, *Free Space,* 30–31. Numerous accounts exist of how participation in groups helped individuals. One DWL woman wrote, "[CR] was a lifesaver for this neurotic." Nevertheless, it was not seen as a replacement for psychotherapy, but rather a tool for women to help distinguish between what they must change in their own lives and what must be struggled against collectively and politically. As such, the idea of developing new types of feminist therapy—complementary to the CR group—was seen as desirable. The DWL author continued, "I only wish I knew of a female psychiatrist who's had her consciousness raised so I could help myself get rid of these neuroses in a way that's acceptable to ME!" "From a Neurotic's Point of View," *DWL News,* November 1972, 3–4.

Researchers in mental health and social work confirmed the distinction between CR and therapy and identified processes developed in CR groups as offering new ways to transform traditional therapy. Cherniss, "Personality and Ideology," 123–25; Eastman, "Consciousness-Raising as a Resocialization Process," 153, 181; Kravetz, "Consciousness-Raising Groups in the 1970s," 180–83.

19. Hanisch, "The Personal Is Political," 76; Peslikis, "Resistances to Consciousness," 379.

20. Kleine interview, 1985.

21. DWL, "Women's Liberation Answers Some Questions," leaflet, [late 1972?]. The resulting process was to be from the bottom up and extremely democratic. It has been argued that this method is in some ways a more true application of Marxist method, as well as an inherent rejection of the Leninist model of the vanguard party. Hartsock, "Fundamental Feminism," 32–43; Rowbotham, "Women's Movement and Organizing for Socialism," 21–155; Hartsock, "Feminism, Power, and Change," 2–24.

22. Morgan interview.

23. Arnold, "Consciousness-Raising," 161. Like the closing formula in Sarah Grimké's correspondence ("Thine in the bonds of womanhood"), a bond has dual meanings: subjugation and solidarity. The term "sisterhood" was used in contrast to the generic "brotherhood," and there was some use of the term "sister" by nineteenth-century feminists. But it was largely inspired by the common usage of "brother" and "sister" in the black community—in churches and in the black women's club movement. Dill, "Race, Class, and Gender," 134. The familial imagery is obvious here. However, Allen argued against the CR group as a surrogate family and for preserving a distance by maintaining a separate private life. *Free Space,* 34. In Dayton, even if it had been considered desirable to maintain a separate private life, the small size of the city and of its feminist community undoubtedly would have made this impossible. In the successive waves, CR group participants recognized the importance of establishing these intimate links outside of friendship networks. However, it was usually assumed that CR group members would become close friends, and a few referred to their group as their family. Grimké, *Letters on the Equality of the Sexes,* 306–16.

24. Sherrie Novick interview.

25. Baxandall, "Catching the Fire," 210. But Baxandall rightly stressed above all the joy of the movement.

26. Sale, *SDS*, 441.

27. DWL, "Directory of Consciousness-Raising Groups," August 1973.

28. Beth Ann Krier, "Latent Feminists List Woes," *JH*, 25 March 1970, 27.

29. "Abortion: Legalize It," leaflet, personal archives. (All unpublished material hereafter is from my personal archives, unless otherwise stated.).

30. According to Brownmiller, Robin Morgan had spoken to journalist Lindsy Van Gelder about the idea of a freedom bonfire in which various instruments of women's oppression might be thrown, including bras. (Younger readers should be reminded that the bras and girdles of the time were much more structured and much less comfortable than the ones available today.) Van Gelder opened her subsequent article on this theme. Brownmiller, *In Our Time*, 37. See also Hanisch, "1968 Miss America Protest," 199.

31. *DDN*, 3 May 1970, 1st ed.; *DDN*, 1 May 1969.

32. Freeman, *Politics of Women's Liberation*, 148.

33. Mary Wiegers, "The New Feminists: Backlash Is Built-in," *JH*, 24 March 1970, 27.

34. Jim Fain, editorial, *DDN*, 4 May 1972.

35. Carol Mattar, "Women Get Place of Their Own," *JH*, 25 August 1973, 33.

36. "Anti-war Demonstration: April 15," leaflet.

37. Suits drew heavily from the Florida Paper for her article "Rebellion," not always crediting the authors. However, she accurately pointed out that much of the New Left at the time "denounced as bourgeois the concept that ideas are personal property that can be stolen," and that the *Minority Report* "prided itself on regularly 'stealing' cartoons, articles, and ideas from both the underground and aboveground press." Suits, letter to the author, 5 August 1985. The Florida Paper: Jones and Brown, "Towards a Female Liberation Movement.".

38. Jones and Brown, "Towards a Female Liberation Movement," 365–66.

39. Ellen Willis, "Women and the Left," printed in the *Guardian* [New York], February 1969, reprinted in *Notes from the Second Year*, April 1970, 55.

40. Morgan, "Goodbye to All That," 129–30. Other key texts include Piercy's "Grand Coolie Damn," 473–92, and Hanisch, "Hard Knocks," 62.

41. Klatch, *Generation Divided*, 8, 170–73.

42. Hole and Levine, *Rebirth of Feminism*, 116.

43. Echols, *Daring to Be Bad*, 52, 101, 3. Note that "feminist" and "radical feminist" are used interchangeably.

44. Gatlin, *American Women since 1945*, 123, 124; Echols, *Daring to Be Bad*, 3; Gatlin, *American Women since 1945*, 124; Ryan, *Feminism and the Women's Movement*, 55.

45. Echols, *Daring to Be Bad*, 245. "The Fourth World Manifesto" declared: "UNDERNEATH THE SURFACE OF EVERY NATIONAL, ETHNIC, OR RACIAL CULTURE IS THE SPLIT BETWEEN THE TWO PRIMARY CULTURES OF THE WORLD—THE FEMALE CULTURE AND THE MALE CULTURE," and "We identify with all women of all races, classes, and countries all over the world. The female culture is the Fourth World." Burris et al., "The Fourth World Manifesto," 112, 118.

46. Freeman, "On the Origins of the Women's Liberation Movement," 185. Interview with Leslie Cagan," in Cluster, ed., *They Should Have Served That Cup of Coffee*, 241.

47. "What Do Women Want, Anyway?" Special issue of *Here and Now* 7:4 (hereafter cited as *HN: Women's Issue*) (July–August 1970).

48. Kathy Kleine, "In Defense of Liberation," *HN: Women's Issue*, 26–27.

49. Kathy Kleine, "We Have a Dream," *HN: Women's Issue*, 15.

50. Mary Morgan, "One Woman, One Vote," *HN: Women's Issue*, 12.

51. Kleine, "We Have a Dream," 15.

52. Nancy Galehouse, "Strike Day," *DWL News*, 27 September 1970, 3–4.

53. Elaine Morrissey, *DDN*, 27 August 1970. Jim Fain, editorial, *DDN*, 27 August 1970.

54. Carden, *New Feminist Movement*, 110.

55. Ibid., 155.

56. Tax, "For the People Hear Us Singing," 312.

57. Daytonians were older than Margaret Strobel's subjects from Chicago Women's Liberation Union, Whittier's radical feminists in Columbus, and "women's liberation" members in Carden's studies (which she separates from the older "women's rights" group). DWL members were slightly less educated than subjects in the Carden, Strobel, and Whittier studies. In part, this may reflect local or regional differences and the fact that Dayton's movement was not university-based. Carden and Strobel showed similar marriage rates. Strobel, "Organizational Learning in the Chicago Women's Liberation Union," 149; Whittier, *Feminist Generations*, 10; Carden, *New Feminist Movement*, 30.

58. Dayton SMSA 1970 census information on the twenty-five to forty-four-year-old age bracket: 85.8 percent married and 5.8 percent divorced. For eighteen to forty-four-year-olds: 75.2 percent married and 5.3 percent divorced. My sample was too small to give any precise figures, but a far larger number of DWL activists were single or divorced.

59. Rosen, *World Split Open*, 46.

60. Diane K. Lewis, "A Response to Inequality," 169n; Hemmons, "Women's Liberation Movement," 297; Rosen, *World Split Open*, 337–38.

61. Based on discussions and personal observations, I suspect that given the emphasis on education among Jews, many Jewish women of my generation left Dayton to go to college. The Catholic University of Dayton was not an option, and the young Wright State was not developed enough. Since many Jewish families had shallow roots in the city, geographic mobility may have been greater; all of my Jewish female friends went to college elsewhere. For older women with memories of the Shoah and of overt antisemitism (many Dayton neighborhoods were closed to Jews well into the sixties), sympathy to feminism may have been overshadowed by a sense of solidarity toward the cosexual community.

62. Carden, *New Feminist Movement*, 20.

63. One 1968 poll showed that 43 percent of the U.S. population went to church on Sunday. O'Neill, *Coming Apart*, 312n.

64. Evans, *Personal Politics*, 110–11n.

65. This point has also been made by Breines in her review of *Personal Politics*.

66. Weigand, *Red Feminism*; Kaplan and Shapiro, *Red Diapers*, 8.

67. Rupp and Taylor, *Survival in the Doldrums*. As this question was not central to my study, I may have missed connections. Irrespective, Rupp and Taylor's book retains its interest as national context, particularly given the geographic mobility of this generation and the national links in many cases, particularly to church groups such as those discussed in Hartmann, *Other Feminists*, 92–131. I found little evidence of older women's organizations playing the role of "movement halfway houses," as Aldon Morris described those isolated groups that develop resources for changing society. Such groups are activated when new social movements with similar goals emerge. Morris, *Origins of the Civil Rights Movement*, 139.

68. Freeman, *Politics of Women's Liberation;* Ferree and Hess, *Controversy and Coalition;* Ryan, *Feminism and the Women's Movement*, 40–41.

69. In her 1975 book, Freeman rejected a women's liberation and women's rights division, as well as the attempts to place these groups on the liberal to Left spectrum. The programs of the so-called reformist groups, she argued, would fundamentally transform society, and radical groups often limit themselves to the traditionally feminine spheres of education, maternity, and sexuality. *Politics of Women's Liberation*, 50–51. Zillah Eisenstein argued that liberal feminism contained "the seeds of its own transformation" because it "involves more than simply achieving the bourgeois male rights earlier denied women." The difference between liberalism and liberal feminism "is that feminism requires a recognition, however implicit and undefined, of the sexual-class identification for women as women." Eisenstein, *Radical Future of Liberal Feminism*, 6–8.

70. "Co-Ordinating Meeting," *DWL News*, November 1972, 5.

71. Echols, *Daring to Be Bad*. Whittier, *Feminist Generations;* Rosenberg, *Divided Lives*, 274; Evans, *Personal Politics;* Reinelt, "Moving onto the Terrain of the State," 84–104; Staggenborg, "Can Feminist Organizations Be Effective?" 345, 353.

72. Feminists also use Iowa as an example of a Middle American spot where feminism had to be toned down to succeed. Robin Morgan advocated using "simple (real) language" to reach "everyone from Queens to Iowa." And the founder of the Women's Equity Action League, Elizabeth Boyer, boasted of a chapter in Iowa, "of all places," proud that the moderate WEAL succeeded "where you couldn't sell 'women's liberation' if you gold plated it." If Dayton is any indication, a study of feminism in Iowa would be in line before accepting such assertions. Rosen, *World Split Open*, 161; Hole and Levine, *Rebirth of Feminism*, 96.

73. Friedan, *It Changed My Life*, 119.

74. DWL, "This is a conference on the 'Status of Women,'" leaflet, [1970].

75. Evans, *Personal Politics*, 21.

CHAPTER 2

1. "Group Forms Rebirth," *Minority Report: Women's Liberation Issue*, 5.

2. While no moral opposition to abortion was ever expressed in any of DWL's writings, by late 1972 two members of a CR group were sympathetic to the antiabortion group Right to Life. One stayed in DWL for a brief time, and the other participated in the CR group for about a year. The latter woman went on to become part of Dayton's Right to Life leadership.

DWL members saw an antichoice position as an unreconcilable difference with the goals of DWL: "[I]t is not possible to be in Dayton Women's Liberation and be against abortion and/or abortion reform." Meetings on the question were convened in late 1972 and early 1973. "Coordinating Meeting," DWL News, 29 October 1972, 9. No attempts were ever made to exclude anyone from DWL's midst.

3. "Abortion," *MR: Women's Issue,* 9.

4. "Abortion Hearings: If They Won't Listen, Maybe They'll Read," *DWL News,* 26 June 1971, 7.

5. Jan Griesinger, "Abortion: Free and Legal," *Here and Now: Women's Issue,* 18, 19.

6. "Gailbraith's Bill Potentially Dangerous," *DWL News,* 9 February 1971, 7.

7. "We Demand Control over Our Own Bodies," *DWL News,* 29 September 1971, 4.

8. "Abortion Conference," *DWL News,* 12 August 1971, 2. The original WITCH (Women's International Terrorist Conspiracy from Hell) was a group born out of New York Radical Women, known for their theatrical "zap actions." This "coven's" first action was to hex the Wall Street stock exchange. Other covens were created around the country. Hole and Levine, *Rebirth of Feminism,* 126–30; Morgan, "Three Articles on WITCH," in *Going Too Far,* 71–81; "Historical Documents: WITCH," in Morgan, *Sisterhood,* 603–21.

9. "We Demand Control," 3. Challenging "expertise" and replacing (male) authorities on women with women's direct testimonies was a technique used across the nation. As Brownmiller put it, in these days when "first-person discourse on a dizzying variety of intimate subjects [has become] a gimmicky staple of the afternoon talk shows," it is hard to remember how crucial it was in the consciousness-raising process, "an original technique and a powerful ideological tool." *In Our Time,* 109.

10. Jan Griesinger, "What's New with Abortion?" *DWL News,* June 1973, 2.

11. "Rebirth," *MR Women's Issue,* 5. The idea that the pill alone led to woman's liberation was denounced as a myth. Betty Peterson (pseudonym), "Bitch Is Beautiful," *MR,* 11–25 November 1969, 3; Elayne Archer, "Another Bitter Pill: The Birth of Conspiracy," reprint from Health Policy Advisory Center, *HN: Women's Issue,* 22.

12. "We Demand Control," 4, 3.

13. Griesinger, "Abortion," 18.

14. Peterson, "Bitch Is Beautiful," 3.

15. Rector, "Woman as Guru," *MR Women's Issue,* 5.

16. Simmons interview; "Un-Armed Forces Day: Women Down Uncle Sam," *DWL News,* 23 May 1971, 3; *DWL News,* 9 April 1971.

17. "Why Children? Are There Any *Good* Reasons to Have Them?" *DWL News,* July 1973, 8.

18. "A Free Choice?" *DWL News,* July 1973, 3ff.

19. Karen DeMasi of the Miami Valley Regional Planning Commission, quoted in Katherine Ullmer, "Day-care Gap Puts Working Mothers in Lots of Company," *DDN,* 13 April 1982, 15; telephone interview with Dixie Yoon, Child Care Action Advisory Committee of Human Services, July 1982; Hart interview.

20. Allyne Rosenthal, "A Proposal for Industrial Day Care," *HN: Women's Issue,* 21; Kleine, "We Have a Dream," 14.

21. "Report from Coordinating Meeting," *DWL News,* 27 September 1972, 7; Morgan interview.

22. "Cooperative Child Care Becoming a Reality," *DWL News,* 9 February

1970, 3; "On Day Care," *DWL News,* 10 March 1970, 3. Reprinted from Liberation News Service.

23. "Day Care Collective Forming," *DWL News,* 25 November 1970, 2.

24. Kleine, "We Have a Dream," 14; Robin Suits, "Economic Exploitation," *HN: Women's Issue,* 11.

25. Deborah Thomas, "A Modest Proposal of Non-Marriage," *DWL News,* June 1973, 8–9. Reprinted from *Women, a Journal of Liberation* 2:2 (Winter 1971), 20–21.

26. "The Utopian Marriage Contract," *DWL News,* March 1972, 3. Reprinted from Susan Edmiston, *Ms.,* Spring 1972.

27. A member of the Ovarian Society, "The Nuclear Family Trap," *DWL News,* June 1973, 11; "We Demand Control," 4.

28. A member of the Ovarian Society, "Once upon a Time in the Past There Was—," *DWL News,* June 1973, 7.

29. Barbara Gregg, "Divorce: Personal and Political," *DWL News,* May 1974, 9–10.

30. Nancy Galehouse, "Sexual Conditioning," *HN: Women's Issue,* 13.

31. "The Myth of the Liberated Female," *DWL News,* 27 September 1972, 1–2.

32. "We Demand Control," 3–4. A six-point platform was prepared for a demonstration in the fall of 1971.

33. Kathy Kleine and Barbara Gregg, "On Heterosexuality," *DWL News,* May 1973, 1, 8–9.

34. Charlotte Bunch, "Lesbian Feminist Politics," *DWL News,* May 1973, 4, reprinted from *off our backs,* April 1973.

35. Perhaps the relatively lesser conflict with the "male Left" from which DWL had emerged had not only produced more gradual political splits, but had also slowed the process insofar as sexual preference was concerned.

36. Marcia Muller, *The Cheshire Cat's Eye* (New York: Mysterious Press, 1983), 66–67.

37. Martin and Lyon, "Realities of Lesbianism," 99–109.

38. Denise Goodman, "Libbers at WSU: Feuding Women Close Ranks," *JH,* 5 August 1972.

39. Morgan, interview; "One evening . . . ," reprint from Gay Women's Liberation, *DWL News,* May 1972, 4.

40. Lesbians had been purged from NOW prior to 1971. Freeman, *Politics of Women's Liberation,* 99; Snitow and Stansell, introduction, in Snitow et al., eds., *Desire,* 24.

41. Before the emergence of the women's movement, the only visible manifestation of lesbians in Dayton had been the bar subculture, which continued during and parallel to the women's liberation movement. These bars were mostly in southeastern part of the city, near the University of Dayton, far from the neighborhoods where most DWL members lived. The bars provided a vital space in which to meet and feel free; the notion of space remained important for lesbians throughout the movement. However, many lesbians found the bar scene inadequate and, with "gay bashing" on the rise, even dangerous. For a good description of the differences between the bar scene and the lesbian feminist community in one city, see Krieger, *Mirror Dance,* 125–41.

42. "Book Report," *DWL News,* November 1972, 1.

43. "Co-ordinating Meeting," *DWL News,* November 1972, 6. Another example came when Wilka's boss discovered she was a lesbian. Wilka had accepted an invitation to speak on a local radio station anonymously as "Jane X," but a colleague recognized her voice and turned the radio up so everyone in her office could hear. DWL members developed contingency plans for how to defend her.

44. "A Marriage Disagreement, or Marriage by Other Means," *Feminist Memoir Project,* 285.

45. Pat Rector, "One Woman's Manifesto," *MR,* April 1970; Pat Rector, "Psychological Conditioning," *Here and Now: Women's Issue,* 11.

46. "Up against the Wall, Betty Crocker," 6.

47. "Justice Begins at Home," *DWL News,* September 1974, 2, reprinted from *Common Lot,* April 1974.

48. See Bartky, "Toward a Phenomenology of Feminist Consciousness," 28–29.

49. Goodman, "Libbers at WSU."

50. Rector, "One Woman's Manifesto"; Kleine, "We Have a Dream," 14.

51. Mary Morgan, Sondra Miller, and Kathy Kleine for DWL, letter to John Schaenzer, Frigidaire Division, GMC, 2 October 1970.

52. Hull, Scott, and Smith, eds., *All the Women Are White.*

53. "White Women's Liberation as It Relates to Non-White Women," *DWL News,* 9 February 1971, 5. See also hooks, *Ain't I a Woman,* 185–88.

54. "You Tell It Like It Is!" *DWL News,* October 1971, excerpted from the *New York Times Magazine,* 22 August 1971. The original article, "What the Black Woman Thinks about Women's Lib," was by Toni Morrison. Giddings, *When and Where I Enter,* 307, 383n.

55. Jan Griesinger, "Response to 'Welfare Mother,'" *DWL News,* February 1972, 5.

56. hooks, *Ain't I a Woman,* 187.

57. Kleine, "In Defense of Liberation," 27. Despite this position, there were individuals in DWL's ranks who worked for the ERA outside of the organization. Several, for example, were members of Fairborn NOW or the Ohio Women's Political Caucus, and Carroll was a member of the American Federation of Government Employees. Carroll said, "I had put a resolution on the floor at my first regional convention [1973] to back the ERA. . . . I had tomatoes thrown at me. My local was the only one who voted for it."

58. "Why E.R.A.," *DWL News,* March–April 1973, 3; Pam Rosenthal, "In the Name of Equality . . . Women Lose Rights," *DWL News,* March–April 1973, 4.

59. "Equal Rights Amendment?" leaflet, attached to *DWL News,* May 1973, 2.

60. Mary Morgan, notes from a speech (Wright State University women's studies class?), 15 February 1972, Department of Archives and Special Collections, Wright State University, Dayton (hereafter cited as WSU archives).

61. The timing of this action proved to be unfortunate: on the same day, four antiwar demonstrators were killed at Ohio's Kent State University. Thus, the rally for Morgan took place simultaneously with a demonstration against the Kent State killings. The choice involved added to the tensions between the left and the women's movement.

62. Gail Levin, "How to Be a City Mother," typed autobiographical text, [1976?], 1, 5. Levin, who believed that she had rarely encountered sexism, said that the local women's movement had no meaning for her. As commissioner, she voted

against funding for the Women's Center. She had more sympathy with the movement nationally, and in later years she contributed to the ERA drive. Levin interviews.

63. Dorothy W. Cousineau, Kathy Ellison, Mary M. Morgan, and Nancy Staub, "Pat Roach for City Commission," letter to women voters, 19 September 1975.

64. Elaine Morrissey, "Women Say 'Give Us Choice,'" *DDN,* 15 February, 1970, C1.

65. Barbara Gregg, "Revolutionary Women," *DWL News,* 1 September 1973, 3.

66. Carden, *New Feminist Movement,* 87.

67. Kathy Kleine and Mary Morgan, "Coordinating Committee," *DWL News,* 27 September 1970, 1.

68. "Decisions between Coordinating Committee Meetings," *DWL News,* May 1972, 7.

69. It is often incorrectly assumed that consensus is synonymous with unanimous agreement. In fact, it means that any individual in a group can prevent a decision from being made.

70. Mary Morgan, "Fireside Chats," *DWL News,* November 1971, 2. Fireside Chats were often accompanied by potlucks, one aspect of DWL's efforts at building community.

71. "Little Sisters . . . ," *DWL News,* 29 October 1972, 1.

72. Kleine and Morgan, "Coordinating Committee," 2.

73. This was undoubtedly a reference to an incident at the University of Dayton. DWL had accepted a speaking engagement for a class, only to discover that the instructor had intentionally excluded the campus feminist group. "We feel that Dayton Women's Liberation unwittingly permitted ourselves to be used to put down our sisters at UD." Mary Morgan with help from several sisters, "Creating Sisterhood," *DWL News,* January 1973, 3–4.

74. "Speakers Collective Workshop," *DWL News,* January 1973, 2.

75. "January Coordinating Meeting," *DWL News,* February 1973, 10. *Ms.,* for example, in its first issues in mid-1972, carried advertisements for professional feminist speakers bureaus.

76. "Educational Outreach," *DWL News,* January 1973, 5; "January Coordinating Meeting," *DWL News,* February 1973, 10.

77. See Rothschild-Whitt, "Conditions for Democracy," 224–27; Kanter, *Commitment and Community,* 78–80; Duberman, *Black Mountain.*

78. Kathy Kleine, "Dear Sisters," *DWL News,* August 1970, 1.

79. Jane Monsbridge, "What is the Feminist Movement?" In Ferree and Martin, eds., *Feminist Organizations,* 27–34.

80. Mary Wiegers, "The New Feminists: Backlash Is Built-in," and Beth Ann Krier, "Shopping Guide: Local Women's Lib Groups," *JH,* 24 March 1970, 27 ff.

81. The various guidelines opposed giving solo interviews, and some suggested giving only first names. Kleine and Morgan, "Coordinating Committee," 3; "Odds and Ends: News Media," *DWL News,* March 1972, 1.

82. Reichert's WYSO program, which analyzed popular music from a feminist perspective, apparently began before a WBAI-New York program that Hole and Levine dubbed "the first and only continuing feminist radio program in the country." *Rebirth of Feminism,* 275.

The impact of WYSO on Dayton was limited at first because reception required a good FM antenna. In the spring of 1973, power was increased to better cover the

Dayton area. As a result of this and outreach work, the number of Dayton listeners increased. In the midseventies, WYSO went from, as one staff member wrote, "a student-faculty sandbox (rock for the kids, classical for the professors) to a true community station." By the early 1980s, the listening audience was at approximately twenty-five thousand, and about 60 percent were from Dayton and the immediate suburbs. From that time on, WYSO became a more important source of information and means of communication for the women's movement and an important inroad for National Public Radio. Jon Herbst, "Culture/Politics on the Air," *Cultural Gazette,* Spring/Summer 1978, 1ff; Sherry Novick interview.

83. Mary Morgan, "This Is a Recorded Message . . . ," *DWL News,* 1 September 1973, 10.

84. Morgan, *Going Too Far,* 216.

85. Griesinger, *Women in the Struggle for Liberation.*

86. Non-DWL members of Women Here and There included Harriet Miller, a professor of Christian education at the United Theological Seminary, and Joan Arnold (Romero), an ex-nun who was then on the faculty at the seminary. Both were involved in feminist activities related to women and religion nationally. *Wholeness of Women,* United Theological Seminary, November 1974; Janet Long, "Romero: 'Why Not Women?'" *DDN,* May 1974. The group later joined with an order of nuns in campaigning on the bottle baby issue. "Local Church Women Take on Big Business," *JH,* 10 September 1977, 18.

87. Kathy Kleine for the newsletter collective, "Movement," *DWL News,* November 1973, 2, 3.

88. "Letter from a Welfare Mother," *DWL News,* December 1971, 2, reprinted from *Women, A Journal of Liberation* 2:3.

89. This was how the radical feminist collective, started in November 1972, was defined. It was "the place for women who want to take stands" and "for reading for discussion and expansion of the mind, and perhaps sharing a new lifestyle living the ideals you have in your head." "Co-Ordinating Meeting," *DWL News,* November 1972, 5.

90. Griesinger, "Response to 'Welfare Mother,'" 5. She added, "If we ever turn a deaf ear to poor sisters who cry for freedom or consent in silence to their misery, then we will in fact have been bought off."

91. Personal testimonies attest to this, as do addresses: shortly after joining DWL, many members moved into the Five Oaks or Dayton View area, some as part of the many group houses.

92. "How We Live and with Whom," *DWL News,* June 1973, 1. The quote is from the winter 1971 issue of *Women, a Journal of Liberation* and was used to introduce the special issue of *DWL News* on the theme.

93. Kleine, "Lifestyles and Liberation," *DWL News,* June 1973, 10.

94. Suits recalled the conflict that led to her departure as also having been linked to a specific incident. Three people, friends of several DWL members, were arrested for possession of drugs. One woman allegedly agreed to inform on the dealer, a male leftist, in exchange for her release. According to Suits, a member of Elizabeth's Sisters defended the woman's informing on a man on feminist grounds. Suits's opposition to informing reinforced suspicions of her lack of independence from men. The debate, Suits pointed out, presaged the national debate over whether ex-Weatherperson Jane

Alpert had informed, or would have been justified in informing, on members of the underground. Suits interview; Suits, letter to the author, 5 August 1985.

95. Hart interview; Holmes interview.

96. "Reflections," *DWL News,* May 1974, 5.

97. Hogeland, *Feminism and Its Fictions,* 26, 29–34, 167–68.

98. B. Schroeder, "The Wilder Sisters Are Getting Wilder!" *DWL News,* August 1973, 9; a member of the Wilder Sisters, "A Year of Change," *DWL News,* August 1973, 11.

99. Lois Bailey, "Trust, Acceptance, Honesty, Confrontation—or: How Does a CR Group Grow?" *DWL News,* June 1974, 6.

100. Bailey, "Trust, 6; Wilma Schroeder, "A Personal Account," *DWL News,* June 1974, 7.

101. This account (and that of the housewife-mother in the previous paragraph) takes some information from unsigned articles and is thus left anonymous.

102. In Anita Shreeve's book on consciousness-raising, one woman cynically stated: "I went out and climbed the ladder. . . . I]f I tried to carry an entire movement around on my shoulders, I would not get very far. They would drag me down, instead of me dragging them up. So the only way to do it is go out and do it for yourself." *Women Together, Women Alone,* 60. Paradoxically, fulltime homemakers could maintain a higher level of commitment to the women's movement.

103. Kleine and Gregg, "On Heterosexuality," 9.

CHAPTER 3

1. "A Women's Center?" *DWL News,* 23 May 1971, 5.

2. "January Coordinating Meeting," 10.

3. "Model Cities," *DWL News,* November 1971, 7.

4. The Center later claimed to be the first in Dayton to offer such services. This was not entirely true: DWL had offered self-defense and automobile mechanics courses for its members and also had done some telephone referrals.

5. DWC proposal, August 1973.

6. Jan Griesinger, "Dayton Women Center: A thing I wrote for some women in church stuff out of town . . . ," 7 February 1974, typed notes, WSU archives.

7. "Up to Date News about the Women's Center," *DWL News,* March–April 1973, 6. Kathy Ellison, notes from speech for Central State University social work class, 12 February 1974.

8. Griesinger, "Dayton Women Center."

9. "Men's Center," editorial, *DDN,* 5 May 1973.

10. Women's Center Collective minutes (hereafter cited as DWC minutes), 7 October 1973; Michael R. Merz, letter to Judge Howell, 31 January 1974; Merz, letter to Roberta Fisher; Mary Ann Balch for DWL, letter to Ron Gatton, 6 February 1974.

11. Griesinger, "Dayton Women Center."

12. Barb Roberts, Barbara Gregg, Sherrie Holmes, Lois Murtaugh, Robin Suits, Roberta Allen, Betty Jean Carroll, Jan Griesinger (DWC Collective), fund-raising letter, 25 April 1973.

13. S. Holmes, "Me: Change Is the RIGHT Word!" *DWL News,* August 1973, 12–13.

14. Ibid.

15. NAM's founding convention took place in 1972, although the organization actually began in 1971. It was one of the groups to "arise out of the ashes of SDS." Judis, "New American Movement," 123. The NAM position that "men are not auxiliary to the struggle against sexism," despite the material advantages that they gain as a result, led to a heated debate over whether or not men can be feminists. "New American Movement," adopted at the national founding convention, June 1972, 2, 5, 6. NAM supported women's organizing both outside and inside the organization. One all-women's chapter was formed in Chapel Hill, North Carolina.

16. The local chapter was strong for a medium-sized city. At the 1975 convention, for example, 42 of the organization's 45 chapters were said to account for 586 members. In addition, an estimated 150–200 people were members either of chapters or at large. Judis, "New American Movement," 132n.

17. Reichert, letter to the author, 8 August 2001.

18. Quoted in Susan Brownmiller, *In Our Time*, 39.

19. Reichert later gained more fame when two documentaries she codirected, *Union Maids* (1976) and *Seeing Red* (1983), both received Academy Award nominations. She has been called one of the godmothers of the American independent and feminist film movement.

20. Whittier, *Feminist Generations*, 56–57; Mueller, "Conflict in Contemporary Feminism," 274.

21. Joreen [Jo Freeman], "Tyranny of Structurelessness," 285–99. Chicago Women's Liberation Union, Hyde Park Chapter, *Socialist Feminism*. On the group's history, see Staggenborg, "Stability and Innovation in the Women's Movement," 75–92, and "Can Feminist Organizations Be Effective?" 339–55; and Strobel, "Organizational Learning," 145–64.

22. Joreen, "Tyranny of Structurelessness."

23. Barbara Tuss, "Political Reality and the Women's Movement," *DWL News*, April 1974, 6.

24. Mary Morgan, "Fireside Chat," *DWL News*, December 1973, 3; Kathy Kleine, "Politics of Feminism," *DWL News*, April 1974, 8.

25. "Dayton Women's Center Staff Positions: Relevant Areas of Inquiry." Typed notes for interviews, WSU archives.

26. Ellison's (and Fisher's) straight style entered into the debate on hiring, but must not be exaggerated. Contrary to what has been reported in other cities, there is no record in Dayton of feminists being criticized because of their personal appearance. Jeans and casual clothes were the rule, but only one person spoke of a "uniform." My experience as a "lipstick feminist" (to borrow a Scandinavian expression) confirms this: it was only upon my arrival in Ann Arbor, Michigan, that I was judged unfeminist because of my eccentric, theatrical style. This had never been my experience in Dayton.

27. Maddi Breslin interview. See also Donahue, *My Own Story*.

28. The composition of the Women's Center collective changed drastically. In April 1973, all members were in DWL, including two socialist feminists. A year later, only half had previous experience in DWL, and an overlapping 50 percent were socialist feminists. By 1976, no DWL women were left. "Women's Center Collective Members," membership lists, 1973–78.

29. Questionnaire distributed to visitors during the first week of events. Results

included in DWC logs, "Opening week survey"; Ellison, notes from speech; "Counseling: Women Moving!" DWC mailing [May 1974?], mimeograph; DWC [Maddi Breslin], "Proposal for a Women's Center for Greater Dayton, Ohio," fund-raising proposal, May 1974, 3–6. Telephone inquiries and services accounted for about 40 percent. Figures cited for calls and class enrollment often are drawn from funding proposals, a fairly unreliable source. However, when cross-checked with internal telephone logs the figures hold up. Other information on utilizers, however, is necessarily impressionistic, based on interviews, general evaluations written at the time, and Center surveys.

30. Ellison, notes from speech.

31. Barbara Kruger, "The Dayton Women's Center," term paper, Wright State University, 7 March 1974, 10.

32. DWC [Breslin], "Proposal for a Women's Center," 3–4.

33. Russell Campbell interview.

34. Ibid. In mid-1974, it was decided that to be a collective member, a woman had to attend three consecutive meetings and ask to join. Anyone missing three meetings without justification was eliminated. Although voting was supposedly the official mode of decision-making, confusion reigned on this point. Breslin recalled DWC as structureless. Some remember voting when consensus seemed impossible. Others remember meetings with motions introduced, seconded, and voted on.

35. See also Rothschild-Whitt, "Conditions for Democracy," 230–32.

36. "Telephone Tips," instructions for volunteers, typed and handwritten instructions in loose-leaf notebook.

37. Peterson, "Bitch Is Beautiful," 3; Sheila Eliseo, "Capsule Commentary," *DWL News,* October 1973, 7.

38. Charlotte M. Holovack, "Counseling and Sexism," *DWL News,* November 1973, 6.

39. Twila Merta, "Communication Lines: Letters to the Newsletter," *DWL News,* December 1973, 14–15. Psychology student Judy Antonelli replied that while some problems were physiological in origin, psychiatrists used medication abusively to "keep mental patients and prisoners so doped up that they can't even think straight (and therefore don't rebel)." Antonelli, "In Response," *DWL News,* January 1974, 8.

40. "Counseling: Women Moving!"

41. Transactional analysis is based on the notion of people playing out scenarios, predetermined scripts, with each individual having in herself or himself three systems of thought with three types of behavior: the parent, the adult, and the child. Communication is seen as a variety of the many possible combinations and interactions between the three. The influence of TA was stressed by respondents and confirmed by the frequent appearance of TA vocabulary in members' language.

42. Tricia Hart, letter to DWC, in "Counseling: Women Moving!"

43. "Counseling," *Women's Service Directory,* 1975, 9. Adapted from a statement by Cleveland Women's Counseling.

44. Catherine Martindale, "Model Cities Lists Projects," *JH,* 1 March 1974. While austerity can reinforce commitment, the ongoing struggle to pay the bills did little to help internal cohesiveness, particularly as the Center increasingly aimed at obtaining funds from external sources. On internal versus external support bases, see Rothschild-Whitt, "Conditions for Democracy," 227–30.

45. DWC [Breslin], "Proposal for a Women's Center."

46. The Comprehensive Employment and Training Act was a Department of Labor job training program. The Center received relatively small amounts of money from a small radical foundation set up by a Dayton woman after she inherited a large sum of money, as well as from the Ms. Foundation and the Playboy Foundation.

47. Available records show an average of eleven hundred to sixteen hundred dollars per month; for the first four years, Suits says eighteen hundred per month. DWC Financial Report, 8 August 1977; Mary Deal, Financial Report to the DWC Collective, 8 August 1977; Financial Statement, attached to DWC minutes, 16 August 1978; Financial Report attached to DWC minutes, 1 September 1978; Suits interview.

48. Interestingly, internal differences paled in the face of outside threats. Between December 1973 and mid-1974, simultaneously with the conflicts at the Center, conflict over control of the newly created abortion clinic united feminists from both sides, including Suits, Holmes, Gregg, and Griesinger.

49. Of the socialist feminists, only Suits and, to a lesser extent, Holmes had any substantial experience in DWL. Both rapidly shifted their primary commitment to the Center, and this was reinforced by their daily presence on staff.

50. "Structural Change?" *DWL News,* December 1973, 2–3.

51. Job descriptions, "Dayton Women's Center Work Program," 19 November 1973; "Data Forecast," form for Model Cities completed by Kathy Ellison, 10 April 1974.

52. "Notes from Jan. 16 Coordinating Meeting," *DWL News,* February 1974, 2.

53. Susan Zurcher, interview with Dorothy Smith, Dayton, 17 February 1984.

54. I have observed this dynamic repeatedly in social movements. It would merit further research. It is also one reason why studying leaders of an organization amplifies conflict and paralysis. No doubt the grass roots remain unaware of many documented conflicts.

55. In March 1974, a discussion on conditions of membership in DWL, and in June, on general strategy.

56. Morgan, "Fireside Chat," *DWL News,* December 1973, 3.

57. "Calendar," *DWL News,* January 1974, 4; "Fireside Chat on Women's Center," *DWL News,* April 1974, 1; *DWL News,* September 1974, 1.

58. The Socialist Feminist CR Group: Sherrie Holmes, Barbara Tuss, Robin Suits, Sharon Trinka, Julia Reichert, Tricia Hart, Nancy Sutton, Sharon Stone, Denise Viall, "Proposal . . . DWL: A Time for a Change!" *DWL News,* September 1974, 4.

59. Socialist Feminist CR Group, "DWL: A Time for a Change!" 4–7.

60. "Education Task Force Proposal," *DWL News,* October 1974, 3–6.

61. "Outline Proposal Submitted by New/Old Group, Fireside Chat, Restructuring DWL," *DWL News,* October 1974, 6.

62. "Education Task Force Proposal," *DWL News,* October 1974, 3.

63. Mary Anne Balch, "Notes from Special Meeting of Dayton Women's Liberation, October 13, 1974, Regarding the Structure and Purpose of DWL," *DWL News,* November 1974, 3.

64. Sappho's Army Speakers Collective, "Our Perspective," *DWL News,* December 1974, 3.

65. Socialist Feminist CR Group, "Revised Proposal," *DWL News,* October 1974, 12.

66. Anita Matthews, Jane Graham, Pam Ediss, Cheryl Radican, Mary Morgan, Roberta Allen, Donna Parker, Barbara Gregg, Mary Ann Balch, Joan Ediss, Charlotte Holovack, Kathy Kleine, Jan Griesinger, Kathy Hinchcliff, "Dear Sisters . . . ," *DWL News,* 1 March 1975, 1.

67. In early 1975, the lesbian community in nearby Lexington, Kentucky, was one of several targeted for investigation in relationship to the supposed developing gay underground and the search for fugitive Susan Saxe, wanted for a bank robbery intended to finance her revolutionary activities. While underground, Saxe had come out as a lesbian.

Grand jury hearings were held, a pretrial process with no lawyers permitted. The Justice Department requested and was granted imposed immunity, eliminating subpoenaed witnesses' recourse to plead the Fifth Amendment. Therefore, refusal to cooperate meant facing charges of contempt of court and imprisonment. A standard question reported was, "Name every meeting you've attended in the past year, and state who was there and what was discussed." Subsequent harassment included questioning a lesbian woman's grandmother and checking with employers. In Lexington, five women and one man were sent to jail for refusing to speak to the FBI, and DWL supported them. The surrounding debate centered on the attitude vis-à-vis the FBI. In Lexington, some less politicized women believed they had nothing to hide, and others with children and economic constraints thought they could not afford to spend time in jail. Looming in the background of this debate was the position of some lesbian separatists nationally who favored speaking with the FBI rather than "taking risks for male supremacists." DWL opposed all cooperation with the FBI or the grand jury. "FBI Harassment Strikes Lexington," *DWL News,* April 1975, 3–4; Kelly, "Grand Juries," 18–19; Brownmiller, *In Our Time,* 231–32.

68. Judy Antonelli, "Steinem-CIA Tie Uncovered," *DWL News,* July 1975, 6–7. Taken from Redstockings, "Gloria Steinem and the CIA," in Redstockings, *Feminist Revolution,* 150–69; Judy Antonelli, "Steinem Reply," *DWL News,* October 1975, 3, including excerpts from Steinem's response published in *off our backs,* September 1975, and letters of support from Rita Mae Brown and Robin Morgan.

69. In a list of seventy-five names and addresses compiled for a 1984 reunion, only thirty-one addresses were from Dayton and the suburbs. An additional thirteen were from Yellow Springs. This sample would overrepresent Daytonians, given that those who had moved away were more difficult to trace. "Addresses of DWL Sisters," in notes from the DWL fifteenth-year reunion, a revived DWL newsletter.

70. Griesinger interview; Carrie Labriola, "'Can't You Get a Man?' 'Women's Libbers' Remember How It Was 15 Years Ago," *JH,* 9 October 1984, 9.

71. Women who rejected feminism would, of course, be less easy to trace and perhaps less likely to be cooperative with this investigation. I was, however, able to investigate all but one such report, and none proved to be founded. Throughout the entire study, there were no dramatic about-faces.

72. This is consistent with national reports: when women drop out of the movement, they apparently do not stop being feminists. See Freeman, *Politics of Women's Liberation,* 143. Carden commented on the demise of CR groups: "When their group breaks up, many women, although they remain committed feminists, cease active participation. With their outlook and attitudes changed, they revise their way of life." *New Feminist Movement,* 72–73.

73. Margo Evans interview.

74. Videotape of DWL reunion, by Diane Graham Teramana, October 1984.

CHAPTER 4

1. Hole and Levine, *Rebirth of Feminism,* 299.

2. Ibid., 301. There was no discussion of actually performing abortions illegally, like Jane, the Chicago group started the previous year, did. Kaplan, *Story of Jane.*

3. Dayton Clergy and Lay Consultation Service on Abortion, "This Woman Has a Problem Pregnancy . . . ," leaflet.

4. Griesinger interview; Elaine Morrissey, "Clergy Answers 40 Calls on Abortion First Week," *DDN,* June 1970; Wade M. Jackson, "What Is Legal?" Letter to the editor, *DDN* [1971?], and editors' reply. This information gives only a partial picture of abortion recipients from the Dayton area. It excludes women who went out of town on their own, obtained illegal abortions in Dayton, or self-aborted. These categories probably included both the poorest and the wealthiest.

5. Griesinger raised the issue in the Dayton group, but many of the clergymen were reluctant at first. "It took some persuasion for them to understand that women should have as many choices as possible," one DWL author wrote, "and that choosing [with] whom one decides to discuss [them] . . . is as important, if not more important than any other choice one must make." Y. H., "Clergy and Lay Consultation Center," *DWL News,* 12 August 1971, 2.

6. Y. H., "Clergy and Lay."

7. Wilson, as discussed below, was later criticized for her attitude toward counseling after becoming director of the abortion clinic. While her potential bias is obvious, she was not alone in taking this position.

8. Boston Women's Health Book Collective, *Our Bodies, Ourselves,* 222; Hole and Levine, *Rebirth of Feminism,* 299–300; Y. H., "Clergy and Lay."

9. Both quoted in Morrissey, "Clergy Answers 40 Calls."

10. Morrissey, "Clergy Answers 40 Calls"; Clergy and Lay, "This Woman Has a Problem Pregnancy . . ."; Ann Heller and Mary Anne Sharkey, "Abortion Change to Be Slow," *JH,* 23 January 1973, 24.

11. It may be that women needing abortions would have made the extra effort to find a less well-publicized service, as well.

12. Stephen Landers, "Abortion Clinics Stymied," *DDN,* 11 February 1972.

13. Heller and Sharkey, "Abortion Change to Be Slow," 23; Landers, "Abortion Clinics Stymied."

14. Jim Bohman, "Hospitals Here Awaiting New Ohio Law on Abortion," *DDN,* 5 May 1973; Henry Harris, "MVH Says Staff against Late Abortions," *DDN,* 14 May 1974.

15. On the discussions within Dayton's Planned Parenthood, see Wattleton, *Life on the Line,* 147–52.

16. Griesinger, "What's New with Abortion?" 2; Landers, "Abortion Clinics Stymied"; Barnum, "After Roe v. Wade," 2.

17. "Chronology-Dayton Women's Health Center" [prepared by community board for lawyer, June 1974, compiled by Robin Suits]. Jan Griesinger, "Dayton Women's Health Center," *DWL News,* October 1973, 3; Barnum, "After Roe v. Wade," 4; Morgan interview; Griesinger interview; Wilson interview. These personal,

high-risk loans with no collateral were in chunks of one thousand to six thousand dollars to be paid back over the first year at 6 percent. Wilson reported that she and Heindal had been offered a personal loan by a member of Heindal's family. However, they preferred to borrow from the community.

18. See, for instance, Ross, "African-American Women and Abortion," 161–207.

19. Wilson and Heindal did a lot of the footwork connecting doctors, but feminists believed that "whatever success they had with the doctors was due to their association with Clergy and Lay." "Chronology-Dayton Women's Health Center.".

20. Wilson interview; Barnum, "After Roe v. Wade," 3.

21. Griesinger, "Dayton Women's Health Center."

22. Wilson interview; DWC logs; Jo Ann Knout, "Abortion: Always Emotional," *DDN,* 30 December 1973, B1; Bonnie Russ, "Abortion Clinic Operating Here," *JH,* 14 September 1973, 16.

23. Barnum, "After Roe v. Wade," 4; Wilson interview; Griesinger, "Dayton Women's Health Center"; Barnum, "After Roe v. Wade," 4; Wilson interview; Dayton Women's Health Center, Inc., Income Statement, September–October 1973.

24. Article 2, Code of Regulations [September 1973?].

25. The speed at which the abortions were performed was criticized for psychological reasons, not medical ones. At no point was the quality of medical care questioned.

26. Parsons and Hodne, "Collective Experiment in Women's Health," 11. The conservatism of Dayton's medical establishment, and even of Planned Parenthood's own doctors, is confirmed in Faye Wattleton's memoirs. *Life on the Line,* 104–6, 141, 149–52.

27. In addition, directors claimed that after the price freeze was lifted, costs increased and the clinic was barely breaking even. Wilson interview; Barnum, "After Roe v. Wade," 4.

28. "Chronology-Dayton Women's Health Center."

29. See Shore, "Feminist Workplace—Ideology in Practice."

30. See Taylor, "Free Medicine," 47; Graubard, "From Free Schools to 'Educational Alternatives,'" 61; and Moberg, "Experimenting with the Future," 287, 292.

31. Wilson interview; Holmes interview, 1981; Griesinger interview.

32. Gregg interview; Holmes interview, 1981; Griesinger interview.

33. Holmes interview, 1981; Gregg interview.

34. This was compounded by the method by which abortion was legalized. The fact that the courts granted women this right, as opposed to the alternative of a legislative, state-by-state strategy, meant that it was perceived by many as a moral victory and a recognition of a human right, as opposed to a victory for feminists resulting from a political battle. This also allowed women with no background in abortion rights work to see this decision as manna from heaven. The specific nature of the legalization of abortion was later to color the development of the movements opposing and defending reproductive freedom.

35. There is some discussion of rape in *Sexual Politics* (1969) and the *Female Eunuch* (1970), but of the spate of feminist anthologies published in 1970, not one contains an article on rape. The New York Radical Feminist "Speakout on Rape" in January 1971, followed in the same year by Susan Griffin's landmark article "Rape: The All American Crime," marked the starting point of serious and ongoing attention to the issue. See also Brownmiller, *In Our Time,* 194–208.

36. Women's Crisis Center of Ann Arbor, *Freedom from Rape.*

37. Breslin, "Attitudes about Rape and Rape Victims in Dayton, Ohio," 23.

38. The first two rape crisis centers were in Washington, D.C., and Berkeley in late 1971 or early 1972. It is estimated that one year later there were forty such centers in existence, by 1974 there were four hundred, and by 1978 there were a thousand. Burt and Gornick, "Ten Years After," 20–21; Pride, "To Respectability and Back."

39. In Nikki Canton, "Women Combine Forces to Aid Rape Victims," *DDN,* 4 April 1974.

40. Ibid.

41. In these references, not only did the Victimization Project get WAR's name wrong, but the word "rape" was usually eliminated. Victimization Project, Discretionary Grant Progress Report to the U.S. Department of Justice Law Enforcement Assistance Administration, 31 July 1975 (hereafter cited as Progress Report), 4; Canton, "Women Combine Forces.".

42. Ellison interview, 1985.

43. While the feminist groups were rejected as "sub-contractors"—that is, as recipients of funding—they were solicited for cooperation on a volunteer basis. A form letter announcing the creation of the Victimization Project was sent to the Women's Center as "probably one of the existing community resources that lends support to victims [of rape]." Bonnie Macauley, letter to Kathy Ellison, 5 June 1974. The letter asked Center members to indicate whether they were interested in "fitting into this network of community resources."

44. Breslin, "Attitudes about Rape," 23.

45. This approach fit in nicely with the rising conservatism that advocated providing services while circumventing attacks on social services. See Pride, "To Respectability and Back," 116.

46. Progress Report, 1; Bonnie Macauley, "The Ombudsman: 223-4613, Office Launches Effort to Aid Victims of Violent Crimes," *DDN,* 6 August 1974; Victim/Witness Division (Victimization Project), Final Report to the LEAA, 31 December 1976 (hereafter cited as Final Report).

47. "Victimization Center," Project Description, attached to letter to Kathy Ellison, 5 June 1974.

48. Victimization Project, Grant Extension, [1975], 1, 3.

49. "Victimization Center," Project Description.

50. This represented 93 percent of the total budget of $126,633; the remainder came from local sources.

51. Progress Report, 53.

52. Ibid., 54.

53. Ibid., 53–70.

54. Ibid., 24.

55. Brooks interview.

56. Final Report, 1976, 17.

57. Rape Crisis Center, "Rape: Medical and Legal Information," in Breslin, "Attitudes about Rape," 47.

58. Nikki Canton, "Victimization Center Catalyst for Change," *DDN,* 17 October 1974.

59. Adding insult to injury, emergency room bills were high—averaging eighty

dollars in 1974, not counting follow-up care. Connie Breece, "Victimization Office Provides Continuing Help to Women," *DDN,* 15 November 1974; Pat Hussey, "Rape Victims Can Sue Attackers for Damages," *DDN,* 21 March 1975. While costs involved in collecting evidence for other crimes were covered by state and local government, all medical expenses incurred by a rape victim were the victim's responsibility.

60. At the Project's initiative, a task force was created in fall 1974 to "improve and standardize the treatment of sexual assault victims" at area hospitals. The group included representatives from the Prosecutor's Office, local police departments, and the Area Hospital Council. Despite the "establishment" nature of the task force, its proposed guidelines were not immediately adopted. The Hospital Council spent months before agreeing, and the completion of a manual took another nine months. Progress Report, 49.

61. The revised criminal code went into effect in January 1974. The definition of lack of consent had been expanded to such an extent that the accused rapist's defense had to prove consent; the notions of sexual contact with erogenous zones and sexual imposition were introduced; and proving that penetration occurred was thus not necessary to convict on a lesser charge than rape. *Ohio Criminal Code,* Chapter 2907: Sexual Offenses, effective 27 August 1975.

62. Ibid.

63. Jan Griesinger, "Rape Law Reform," *DWL News,* May 1975, 5.

64. "Some Questions about the Victimization Center: or, Is the Women's Movement Being Co-opted?" *DWL News,* May 1975, 3.

65. Jim Nichols, "Attitude Is a Woman's Best Defense against Rape, Says Lecturer," *DDN* [May 1975], from Progress Report, 20k.

66. Brownmiller, *Against Our Will,* 361.

67. In a civil suit, "the preponderance of evidence" must be on the victim's side, as opposed to the proof "beyond a reasonable doubt" necessary in a criminal case. Progress Report, 42.

68. "Four Ways to Kill an Unborn Child," leaflet, New Haven.

69. In an article written by a staff person, she repeated a policeman's warning to be particularly "mindful of the women in the grand jury." She went on to quote a victim on the "cold eyes" of the women and on one juror who "made me feel like a tramp." Connie Breece, "Rape Victims Warned of Grand Jury Strain," *DDN,* 28 March 1975.

70. Progress Report, 35; Final Report, 1976, 54–70; "Final Report: Pilot Survey of Sexual Assault Reporting Rate," compiled by Connie Breece and Mary Brooks, July 1975.

71. In the first thirty months of operation, 493 rapes were reported and 135, or 27.4 percent, were accepted for prosecution. In the subsequent thirty months, only 21.2 percent of the 704 reported cases were accepted. Data compiled from Final Report, 1976. The reluctance of one key prosecutor no doubt contributed to this, but as women were encouraged to report rape, a larger percentage were "difficult cases," such as casual acquaintance rape. The number of rapes reported continued to increase, from 187 in 1972 to 203 in 1974 and 1975, 349 in 1976, 518 in 1979, and dropping slightly to 449 in 1980. Final Report, 66–70; 1979 and 1980 figures compiled by Victim/Witness. Increases no doubt came from changes in attitudes nationwide that decreased women's feelings of guilt and defined rape as a violent crime, and from broadened definitions of sexual offenses. Perhaps there also was an increase in

the crime itself. However, Victim/Witness's work undoubtedly contributed, as well. By 1981, Dayton ranked among the highest of U.S. cities in percentage of arrests per rape (considerably better than its record on arrests for violent crime in general), and the prosecution rate (58.95 percent) was tenth out of seventy-seven cities ranked. John Tepper Marlin and James S. Avery, *The Book of American City Rankings* (New York: Facts on File, 1983). However, it is difficult to draw any conclusions from this type of comparison because of differences in urbanization patterns and in state laws defining rape.

72. From a survey mailed to recipients (40 percent return rate), cited in Progress Report, 28.

73. Lisa C. Hardin, "What Do Victims Do a Year from Now." Letter to the editor, *JH*, 10 June 1975.

74. Final Report, 1976, 42.

75. Ibid., 35.

76. Progress Report, 8, 26.

77. Canton, "Victimization Center Catalyst"; Progress Report, 24; Final Report, 1976, 1.

78. Martindale, "Proposed Rape Law."

79. Pat Hussey, "Rape Cases Difficult for Polygraph Tests," *DDN*, 11 April 1975.

80. Cases can be deemed unfounded for many reasons, ranging from the decision by police not to advise prosecution, for whatever reason, to actual proof of falsified testimony. The police have leeway in categorizing complaints. The FBI estimates 19 percent of reported rape cases are registered as unfounded. Other estimates go up to 50 percent. Unfounding, thus, may have little to do with false accusation. In New York, when a special squad of policewomen was created to interview complainants, the number of false accusations recorded dropped to 2 percent—precisely the same rate for other violent crimes. When the low rate of reporting is taken into account (estimated at about one in ten rapes reported), it would seem that the commonly held idea of a high rate of false accusations of rape might be an "unfounded" fear. Herman, "Rape Culture," in *Women,* ed. Freeman, 52–53; Brownmiller, *Against Our Will,* 387.

81. Pat Hussey, "'Victim-Is-Guilty' Syndrome Interferes with Reporting of Crime," *DDN*, 20 September 1974.

82. Few feminist experiences in counterinstitutions have avoided the pressures or opposition of established institutions. Lois Ahrens gives a good illustration of the transformation of a Texas battered women's shelter from a community-based, feminist organization to an institutionalized social service. See Ahrens, "Battered Women's Refuges," 41–47. One striking exception was the Pennsylvania Coalition against Domestic Violence, started and maintained by feminists, which was administering approximately $2 million a year by 1982.

See Schecter, *Women and Male Violence,* 113. A feminist antirape group in Columbus with little effort won a $425,000 grant from the National Institute of Mental Health for research on rape prevention. Whittier, *Feminist Generations,* 37.

83. Novick also pointed out some less positive reasons that may have contributed to her being treated well: hers was a clear-cut case involving an armed stranger; she is white and was attacked by a black man; and as an activist working at a local radio station, she was known in the community.

CHAPTER 5

1. The above figures on calls, staff, and so on are culled from membership lists, logs, minutes of the collective meetings, and correspondence with the Women's Center. Given the fifteen thousand to twenty thousand calls noted in the logs, it is impossible to calculate overlap.

2. Only a small fraction of Center participants came from DWL. Surveys in the first months showed 10–40 percent were on the DWL mailing list, and the lower figure rapidly proved to be most accurate. Opening week survey, reported in DWC logs; January 1974 evaluations.

3. Gloria Koch interview; Joann Kleinehenz interview.

4. "New American Movement," 6. Years later, in a contest for a new Center logo, Russell-Campbell submitted the winner, conceived of jointly with her husband but designed by him. This sparked debate, including an angry letter from Mary Morgan, who nominated the Center for its own Porky Award for perpetuating sexism. Sisterly to the end, she sent in her financial contribution with a note criticizing the Center "for selecting a Women's Center Logo designed by a man who was creatively inspired by his wife. So what else is new." Morgan, letter to the Women's Center, 30 January 1979, WSU archives.

5. Although this may represent a change in comparison to DWL, it highlights the radical identity of the Dayton movement. A national study of NOW members showed an identical 71 percent from liberal to Left, but with only 9 percent identifying as radicals. Freeman, *Politics of Women's Liberation,* 91–92.

6. The remaining percent was a hodgepodge (don't believe in government, disillusioned, mild, undefinable, people power, and so on). Seventy-six questionnaires were returned, with sixty-four extremely diverse answers to the above question. No details were recorded on the distribution methods or response rate of this survey, and no other such surveys were carried out at any other time in the movement.

Informants noted where they lived, offering an approximate geopolitical map of the organized feminist movement. Feminists from South Dayton, or the more affluent area, could be mainly characterized as liberal, with several slightly to the right or left but no radicals. Feminists from East Dayton, a more working-class and Appalachian community, tended to range from conservative to liberal. Northwest Dayton (Dayton View excluded) was liberal, with few conservatives and several leftists. More than two-thirds of Dayton View and Five Oaks feminists, on the other hand, considered themselves left of center or radicals, with not one self-defined conservative in the crowd. Dayton View, a racially, ethnically, and economically mixed area, was confirmed along with parts of Five Oaks as the Left and feminist "ghetto."

7. Approximately one-third of the DWC women interviewed connected the church or their religious teachings to their political awareness or activism. However, this was far less than for the DWL sample.

8. One survey showed 43 percent in the northwest area The remainder came from all parts of the city except the black West Side. A surprising 10 percent of the total came from neighboring towns. Ellison, notes from speech; Women's Center Profile and Evaluation Questionnaire, May 1976.

9. See Ellison, notes from speech. Other than my interviews, no data exist on socioeconomic status.

10. Kruger, "Dayton Women's Center."

11. DWC [Breslin], "Proposal for a Women's Center," 8.

12. DWC minutes, 27 February 1974; Suits interview.

13. Ellison interview, 1985.

14. "Evaluation Meeting," DWC minutes, 28 April 1974.

15. Carol Weisbecker, letter to the Women's Center; Nancy Thompson, letter to the Women's Center, 3 August 1977.

16. Description of DWC from the DWC Collective, *Dayton Gay Center News* 2 [Winter 1973–74?].

17. Barbara Baird, letter to the Women's Center, 19 March 1974, WSU archives.

18. Ellison, notes from speech.

19. *Dayton Women's Center Newsletter* (hereafter cited as *DWC News*), April 1975. The Center sent out three or four short newsletters of one to three mimeographed pages per year. The articles were short, impersonal, and unsigned, and mostly were aimed at advertising the Center's services and events.

20. Maddi Breslin, notes for her assertiveness workshop, [1974?].

21. Grigsby interview; Simmons interview; Maureen Lynch interview.

22. Job descriptions, "Dayton Women's Center Work Program," 19 November 1973.

23. *DWC News*, August 1975; *DWC News*, January 1976.

24. DWC [Breslin], "Proposal for a Women's Center," 6.

25. Ibid.; Center logs. Logs show around twenty thousand calls over the years. Letter to the Women's Center, 5 September 1978.

26. Instructions for volunteers. .

27. *Dayton Women's Yellow Pages*, 3–8.

28. Instructions for volunteers.

29. Like several other Center projects, the service directory served as a model for at least one other group. Ann Bach wrote from North Carolina to thank the Center for not having copyrighted the directory; she had used it as a model for a similar guide. Letter to the Women's Center, 7 March 1977.

30. *Dayton Women's Yellow Pages*, 51.

31. On the Playboy funding of feminist projects, see Pride, "To Respectability and Back," 117; Lederer, "*Playboy* Isn't Playing," in *Take Back the Night*, ed. Lederer, 122.

32. In October 1973, when the emergency room administration at a local hospital was contracted to a private company, twenty-one of twenty-eight emergency room nurses walked out to protest poor hospital conditions. Under threat, eleven returned to work. The remaining ten were fired and filed suit against the hospital. Center members, many of whom were health-care workers, had supported them by holding a benefit and helping to produce a WYSO program. After receiving the Susan B. Award, the nurses wrote in thanks, declaring, "[I]t has been the Dayton Women's Center and WYSO who have had the stamina to publicly endorse our patient advocacy," and stating that the support had helped them stand their ground. Sandy Doyle, spokeswoman for the ten fired nurses, letter to the Women's Center, 17 February 1975.

33. Dayton Socialist Feminist Group, proposal for the conference, attached to letter sent to socialist feminist groups around the country; Suits interview; Tuss interview.

34. "Socialist Feminist Conference," preregistration bulletin.

35. At the last minute, an additional hundred women showed up. Contrary to

written versions (e.g., Deckard, *Women's Movement*, 334–35; Hansen, "Women's Unions and the Search for a Political Identity," 90), these women were not turned away. In this small Ohio village with no available hotel rooms, and under the pouring hail, arrangements were made for all of the unexpected arrivals. Suits interview; Reichert interview.

36. The introductory speeches for the theory panel, by Barbara Ehrenreich, the Berkeley-Oakland Women's Union, and Michelle Russell, are reprinted in *Socialist Revolution* 26 (October–December 1975): 85–107. An expanded and revised version of a speech by Charlotte Bunch is reprinted as "Not for Lesbians Only" in Quest staff, eds., *Building Feminist Theory*, 67–73.

37. Memo from Diane and Jenny to the conference steering committee, notes from evaluation meeting, 22 July 1975. For other accounts of the conference, see Dudley, "Report on the Conference," 107–16; Hansen, "Women's Unions," 90–91; and "Socialist Feminism in America," in Eisenstein, ed., *Capitalist Patriarchy*, 349–53. Hartsock's "Fundamental Feminism" was written as the result of discussions by women from Quest about the conference, as was, to an extent, Bunch's "Beyond Either/Or." The impact of the conference also is mentioned in Combahee River Collective, "Black Feminist Statement," 370.

38. For example, a network for women in radio (Novick interview) and the Columbus Women's Union were founded (Mary Anne Hay for the Columbus Women's Union, "First Organizational Report," letter to the conference steering committee, [July–August 1975]).

39. Dudley, "Report on the Conference," 109.

40. Hansen, "Women's Unions," 67–95.

41. One such project, Summer Lights, came out of the Media House and NAM. Community activists created slide tapes on issues raised in different neighborhoods and presented them at weekend socials—half picnic, half politics. Among the productions was one on the Women's Center and another on utilities problems and organizing in conjunction with the Miami Valley Power Project. The Power Project favored public ownership of the utilities companies, opposed rate hikes, and supported striking utility workers. MacLean, "NAM Conference Draws Up Alternative Energy Program," 8–11.

42. Issel, *Social Change in the United States*, 148; Alinsky, *Reveille for Radicals*, 86.

43. Holmes interview, 1981.

44. A strong, active NOW chapter had existed in neighboring Fairborn since 1973, and several women from DWL and the Center had participated. Lines of communications existed; interested Daytonians who called the phone line were referred to Fairborn NOW, and there were joint projects with Dayton groups.

45. For one article, written by a NAM member, that argues for socialists to relate to NOW, see MacLean, "N.O.W.," 39–50.

46. New people did not become active. For example, Noel Vaughn, whose name is on the membership list, later stated in an interview with me that no local chapter existed at the time.

47. Russell-Campbell interview; Deckard, *Women's Movement*, 162–64.

48. Pete Fusco, "Feminist Aims to Corral Sacred Cow: Sports," *DDN*, 13 October 1974, B1.

49. Fusco, "Feminist Aims to Corral Sacred Cow."

50. Department of Health, Education, and Welfare, *Federal Register* 40:108, 86.1 (4 June 1975), 24128.

51. Fisher, indirect quote, in Fusco, "Feminist Aims to Corral Sacred Cow." Department of Health, Education, and Welfare, Office for Civil Rights, *Final Title IX Regulation Implementing Education Amendments of 1972: Prohibiting Sex Discrimination in Education,* June 1975, 4. These guidelines were, according to some, the result of intense lobbying efforts by spokespeople for men's sports. They were somewhat modified in guidelines announced in 1979 that required, among other items, that athletic scholarship money be divided proportionally among men and women according to their representation in a given sport. Deckard, *Women's Movement,* 406, 177–78.

52. Department of Health, Education, and Welfare, *Federal Register* 40:108, 86.3 (4 June 1975), 24138. .

53. Cutler, "Ridding the Schools of Sexism," 40ff; Kathy Kleine, "School Supt. Finds Women's Rights Irrelevant!" *DWL News,* October 1973, 4.

54. Maddi Breslin, notes from speech for Title IX seminar, [1976].

55. Maida Odom, "HEW Probes Charges of Sex Bias in Area Schools," *DDN,* March 1977.

56. Maida Odom, "City Schools under Pressure to Answer Sex Bias Charges," *DDN,* 10 April 1977, A1ff.

57. Odom, "City Schools under Pressure," A10.

58. He later retracted the statement but continued to claim that total, immediate compliance was not necessary. Ibid.

59. Kenneth G. Mines, director of HEW's Office for Civil Rights, Region V, letter to John B. Maxwell, 5 September 1978.

60. O. O. Barr, director, Elementary and Secondary Education Division of HEW's Office for Civil Rights, Region V, letter to Roberta Fisher, 27 September 1979.

61. Local officials weren't the only ones dragging their feet. Nationally, HEW's Office for Civil Rights had proved to be a reluctant partner. It had taken three years since the adoption of the bill before guidelines and enforcement provisions went into effect, and four years for the compliance deadlines. Even the statement by HEW secretary Caspar Weinberger, included in the booklet sent to local school officials around the country, soft-pedaled on enforcement: "We want to achieve the goals of the Title as soon as possible, rather than undergo a series of futile confrontations and endless law suits. We call upon schools and colleges to do their utmost in the same spirit." HEW, Office for Civil Rights, *Final Title IX Regulation,* 6. It took HEW more than two years to even acknowledge that the Dayton school board had not submitted the required evaluations, a fact that easily could have been ascertained by checking the department's own records—or by school officials' statements to the press. Dayton was but one example of an only slightly veiled federal policy to resist Title IX enforcement. In the fall of 1977, national NOW came to much the same conclusion. A year-long study of the complaints received under Title IX showed that only 179 out of 900 complaints made in a period of more than four years had been investigated and resolved. The study cited information from Dayton substantiating the claims. Hal Lipper, "Dayton Cases Cited in Sex-Bias Report," *DDN,* 7 November 1977. Lack of enforcement was again confirmed in 1978 in a report on HEW's Title IX enforcement, which stated, "[R]ules and policies that perpetuate unequal treatment

of males and females—which are now clearly illegal—are still going on uncorrected in the nation's schools." "Stalled at the Start: Government Action on Sex Bias in the Schools" (Washington, D.C.: Project on Equal Educational Rights, 1978), 13, quoted in Weitzman, "Sex Role Socialization," 180.

62. Dayton NOW raised the issue when the organization was contacted by a woman to lodge a complaint against a local bar that had forbidden her to use its pool table. Ten NOW members descended upon the establishment to attempt to play pool. The proprietor refused to allow them to play, and later stated to the press that women take far too long to play a game and that, according to the press, "Ya let women play on a pool table and they rip it up." It was only after a complaint was filed with the Ohio Civil Rights Commission that the infamous pool table went coed. Pete Fusco, "Pool Table a NOW Battlefield," *DDN,* 21 November 1975.

63. Anne Saunier interview.

64. Comparisons with other studies of the period indicate that the midseventies Dayton NOW chapter was atypical. See profiles of NOW members in Carden, *New Feminist Movement,* 19–30, and Freeman, *Politics of Women's Liberation,* 92–93. Freeman points out, however, that NOW had become "an umbrella group for all kinds of feminists, even those whose primary loyalty lies elsewhere."

65. Fall 1976 collective meeting.

66. DWC minutes, 12 November 1975.

67. Maddi Breslin, letter to the DWC Collective, 12 October 1976.

68. Suits also questioned Scalia's eligibility for CETA. Scalia was not a "typical low-income person"; her middle-class family had been shaken by her husband's health problems. Nationally, civil rights groups worried about funds being funneled into displaced homemaker (job reentry) programs and being used for wives of middle-class and upper-middle-class men instead of the low-income people, many of them blacks, for whom they originally had been intended. See Nelson, "CETA Displaced Homemakers," 18–19.

Later, a more "typical" CETA employee (a black, unemployed, single mother) was hired. One collective member vaguely remembered that she "embezzled CETA money," apparently referring to her arriving late at work, a comment that reflected race and class bias. These were but two examples of an ongoing dynamic in the Center that arose from the ambiguity of its relationship with institutions. If questioned, most activists said that resources from the state should be put to use as they saw fit. However, there was constant interference between goals defined to fill administrative requirements and the activists' original intentions.

69. Suits interview; Michael R. Merz, letter to James R. Kirland, 12 August 1976.

70. Roberta Fisher, letter to the NAM women's caucus, 17 January 1977; NAM women's caucus, letter to the DWC collective, [January 1977].

71. Robin Suits, letter to the author, 5 August 1985.

72. Robin Suits, prepared with Donna Crawl, typed handout for the DWC collective meeting, [January 1977]; Robin Suits, letter to the DWC collective, 4 April 1977.

73. Statement of purpose attached to DWC minutes, 13 July 1977.

74. "The Needs of Women in the Miami Valley: A Conference Sponsored by the Dayton Women's Center," conference brochure, 12 November 1977. DWC minutes, February–November 1977.

75. Concept paper for a career center, 31 July 1975.

76. Patsy Sitzman, Maddi Breslin, and Kathy Ellison for DWC, "Women in Employment and Careers Project," proposal to CETA, [February 1975].

77. Grigsby interview; battered woman committee minutes, 21 March, 11 April, and 9 May 1977; Jo Ann Knout, "Battered Women Refuge," *DDN,* 23 June 1977, 14; Sue Gasper, update on shelter, in "Needs of Women in the Miami Valley.".
Original funding came from the United Way, CETA, and the LEAA. In 1980, a new system went into effect in the state: an additional ten dollars was charged for each marriage license delivered, which was given to the shelters, a surprising recognition of the link between marriage and violence. Carol Cancila, "Shelter Provides Help, Hope for Victims of Violence," *JH,* 2 January 1982, 15.

78. YWCA Battered Women Project, problems statement, mimeographed, [1978–79?].

79. Grigsby interview. However, she also stressed her relative independence. For example, when a local prosecutor refused to accept cases involving battering, she was allowed to alert the press in the name of the shelter. Ken Kraus, "Handling of Domestic Violence Cases Criticized," *JH,* 22 April 1981, 1ff; Grigsby interview; Simmons interview. Interestingly, in this case, the battered woman was represented by Jeri Simmons, former DWL and Sappho's Army activist who had become a lawyer for the Legal Aid Society.

80. Jan Hofman, "Feminism's Future: Women's Center Closing Prompts Soul-Searching Questions," *DDN,* 9 January 1981, 25.

81. DWC financial report, 8 August 1977; DWC financial report, attached to DWC minutes, 1 September 1978.

82. Sue Mumpower, letter to the DWC collective, [April 1978].

83. Center activist Ellison applied for jobs at Victim/Witness and the Career Development Center. For the latter, she recalled being asked for a character witness who could testify that she was not too aggressively feminist. "The gist of it was, do I stand up too strongly for women's rights," she said. "Was I going to terrify people or be unable to function in normal settings." She was not hired.

84. Scholars of alternative institutions have identified two approaches: adversary, which critique and pressure institutions to change, and exemplary, which seek to create institutions that prefigure those desired in the future. It has been argued that attempting to mix the two strategies leads to failure. Starr, "Phantom Community," 245–73. However, the study of the Women's Center suggests that it is necessary to blend the two to maintain an alternative institutions' vigor. Hedman's study of an experimental school also supports this idea. "Adversaries and Models," 41–51.

CHAPTER 6

1. U.S. Bureau of the Census, *Statistical Abstract of the United States: 1981,* 401; U.S. Bureau of Labor Statistics, *Perspectives on Working Women,* 9–11.

2. Belkin, "Drowning in the Steno Pool," 77–82; Ann, "Secretarial Proletariat," 94–110.

3. Ann, "Secretarial Proletariat," 109.

4. Glenn and Feldberg, "Clerical Work," 328–31.

5. Ann, "Secretarial Proletariat," 109.

6. For descriptions of a number of these caucuses and actions, see Tepperman, *Not Servants, Not Machines,* 63–78.

7. Union WAGE: Women's Alliance to Gain Equality. Maupin, quoted in Tepperman, *Not Servants, Not Machines*, 128.

8. Baxandall et al., eds., *America's Working Women*, 389.

9. Seifer and Wertheimer, "New Approaches to Collective Power," 160–61.

10. "Workshop Minutes: Women as Clerical Workers," *NAM Women's Newsletter*, December 1972, n.p.; Evans, "American Women in a New Millennium," 68–69; Tepperman, *Not Servants, Not Machines*, 88.

11. "Letter of Understanding: Working Women and Local Organizations," [1979?].

12. Daytonians had read, for instance, the personal letter sent to conference organizers by feminist labor historian Rosalyn Baxandall: "I'm a member of CLUW and [am] almost giving up on it" (10 May [1975].) In the months following the conference, public criticisms of CLUW by prominent socialist feminists began appearing. See in particular Troger, "Coalition of Labor Union Women," 85–110; Reverby, "Epilogue . . . ," 111–14; Withorn, "Death of CLUW," 47–51.

13. Graff had supported the NOW strategy in the NAM socialist feminist commission. Novick interview. MacLean had written a position paper encouraging socialist feminists to get involved in NOW. MacLean, "N.O.W.," 39–50. In the upcoming years, national leadership was divided over this "new populism." MacLean continued to support it. "Toward a Balanced Approach to the New Populists," 109–14.

14. Holmes interview; Karen Nussbaum interview, in Tepperman, *Not Servants, Not Machines*, 91–92; Goldberg, *Organizing Women Office Workers*, 36.

15. "Agreed: Pay Inadequate," *Dayton Women Working Newsletter* (hereafter cited as *DWW News*), [February–March 1976?].

16. The working women's movement may not have been the first to appropriate National Secretaries Week. Brownmiller tells of an 1972 action at NBC. Management gave each female employee a red rose, and hundreds of angry women protested the blatant discrimination by sending the roses back. *In Our Time*, 155.

17. Sherrie Holmes, Dayton NAM, "Summary of Clerical Organizing in Dayton," mimeographed handout for clerical organizing workshop, NAM convention, 1976.

18. The four sources of money were church groups, which accounted for between 9 percent and 18 percent of the total; foundations, between 25 percent and 32 percent; the national consortium (NWEP), from 23 percent to 42 percent; and grass-roots fund-raising, 17 percent to 35 percent. Aside from providing staff salaries, no money was obtained directly from federal funds. DWW financial reports, 1977–79.

19. The new headquarters consisted of one small and impersonal room (later, two rooms) in the large Downtown YWCA building. The YWCA was centrally located and charged only thirty-five dollars a month in 1977, around 5 percent of DWW's budget over the years. DWW financial reports, 1977–79. Other working women's organizations had had ties to this institution: Women Employed and 9 to 5 both came out of conferences held at their YWCAs. Seifer and Wertheimer, "New Approaches to Collective Power." Cleveland's office also was in a Y.

20. Submitting monthly progress reports was a requirement for DWW's national funding. Copies were sent to the Youth Project, the other working women's organizations, and NAM.

21. Monthly Progress Report, 1976.

22. CLUW, Union WAGE, 9 to 5, and Chicago Women Employed. Seifer and Wertheimer, "New Approaches to Collective Power," 171.

23. Tepperman, "Organizing Office Workers," 17–18.

24. Balser, *Sisterhood and Solidarity,* 27; Goldberg, *Organizing Women Office Workers,* 27–28.

25. For example, in 1974, more new groups of white-collar workers voted in unions than in any previous year since records were kept, and the fastest growing unions were those with a high percentage of office workers. Glenn and Feldberg, "Clerical Work," 334; Tepperman, *Not Servants, Not Machines,* 94–130.

26. Foner, *Women and the American Labor Movement,* 497.

27. Wertheimer, "'Union Is Power,'" 355.

28. Noreen Willhelm, "There is a movement growing . . ." Undated notes from a speech.

29. Notes from NWEP meeting, 4 January [1978].

30. Ibid.

31. Ibid.

32. DWW financial records; Ellison interview, 1985.

33. Tepperman, "Organizing Office Workers," 14.

34. Sherrie Holmes interview with Dorothy Smith, San Rafael, California, 30 June 1983, WSU archives.

35. Sherrie Holmes, Dayton NAM, Progress Report, 1977.

36. Holmes, "Summary of Clerical Organizing in Dayton."

37. Noreen Willhelm, proposed contract, September 1979–September 1980, WSU archives.

38. Deckard, *Women's Movement,* 403–4.

39. Monthly Progress Report, 1976. The OFCCP oversaw enforcement of the executive orders that prohibited discrimination by federal contractors.

40. Progress Report, December 1976; Helen Williams for Cleveland Women Working and Sherrie Holmes for Dayton Women Working, joint fund-raising project, March 1977, 13.

41. Historians have neglected Dayton's role. Roberta Goldberg makes no mention in her book of DWW. Goldberg, *Organizing Women Office Workers,* 33.

42. Seifer and Wertheimer, "New Approaches to Collective Power," 177.

43. Williams and Holmes, joint fund-raising project, 23. There were 120 women in attendance.

44. NWEP, typewritten report, [1978].

45. Ibid.; Ellen Cassedy, letter to NWEP board members, 10 May 1979; Cassedy, letter to NWEP board members, 2 July 1979; Working Women, memo, August 1979. In 1981, Working Women had twelve local affiliates and a total of some ten thousand individual members from nearly every state in the country. Bob Downing, "The Original '9-to-5er' Hopes Awareness Is a Result of Film," *DDN,* 13 January 1981, 15.

46. Ellen Cassedy, letter to NWEP affiliate organizations and Karen Nussbaum and Janet Selcer of Working Women, 2 October 1979.

47. Sherrie Holmes, "Fund-raising—Sherrie Holmes's Opinion," typed internal DWC memo [1977?].

48. Williams and Holmes, joint fund-raising project, 22.

49. "Join the Movement of the '80s," leaflet [1980?].

50. Holmes, "Summary of Clerical Organizing," Youth Project Progress Report, January–July 1978; Foner, *Women and the American Labor Movement*, 551–54. DWW also supported the national Sears boycott. At the time of the group's creation, the EEOC had charged Sears and Roebuck, the largest retailer of merchandise in the world and one of the largest private employers of women in the U.S., with discrimination by race and sex. While still a NOW task force, DWW endorsed a consumer boycott, picketing the store and distributing balloons with the inscription "Sears Discriminates." "Sears' Bias Challenged," *DWW News* [February–March 1976?]; Kessler-Harris, "Equal Employment Opportunity Commission v. Sears, Roebuck and Company," 432–46.

51. Including the Ohio AFL-CIO, the National Hospital Union 1199, locals of the Communication Workers of America, the Retail Clerks Union, and the Sheet Metal Workers.

52. Holmes, Progress Report, 1977.

53. Notes from NWEP meeting, 4 January [1978].

54. Working Women, "Race against Time: An Overview of Office Automation," printed leaflet, [1980]; Sid Karpoff, "Study Probes Computer Drawbacks," *DDN*, 24 April 1980; Judith L. Schultz, "Office Automation 'Dehumanizing,'" *JH*, 4 April 1980.

55. Kinder, funding proposal to People's Resources, 2.

56. Progress Report, February 1977.

57. Jerry Heaster, "Loser: 'Tote That Sprinkler, Buy That Plunger' Orders Make 'Winner' a Petty Sight to Office Workers," *JH*, 5 May 1978; Karla Garret, "Boss a Winner-Loser: Working Women Hand Out Pettiness Prizes," *DDN*, 5 May 1978; "Three Winners Declared Losers," *DWW News*, Spring/Summer 1978.

58. Heaster, "Loser."

59. "National Secretaries Week: Raises, Not Roses!" *DWW News*, Summer 1977; Progress Report, April, June, and July 1977; "E. F. MacDonald WINNER! Female Employees LOSERS!" leaflet [June 1977]; Tepperman, *Not Servants, Not Machines*, 91–92.

60. Progress Report, August 1977.

61. During this period, four major federal measures and a myriad of state laws forbade discrimination against workers on the basis of sex and race: Title VII of the 1964 Civil Rights Act, the Equal Pay Act, and Executive Orders 11246 (as amended by E.O. 11375) and 11478. These measures were enforced by several agencies (with some changes over the years). The most comprehensive, Title VII, which covered all private and public educational institutions and private employers of more than fifteen people, was enforced by the Equal Employment Opportunity Commission. Executive Order 11246, for federal contractors, was under the Department of Labor's Office of Federal Contract Compliance Programs. The Equal Pay Act was enforced by the Wage and Hour Division of the Department of Labor until July 1979, when it was taken over by the EEOC. These agencies worked primarily through regional offices. In addition, the Ohio Civil Rights Commission had a work-sharing agreement with the EEOC, and some complaints from within the city limits were handled by the Dayton Human Relations Council. Working Women Organizing Project, "How to Start a Group in Your City," 1; Ross, *Rights of Women*, 90; Hole and Levine, *Rebirth of Feminism*, 44–45; Fox and Hesse-Biber, *Women at Work*, 92.

62. According to a General Accounting Office investigation, cited in "Working Women's Groups Launch Equal Rights Campaign," *DWW News,* Summer 1977.

63. Williams and Holmes, joint fund-raising project, 8.

64. "Working Women's Groups Launch Equal Rights Campaign"; "Action Alert," letter to DWW members, [1977].

65. Progress Report, April, May, July, and August 1977; Holmes, Progress Report, 1977.

66. Cleveland Women Working, "Ohio Campaign for Equal Employment," mimeographed.

67. Cleveland Women Working, "Ohio Campaign"; "Equal Employment Campaign Launched," *DWW News,* Spring 1979.

68. Willhelm, proposed contract.

69. Judith L. Schultz, "EEOC Opens Dayton Office," *JH,* 19 July 1979. NWEP, typewritten report, [1978?].

70. Quoted in Tepperman, *Not Servants, Not Machines,* 49.

71. *Banks Shortchange Women* (Chicago: Women Employed, April 1974); *Discrimination against Women and Minorities at Harris Trust and Savings Bank* (Chicago: Women Employed, June 1976); *Testimony on Employment Practices in the Banking Industry* (Boston: 9 to 5, February 1976); *Bank Discrimination: Treasury Inaction* (Boston: 9 to 5, August 1976), cited in *A Dayton Women Working Study: Employment Discrimination in Dayton's Three Largest Commercial Banks* (Dayton: Dayton Women Working, 10 July 1978) (hereafter cited as *DWW Bank Study*).

72. DWW, "Women in Banking: Job Survey," leaflet. Results had no statistical value, as the distribution methods were not scientific and no information was recorded on response rate. Progress Report, May 1977.

73. Appendix C, *DWW Bank Study.*

74. Quoted by Holmes in Diana Kunde, "Banking Bias Charges Bring U.S. Probe," *JH,* 11 July 1978.

75. *DWW Bank Study.*

76. Ibid.

77. Kunde, "Banking Bias Charges"; Karla Garret, "Labor Department to Investigate Affirmative Action at Local Banks," *DDN,* 11 July 1978.

78. "Banks: Update." *DWW News,* Spring 1979.

79. Sid Karpoff, "U.S. Finds Job Bias at Third National," *DDN,* 29 May 1980.

80. Kinder, funding proposal to People's Resource, 3.

81. Mickey Davis, "She's Done Her Part for Working Women," *JH,* 23 March 1979.

82. Furthermore, overhead was low, but the nature of DWW made fund-raising easier for many reasons. DWW had little competition in its field of action. Emphasizing implementation of existing laws and traditional lobbying made the subject matter relatively safe (except for those foundations whose donors were targeted by DWW). The hierarchical structure made interactions with foundations and government easier. There was less need to "stretch the truth" in proposals (thus less goal displacement, or interference between internal goals and bureaucratic requirements). DWW activities, divided into specific campaigns, lent themselves more to blow-by-blow funding requests. Staff salaries represented the main expense, and staff could be cut back.

83. DWW's unbridled optimism led the group to continue its increase in spending from year to year. Experts at portraying a winning image to the public, DWW

seemed to have fallen victim to its own propaganda. In early 1980, DWW's director discovered that the group was in serious debt and cut staff down to one person.

84. DWW, memo on funding sources, 21 March 1979.

85. DWW bylaws, adopted by the executive committee, 1 March 1979.

86. Handwritten notes from a Working Women leadership seminar, 26 August 1979.

87. Notes from NWEP meeting, 4 January [1978].

88. "Dress code" defined in Working Women, "Personnel Policies," memo, n.d.

89. Sherrie Holmes interview with Dorothy Smith. WSU archives.

90. Tepperman, "Organizing Office Workers," 17–18.

91. Kathy Ellison, when asked to speak on the issue of equal pay at a DWW meeting toward the end of its existence, tried to explain the problems involved in determining the monetary value of a job or a person's worth. She was met with incomprehension.

92. The position toward the unemployed gives another example of deradicalization. In 1974, socialist feminists had criticized CLUW for cutting off a base by not accepting the unemployed. Over the following years, some affiliates of Working Women decided not to include the unemployed, or workers other than clericals, and the president, Karen Nussbaum, recommended this for the national bylaws. Nussbaum, letter to Working Women affiliates, 3 December 1979.

93. Notes from NWEP meeting, 4 January [1978].

94. Jean Kappell, "On-the-Job 'Favors': Equal Rightists Say Sexual Harassment Issue Is Overplayed." *DDN,* 9 January 1978.

95. While interest in the issue of sexual harassment heightened in the late 1970s, sufficient attention had been paid to the question that the Working Women's organizations could not plead ignorance. The Alliance against Sexual Coercion, for example, had been functioning since 1976. In the same year, the women's magazine *Redbook* published the results of a survey (based on questionnaires returned by nine thousand of its readers) in which 88 percent reported unwanted sexual attention on the job. While there was no statistical value to this, it was enough to suggest that the problem might not be as infrequent as these organizers seemed to think. See Alliance against Sexual Coercion, "Organizing against Sexual Harassment," 17–34.

96. James Oppenheim (1882–1932) wrote the poem "Bread and Roses," first published in the IWW newspaper in April 1946. Kornbluh, ed., *Rebel Voices,* 195. Rose Schneiderman used the expression much earlier, as a 1912 flyer for a speech confirms. Rose Schneiderman Meeting Flyer, Milwaukee, October 1912, Rose Schneiderman Papers, Tamiment Library, New York University (WTUL microfilm, reel 2, #226), www.binghamton.edu/~womhist/law/doc20.htm.

97. Progress Report, May 1977.

98. DWW letter, n.d.

99. Willhelm, notes for a speech.

100. Ibid.

101. NWEP, typewritten report, [1978?].

CHAPTER 7

1. Susan Kelleher, "Akron Law Spurs Pro-Choice Group Mobilization Here," *Times Publications* [Kettering], 2 August 1978, B1.

2. Kelleher, "Akron Law Spurs Pro-Choice Group Mobilization Here." Footnote 67, a loophole in the 1973 *Roe v. Wade* decision, stated that the court had not taken a position on whether minors could be required to obtain parental consent. Glen, "Abortion in the Courts," 9.

3. Scholar Rebecca Klatch believes the New Right has two strains, the social and the laissez-faire conservatives. Despite a "common symbolism" that gives unity, antifeminism is crucial for the former. Klatch, *Women of the New Right,* 4–6, 119. Similarly, despite overlap, the antiabortion movement is not the same as the New Right. Many laissez-faire conservatives, according to Klatch, support abortion provided that "big government" stays out of it. 149–50. Inversely, a minority of antiabortion activists reject a link with the Right. For instance, Thea Rossi Barron, chief lobbyist for the National Right to Life Committee, resigned to protest the growing collaboration between the antiabortion movement and the right wing. See www.feminist.org/research /chronicles/fc1978.html. However, the public face of the movement, as it appeared to Dayton liberals and feminists, was this socially conservative and antifeminist New Right.

4. Sheila Rowbotham describes these developments well in *Century of Women,* chapters 8–9. Articles on the New Right and its antifeminism were appearing concomitantly with the creation of FOC; see Brady and Tedin, "Ladies in Pink," 564–75; Gordon and Hunter, "Sex, Family and the New Right," 9–25; Ehrenreich, "Women's Movements," 93–101; Harding, "Family Reform Movements," 57–75; Oliker, "Abortion and the Left," 71–95; Eisenstein, "Antifeminism in the Politics and Election of 1980," 187–205; Petchesky, "Antiabortion, Antifeminism, and the Rise of the New Right," 206–46.

5. Pat Rooney, "'Ohio Statute Violates Privacy,'" *DDN,* 15 February 1973, 31.

6. This idea that feminists dropped the issue was expressed by several members of FOC. Ironically, it is precisely those persons who had not been previously involved in either the women's movement or in work for reproductive freedom who spoke of how "we" had felt the fight was won and had stopped working on the issue.

7. Jim Nichols, "Things Are Better Now: Dayton Feminists Weather First Throes of Conservatism," *DDN,* 15 September 1977.

8. According to Novick, memories of how clinic directors "offed the community board that originally controlled the clinic" remained throughout this period. Feminists' impressions since that battle, she believed, had not improved their dispositions toward the clinic: "So while people really support their existence, . . . (and have done stuff to head off Right to Life), no one feels very good about that clinic. And it's been a weird dynamic at Freedom of Choice."

9. Brim, "Abortion Clinics under Siege," 23–24. In the following six months, two Ohio clinics were victims of arson: a Cincinnati Planned Parenthood clinic (which did not perform abortions) in November 1977 and a Cleveland clinic in February 1978.

10. "Both Sides Claim Victory at Ohio Women's Meet," *DDN,* [May 1977].

11. DWW Progress Report, May 1977; Whittier, *Feminist Generations,* 44–45.

12. Van Gelder, "Countdown to Houston," 61.

13. DWW Progress Report, May 1977.

14. DWC minutes, 16 November 1977; "Building an Inclusive Movement," in Kahn, ed. *Frontline Feminism,* 433–34.

15. Only weeks after the Akron ordinance, antiabortionists marked a goal when the Supreme Court handed down decisions on three cases authorizing restrictions to abortion. One decision declared the Hyde Amendment constitutional. Other provisions allowed the "encouragement of normal childbirth" and let publicly funded hospitals refuse to perform "elective" abortions.

16. DWC minutes, 8 February 1978.

17. Sheehy, "Women in Passage," 249. In the following years, several feature articles about Saunier appeared: Diane Dorrans Saeks, "Kettering Woman Gets Acclaim after Houston," *DDN,* 8 December 1977, 17; "'Knowing Who I Am . . . Feeling Confident . . . and Keeping My Self-Esteem': That's Anne Saunier's Formula for Success," *JH,* 9 March 1979, 27; Carol Cancila, "'Know Yourself,' Mead's Saunier Advises Women," *DDN,* 14 September 1982, 16.

18. Hole and Levine, *Rebirth of Feminism,* 290.

19. Lynch interview.

20. Wattleton, *Life on the Line,* 109–11.

21. "Conception or Fertilization," *Right to Life of Greater Cincinnati Newsletter,* January 1977, 3.

22. A representative of the *Life Advocate,* interviewed by Lithicum and Novick, WYSO radio program on the national Right to Life convention.

23. Ginny Folsom, letter to Leonard T. Roberts, chairperson of the Dayton Area Chamber of Commerce, 24 May 1978. This Right to Life position followed that of the Dayton Association of Southern Baptists. The previous year, its executive board had written to Planned Parenthood, "in the name of our Lord Jesus Christ," to protest its sex education programs. "We believe that sexual permissiveness destroys the moral fabric of our society and contributes to the grave moral and spiritual error of abortion-on-demand for selfish non-therapeutic abortions. We are grieved that Planned Parenthood . . . has chosen to emphasize the unwholesome prurient aspects of human sexual behavior." Robert D. Hopkins and Joe Baker for the Greater Dayton Association of Baptists, SBC, letter to Frederick C. Smith, president of Planned Parenthood of Miami Valley, 10 February 1977. Right to Life, according to Maureen Lynch, also put pressure on the United Way to stop funding organizations (such as the YWCA) with prochoice positions.

24. Jean Kappell, "Planned Parenthood Chief Sees New Post as Reflection of Area Feats," *DDN,* 30 January 1978, 23.

25. "New Planned Parenthood Chief: Dayton Woman Promises 'Aggressive Stance,'" copy of AP wire service article from PPMV files [January 1978]. "A Five Year Plan: 1976–1980 for the Planned Parent Federation of America, Inc.," approved by PPFA membership, Seattle, Washington, 22 October 1975, 11.

26. "A Meeting of Concerned Pro-Choice Supporters," 6 March 1978.

27. "The purpose of the coalition is to 1) work together to stop the ordinance, 2) support women's rights to choose and safeguard reproductive rights, and 3) oppose the violence committed in the name of 'life.'" "Meeting of Concerned Pro-Choice Supporters," 13 March 1978.

28. "Meeting of Concerned Pro-Choice Supporters," 13 March 1978.

29. DWC minutes, 8 March 1978.

30. Information on membership is based on attendance sheets from general and board meetings, petitions, articles, newsletters, and interviews. Membership files

were not available for consultation, out of respect for those who wished to remain anonymous.

31. One founding member estimated active participation of men at between 5 percent and 10 percent. Three men appear on the fourteen-member steering committee during the group's organizational period. Only once was there more than one man in attendance at board meetings, attended by between eight and seventeen people, in the period to 1981. Four different men participated on the board (including a long-time activist from the Dayton Left, the director of the Free Clinic, and one member's husband).

32. Ross, "African-American Women and Abortion," 165.

33. Ibid., 186–87.

34. Ibid. See also Davis, *Women Race and Class,* 202–21; Davis, "Racism, Birth Control, and Reproductive Rights," 15–26; and Solinger, *Wake Up Little Susie.*

35. What Silverman described apparently was true for many FOC members. She did, however, become active in FOC.

36. "Feminists" refers to activists from the women's movement previously to FOC. "Liberals" refers to those who came out of liberal political activism, but not radical or feminist movements. It thus indicates a history of activism and affiliation, not political philosophy. Most of the liberals identified themselves as such. Some also espoused feminist views; others did not. The latter lacked even in gender consciousness, rejecting the idea that women formed a group and that they belonged to this group. Calling the latter nonfeminist must not be misconstrued as a moral judgment.

37. FOC had considerable support from the Jewish community. In general, polls showed a higher percentage of support for legal abortion among Jews than among Christians, consistent with the liberal leanings of a large majority of Jews. However, it probably also was due to perceptions of the Right as antisemitic. See Skerry, "Class Conflict over Abortion," 74n.

38. Vaughn, upon graduation in 1979, cofounded an all-women's law firm with four other recent graduates, among them Kathy Ellison.

39. Marie Ferguson interview.

40. The profile of this group of women would seem to correspond closely to a 1979 report on NARAL membership showing the group to be white, urban, disproportionally Jewish, in the twenty-five to forty-four age bracket, and professionally educated and employed. The membership identified as liberal and had considerable overlapping membership with groups such as NOW, the ACLU, and Planned Parenthood. See Gelb and Palley, *Women and Public Policies,* 147.

41. The subsequent superintendent also was known to early feminists for, among other things, having called the police on peaceful antiwar demonstrators at the high school where he was then principal, having eliminated the board of education's women's rights committee, and having been less than enthusiastic about the implementation of Title IX.

42. Paying dues to NOW—that is, sending in a contribution—was the sole requirement for NOW membership. It did not imply a relationship to a local chapter or any other form of involvement. Thus, card-carrying NOW members were not automatically considered to be feminist activists.

43. This belief that sexism is more acute among the working class is debatable. One study confirmed that support for legal abortion rose with educational level and

income. Skerry, "Class Conflict over Abortion," 75. However, a study on activists in the anti-ERA movement found participants to be highly educated and middle to upper middle class. (The factors that most strikingly distinguished these women from feminists were provincialism and commitment to fundamentalist Protestantism.) Brady and Tedin, "Ladies in Pink." Jo Freeman argued that male dominance existed among professional men, but was more subtle. She cited one study that stated that "lower-class men concede fewer rights ideologically than their women in fact obtain, and the more educated men are likely to concede more ideologically than they in fact grant." *Politics of Women's Liberation,* 32. Quote from Goode, *World Revolution and Family Patterns,* 21–22.

44. Feminists were certainly closer to the truth. A poll done by Planned Parenthood of Ohio showed 38 percent of the sample acknowledged knowing friends or family members who had "had or had been involved in an abortion"—and a full 63 percent of the respondents aged eighteen to twenty-nine. Planned Parenthood Affiliates of Ohio, *Public Attitudes towards Issues of Reproductive Freedom in Ohio,* 14. These figures are low, since many abortion recipients do not speak of their experience. Furthermore, given the level of antiabortion harassment, some respondents may not have answered truthfully.

45. Contrary to the situation in some cities, the new group was not seen as a rival, no doubt due to overlapping membership.

46. "Position Statement," mimeographed, n.d.. Reprinted in FOC petition-advertisement, *DDN,* 27 September 1981, B8.

47. As a result of Novick's and other activists' efforts, WYSO addressed the issue on several occasions in 1979 and 1980, and the FOC newsletter also carried a related article. "Who's Who on the Far Right," *Freedom of Choice Newsletter* (hereafter cited as *FOC News*), Winter 1981, 3.

48. The role of the Catholic Church—the largest, richest, and most centralized denomination in the United States—in the antiabortion movement has been documented, showing not only ideological influence but financial investment and use of church infrastructure in diffusing information and mobilizing activists. See Gelb and Palley, *Women and Public Policies,* 125–53; Oliker, "Abortion and the Left," 82–87; Deckard, *Women's Movement,* 423. Catholic opinion, however, shows only slightly more opposition to abortion than among Protestants in opinion polls. Gelb and Palley, *Women and Public Policies,* 137.

The director of the Dayton abortion clinic reported having had as patients women whom she had seen at Right to Life demonstrations. Reflecting on similar reports, Diedre English suggests that it is not abortion or contraception itself that was the key to the Catholic Right to Lifers' opposition, but rather "a frank and open justification of these sexual freedoms." English, "War against Choice," 19. To a certain extent, Right to Life and the confessional could serve as an escape hatch for the sinners.

49. Editorial, *FOC News* [early 1979?].

50. Karla Garrett, "Inspired by Akron Action: Local Abortion Group Organizes," *DDN,* 21 March 1978.

51. "A Meeting of Concerned Pro-Choice Supporters," 6 March 1978; Kelleher, "Akron Law," B1–2. Most of the clauses of the Akron ordinance were later overturned.

52. Arnold, "Dilemmas of Feminist Coalitions," 288.

53. Handwritten note on minutes from FOC meeting, [3 September 1980?].

54. Antiabortionists did, however, regularly picket the clinic and harass the patients. In 1981, in order to stop this practice, clinic directors pressed charges against picketers for trespassing. The lawyer for the accused requested a subpoena of the clinic's files, arguing that they were needed to support his defense of the "doctrine of necessity"—that is, to show that the picketers were trespassing to save lives. Clinic directors argued that medical confidentiality covered them, but a Kettering judge did subpoena records, contending that only information given in the presence of a physician was confidential. Prochoicers knew that giving the files with the names and addresses of abortion recipients to the Right to Life supporters exposed the women to possible harassment. It was thus, Wilson explained, a choice between dropping charges or refusing to turn over the files and being in contempt of court. Wilson decided to drop charges. Sandra A. Holden, "'Open Season': Anti-Abortion Activists See More Protests after Decision," *JH*, 7 August 1981; Simmons interview; Wilson interview. This was an early example of what became a more common tactic of subpoenaing files from alternative institutions where medical practices and/or counseling took place. See, for example, Gorchov, "Rape Crisis Records Subpoenaed," 13.

55. Wade M. Jackson, treasurer of the Greater Dayton Pro-Life Education Foundation, letter to Mead, 4 August 1978.

56. "Pro-Choice Rally Big Success, *FOC News*, Summer 1979, 3.

57. Minutes from FOC board meeting, 2 October 1979.

58. Karen Ray, "Pro-Life, Pro-Choice Groups Rally; Clash One of Words, Ideas," *DDN*, 28 October 1979, A1ff.

59. "Abortion Restrictions Opposed by Voters," *JH*, 16 May 1978, 6. An in-depth poll conducted throughout Ohio for Planned Parenthood affiliates showed this state to be no exception: only 13 percent opposed abortion in all cases, 39 percent favored abortion to save the mother's life, for deformed fetuses, or in cases of rape or incest, and 42 percent were either in favor under all circumstances or considered it a matter of the woman's choice. Planned Parenthood, *Public Attitudes*, 13.

60. Virginia Slims poll, cited in Gelb and Palley, *Women and Public Policies*, 14.

61. Bers and Mezey, "Support for Feminist Goals among Leaders of Women's Community Groups," 737–48.

62. Ellison felt this also applied to their involvement in the civil rights movement. They believed that the most overt racism came from alien lower classes, particularly the Appalachian community in East Dayton. Middle-class liberals, she contended, could oppose racism without threatening their class status.

CONCLUSION

1. NOW was the first identifiable and the oldest of the groups started nationally, but it was initially a superstructure without a grass roots. Freeman, *Politics of Women's Liberation*, 73. Furthermore, as this study has demonstrated, organizational stability is not necessarily a goal or a measure of the success of social movements.

2. Red Apple Collective, "Socialist-Feminist Unions," 42.

3. Bouchier, "Deradicalization of Feminism," 397.

4. For a review of the critical literature, see Staggenborg, "Can Feminist Organizations Be Effective?" 343.

5. Luttrell, "Beyond the Politics of Victimization," 44.

6. Haber, "Is Personal Life Still a Political Issue?" 425.

7. Gordon and Hunter, "Sex, Family, and the New Right," 21–22.

8. The ways in which the YWCA and Planned Parenthood incorporated feminist ideas would be an interesting study. The former, it would seem, was subject to pressure from the national level at one point, which apparently created space that was seized by the more feminist staff members. In Planned Parenthood, the process resulted from local, internal pressure. Several Daytonians, as national board members, helped set national orientations.

9. The term "all-inclusive sisterhood" is from Dill, "Race, Class, and Gender."

10. Bernice McNair Barnett has argued that "when standard categories of feminist organizations are applied to Black women's historical experiences, they are simply inadequate." "Black Women's Collectivist Movement Organizations," 199–219. Sherna Berger Gluck and her coauthors also see the exclusion of women of color as methodological and historiographical. "Whose Feminism, Whose History?" I tried hard, as they suggest, to "listen carefully" to the voices of community activists. Interviews included a head of the YWCA in the black community, a feminist in the Urban League, the cofounder of an all-women's organization that identified with the club tradition, and a member of a black women's cultural group. Although the latter two groups did not use the label feminist, examining them might or might not have offered ideas about how to redefine the object of this study. However, they were started well into the 1980s, after the period examined, and the members with whom I spoke did not consider their groups a part of the women's movement. For instance, Audrey Davis qualified her group, the Quality of Sharing, as a support group for reinforcing sisterhood, but said that none of the participants would label it feminist and that the women's movement had had no influence on their lives. Perhaps the definition of the movement used here contains a white bias, yet I prefer to maintain the universalistic pretensions of the title and be open to constructive criticism, rather than hide behind a safe qualification of "white" feminism.

11. Statement of purpose, Women's Network membership list. Anita Shreve also describes networks of this kind in *Women Together, Women Alone*, 191–92.

12. Laura Eblin, "Area Women Establish Links for Support System," *DDN*, 3 May 1980.

13. Evans interview.

14. Levin interview.

15. In Robinson, "Socialism and Feminism," 202.

RESEARCH METHODS AND SOURCES

1. See Reinharz, *Feminist Methods in Social Research*, 7–30, 258–63.

RESEARCH METHODS AND SOURCES

THE RESEARCH for this book was conducted over nearly twenty years, first from 1980 to 1985 (in collaboration with Dominique Loeillet until 1982), and then during several periods in the 1990s, including in 1994 as a visiting scholar at Stanford's Institute for Research on Gender and Women.

WRITTEN SOURCES

No public archives on the Dayton movement existed at the outset of my research. Feminists scoured their attics and scrapbooks and donated the more than ten thousand pages that make up my personal archives. They include full collections of all the newsletters produced by all groups, minutes from meetings, leaflets, articles, position papers, fund-raising documents, studies, surveys, notes from speeches, legal documents, and more. I was given unlimited access to the Women's Center's massive internal files before it closed, and partial access to Dayton Women Working's files. Many other organizational archives were confidential for obvious reasons: those of the YWCA's Battered Women's Shelter, the Victim/Witness Division, and Planned Parenthood's clinic. However, even in these cases many files in which clients' names did not figure were made available. Other particularly noteworthy sources were the Women's Center logs that summarized every call received and responses provided over its history. Minutes from the Women's Center collective meetings from September 1973 through mid-1979 were found, including the "official" records and often several other versions (none are signed, and all are cited as DWC minutes). These materials will be donated to appropriate archives. After I established this collection, Dorothy Smith of Wright State University's special archives began amassing what is now a fairly extensive collection on several Dayton feminist organizations.

Little information was available on the history of Dayton other than several master's theses and hagiographic works on famous sons (or fathers) and histories produced by the chamber of commerce. Most of my information on local history thus comes from interviews and other personal research.

LOCAL MEDIA COVERAGE

I could not read Dayton's two major daily newspapers extensively (nearly ten thousand issues, not counting the various editions). To evaluate changes in coverage of women's issues over the years, I read one week's papers per year from 1969 through 1980. For coverage of specific issues, I compiled a detailed chronology and read newspapers during important periods. The public library maintained files of clippings on specific themes, several of which were relevant to my research, and I read these in entirety. Finally, while at Stanford in 1994, I was able to survey online databases such as Lexis-Nexis.

Of the local audio-visual media, only one radio station irregularly kept copies of programs, but copies of only several programs were to be found. I also viewed local media productions and a videotape of a DWL reunion.

OBSERVATION AND PERSONAL INVOLVEMENT

During the research period my direct observation was limited. At the beginning of my fieldwork, one of the four major organizations studied had folded and two were nearing their end. I visited the offices of the Dayton Women's Center (in St. Andrew's Church), Dayton Women Working, the Victim/Witness Division of the Prosecutor's Office, the YWCA Battered Women's Shelter, and the abortion clinic. I also attended a Women's Center collective meeting, a Freedom of Choice public debate, and a DWW benefit concert.

My involvement in the Dayton movement prior to this study deserves mention. I lived in Dayton through the spring of 1973 and again during the summers of 1974 and 1975. My family and I were not unknown to many of the informants, although, because I left the city at a young age, I was not involved in any of the conflicts described in this book.

I grew up in a racially integrated, and later predominantly black, part of Dayton View, where my parents were active in community politics. It was only as a teenager that I discovered that below the surface of what I saw as their mainstream liberal politics lay a complex family history. My maternal grandfather had been an ever optimistic union organizer and Communist sympathizer, repeatedly blacklisted. My father's grandmother devoted her life to women's rights, including serving as secretary to suffragist Carrie Chapman Catt. Both parents had fought for open housing and neighborhood improvement and against the segregationist, radical Right.

My elder brother was the path-breaker. A serious student in high school, he went off to the University of Michigan in 1967 and came back a long-haired radical. During his first summer home, he joined Summer in the City, a group created to fight white racism, and was among those arrested for distributing antiwar leaflets. It was a defining moment for me when, during my seventh-grade current events class, my classmates taunted, "Ezekiel's brother's a commie." That's when I crossed the line into the movement.

I became an active follower, participating in antiwar demonstrations and attending countercultural music festivals and other events. Feminism was a logical extension for me. I attended several DWL events, including a one-shot consciousness-raising-type discussion group held at my high school. I participated in another DWL presentation as the organization's token high school student. I had visited the Women's Center in its original house on Main Street on several occasions and used its referral services once or twice. I attended a few of the Center's community events and a benefit.

I left for the University of Michigan in the spring of 1973, but I returned for several summers. I participated in a community media project in the summer of 1975 and befriended several participants. I attended the Socialist Feminist Conference in Yellow Springs as a member of the Ann Arbor contingent.

Informants' familiarity with me and my family certainly opened doors. Being a former Dayton View inhabitant, a Jew, and my father's daughter, officials from the traditional black organizations, such as the NAACP and the West Side YWCA opened their doors. One black leader stated that he had only agreed to interview because of my last name. Similarly, among the liberal contingent, my family name made access easy.

iПTERVIEWS

I attempted to interview people from all the different groups, subgroups, periods, and positions. For institutions, I sought balance between women in official leadership and self-identified feminists in the ranks. I favored women with relatively long experience, although I also tried to contact all those who reportedly left in conflict. I was able to trace all but two of the people targeted, and with one exception, they cooperated fully.

I obtained lists of names in two ways. First, I showed each individual contacted the list I was compiling and asked for suggestions. Second, I established an index and created an entry for each person mentioned in interviews or written documents. In this manner, I was able to identify important protagonists while going beyond friendship networks.

Many of the people targeted no longer lived in the Dayton area. To interview several key protagonists, I traveled to Oregon, Indiana, New Hampshire, and California. I was not able to conduct interviews with six key people: the two who could not be traced; two who repeatedly cancelled appointments, ostensibly for reasons that were independent of the research itself; and two out-of-towners due to scheduling problems.

I conducted interviews with fifty-nine people. The average time was approximately two hours and forty minutes, with the range between one-half to seven and one-half hours (over two days). All interviews were recorded, and about one-third were entirely transcribed. The remainder were transcribed selectively and indexed. All direct quotes are based on the original audio tape. Both Dominique Loeillet and I conducted most of the interviews in the 1980–82 period. The interviews thereafter I conducted alone.

An earlier version of this manuscript was made available for comments. Several of the subjects responded in follow-up discussions and by mail, e-mail, and telephone, and I have incorporated their comments.

Armed with what I saw as healthy skepticism, I felt compelled to check and double-check information obtained through interviews and to reflect on how to interpret oral narratives. I was repeatedly impressed—and moved—by the subjects' accuracy, honesty, and evenhandedness.

In addition to the formal interviews, I continued dialogues throughout the

1990s with several protagonists via informal discussions, letters, phone calls, and e-mail.

LIST OF INTERVIEWS

Interviews were conducted by Ezekiel and Loeillet in the Dayton area and at each person's home unless otherwise indicated. Interviews followed by an asterisk were conducted by Ezekiel alone.

Breslin, Maddi	July 1980, 3 hours, in Ezekiel's home
Brooks, Mary	August 1981, 2.5 hours, with Reck, in her office
Carroll, Betty Jean	August 1981, 3 hours
	July 1985, 2 hours*
Collins, Sallie	July 1982, 1 hour, in her office
Crawl, Donna	August 1981, 3 hours, Marion, Indiana
Davis, Audrey	July 1982, 2 hours
Doe, Brenda	August 1981, 1 hour, public park
Drennen, Sheila	July 1985, 4 hours, Yellow Springs, Ohio*
Ediss, Joan	August 1980, 4.5 hours, with Kleine, in Kleine's home
	July 1981, 1 hour, Yellow Springs, Ohio
	July 1985, 1 hour, Yellow Springs*
Ellison, Kathy	August 1981, 3 hours, in her office
	July 1985, 2 hours, in her office*
	July 1999, by telephone*
Evans, Margo	July 1982, roundtable
Ferguson, Marie	July 1982, roundtable
Fisher, Roberta	August 1981, 3 hours, Waynesville, Ohio
Ford, Cathy	July 1982, 2 hours, in her office
Gooding, Jesse	July 1985, 2 hours, in his office*
Gregg, Barbara New	March 1982, 4.5 hours, by Loeillet only, Wilmott, New Hampshire
Griesinger, Jan	July 1980, 7.5 hours over two days, with Morgan, Millfield, Ohio
	July 1985, 5 hours, with Morgan, Millfield*
Grigsby, Nancy	August 1981, 3 hours, with Kanapke
Harris, Sarah	July 1982, roundtable
Hart, Tricia	August 1981, 3 hours
Haycock, Dana	July 1982, 1 hour, in her office
Holmes, Sherrie	July 1980, 1.5 hours, in her office, San Francisco, California
	September 1981, 3 hours, Mill Valley, California*
Kanapke, Peg	August 1981, 3 hours, with Grigsby, in Grigsby's home
Kinder, Claudia office	July 1980, 2.5 hours, in her office; .75 hours in her with Koch and McGuire
Kleine, Kathy	August 1980, 4.5 hours, with Ediss
	July 1985, 2 hours, Berkeley, California*

Kleinehenz, Joann	July 1985, 1 hour
Koch, Gloria	July 1980, .75 hours, with Kinder and McGuire, in Kinder's office
	[date] 1.5 hours, in her office
Levin, Gail	July 1982, roundtable
	July 1982, 2 hours, in her office
Lizak, Leslie	July 1982, 3 hours
Lynch, Maureen	July 1982, 1.5 hours
Macauley, Bonnie	July 1982, roundtable
MacIlwaine, Paula	July 1982, roundtable
McGuire, Sandy	July 1980, .75 hours, with Kinder and Koch, in Kinder's office
Merz, Margo	July 1982, 3 hours
Mescher, Maggie	July 1985, 3 hours*
Mooney, Bill	July 1982, 1 hour at Museum of Natural History*
Morgan, Mary	July 1980, 7.5 hours over two days, with Griesinger, Millfield, Ohio
	July 1985, 5 hours, with Griesinger, Millfield*
Novick, Sherrie	August 1982, 7.5 hours over two days, with Tuss
Parker, Donna	July 1985, 3 hours, Yellow Springs, Ohio*
Radican, Chewerl	September 1981, 4.5 hours, Portland, Oregon*
Reck, Maggie	August 1981, 2.5 hours, with Brooks, in her office
	August 1981, .5 hours, in her office
Reichert, Julia	August 1978, 3 hours (for a previous article)*
	July 1982, 2 hours
Reisner, Elsa	July 1982, 3 hours, with Konrad Reisner, in their home
Reisner, Konrad	July 1982, 3 hours, with Elsa Reisner, in their home
Roach, Pat	[1981 or 1982,] .5 hours, in her office
Roberts, Michele	July 1985, 3 hours, in Ezekiel's home*
Russell-Campbell, Pat	July 1985, 3 hours, in Ezekiel's home*
Saunier, Anne	July 1982, 3 hours
Silverman, Sybil	August 1981, 4.5 hours
Simmons, Jeri	August 1981, 3 hours
Suits, Robin	July 1980, 4.5 hours over two days
Teramana, Diane Graham	July 1985, by telephone*
Tobias, Judy	July 1982, .5 hours, in her office
Tuss, Barbara	August 1982, 7.5 hours over two days, with Novick
Vaughn, Noelle	August 1981, 1.5 hours
Walker, Deborah	August 1980, .5 hours, in a restaurant
Whitney, Betsy	July 1982, .5 hours, in her office
Willhelm, Noreen	July 1999, 1.5 hours, in her office*
	July 1999, 1.5 hours, in a restaurant*
Wilson, Anita	August 1981, 3 hours, in her office

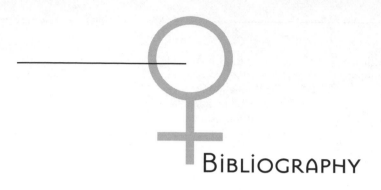

BIBLIOGRAPHY

BOOKS AND PERIODICALS
(See also Research Methods and Sources)

Abel, Elizabeth, and Emily K. Abel, eds. *The Signs Reader: Women, Gender, and Scholarship*. Chicago: University of Chicago Press, 1983.

Ackerman, Frank. "Dare to Struggle, Dare to Influence People." *Radical America* 12:2 (March–April 1978): 56–61.

AH and JK [Alice Henry and Janis Kelly?]. "National Women's Conference." *off our backs* (January 1978): 2–5.

Ahrens, Lois. "Battered Women's Refuges: Feminist Cooperatives vs. Social Service Institutions." *Radical America* 14:3 (May–June 1980): 41–47.

Alinsky, Saul D. *Rules for Radicals: A Practical Primer for Realistic Radicals*. New York: Vintage, 1972.

Allen, Pamela. *Free Space: A Perspective on the Small Group in Women's Liberation*. Rev. ed. New York: Times Change, 1970.

Alliance against Sexual Coercion. "Organizing against Sexual Harassment." *Radical America* 15:4 (July–August 1981): 17–34.

Almquist, Elizabeth M. "Black Women and the Pursuit of Equality." In Freeman, ed. *Women*, 430–46.

Alpert, Jane. *Growing Up Underground*. 1981. New York: Citadel, 1990.

———. "Mother Right: A New Feminist Theory." *Ms.* (August 1973): 52+.

Amatniek, Kathie. "Funeral Oration for Traditional Womanhood." 1968. In Tanner, ed. *Voices from Women's Liberation*, 138–42.

Amott, Teresa, and Julie Matthaei. "Comparable Worth, Incomparable Pay." *Radical America* 18:5 (September–October 1984): 21–28.

Ann, Judith. "The Secretarial Proletariat." In Morgan, ed. *Sisterhood Is Powerful*, 94–110.

Arnold, Gretchen. "Dilemmas of Feminist Coalitions: Collective Identity and Strategic Effectiveness in the Battered Women's Movement." In Ferree and Martin, eds. *Feminist Organizations*, 276–90.

Arnold, June. "Consciousness-Raising." In Stambler, ed. *Women's Liberation*, 155–61.

Atkinson, Ti-Grace. "Radical Feminism." *Notes from the Second Year* (April 1970): 32–37.

Babcox, Deborah, and Madeline Belkin. *Liberation Now! Writings from the Women's Liberation Movement*. New York: Dell, 1971.

Bachrach, Amy, and Carisa Cunningham. "What Do You Mean the Party's Over? We Just Got Here!" *Socialist Review* 81 (May–June 1985): 53–63.

Baker, Andrea J. "The Problem of Authority in Radical Movement Groups: A Case Study of Lesbian-Feminist Organization." In Heller et al., eds. *Leaders and Followers*, 135–55.

Balser, Diane. *Sisterhood and Solidarity: Feminism and Labor in Modern Times.* Boston: South End, 1987.

Banks, Olive. *Faces of Feminism: A Study of Feminism as a Social Movement.* 1981. Oxford: Basil Blackwell, 1986.

Barbour, Floyd B., ed. *The Black Power Revolt: A Collection of Essays.* 1968. Toronto: Macmillan, 1969.

Barnum, Ann P. "After Roe v. Wade: An Exclusive Look inside an Abortion Clinic." *Arete* (Winter 1975): 2–4.

Bartky, Sandra Lee. "Toward a Phenomenology of Feminist Consciousness." 1975. In Vetterling-Braggin et al., eds. *Feminism and Philosophy,* 22–23.

Batchelder, Eleanor Olds, and Linda Nathan Marks. "Creating Alternatives: A Survey of Women's Projects." *Heresies* 7 (Spring 1979): 97–127.

Baxandall, Rosalyn. "Who Shall Care for Our Children? The History and Development of Day Care in the United States." In Freeman, ed. *Women,* 134–49.

Baxandall, Rosalyn Fraad. "Catching the Fire." In DuPlessis and Snitow, eds. *Feminist Memoir Project,* 210.

Baxandall, Rosalyn, and Linda Gordon, eds. *Dear Sisters: Dispatches from the Women's Liberation Movement.* New York: Basic Books, 2000.

Baxandall, Rosalyn, Linda Gordon, and Susan Reverby, eds. *America's Working Women.* New York: Vintage, 1976.

Bay Area Women against Rape. *B.A.W.A.R.'s Packet.* Berkeley, Calif.: 1974.

Beale, Frances M. "Double Jeopardy: To Be Black and Female." In Cade, ed. *Black Woman,* 90–100.

———. "Slave of a Slave No More: Black Women in Struggle." *Black Scholar* 6:5 (March 1975): 2–10.

Belkin, Madeline. "Drowning in the Steno Pool." 1970. In Babcox and Belkin, eds. *Liberation Now!* 77–82.

Benson, Susan Porter. "'The Clerking Sisterhood': Rationalization and the Work Culture of Saleswomen in American Department Stores, 1890–1960." *Radical America* 12:2 (March–April 1978): 41–55.

Benston, Margaret. "The Political Economy of Women's Liberation." 1969. In Tanner, ed. *Voices from Women's Liberation,* 279–92.

Berkeley-Oakland Women's Union, "Speech at the National Conference on Socialist Feminism." *Socialist Revolution* 26 (October–December 1975): 93–100.

Bers, Trudy Haffron, and Susan Gluck Mezey. "Support for Feminist Goals among Leaders of Women's Community Groups." *Signs* 6 (1981): 737–48.

Bishop, Nadean. "Abortion: The Controversial Choice." In Freeman, ed. *Women,* 64–80.

"The Black Sexism Debate." *Black Scholar* 10:8–9 (May–June 1979).

Blau, Francine D. "Women in the Labor Force: An Overview." In Freeman, ed. *Women,* 265–89.

Boles, Janet K. "Form Follows Function: The Evolution of Feminist Strategies." *Annals AAPSS* 515 (May 1991): 38–49.

Boston Women's Health Book Collective. *Our Bodies, Ourselves.* 2nd ed. New York: Simon and Schuster, 1976.

Bouchier, David. "The Deradicalization of Feminism: Ideology and Utopia in Action." *Sociology* [London] 13 (1979): 387–402.

———. *The Feminist Challenge: The Movement for Women's Liberation in Britain and the USA.* New York: Schocken, 1984.

Brady, David W., and Kent L. Tedin. "Ladies in Pink: Religion and Political Ideology in the Anti-ERA Movement." *Social Science Quarterly* 56 (March 1976): 564–75.

Brady, Ellen, and Janet Selcer. "9 to 5: The Typing Rebellion." *Seven Days* sample issue [New York], 7 (December 1974): 9.

Breines, Wini. Review of *Personal Politics* by Sara Evans. *Feminist Studies* 5:3 (Fall 1979): 496–506.

Breines, Winifred. *Community and Organization in the New Left: The Great Refusal.* 2d ed. New Brunswick, N.J.: Rutgers University Press, 1989.

———. "Who'se New Left." *Journal of American History* 75:2 (September 1988): 528–45.

Breslin, Madeline J. "Attitudes about Rape and Rape Victims in Dayton, Ohio." Research proposal and term paper. Wright State University, Dayton, 1974.

Brim, Christine. "Abortion Clinics under Siege: The Assaults against a Hard-Won Right." *Seven Days* [New York] (5 May 1978): 23–24.

Brooke. "The Chador of Women's Liberation: Cultural Feminism and the Movement Press." *Heresies* 9 (1980): 70–74.

———. "The Retreat to Cultural Feminism." In Redstockings. *Feminist Revolution,* 65–69.

Brownmiller, Susan. *Against Our Will: Men, Women, and Rape.* 1975. Harmondsworth, England: Penguin, 1976.

———. *In Our Time: Memoir of a Revolution.* New York: Dial/Random, 1999.

———. "Sisterhood Is Powerful." In Stambler, ed. *Women's Liberation,* 141–55.

Buechler, Steven. *Women's Movements in the United States: Woman Suffrage, Equal Rights, and Beyond.* New Brunswick, N.J.: Rutgers University Press, 1990.

Buhle, Mari Jo, Paul Buhle, and Dan Georgakas, eds. *Encyclopedia of the American Left.* Urbana: University of Illinois Press, 1992.

"Building an Inclusive Movement." In Kahn, ed. *Frontline Feminism,* 433–34.

Bularzik, Mary. "Sexual Harassment at the Workplace: Historical Notes." *Radical America* 12:4 (July–August 1978): 25–44.

Bunch, Charlotte. "Beyond Either/Or: Feminist Options." 1976. In *Quest* staff, eds. *Building Feminist Theory,* 44–56.

———. Introduction. In *Quest* staff, eds. *Building Feminist Theory,* xv–xxiii.

———. "Learning from Lesbian Separatism." *Ms.* (November 1976): 60ff.

———. "Not for Lesbians Only." 1975. In *Quest* staff, eds. *Building Feminist Theory,* 67–73.

Bunch-Weeks, Charlotte. "Asian Women in Revolution." In Stambler, ed. *Blueprint,* 343–63.

———. "A Broom of One's Own." In Cooke et al., eds. *New Women,* 164–86.

Burns, Stewart. *Social Movements of the 1960s.* Boston: Twayne, 1990.

Burris, Barbara, in agreement with Kathy Barry et al. "The Fourth World Manifesto." 1971. In Koedt et al., eds. *Radical Feminism,* 322–57.

Burt, Martha, and Janet Gornick. "Ten Years After: Rape Crisis Centers." *off our backs* (August–September 1984): 20–21.

Cade, Toni, ed. *The Black Woman: An Anthology.* New York: Mentor, 1970.

———. "The Pill: Genocide or Liberation." 1969. In Cade, ed. *Black Woman,* 162–69.

CARASA and Susan E. Davis, ed. *Women under Attack: Victories, Backlash, and the Fight for Reproductive Freedom.* Boston: South End, 1988.

Carden, Maren Lockwood. *The New Feminist Movement.* New York: Sage, 1974.

Carmichael, Stokely. "Power and Racism." 1966. In Barbour, ed. *Black Power Revolt,* 63–77.

Carroll, Peter N. *It Seemed like Nothing Happened: The Tragedy and Promise of America in the 1970s.* New York: Holt, 1982.

Carson, Clayborne. *In Struggle: SNCC and the Black Awakening of the 1960s.* Cambridge, Mass.: Harvard University Press, 1981.

Case, John, and Rosemary C. R. Taylor, eds. *Co-ops, Communes, and Collectives: Experiments in Social Change in the 1960s and 1970s.* New York: Pantheon, 1979.

Cerullo, Margaret. "Autonomy and the Limits of Organization: A Socialist-Feminist Response to Harry Boyte." *Socialist Review* 43 (January–February 1979): 91–101.

Chafe, William H. *The American Woman: Her Changing Social, Economic, and Political Roles, 1920–1970.* Oxford: Oxford University Press, 1972.

Chapman, Anne. "Feminist Men and the Male Role: Some Thoughts on the Seventh National Conference on Men and Masculinity." *Women's Studies Quarterly* 10:1 (Spring 1982): 17–18.

Cherniss, Cary. "Personality and Ideology: A Personological Study of Women's Liberation." *Psychiatry* 35 (May 1972): 109–25.

Chesler, Phyllis. *Women and Madness.* New York: Avon, 1973.

Chicago Women's Liberation Union, Hyde Park Chapter. *Socialist Feminism: A Strategy for the Women's Movement.* Chicago, 1972.

Chisholm, Shirley. "Race, Revolution, and Women" *Black Scholar* 3:4 (December 1971): 17–21.

Chow, Esther Ngan-Ling, Doris Wilkinson, and Maxine Baca Zinn. *Race, Class, and Gender: Common Bonds, Different Voices.* Thousand Oaks, Calif.: Sage, 1996.

Cisler, Lucinda. "Abortion Law Repeal (sort of): A Warning to Women." In Stambler, ed. *Women's Liberation,* 72–81.

———. "Unfinished Business: Birth Control and Women's Liberation." 1969. In Morgan, ed. *Sisterhood Is Powerful,* 274–323.

Clark, Adele, and Alice Wolfson. "Socialist-Feminism and Reproductive Rights: Movement Work and Its Contradictions." *Socialist Review* 78 (November–December 1984): 110–20.

Clark, Terri. "Houston: A Turning Point?" *off our backs* (March 1978): 2.

Cluster, Dick, ed. *They Should Have Served That Cup of Coffee.* Boston: South End, 1979.

Collins, Patricia Hill. *Black Feminist Thought: Knowledge, Consciousness, and the Politics of Empowerment.* Boston: Unwin Hyman, 1990.

Combahee River Collective. "A Black Feminist Statement." 1977. In Eisenstein, ed. *Capitalist Patriarchy,* 362–72.

Cooke, Joanne. "Editorial: Here's to You, Mrs. Robinson." *motive* 29 (March–April 1969): 4–5.

Cooke, Joanne, Charlotte Bunch-Weeks, and Robin Morgan, eds. *The New Women.* Greenwich, Conn.: Fawcett, 1971.

Costain, Anne N. *Inviting Women's Rebellion: A Political Process Interpretation of the Women's Movement.* Baltimore, Md.: Johns Hopkins University Press, 1992.

Crowther, Samuel. *John H. Patterson: Pioneer in Industrial Welfare.* Garden City, N.Y.: Doubleday, 1923.

Cummings, Bernice, and Victoria Schuck, eds. *Women Organizing: An Anthology.* Metuchen, N.J.: Scarecrow, 1979.

Cutler, Marilyn H. "Ridding the Schools of Sexism: A Mixed Bag." *American School Board Journal* (October 1973): 40ff.

Daley, Richard Emmet. "City Manager Government in Dayton, Ohio, 1914–1968: An Analysis of Its Performance in Relation to the Community Power Structure." Master's thesis. Ohio State University, 1968.

Daly, Mary. *Beyond God the Father: Toward a Philosophy of Women's Liberation.* Boston: Beacon, 1974.

Damon, Gene. "The Least of These: The Minority Whose Screams Haven't Yet Been Heard." In Morgan, ed. *Sisterhood Is Powerful,* 333–43.

Davies, Margery. "Women's Place Is at the Typewriter: The Feminization of the Clerical Work Force." *Radical America* 8:4 (July–August 1974): 1–28.

Davies, Philip. *The Metropolitan Mosaic: Problems of the Contemporary City.* Durham: British Association for American Studies, 1980.

Davis, Angela. "Racism, Birth Control, and Reproductive Rights." In Fried, ed. *From Abortion to Reproductive Freedom,* 15–26.

———. "Reflection on Black Woman's Role in the Community of Slaves." *Black Scholar* 3:4 (December 1971): 3–15.

———. *Women, Race, and Class.* New York: Vintage, 1983.

Davis, Flora. *Moving the Mountain: The Women's Movement in America since 1960.* New York: Touchstone, 1991.

"A Dayton Women Working Study: Employment Discrimination in Dayton's Three Largest Commercial Banks." Dayton: Dayton Women Working, 10 July 1978.

"Dayton Women's Yellow Pages: Women's Service Directory." Dayton: Dayton Women's Center, 1975.

"Dayton Women's Yellow Pages: Women's Service Directory." 2nd ed. Dayton: Dayton Women's Center, [1977].

de Beauvoir, Simone. *The Second Sex.* 1949 (France). 1953 (U.S.). Trans. and ed. H. M. Parshley. New York: Vintage, 1974.

Deckard, Barbara Sinclair. *The Women's Movement: Political, Socioeconomic, and Psychological Issues.* New York: Harper, 1983.

Delacoste, Frederique, and Felice Newman, eds. *Fight Back: Feminist Resistance to Male Violence.* Minneapolis: Cleis, 1981.

Diamant, Anita. "ERA RIP. But how hard should we cry at the funeral?" *Radical America* 16:1–2 (January–April 1982): 168–71.

Dill, Bonnie Thornton. "Race, Class, and Gender: Prospects for an All-Inclusive Sisterhood." *Feminist Studies* 9:1 (Spring 1983): 131–50.

Discover (the Unexpected in) Dayton: Dayton Data Book. Dayton: Dayton Development Council, [1977].

Dixon, Marlene. *The Future of Women's Liberation*. San Francisco: Synthesis, 1980.

———. "The Restless Eagles: Women's Liberation." *motive* 29 (March–April 1969): 18–23.

———. "Why Women's Liberation?" 1969. In Babcox and Belkin, eds. *Liberation Now!* 9–25.

Donahue, Phil. *My Own Story*. New York: Simon and Schuster, 1979.

Dreifus, Claudia. *Seizing Our Bodies: The Politics of Women's Health*. New York: Vintage, 1978.

———. "Women's Lib Hits the Courts: The Great Abortion Suit." In Stambler, ed. *Blueprint*, 57–72.

Duberman, Martin. *Black Mountain: An Exploration in Community*. New York: Dutton, 1972.

Dubois, Ellen Carol. *Feminism and Suffrage: The Emergence of an Independent Women's Movement in America, 1848–1869*. Ithaca, N.Y.: Cornell University Press, 1978.

Dubois, Ellen, Mari Jo Buhle, Temma Kaplan, Gerda Lerner, and Carroll Smith-Rosenberg. "Politics and Culture in Women's History: A Symposium." *Feminist Studies* 6:1 (Spring 1980): 26–64.

DuBois, Ellen Carol, and Vicki L. Ruiz, eds. *Unequal Sisters: A Multicultural Reader in U.S. Women's History*. New York: Routledge, 1990.

Dudley, Barbara (for the Berkeley-Oakland Women's Union). "Report on the Conference." *Socialist Revolution* 26 (October–December 1975): 107–16.

Dunbar, Roxanne. "Female Liberation as the Basis for Social Revolution" In Morgan, ed. *Sisterhood Is Powerful*, 536–53.

DuPlessis, Rachel Blau, and Ann Snitow, eds. *The Feminist Memoir Project: Voices from Women's Liberation*. New York: Three Rivers, 1998.

Eastman, Paula Costa. "Consciousness-Raising as a Resocialization Process for Women." *Smith College Studies in Social Work* 43:3 (June 1973): 153–83.

Easton [Epstein], Barbara. "Feminism and the Contemporary Family." *Socialist Review* 39 (May–June 1978): 11–36.

———. "Socialism and Feminism 1: Towards a Unified Movement." *Socialist Revolution* 19 (January–March 1974): 59–67.

Echols, Alice. *Daring to Be Bad: Radical Feminism in America 1967–1975*. Minneapolis: University of Minnesota Press, 1989.

———. "The New Feminism of Yin and Yang." In Snitow et al., eds. *Desire*, 62–81.

———. "'We Gotta Get Out of This Place': Notes toward a Remapping of the Sixties." *Socialist Review* 22:9 (April 1992), 9–33.

Eckert, Allan W. *Dayton: A History in Pictures*. Dayton: Junior League, 1976.

Ehrenreich, Barbara. *For Her Own Good: 150 Years of the Experts' Advice to Women*. Garden City, N.Y.: Anchor-Doubleday, 1978.

———. *The Hearts of Men: American Dreams and the Flight from Commitment*. Garden City, N.Y.: Anchor-Doubleday, 1983.

———. "Life without Father: Reconsidering Socialist-Feminist Theory." *Socialist Review* 73 (January–February 1984): 48–57.

———. Speech at the National Conference on Socialist Feminism. *Socialist Revolution* 26 (October–December 1975): 85–93.

———. "The Women's Movements: Feminist and Antifeminist." *Radical America* 15:1, 2 (Spring 1981): 93–101.

Eichler, Margrit. *Nonsexist Research Methods: A Practical Guide.* Boston: Allen and Unwin, 1988.

Eisenstein, Zillah. "Antifeminism in the Politics and Election of 1980." *Feminist Studies* 7:2 (Summer 1981): 187–205.

———. "Developing a Theory of Capitalist Patriarchy and Socialist Feminism." In Eisenstein, ed. *Capitalist Patriarchy,* 5–40.

———. *The Female Body and the Law.* Berkeley: University of California Press, 1988.

———. *Feminism and Sexual Equality: Crisis in Liberal America.* New York: Monthly Review, 1984.

———. *The Radical Future of Liberal Feminism.* New York: Longman, 1981.

———, ed. *Capitalist Patriarchy and the Case for Socialist Feminism.* New York: Monthly Review, 1979.

English, Dierdre. "The Fear That Feminism Will Free Men First." In Snitow et al., eds. *Desire,* 97–104.

———. "The War against Choice: Inside the Antiabortion Movement." *Mother Jones* (February/March 1981): 16–31.

English, Jane. "Abortion and the Concept of a Person." 1975. In Vetterling-Braggin et al., eds. *Feminism and Philosophy,* 417–28.

Evans, Sara M. *Born for Liberty: A History of Women in America.* New York: Free Press, 1989.

———. "The Origins of the Women's Liberation Movement." *Radical America* 9:2 (March–April 1975): 1–12.

———. *Personal Politics: The Roots of Women's Liberation in the Civil Rights Movement and the New Left.* New York: Vintage, 1980.

Faludi, Susan. *Backlash: The Undeclared War against American Women.* New York: Crown, 1991.

Farrel, Amy Erdman. *Yours in Sisterhood: Ms. Magazine and the Promise of Popular Feminism.* Chapel Hill: University of North Carolina Press, 1998.

Faux, Marian. *Roe v. Wade: The Untold Story of the Landmark Supreme Court Decision That Made Abortion Legal.* New York: Mento, 1988.

Feldberg, Roslyn L. "'Union Fever': Organizing among Clerical Workers, 1900–1930." *Radical America* 14:3 (May–June 1980): 53–67.

Ferree, Myra Marx, and Beth B. Hess. *Controversy and Coalition: The New Feminist Movement across Three Decades of Change.* 3d ed. New York: Routledge, 2000.

Ferree, Myra Marx, and Patricia Yancey Martin, eds. *Feminist Organizations: Harvest of the New Women's Movement.* Philadelphia: Temple University Press, 1995.

Firestone, Shulamith. *The Dialectic of Sex: The Case for Feminist Revolution.* New York: Morrow, 1970.

———. "Love." *Notes from the Second Year* (April 1970): 16–27.

Fisher-Manick, Beverly. "Race and Class: Beyond Personal Politics." 1977. In Quest staff, eds. *Building Feminist Theory,* 149–60.

Flacks, Richard. "The Liberated Generation: An Exploration of the Roots of Student Protest." 1967. In Gadlin and Garskof, eds. *Uptight Society,* 284–98.

———. *Making History: The American Left and the American Mind.* 1988. New York: Columbia University Press, 1990.

Flexner, Eleanor. *Century of Struggle: The Woman's Rights Movement in the United States.* 1959. Rev. ed. Cambridge, Mass.: Belknap-Harvard University Press, 1975.

Foner, Philip S. *Women in the American Labor Movement: From World War I to the Present.* New York: Free Press, 1980.

Fox, Mary Frank, and Sharlene Hesse-Biber. *Women at Work.* Palo Alto, Calif.: Mayfield, 1984.

Freeman, Jo. "A Model for Analyzing the Strategic Options of Social Movement Organizations." In Freeman, ed. *Social Movements of the Sixties and Seventies,* 193–210.

———. "On the Origins of Social Movements." In Freeman, ed. *Social Movements of the Sixties and Seventies,* 8–30.

———. "On the Origins of the Women's Liberation Movement from a Strictly Personal Perspective." In DuPlessis and Snitow, eds. *Feminist Memoir Project,* 185.

———. *The Politics of Women's Liberation: A Case Study of an Emerging Social Movement and Its Relation to the Policy Process.* New York: Longman, 1975.

———. ed. *Social Movements of the Sixties and Seventies.* New York: Longman, 1983.

———, ed. *Women: A Feminist Perspective.* 2d ed. Palo Alto, Calif.: Mayfield, 1979.

Fried, Marlene Gerber, ed. *From Abortion to Reproductive Freedom: Transforming a Movement.* Boston: South End, 1990.

Friedan, Betty. *It Changed My Life: Writings on the Women's Movement.* New York: Dell, 1977.

———. *The Feminine Mystique.* 1963. Harmondsworth, England: Penguin, 1972.

———. *The Second Stage.* New York: Summit-Simon, 1981.

Frye, Marilyn. "Who Wants a Piece of the Pie?" 1976–77. In Quest staff, eds. *Building Feminist Theory,* 94–100.

Gadlin, Howard, and Bertram E. Garskof, eds. *The Uptight Society: A Book of Readings.* Belmont: Brooks/Cole, 1970.

Gatlin, Rochelle. *American Women since 1945.* Houndsmills, England: Macmillan, 1987.

Gelb, Joyce, and Marian Lief Palley. *Women and Public Policies.* Princeton, N.J.: Princeton University Press, 1982.

Gerhard, Jane. *Desiring Revolution: Second-Wave Feminism and the Rewriting of American Sexual Thought, 1920–1982.* New York: Columbia University Press, 2001.

Gibson, Anne, and Timothy Fast. *The Women's Atlas of the United States.* New York: Facts on File, 1986.

Giddings, Paula. *When and Where I Enter: The Impact of Black Women on Race and Sex in America.* 1984. New York: Bantam, 1985.

Ginsburg, Faye. *Contested Lives: The Abortion Debate in an American Community.* Berkeley: University of California Press, 1989.

Gitlin, Tod. *The Sixties: Years of Hope, Days of Rage.* New York: Bantam, 1989.

Glen, Kristin Booth. "Abortion in the Courts: A Laywoman's Historical Guide to the New Disaster Area." *Feminist Studies* 4:2 (February 1978): 1–26.

Glenn, Evelyn Nakano, and Roslyn L. Feldberg. "Clerical Work: The Female Occupation." In Freeman, ed. *Women,* 313–38.

Gluck, Sherna. "What's So Special about Women? Women's Oral History." *Frontiers* 2:2 (Summer 1977): 3–14.

Gluck, Sherna Berger, et al. "Whose Feminism, Whose History?" In Naples, ed. *Community Activism and Feminist Politics,* 31–56.

Gluck, Sherna Berger, and Daphne Patai, eds. *Women's Words: The Feminist Practice of Oral History.* New York: Routledge, 1991.

Goldberg, Roberta. *Organizing Women Office Workers: Dissatisfaction, Consciousness, and Action.* New York: Praeger, 1983.

Gorchov, Lynn. "Rape Crisis Records Subpoenaed; Director Jailed." *off our backs* (February 1983): 13.

Gordon, Linda. "Individual and Community in the History of Feminism." In Proceedings from the Second Sex—Thirty Years Later: Conference on Feminist Theory, 27–29 September 1979, 120–28.

———. "The Long Struggle for Reproductive Rights." *Radical America* 15:1, 2 (Spring 1981): 78–88.

———. "The Politics of Sexual Harassment." *Radical America* 15:4 (July–August 1981): 7–14.

———. *Woman's Body, Woman's Right: A Social History of Birth Control in America.* 1976. Harmondsworth, England: Penguin, 1977.

———. "Women's Freedom, Women's Power: Notes for Reproductive Rights Activists." *Radical America* 19:6 (November–December 1985): 31–37.

Gordon, Linda, and Allen Hunter. "Sex, Family, and the New Right: Anti-Feminism as a Political Force." *Radical America* 11:6 and 12:1 (November 1977–February 1978): 9–25.

Gornick, Vivian, and Barbara K. Moran, eds. *Women in Sexist Society: Studies in Power and Powerlessness.* New York: Mentor, 1971.

Graubard, Allen. "From Free Schools to 'Educational Alternatives.'" In Case and Taylor, eds. *Co-ops, Communes, and Collectives,* 49–65.

Griesinger, Jan. *Women in the Struggle for Liberation.* Geneva: World Student Christian Federation, 1973.

Griffin, Susan. "Rape: The All-American Crime." 1971. In Vetterling-Braggin et al., eds. *Feminism and Philosophy,* 313–32.

Grimstad, Kirsten, and Susan Rennie, eds. *The New Women's Survival Catalog.* New York: Coward/Berkeley, 1973.

Gross, Louise, and Phyllis MacEwan. "On Day Care." In Tanner, ed. *Voices from Women's Liberation,* 199–207.

Grossholtz, Jean. "Shelters: View from a U.S. Tour." *off our backs* (November 1982): 18.

Haber, Barbara. "Is Personal Life Still a Political Issue?" *Feminist Studies* 5:3 (Fall 1979): 417–30.

Hanisch, Carol. "Hard Knocks: Working for Women's Liberation in a Mixed (Male-Female) Movement Group." *Notes from the Second Year* (April 1970): 59–68.

———. "The 1968 Miss America Protest: The Origins of the 'Bra-Burner' Moniker." In DuPlessis and Snitow, eds. *Feminist Memoir Project,* 199.

———. "The Personal Is Political." *Notes from the Second Year* (April 1970): 76–78.

———. "What Can Be Learned: A Critique of the Miss America Protest." In Tanner, ed. *Voices from Women's Liberation,* 132–38.

Hansen, Karen V. "The Women's Unions and the Search for a Political Identity." *Socialist Review* 86 (March–April 1986): 67–95.

Hansen, Karen V., and Ilene J. Philipson. *Women, Class, and the Feminist Imagination: A Socialist Feminist Reader.* Philadelphia: Temple University Press, 1990.

"The Hard-Fought Resolutions of Houston." *Ms.* (March 1978): 19ff.

Harding, Sandra, ed. *Feminism and Methodology: Social Science Issues.* Bloomington: Indiana University Press, 1987.

Harding, Susan. "Family Reform Movements: Recent Feminism and its Opposition." *Feminist Studies* 7:1 (Spring 1981): 57–75.

Hartmann, Heidi. "The Unhappy Marriage of Marxism and Feminism: Towards a More Progressive Union." In Sargent, ed. *Women and Revolution,* 1–42.

Hartmann, Susan M. *The Other Feminists: Activists in the Liberal Establishment.* New Haven, Conn.: Yale University Press, 1998.

Hartsock, Nancy. "Feminism, Power, and Change: A Theoretical Analysis." In Cummings and Schuck, eds. *Women Organizing,* 2–24.

———. "Fundamental Feminism: Process and Perspective." 1975. In *Quest* staff, eds. *Building Feminist Theory,* 32–43.

———. "Political Change: Two Perspectives on Power." 1974. In *Quest* staff, eds. *Building Feminist Theory,* 3–19.

———. "Staying Alive." Winter 1976–77. In *Quest* staff, eds. *Building Feminist Theory,* 111–22.

Hayden, Casey, and Mary King. "Sex and Caste." *Liberation* [New York] (April 1966): 35–36.

Hedman, Carl. "Adversaries and Models: Alternative Institutions in an Age of Scarcity." *Radical America* 15:5 (September–October 1981): 41–51.

Heller, Trudy, Jon Van Til, and Louis A. Zurcher, Jr., eds. *Leaders and Followers: Challenges for the Future.* Contemporary Studies in Applied Behavioral Science, vol. 4. Greenwich, Conn.: JAI, 1986.

Hemmons, Willa Mae. "The Women's Liberation Movement: Understanding Black Women's Attitudes." In Rodgers-Rose, ed. *Black Woman,* 285–98.

Hercus, Cheryl. "Identity, Emotion, and Feminist Collective Action." *Gender and Society* 13:1 (February 1999): 34–55.

Heresies Collective. "True Confessions." *Heresies* 8 (Spring 1979): 93–96.

Herman, Dianne. "The Rape Culture." In Freeman, ed. *Women,* 41–63.

Hess, Beth B., and Myra Marx Ferree, eds. *Analyzing Gender: A Handbook of Social Science Research.* Newbury Park, Calif.: Sage, 1987.

Hirschhorn, Larry. "Alternative Services and the Crisis of Professionals" In Case and Taylor, eds. *Co-ops, Communes, and Collectives,* 153–93.

Hogeland, Lisa Maria. *Feminism and Its Fictions: The Consciousness-Raising Novel and the Women's Liberation Movement.* Philadelphia: University of Pennsylvania Press, 1998.

Hole, Judith, and Ellen Levine. *Rebirth of Feminism.* New York: Quadrangle/New York Times, 1971.

hooks, bell [Gloria Watkins]. *Ain't I a Woman: Black Women and Feminism.* Boston: South End, 1982.

———. *Feminist Theory: From Margin to Center.* Boston: South End, 1984.

Hull, Gloria T., Patricia Bell Scott, and Barbara Smith, eds. *All the Women Are*

White, All the Blacks Are Men, But Some of Us Are Brave: Black Women's Studies. New York: Feminist Press, 1982.

Hunter, Allen. "In the Wings: New Right Ideology and Organization." *Radical America* 15:1–2 (Spring 1981): 113–38.

"The Impasse of Socialist-Feminism: A Conversation with Dierdre English, Barbara Epstein, Barbara Haber, and Judy MacLean." *Socialist Review* 79 (January–February 1985): 93–110.

Issel, William. *Social Change in the United States 1945–1983*. Houndsmills, England: Macmillan, 1985.

Jacobs, Paul, and Saul Landau. *The New Radicals: A Report with Documents*. New York: Vintage-Random, 1966.

Jaggar, Alison M. *Feminist Politics and Human Nature*. Totowa, N.J.: Rowman, 1983.

———. "Political Philosophies of Women's Liberation." 1977. In Vetterling-Braggin et al., eds. *Feminism and Philosophy*, 5–21.

Jaggar, Alison M., and Paula S. Rothenberg, eds. *Feminist Frameworks: Alternative Theoretical Accounts of the Relations between Women and Men*. 2d ed. New York: McGraw-Hill; 1984.

Jenkins, Lee, and Cheris Kramer. "Small Group Process: Learning from Women." *Women's Studies International Quarterly* 1 (1978): 67–84.

Jones, Beverly, and Judith Brown. "Towards a Female Liberation Movement." 1968. In Tanner, ed. *Voices from Women's Liberation*, 362–415.

Jones, Jacqueline. *Labor of Love, Labor of Sorrow: Black Women, Work, and the Family, from Slavery to Present*. New York: Vintage, 1986.

Joreen [Jo Freeman]. "Trashing: The Dark Side of Sisterhood." *Ms.* (April 1976): 49ff.

———. "The Tyranny of Structurelessness." *Second Wave* 2:1. 1972. Rpt. in Koedt et al., eds. *Radical Feminism*, 285–99.

Joseph, Gloria. "The Incompatible Ménage à Trois, Marxism, Feminism, and Racism." In Sargent, ed. *Women and Revolution*, 91–107.

Joseph, Gloria I., and Jill Lewis. *Common Differences: Conflicts in Black and White Feminist Perspectives*. Garden City, N.Y.: Anchor, 1981.

Judis, John. "New American Movement, 1975." *Socialist Revolution* 26 (October–December 1975): 117–42.

Kahn, Karen, ed. *Frontline Feminism, 1975–1995: Essays from Sojourner's First 20 Years*. San Francisco: Aunt Lute, 1995.

Kahn, Kim Fridkin, and Edie N. Goldenberg. "The Media: Obstacle or Ally of Feminists?" *Annals AAPSS* 515 (May 1991): 104–13.

Kaledin, Eugenia. *Mothers and More: American Women in the 1950s*. Boston: Twayne, 1984.

Kanter, Rosabeth Moss. *Commitment and Community: Communes and Utopias in Sociological Perspective*. Cambridge, Mass.: Harvard University Press, 1972.

———. "Communes in Cities." In Case and Taylor, eds. *Co-ops, Communes, and Collectives*, 112–35.

Kaplan, Judy, and Linn Shapiro. *Red Diapers: Growing Up in the Communist Left*. Urbana: University of Illinois Press, 1998.

Kaplan, Laura. *The Story of Jane: The Legendary Underground Feminist Abortion Service*. New York: Pantheon, 1995.

Katzenstein, Mary Fainsod. "Feminism within American Institutions: Unobtrusive Mobilization in the 1980s." *Signs* 16:1 (Autumn 1990): 27–54.

Katzenstein, Mary Fainsod, and Carol McClurg Mueller, eds. *The Women's Movements of the United States and Western Europe: Consciousness, Political Opportunity, and Public Policy.* Philadelphia: Temple University Press, 1987.

Kelly, Janis. "Grand Juries: We All Know Too Much." *off our backs* (December 1981): 19.

Keniston, Kenneth. *Young Radicals: Notes on Committed Youth.* New York: Harcourt, 1968.

Kessler-Harris, Alice. "Equal Employment Opportunity Commission v. Sears, Roebuck, and Company: A Personal Account." In DuBois and Ruiz, eds. *Unequal Sisters*, 432–46.

King, Mary. *Freedom Song: A Personal Story of the 1960s Civil Rights Movement.* New York: Quill, 1987.

Klagsbrun, Francine, ed. *The First Ms. Reader.* New York: Warner, 1973.

Klandermans, Bert. "The Social Construction of Protest and Multiorganizational Fields." In Morris and Mueller, eds. *Frontiers in Social Movement Theory*, 77–103.

Klatch, Rebecca. "Coalition and Conflict among Women of the New Right." *Signs* 13:4 (Summer 1988).

———. *A Generation Divided: The New Left, the New Right, and the 1960s.* Berkeley: University of California Press, 1999.

———. *Women of the New Right.* Philadelphia: Temple University Press, 1987.

Know Montgomery County. Dayton: League of Women Voters of the Greater Dayton Area, 1982.

Koedt, Anne. "Lesbianism and Feminism." 1971. In Koedt et al., eds. *Radical Feminism*, 246–58.

———. "The Myth of the Vaginal Orgasm." In Tanner, ed. *Voices from Women's Liberation*, 158–66.

Koedt, Anne, Ellen Levine, and Anita Rapone, eds. *Radical Feminism.* New York: Quadrangle, 1973.

Kopkind, Andrew. "'Sea-Level' Media: Up from Underground." In Case and Taylor, eds. *Co-ops, Communes, and Collectives*, 66–88.

Kravetz, Diane. "Consciousness-Raising Groups in the 1970s." *Psychology of Women Quarterly* 3:2 (Winter 1978): 168–86.

Kravetz, Diane, Jeanne Marecek, and Stephen E. Finn. "Factors Influencing Women's Participation in Consciousness-Raising Groups." *Psychology of Women Quarterly* 7:3 (Spring 1983): 257–71.

Kreps, Juanita Morris, ed. *Women and the American Economy: A Look to the 1980s.* Englewood Cliffs, N.J.: Prentice-Hall, 1976.

Krieger, Susan. *The Mirror Dance: Identity in a Women's Community.* Philadelphia: Temple University Press, 1983.

La Feber, Walter, and Richard Polenberg. *The American Century: A History of the United States since the 1890s.* New York: Wiley, 1975.

Langer, Elinor. "Why Big Business Is Trying to Defeat the ERA: The Economic Implications of Equality." *Ms.* (May 1976): 64ff.

League of Women Voters of Greater Dayton Area. "This Is Dayton." Rev. ed. Dayton, 1976. Mimeograph.

Lederer, Laura, ed. *Take Back the Night: Women on Pornography.* Toronto: Bantam, 1980.

Lenhoff, Donna. "Equal Pay for Work of Comparable Value." *Women: A Journal of Liberation* 7:1 (1980): 50–52.

Leon, Barbara. "Separate to Integrate." In Redstockings. *Feminist Revolution,* 139–44.

Leone, Vivian. "Domestics." In Stambler, ed. *Women's Liberation,* 39–44.

Lerner, Gerda, ed. *Black Women in White America: A Documentary History.* New York: Vintage, 1973.

Lewis, Diane K. "A Response to Inequality: Black Women, Racism, and Sexism." 1977. In Abel and Abel, eds. *Signs Reader,* 169–91.

Lewis, Roger. *Outlaws of America: The Underground Press and its Context.* Harmondsworth, England: Penguin, 1972.

Lieberman, Morton A., and Gary R. Bond. "The Problem of Being a Woman: A Survey of 1,700 Women in Consciousness-Raising Groups." *Journal of Applied Behavioral Science* 12 (1976): 363–79.

Lootens, Tricia. "National Organizing against Domestic Violence; Funding for Survival and Independence." *off our backs* (November 1982): 16–17.

Luker, Kristin. *Abortion and the Politics of Motherhood.* Berkeley: University of California Press, 1985.

Luttrell, Wendy. "Beyond the Politics of Victimization." *Socialist Review* 73 (January–February 1984): 42–47.

MacLean, Judy. "NAM Conference Draws Up Alternative Energy Program." *Moving On* (May 1977): 8–10.

———. "N.O.W." *Socialist Revolution* 29 (July–September 1976): 39–50.

———. "Toward a Balanced Approach to the New Populists." *Socialist Review* 38 (March–April 1978): 109–14.

Magar, Michelle. "Two Rights Make a . . . : The New Right Has Wooed and Almost Won the Right-to-Lifers." *Seven Days* [New York] (26 October 1979): 20–21.

Mainardi, Pat. "The Politics of Housework." In Morgan, ed. *Sisterhood Is Powerful,* 501–10.

Malcolm X and Alex Haley. *The Autobiography of Malcolm X.* New York: Grove, 1964.

Mansbridge, Jane J. "The Agony of Inequality." In Case and Taylor, eds. *Co-ops, Communes, and Collectives,* 194–214.

———. "What Is the Feminist Movement?" In Ferree and Martin, eds. *Feminist Organizations,* 27–34.

Martin, Del, and Phyllis Lyon. *Lesbian Woman.* Rev. ed. Toronto: Bantam, 1983.

———. "The Realities of Lesbianism." *motive* 29 (March–April 1969): 61–67.

Martin, Gloria. *Socialist Feminism: The First Decade, 1966–76.* Seattle: Freedom Socialist Publications, 1978.

Matthaei, Julia A. *An Economic History of Women in America: Women's Work, the Sexual Division of Labor, and the Development of Capitalism.* New York: Schocken, 1982.

Maupin, Joyce. *Working Women and their Organizations: 150 Years of Struggle.* Berkeley: Union WAGE Educational Committee, 1974.

McAdam, Doug. *Freedom Summer.* New York: Oxford University Press, 1988.

McAfee, Kathy, and Myrna Wood. "Bread and Roses." 1969. In Tanner, ed. *Voices from Women's Liberation*, 415–33.

———. *What Is the Revolutionary Potential of Women's Liberation?* 1969. Somerville, Mass.: New England Free Press, n.d.

McGrath, Colleen. "The Crisis of Domestic Order." *Socialist Review* 43 (January–February, 1979): 11–30.

McKee, Don M., and Phillip J. Obermiller. "From Mountain to Metropolis: Urban Appalachians in Ohio." Cincinnati: Ohio Urban Appalachian Awareness Project, 1978. Mimeograph.

Mehrhof, Barbara, and Pamela Kearon. "Rape: An Act of Terror." 1971. In Koedt et al., eds. *Radical Feminism*, 228–33.

Melucci, Alberto. "Getting Involved: Identity and Mobilization in Social Movements." *International Social Movement Research* 1 (1988), 329–48.

Merton, Andrew H. *Enemies of Choice: The Right to Life Movement and Its Threat to Abortion.* Boston: Beacon, 1981.

Miles, Angela. "The Integrative Feminine Principle in North American Feminist Radicalism: Value Basis of a New Feminism." *Women's Studies International Quarterly* 4:4 (1981): 481–95.

Milkman, Ruth. "Women's History and the Sears Case." *Feminist Studies* 12:2 (Summer 1986): 375–400.

Miller, James. *Democracy Is in the Streets: From Port Huron to the Siege of Chicago.* New York: Simon and Schuster, 1987.

Millet, Kate. *Sexual Politics.* 1969, 1970. New York: Ballantine-Random, 1978.

Mitchell, Juliet. *Woman's Estate.* New York: Pantheon, 1971.

———. *Women: The Longest Revolution.* 1966. Somerville, Mass.: New England Free Press, n.d.

Moberg, David. "Experimenting with the Future: Alternative Institutions and American Socialism." In Case and Taylor, eds. *Co-ops, Communes, and Collectives*, 274–311.

Mohr, James C. *Abortion in America: The Origins and Evolution of National Policy, 1800–1900.* Oxford: Oxford University Press, 1978.

Moira, Fran, and Carol Anne Douglass. "Ten Years of *off our backs.*" *off our backs* (February 1980): 2ff.

Moon, Rebecca, Leslie B. Tanner, and Susan Pascale. "Karate as Self-defense for Women." In Tanner, ed. *Voices from Women's Liberation*, 256–64.

Moraga, Cherrie, and Gloria Anzaldua, eds. *This Bridge Called My Back: Writings by Radical Women of Color.* Watertown, Mass.: Persephone, 1981.

Morgan, Robin. *Going Too Far: The Personal Chronicle of a Feminist.* New York: Vintage, 1978.

———. "Goodbye to All That." 1970. In Morgan, ed. *Going Too Far*, 115–30.

———. "Theory and Practice: Pornography and Rape." 1974. In Morgan, ed. *Going Too Far*, 163–69.

———, ed. *Sisterhood Is Powerful: An Anthology of Writings from the Women's Liberation Movement.* New York: Vintage, 1970.

Morris, Aldon. *The Origins of the Civil Rights Movement: Black Communities Organizing for Change.* New York: Free Press, 1984.

Morris, Aldon D., and Carol McClurg Mueller, eds. *Frontiers in Social Movement Theory.* New Haven, Conn.: Yale University Press, 1992.

motive. Special issue on women's liberation. *motive* 29 (March–April 1969).

Mueller, Carol. "Building Social Movement Theory." In Morris and Mueller, eds. *Frontiers in Social Movement Theory,* 3–25.

———. "Conflict in Contemporary Feminism." In Ferree and Martin, eds. *Feminist Organizations,* 274.

———. "The Organizational Basis of Conflict in Contemporary Feminism." In Ferree and Martin, eds. *Feminist Organizations,* 263–75.

Mungo, Raymond. *Famous Long Ago: My Life and Hard Times with Liberation News Service.* Boston: Beacon, 1970.

Naples, Nancy A., ed. *Community Activism and Feminist Politics: Organizing across Race, Class, and Gender.* New York: Routledge, 1998.

Nasman, Victoria Tepe. "A Survey of Ohioans Receiving Abortion Care at Dayton Women's Services, January–May 1992." Report released July 1992.

Nassi, Alberta J., and Stephen I. Abromowitz. "Raising Consciousness about Women's Groups: Process and Outcome Research." *Psychology of Women Quarterly* 3:2 (Winter 1978): 139–56.

National Advisory Commission on Civil Disorders. "Summary of the Report." (Report of the National Advisory Commission on Civil Disorders.) Washington, D.C.: GPO, 1968.) In Gadlin and Garskof, eds. *Uptight Society,* 85–101.

Nelson, Jill. "CETA Displaced Homemakers: Who's Displacing Whom?" *Encore American and Worldwide News* (16 April 1979): 18–19.

"New American Movement: The Political Perspective." June 1972. Adopted at the national founding convention.

Notes from the First Year [New York], June 1968.

Notes from the Second Year: Women's Liberation—Major Writings of the Radical Feminists [New York], April 1970.

Notes from the Third Year: Women's Liberation [New York], 1971.

Nussbaum, Karen. "Shifting Investment and the Rise of the Service Sector." *Radical America* 15:4 (July–August 1981): 49–53.

O'Brien, Jim. "American Leninism in the 1970s." *Radical America* 11:6 and 12:1 (November 1977–February 1978): 27–62.

O'Neill, William. *Coming Apart: An Informal History of America in the 1960s.* New York: Quadrangle/New York Times, 1979.

O'Reilly, Jane. "The Housewife's Moment of Truth." 1972. In Klagsbrun, ed. *First Ms. Reader,* 11–22.

off our backs Collective. "OOB Bares Some." *off our backs* (October 1978).

———. "Ten Years Growing." Tenth anniversary issue. *off our backs* (February 1980).

Ohio Task Force for the Implementation of the Equal Rights Amendment. ERA Ohio. Columbus: July 1975.

Oliker, Stacey. "Abortion and the Left: the Limits of 'Pro-Family' Politics." *Socialist Review* 56 (March–April 1981): 71–95.

Paige, Connie. *The Right to Lifers: Who Are They? How They Operate. Where They Get their Money.* New York: Summit, 1983.

Parsons, Patricia, and Carol Hodne. "A Collective Experiment in Women's Health." *Science for the People* 14:4 (July–August 1982): 9–13.

Payne, Carol Williams. "Consciousness Raising: A Dead End?" 1971. In Koedt et al., eds. *Radical Feminism,* 282–84.

Peck, Abe. *Uncovering the Sixties: The Life and Times of the Underground Press.* New York: Pantheon, 1985.

Perks, Robert, and Alistair Thomson, eds. *The Oral History Reader.* London: Routledge, 1998.

Peslikis, Irene. "Resistances to Consciousness." 1969. In Morgan, ed. *Sisterhood Is Powerful,* 379–81.

Petchesky, Rosalind Pollack. *Abortion and Women's Choice: The State, Sexuality, and Reproductive Freedom.* Boston: Northeastern University Press, 1985.

———. "Antiabortion, Antifeminism, and the Rise of the New Right." *Feminist Studies* 7:2 (Summer 1981): 206–46.

———. "Reproductive Freedom: Beyond 'A Woman's Right to Choose.'" In Stimpson et al., eds. *Women,* 92–116.

Piercy, Marge. "The Grand Coolie Damn." 1969. In Morgan, ed. *Sisterhood Is Powerful,* 473–92.

Pilpel, Harriet F. "The Collateral Legal Consequences of Adopting a Constitutional Amendment on Abortion." *Family Planning/Population Reporter* 5:3 (June 1976): 44–48.

Planned Parenthood Affiliates of Ohio. "Public Attitudes towards Issues of Reproductive Freedom in Ohio." [Columbus]: 1982.

Planned Parenthood Association of Miami Valley. "The History of the Planned Parenthood Association of Miami Valley, Inc., 1965–1978." Revised. Dayton: [1984]. Mimeograph.

Planned Parenthood Federation of America. "A Five Year Plan: 1976–1980." Adopted by the PPFA membership in Seattle, 22 October 1975.

Plutzer, Eric. "Work Life, Family Life, and Women's Support of Feminism." *American Sociological Review* 53 (1988): 640–49.

Pohli, Carol Virginia. "Church Closets and Back Doors: A Feminist View of Moral Majority Women." *Feminist Studies* 9:3 (Fall 1983).

Polatnick, M. Rivka. "Diversity in Women's Liberation Ideology: How a Black and a White Group of the 1960s Viewed Motherhood." *Signs* 21:3 (Spring 1996): 679–706.

Popkin, Annie, "The Social Experience of Bread and Roses: Building a Community and Creating a Culture." In Hansen and Philipson, eds. *Women, Class, and the Feminist Imagination,* 182–212.

Pride, Anne. "To Respectability and Back: A Ten Year View of the Anti-Rape Movement." In Delacoste and Newman, eds. *Fight Back,* 114–18.

Quest staff, eds. *Building Feminist Theory: Essays from Quest, a Feminist Quarterly.* New York: Longman, 1981.

Radicalesbians. "The Woman-Identified-Woman." 1970. In Babcox and Belkin, eds. *Liberation Now!* 287–93.

Randall, Vicky. *Women and Politics.* New York: St. Martin's, 1982.

Rape Crisis Center. "Rape: Medical and Legal Information." Boston: [1973?].

Red Apple Collective. "Socialist-Feminist Women's Unions: Past and Present." *Socialist Review* 38 (March–April 1978): 37–57.

Redstockings. *Feminist Revolution.* New Paltz, N.Y.: Redstockings, 1975.

———. "Gloria Steinem and the CIA." In Redstockings. *Feminist Revolution,* 150–69.

Reichert, Julia, and Jim Kleine, directors. *Growing Up Female.* New Day Films. 1970.

Reichert, Julia, Jim Kleine, and Miles Mogulescu, directors. *Union Maids.* New Day Films. 1976.

Reinelt, Claire. "Moving onto the Terrain of the State: The Battered Women's Movement and the Politics of Engagement." In Ferree and Martin, eds. *Feminist Organizations,* 84–104

Reinharz, Shulamit. *Feminist Methods in Social Research.* New York: Oxford University Press, 1992.

"Religion." Special issue of Canadian Woman Studies/les cahiers de la femme [Downsview, Ontario] 5:2 (Winter 1983).

Reverby, Susan. "An Epilogue . . . or Prologue to CLUW?" *Radical America* 9:6 (November–December 1975): 111–14.

Rich, Adrienne. "Compulsory Heterosexuality and Lesbian Existence." In Stimpson et al., eds. *Women,* 62–91.

Richardson, Laurel, and Verta Taylor, eds. *Feminist Frontiers II: Rethinking Sex, Gender, and Society.* 2d ed. New York: Random, 1989.

Riddiough, Christine. "Women, Feminism, and the 1980 Elections." *Socialist Review* 56 (March–April 1981): 37–54.

Riger, Stephanie. "Challenges of Success: Stages of Growth in Feminist Organizations." *Feminist Studies* 20:2 (Summer 1994): 275–301.

Robins, Joan. *Handbook of Women's Liberation.* North Hollywood, Calif.: NOW Library, 1970.

Robinson, Patricia. "Socialism and Feminism: Joining Two Great Traditions." *Socialist Review* 75–76 (May–August 1984): 200–202.

Ronald, Bruce, and Virginia Ronald. *Dayton, the Gem City.* Tulsa: Continental Heritage, 1981.

Rodgers-Rose, LaFrances, ed. *The Black Woman.* Beverly Hills, Calif.: Sage, 1980.

Rosen, Ruth. *The World Split Open: How the Modern Women's Movement Changed America.* New York: Viking, 2000.

Rosenberg, Rosalind. *Divided Lives: American Women in the Twentieth Century.* New York: Hill and Wang, 1992.

Ross, Loretta J. "African-American Women and Abortion." In Solinger, ed. *Abortion Wars,* 161–207.

Ross, Susan Deller. *The Rights of Women: The Basic ACLU Guide to a Woman's Rights.* New York: Avon, 1973.

Rossi, Alice S., ed. *The Feminist Papers: From Adams to de Beauvoir.* 1973. Toronto: Bantam, 1974.

Rothschild, Mary Aickin. "White Women Volunteers in the Freedom Summers: Their Life and Work in a Movement for Social Change." *Feminist Studies* 5:3 (Fall 1979): 466–95.

Rothschild-Whitt, Joyce. "Conditions for Democracy: Making Participatory Organizations Work." In Case and Taylor, eds. *Co-ops, Communes, and Collectives,* 215–44.

Rothstein, Richard. "What Is an Organizer?" Chicago: Midwest Academy, March 1974. Mimeograph.

Rowbotham, Sheila. *A Century of Women.* New York: Penguin, 1999.

————. *Woman's Consciousness, Man's World.* 1973. Harmondsworth, England: Penguin, 1974.

————. "The Women's Movement and Organizing for Socialism." In Rowbotham et al., eds. *Beyond the Fragments,* 21–155.

Rowbotham, Sheila, Lynne Segal, and Hilary Wainwright. *Beyond the Fragments: Feminism and the Making of Socialism.* London: Merlin, 1979.

Ruether, Rosemary Radford, and Rosemary Skinner Keller, eds. *Women and Religion in America.* Cambridge, Mass.: Harper and Row, 1981–86.

Rupp, Leila J., and Verta Taylor. *Survival in the Doldrums: The American Women's Rights Movement, 1945 to the 1960s.* New York: Oxford University Press, 1987.

Russell, Michelle. Speech at the National Conference on Socialist Feminism. *Socialist Revolution* 26 (October–December 1975): 100–107.

Russell, Valerie. "Racism and Sexism. A Collective Struggle: A Minority Woman's Point of View." Know reprints, n.d.

Ryan, Barbara. *Feminism and the Women's Movement: Dynamics of Change in Social Movement Ideology and Activism.* New York: Routledge, 1992.

Sabaroff, Nina. "It's Dark but It's Gonna Get Light." In Stambler, ed. *Women's Liberation,* 230–33.

Sager, Anthony P. "Radical Law: Three Collectives in Cambridge." In Case and Taylor, eds. *Co-ops, Communes, and Collectives,* 136–50.

Sale, Kirkpatrick. *SDS.* New York: Vintage-Random, 1974.

Samuel, Raphael, ed. *People's History and Socialist Theory.* London: Routledge, 1981.

Sanders, Fran. "Dear Black Man." In Cade, ed. *Black Woman,* 73–79.

Sanders, William L. *Dayton, Gem City of Ohio.* Dayton: Dayton Daily News, 1963.

Sanford, Wendy Coppedge. "Working Together, Growing Together: A Brief History of the Boston Women's Health Book Collective." *Heresies* 8 (Spring 1979): 83–92.

[Santa Cruz Women against Rape.] "Confrontation as an Anti-Rape Tactic." *off our backs* (August–September 1984): 22–23.

Sapiro, Virginia. "Feminism: A Generation Later." *Annals AAPSS* 514 (March 1991): 10–22.

————. *The Political Integration of Women: Roles, Socialization, and Politics.* Urbana: University of Illinois Press, 1984.

Sarachild, Kathie. "Consciousness Raising: A Radical Weapon." In Redstockings. *Feminist Revolution,* 131–37.

————. "Going for What We Really Want." In Redstockings. *Feminist Revolution,* 145–47.

————. "The Power of History." In Redstockings. *Feminist Revolution,* 7–29.

Sargent, Lydia. "New Left Women and Men: The Honeymoon Is Over." In Sargent, ed. *Women and Revolution,* xi–xxxii.

————, ed. *Women and Revolution: A Discussion of the Unhappy Marriage of Marxism and Feminism.* Boston: South End, 1981.

Sayres, Sohnya, et al., eds., *The 60s without Apology.* Minneapolis: University of Minnesota Press, 1984.

Schechter, Susan. *Women and Male Violence: The Visions and Struggles of the Battered Women's Movement.* Boston: South End, 1982.

Schmitt, Frederika E., and Patricia Yancey Martin. "Unobtrusive Mobilization by an Institutionalized Rape Crisis Center: 'All We Do Comes from Victims.'" *Gender and Society* 13:3 (June 1999): 364–84.

Schneider, Beth E. "Political Generations and the Contemporary Women's Movement." *Sociological Inquiry* 58 (1988): 4–21.

Schwind, Ida R., and Ruth H. Detrick. *One Hundred Years: The Story of the Young Women's Christian Association of Dayton, Ohio.* Dayton: Otterbein, 1969.

Sealander, Judith, and Dorothy Smith. "The Rise and Fall of Feminist Organizations in the 1970s: Dayton as a Case Study." *Feminist Studies* 12:2 (Summer 1986): 321–41.

Seese, Linda. "You've Come a Long Way, Baby—Women in the Movement." 1969. In Cooke et al., eds. *New Women,* 155–63.

Seifer, Nancy, and Barbara Wertheimer. "New Approaches to Collective Power: Four Working Women's Organizations." In Cummings and Cshuck, eds. *Women Organizing,* 160–61.

"Sex Issue." *Heresies* 12 (1981).

Shelley, Martha. "Lesbianism and the Women's Liberation Movement." In Stambler, ed. *Women's Liberation,* 123–29.

Shore, Merle. "The Feminist Workplace—Ideology in Practice: A Study of Feminist Collective Experimentation in the San Francisco Bay Area." Ph.D. diss. Université de Paris VII, 1985.

Shreeve, Anita. *Women Together, Women Alone: The Legacy of the Consciousness-Raising Movement.* New York: Viking, 1989.

Shulman, Alix Kate. "Sex and Power: Sexual Bases of Radical Feminism." In Stimpson et al., eds. *Women: Sex and Sexuality,* 21–35.

Silverman, Sibyl. "A Descriptive Study of Southern Appalachian Migration to Dayton." Dayton: Dayton Human Relations Commission, [1965]. Report on a research project. Mimeograph.

Sirianni, Carmen. "Democracy and Diversity in Feminist Organizations: Learning from Three Decades of Practice." 1995. www.cpn.org/sections/topics/family-intergen/civic_perspectives/feminist_democracy1.html.

Skerry, Peter. "The Class Conflict over Abortion." *Public Interest* 52 (Summer 1978): 69–84.

Smith, Dorothy. "Creating a Women's Space: The Life Cycle of the Dayton Women's Center." Text of paper presented at the Sixth Berkshire Conference on the History of Women. Northampton, Mass., 1 June 1984.

Smith, Leslie, and Toni White. "'Ourstory/Herstory': The Washington, D.C., Feminist Community from 1969 to 1979." *off our backs* (February 1980): 12ff.

Snitow, Ann, Christine Stansell, and Sharon Thompson, eds. *Desire: The Politics of Sexuality.* 1983. London: Virago, 1984.

"Socialism/Feminism. Papers from the New American Movement Conference on Feminism and Socialism." Durham, N.C., November 1972.

Solinger, Rickie. *Wake Up Little Susie: Single Pregnancy and Race before Roe v. Wade.* New York: Routledge, 1992.

———, ed. *Abortion Wars: A Half Century of Struggle, 1950–2000.* Berkeley: University of California Press, 1998.

Staggenborg, Suzanne. "Can Feminist Organizations Be Effective?" In Ferree and Martin, eds., *Feminist Organizations,* 339–55.

———. *The Pro-Choice Movement: Organization and Activism in the Abortion Conflict.* New York: Oxford University Press, 1991.

———. "Stability and Innovation in the Women's Movement: A Comparison of Two Movement Organizations." *Social Problems* 36:1 (February 1989): 75–92.

Stambler, Sookie, ed. *Women's Liberation: Blueprint for the Future.* New York: Ace, 1970.

Starr, Paul. "The Phantom Community." In Case and Taylor, eds. *Co-ops, Communes, and Collectives,* 245–73.

Steinman, Richard, and Donald M. Traunstein. "Redefining Deviance: The Self-Help Challenge to the Human Services." *Journal of Applied Behavioral Science.* 12:3 (1976): 347–61.

Stetson, Dorothy McBride. *Women's Rights in the USA: Policy Debates and Gender Roles.* Pacific Grove, Calif.: Brooks/Cole, 1991.

Stevens, Wendy. "Women Organizing the Office." *off our backs* (April 1979): 10.

Stimpson, Catherine. "'Thy Neighbor's Wife, Thy Neighbor's Servants': Women's Liberation and Black Civil Rights." In Gornick and Moran, eds. *Women in Sexist Society,* 622–57.

Stimpson, Catherine R., and Ethel Spector Person. *Women: Sex and Sexuality.* Chicago: University of Chicago Press, 1980.

Stimpson, Catherine R., et al., eds. *Women and the American City.* Chicago: University of Chicago Press, 1981.

Stone, Pauline Terrelonge. "Feminist Consciousness and Black Women." In Freeman, ed. *Women,* 575–87.

Strobel, Margaret. "Organizational Learning in the Chicago Women's Liberation Union." In Ferree and Martin, eds. *Feminist Organizations,* 145–64.

Susan, Barbara. "About My Consciousness Raising." In Tanner, ed. *Voices from Women's Liberation,* 238–43.

Sutheim, Susan. "The Subversion of Betty Crocker." *motive* 29 (March–April 1969): 43–47.

Syfers, Judy. "San Francisco School Workers' Union Struggle." *Radical America* 12:2 (March–April 1978): 62–71.

Tanner, Leslie B., ed. *Voices from Women's Liberation.* 1970. New York: Signet, 1971.

Tax, Meredith. "For the People Hear Us Singing, 'Bread and Roses! Bread and Roses!'" In DuPlessis and Snitow, eds. *Feminist Memoir Project,* 312.

———. "Learning How to Bake." *Socialist Review* 73 (January–February 1984): 36–41.

Taylor, Rosemary C. R. "Free Medicine." 1976. In Case and Taylor, eds. *Co-ops, Communes, and Collectives,* 18–48.

Taylor, Verta. "The Future of Feminism: A Social Movement Analysis." In Richardson and Taylor, eds. *Feminist Frontiers II,* 473–90.

———. "Gender and Social Movements: Gender Processes in Women's Self-Help Movements." *Gender and Society* 13:1 (February 1999): 8–33.

TD [Tacie Dejanikus?]. "Reproductive Rights National Network: Rough Road Ahead." *off our backs* (August–September 1981): 10ff.

Tepperman, Jean. *Not Servants, Not Machines: Office Workers Speak Out!* Boston: Beacon, 1976.

Tepperman, Jean. "Organizing Office Workers." *Radical America* 10:1 (January–February 1976): 3–20.

———. Reply to Bahr letter. *Radical America* 10:3 (May–June 1976), 76–77.

Thomas, Jan E. "Everything about Us Is Feminist: The Significance of Ideology in Organizational Change." *Gender and Society* 13:1 (February 1999): 101–19.

Thompson, Paul. "The New Oral History in France." In Samuel, ed. *People's History and Socialist Theory*, 67–77.

———. *The Voice of the Past: Oral History.* Oxford: Oxford University Press, 1978.

Torrey, Jane. "Racism and Feminism: Is Women's Liberation for Whites Only?" *Psychology of Women Quarterly* (Winter 1977).

Troger, Annemarie. "Coalition of Labor Union Women: Strategic Hope, Tactical Despair." *Radical America* 9:6 (November–December 1975): 85–110.

United States Bureau of the Census. *A Statistical Portrait of Women in the United States: 1978.* Washington, D.C.: Government Printing Office, 1980.

———. *Census of the Population: 1970. Vol. 1, Characteristics of the Population.* Part 37, Ohio Section 2. Washington, D.C.: Government Printing Office, 1973.

———. *Census of the Population: 1980. Vol. 1, Characteristics of the Population.* Part 37, Ohio Sections 1–2. Washington, D.C.: Government Printing Office, 1983.

———. *Statistical Abstract of the United States: 1981.* 102nd ed. Washington, D.C.: Government Printing Office, 1981.

United States Bureau of Labor Statistics. *Perspectives on Working Women: A Databook.* Washington, D.C.: Government Printing Office, 1982.

———. *Women in the Labor Force: Some New Data Series.* Prepared by Janet L. Norwood and Elizabeth Waldman. Washington, D.C.: Government Printing Office, 1979.

United Way. "Key Informants Survey." Survey and analysis on community needs to determine United Way funding. Dayton: [1983?].

Valeska, Lucia. "The Future of Female Separatism." 1975. In Quest staff, eds. *Building Feminist Theory*, 20–31.

Van Gelder, Lindsy. "Countdown to Houston." *Ms.* (November 1977): 106ff.

———. "Four Days That Changed the World." *Ms.* (March 1978): 52ff.

Vetterling-Braggin, Mary, Frederick A. Elliston, and Jane English, eds. *Feminism and Philosophy.* 1977. Totowa, N.J.: Littlefield, Adams, 1978.

Victim/Witness Division, Montgomery Count Prosecutor's Office. *Handbook for Victims of Sexual Assault.* Dayton: n.d.

Vogel, Alfred. "Your Clerical Workers Are Ripe for Unionism." Harvard Business Review 49 (March–April 1971). Rpt. in Baxandall et al., eds. *America's Working Women*, 351–53.

Walker, Alice. "Advancing Luna—and Ida B. Wells." In Walker, *You Can't Keep a Good Woman Down*, 85–104.

———. *You Can't Keep a Good Woman Down.* London: Women's Press, 1982.

Wallace, Michele. *Black Macho and the Myth of the Superwoman.* New York: Warner, 1980.

Wallace, Phyllis A. "Impact of Equal Employment Opportunity Laws." In Kreps, ed. *Women and the American Economy*, 123–46.

Wandersee, Winifred D. *On the Move: American Women in the 1970s.* Boston: Twayne, 1988.

Ware, Celestine. *Woman Power: The Movement for Women's Liberation.* New York: Tower Publications, 1970.

Watkins, Bonnie, and Nina Rothchild. *In the Company of Women: Voices from the Women's Movement.* St. Paul: Minnesota Historical Society Press, 1996.

Wattenberg, Ben J., and Richard M. Scammon. *The Real Majority.* New York: Coward, 1970.

Wattleton, Faye. *Life on the Line.* New York: Ballantine, 1966.

Webb, Marilyn Salzman. "Woman as Secretary, Sexpot, Spender, Sow, Civic Actor, Sickie." *motive* 29 (March–April 1969): 48–59.

Weigand, Kathleen. *Red Feminism: American Communism and the Making of Women's Liberation.* Baltimore, Md.: Johns Hopkins University Press, 2001.

Weingart, Sherry. "Thoughts on the ERA Abortion." *Radical America* 12:5 (September–October 1978): 22–25.

Weisstein, Naomi. "'Kinde, Kuche, Kirche' as Scientific Law: Psychology Constructs the Female." 1968. In Morgan, ed. *Sisterhood Is Powerful,* 228–45.

———. "Woman as Nigger." 1969. In Tanner, ed. *Voices,* 296–303.

Weisstein, Naomi, and Heather Booth. "Will the Women's Movement Survive?" Rpt. from *Sister* [New Haven] 4:12. N.d.

Weitzman, Leonore J. *The Divorce Revolution: The Unexpected Social and Economic Consequences for Women and Children in America,* New York: Free Press, 1985.

———. "Sex Role Socialization." In Freeman, ed. *Women,* 153–216.

Wertheimer, Barbara M. "'Union Is Power': Sketches from Women's Labor History." In Freeman, ed. *Women,* 339–58.

West, Guida, and Rhoda Lois Blumberg. *Women and Social Protest.* New York: Oxford University Press, 1990.

"What Do Women Want Anyway?" Special issue of *Here and Now: A Journal of the New World* [Dayton] 7:4 (July–August 1970).

White, Aaronette M. "Talking Feminist, Talking Black." *Gender and Society* 13:1 (February 1999): 77–100.

White, E. Frances. "Listening to the Voices of Black Feminism." *Radical America* 18:2–3 (March–June 1984): 7–25.

Whittier, Nancy. *Feminist Generations: The Persistence of the Radical Women's Movement.* Philadelphia: Temple University Press, 1995.

———. "Turning It Over: Personnel Change in the Columbus, Ohio, Women's Movement, 1969–1984." In Ferree and Martin, eds. *Feminist Organizations,* 180–98.

Willis, Ellen. "Abortion: Which Side Are You On?" *Radical America* 15:1–2 (Spring 1981): 78–88.

———. "Feminism, Moralism, and Pornography." 1979. In Snitow et al., eds. *Desire,* 82–96.

———. "Women and the Left." 1989. *Notes from the Second Year* (April 1970): 55–58.

Withorn, Ann. "The Death of CLUW." *Radical America* 10:2 (March–April 1976): 47–51.

———. "For Better and for Worse: Social Relations among Women in the Welfare State." *Radical America* 18:4 (July–August 1984): 37–47.

———. "Helping Ourselves: The Limits and Potential of Self Help." *Radical America* 14:3 (May–June 1980): 25–39.

Withorn, Ann. "Surviving as a Radical Service Worker: Lessons from the History of Movement-Provided Services." *Radical America* 12:4 (July–August 1978): 9–23.

Women's Crisis Center of Ann Arbor. *Freedom from Rape*. Ann Arbor: 1973.

"Women's Oral History." Special issue. *Frontiers: A Journal of Women's Studies* [Boulder, Colo.] 2:2 (Summer 1977).

"Working with Men: Feminists in N.A.M." *Women: A Journal of Liberation* 7:1: 60–63.

Working Women's Shopper's Guide to Dayton. Dayton: Dayton Women Working, [1978].

Young, Iris. "Beyond the Unhappy Marriage: A Critique of the Dual Systems Theory." In Sargent, ed. *Women and Revolution*, 43–69.

———. "Socialist Feminism and the Limits of Dual Systems Theory." *Socialist Review* 50–51 (March–June 1980): 169–88.

Zald, Meyer N., and Roberta Ash. "Social Movement Organizations: Growth, Decay, and Change." *Social Forces* 44 (March 1966): 327–41.

Zald, Meyer N., and John D. McCarthy, eds. *The Dynamics of Social Movements: Resource Mobilization, Social Control, and Tactics*. Lanham, Md.: University Press of America, 1988.

Zinn, Howard. *A People's History of the United States*. New York: Harper, 1980.

———. *SNCC: The New Abolitionists*. Boston: Beacon, 1964.

NATIONAL PERIODICALS (READ IN ENTIRETY)

Feminist Studies
Heresies
Mother Jones
Ms.
off our backs
Radical America
Seven Days
Signs
Socialist Review
Women: A Journal of Liberation
Women's Studies Abstracts

DAYTON PERIODICALS (READ IN ENTIRETY)

Dayton Women's Center Newsletter
Dayton Women's Liberation Newsletter
Dayton Women Working Newsletter
Freedom of Choice Newsletter
Minority Report

DAYTON PERIODICALS (SURVEYED)

Dayton Daily News
Journal Herald

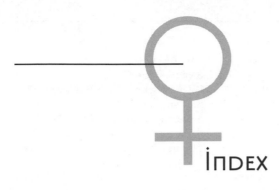

Index

abortion, 8, 9, 10, 27, 40, 41, 44, 49, 95, 117–26, 150, 230; and class, 229; counseling, 118–20, 127, 271n. 7; illegal abortions, 9, 41–43, 118–19, 231, 271n. 4; for "other women," 41, 228, 230; personal experience with, 41, 125, 230–31, 290n. 44. *See also* Roe v. Wade

abortion clinics. *See* Dayton Women's Health Center

Abortion Rights Action Week, 236

abortion rights, 18, 70, 113, 116–17, 213, 215–41; as antechamber to women's movement, 240; broad appeal of issue, 121, 226–27, 230–31, 238; feminist opposition to, 260–61n. 2; idea that feminists dropped issue after *Roe*, 43, 287n. 6; like manna from heaven, 272n. 34; protests, 19, 43, 217, 236, 237–38, 240; public support for, 217, 224, 238–39, 290n. 48, 291n. 59; restrictions, 126, 215, 216, 217, 218, 288n. 15

Abzug, Bella, 60, 203, 235

ACLU (American Civil Liberties Union), xv, 15, 30, 37, 70, 223, 227

AFDC (Aid to Families with Dependent Children). *See* welfare

affirmative action, 57, 65, 198, 206–8

African Americans. *See* black

AFSC (American Friends Service Committee), 171, 224. *See also* Quakers

Against Our Will: Men, Women and Rape (Brownmiller), 135

Aid to Families of Dependent Children. *See* welfare

Akron antiabortion ordinance, 215, 218, 221, 234, 236

Alinsky, Saul, 155, 162, 188, 210, 255n. 17

Allen, Pam. *See Free Space*

Alliance Against Sexual Sexual Coercion, 286n. 95

Alpert, Jane, 265n. 94

alternative institutions, 73, 80, 99, 116, 126, 246, 275n. 80; adversary and exemplary approaches, 281n. 84; dumping, 126, 150; interference between goals and institutional requirements, 280n. 68, 285n. 82; successfully maintaining control of, 275n. 82; subpoenaing records from, 291n. 54; volunteer-staff tensions, 97, 162–63. *See also* Dayton Women's Center; social movements

Amatniek, Kathie, 256n. 12

American Association of University Women, 223

humor, 14, 152, 204
Hunter, Allen, 246
Hupp, George, 120
Hussey, Patricia, 133, 138
Hyde Amendment, 216, 217, 288n. 15

In Our Time (Brownmiller), 258n. 30, 261n. 9, 282n. 16
Indochina Peace Campaign, 64
international feminism, 70
International Socialist Organization, 236
International Women's Year, 183, 213, 217, 218; Houston conference (1977), 183, 218, 235; Ohio preparatory conference, 217–18, 233
Iowa. *See* Heartland

Jewish Family Service, 176
Jews, 87–88, 226, 227, 228, 229; involvement in the women's movement, 35, 89, 94, 227, 229, 289n. 40; lack of Jewish women in movement, 259n. 61; support of abortion rights, 289n. 37; synagogues' support of activism, 118, 223
Jones, Beverly. *See* Florida Paper
Joreen. *See* Freeman, Jo
Journal Herald, vii
Junior League, 95, 131, 177, 230

Kennedy, Florence, 69
Kennedy, John F., 2
Kennedy, Robert, 194
Kent State University, 20, 263n. 61
Kinder, Claudia, 187, 191–92, 197, 198, 208, 209, 211, 212
King, Martin Luther, 4, 194
Klatch, Rebecca, 24, 287n. 3
Kleine, Jim, 88
Kleine, Kathy, 3, 6–7, 13, 16, 26, 27, 28, 34, 46, 55, 58, 66, 74, 78, 94, 108, 110, 111, 115, 217
Kleinehenz, Joann, 181, 183
Koch, Gloria , 190–91, 192, 211
Kurran, Charles, 83

labor force. *See* work
labor movement, 56, 186, 196, 199, 210, 213; democratization of, 213; history of, 195, 286n. 96; relationship to women's movement, 245; strike support, 57, 71, 152, 195, 202, 277n. 32
labor unions, 56, 175, 180, 194, 195–96, 202, 213, 214; distrust of, 56, 57–58, 196, 213; sexism in, 195–96; white collar organizing, 283n. 25
Law Enforcement Assistance Administration. *See* LEAA
law, 94, 226; all-women's practice, 289n. 38; illegal practice of, 84, 165
LEAA (Law Enforcement Assistance Administration), 129, 131, 134, 137; funding for battered women's shelter, 281n. 77
leadership, 74–75, 93, 155–56, 159, 185, 187, 193, 198, 200, 208, 209–11, 222, 224, 242, 244. *See also* elitism; organizational structure; "Tyranny of Structurelessness"
League of Women Voters, 6, 37, 61, 161
legislation: abortion, 19, 215, 216, 218, 234–35; Ohio legislature 43, 60; Ohio State changes in law, 133–34, 157, 164; rape, 133–34, 137, 274n. 61
Leonard, Paul, 134
lesbianism, 16, 48, 50–52, 73, 111–12, 146, 147, 149, 150, 174–75, 180, 181; and class, 53, 174, 245; in the closet, 175; coming out, 50, 51, 52–53, 263n. 43; and feminism, 53, 219, 238; lesbian-baiting, 51, 235; Lexington, Kentucky, supposed underground, 270n. 67; and the media, 68; NOW purge, 262n. 35; subculture, 53, 147, 262n. 41; as vanguard, 50. *See also* homophobia; Sappho's Army